SEVEN SEAS ENTERTAINMENT PRESENTS

MADE IN ABYSS

story and art by AKIHITO TSUKUSHI VOLUME 1

P9-DXM-919

TRANSLATION
Beni Axia Conrad

ADAPTATION
Jake Jung

LETTERING AND RETOUCH
James Gaubatz

LOGO DESIGN
Andrea Rodriguez

COVER DESIGN
Nicky Lim

PROOFREADER
Brett Hallahan
Shanti Whitesides

ASSISTANT EDITOR
Jenn Grunigen

PRODUCTION ASSISTANT
CK Russell

PRODUCTION MANAGER
Lissa Pattillo

EDITOR-IN-CHIEF
Adam Arnold

PUBLISHER
Jason DeAngelis

MADE IN ABYSS VOLUME 1
©Akihito Tsukushi/TAKESHOBO
Originally published in Japan in 2013 by Takeshobo Co. LTD., Tokyo.
English translation rights arranged with Takeshobo Co. LTD., Tokyo,
through TOHAN CORPORATION, Tokyo.

Seven Seas books may be purchased in bulk for promotional, educational, or
business use. Please contact your local bookseller or the Macmillan Corporate
and Premium Sales Department at 1-800-221-7945, extension 5442, or by
e-mail at MacmillanSpecialMarkets@macmillan.com.

Seven Seas and the Seven Seas logo are trademarks of
Seven Seas Entertainment, LLC. All rights reserved.

ISBN: 978-1-626927-73-5

Printed in Canada

First Printing: January 2018

10 9 8 7 6 5 4 3 2

FOLLOW US ONLINE: *www.gomanga.com*

READING DIRECTIONS

This book reads from *right to left*, Japanese style. If
this is your first time reading manga, you start
reading from the top right panel on each page and
take it from there. If you get lost, just follow the
numbered diagram here. It may seem backwards at
first, but you'll get the hang of it! Have fun!!

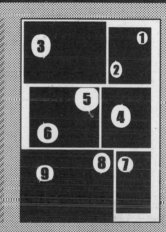

I'd originally thought up this story for a doujinshi and had intended it to be a picture book with a bit of pop-up action.

So when I set out to take that idea and make it into a serialized manga, I started by creating an overarching plot that would be suitable for the medium. According to that plan, the content of the first volume was supposed to fit into three chapters.

However, my plans fell apart, one after the other...

Things I thought I'd have no problem handling by myself have turned out to be really tough. Plus, the storyboards take a lot of time to create, and my editor keeps calling the benikuchinawa (crimson splitjaw) the benichikuwa (crimson fish-paste cake), so it feels like nothing is going as planned. However, I have been able to write and illustrate in the way I want, so I'm managing somehow.

Hopefully, I'll be able to write and illustrate the story all the way to its end. I plan on making it more and more exciting.

Akihito Tukushi

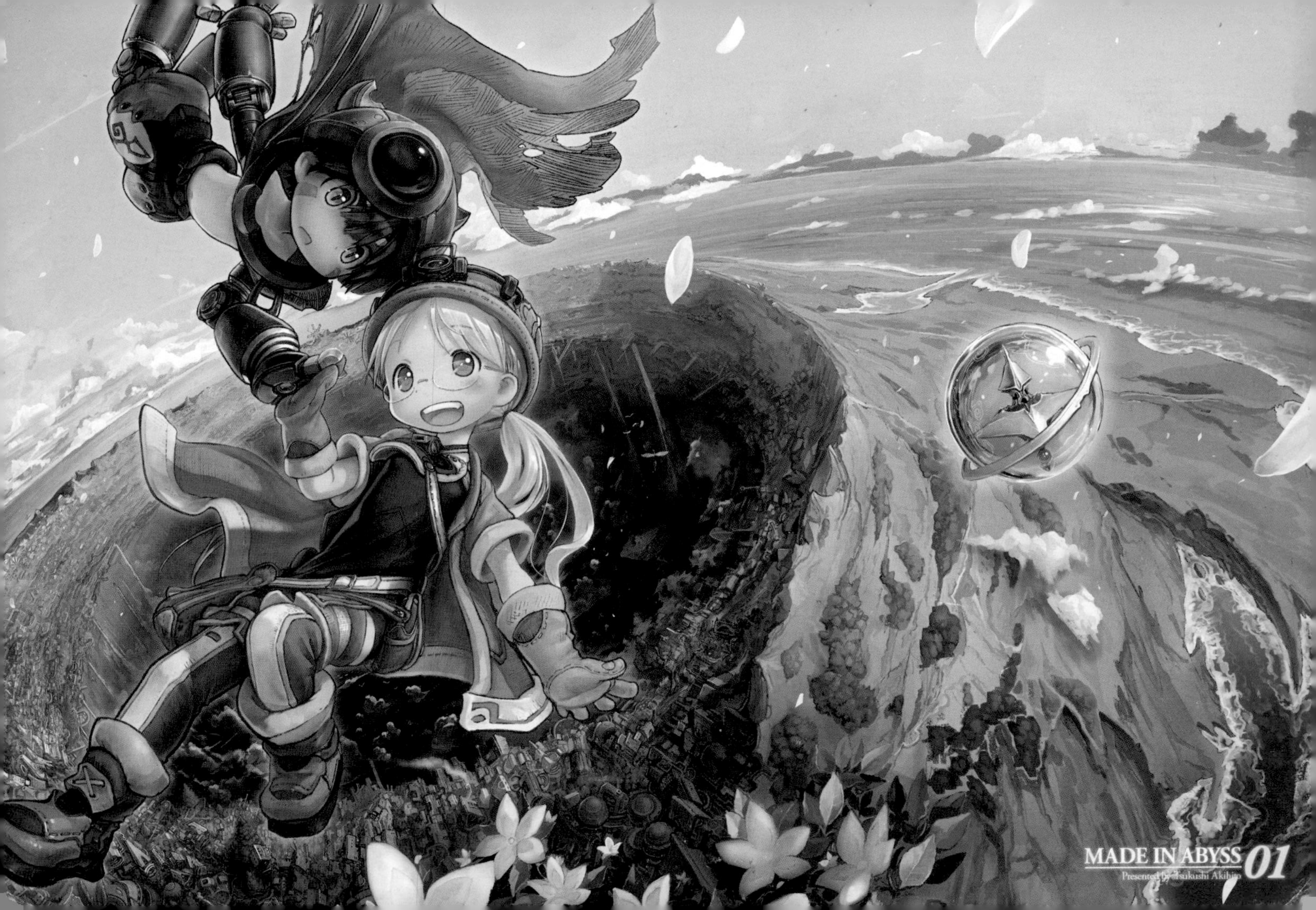
MADE IN ABYSS 01
Presented by Tsukushi Akihito

THE CURSE OF THE ABYSS

This refers to the strains experienced in the Abyss that only occur when ascending. The more proper name for these is "strains of ascending." However, as their true cause is a mystery and they seem to prevent those who venture deep into the pit from returning home, the general populace has taken to calling them the Curse of the Abyss.

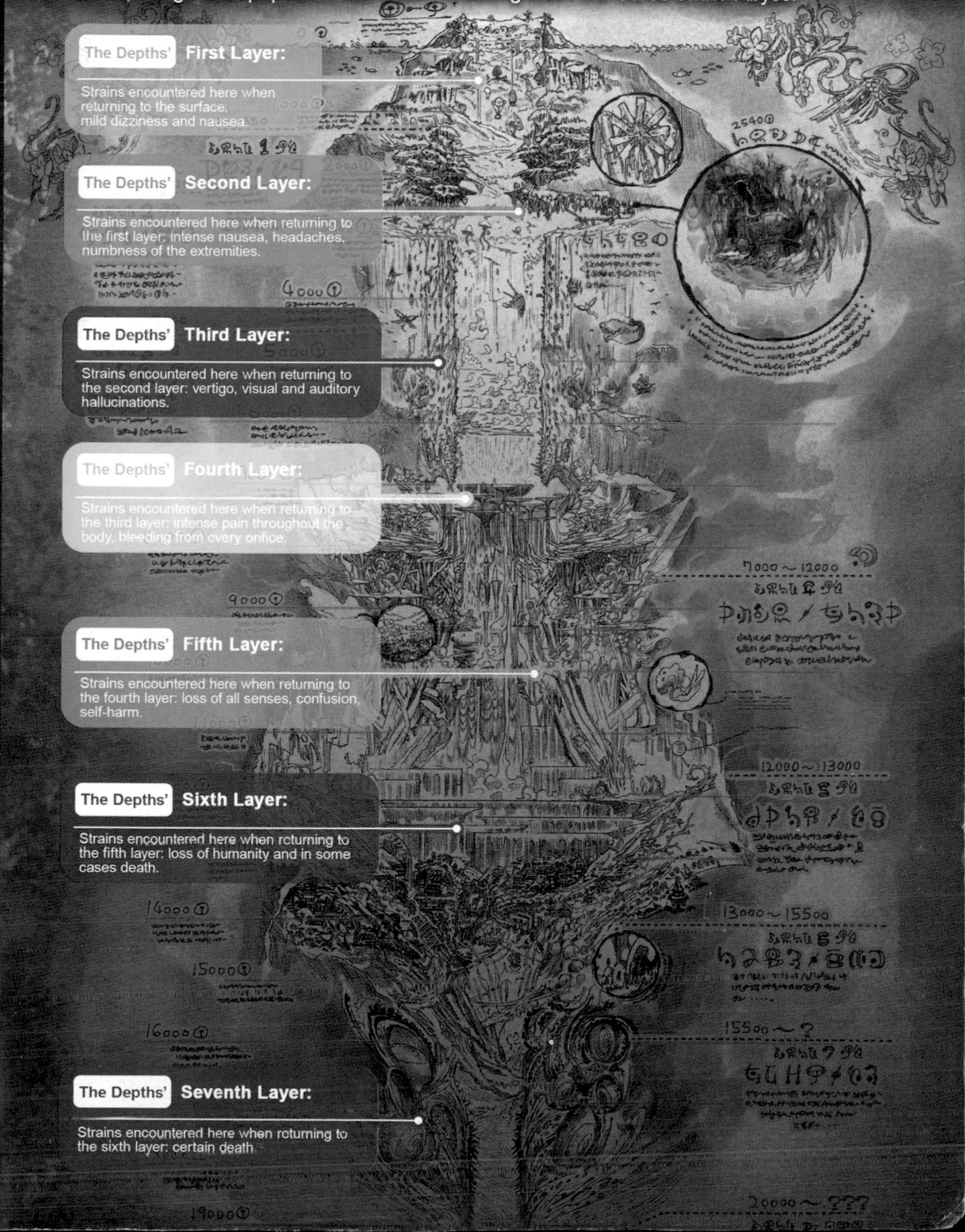

The Depths' First Layer:
Strains encountered here when returning to the surface: mild dizziness and nausea.
The Depths' Second Layer:
Strains encountered here when returning to the first layer: intense nausea, headaches, numbness of the extremities.
4000①
The Depths' Third Layer:
Strains encountered here when returning to the second layer: vertigo, visual and auditory hallucinations.
The Depths' Fourth Layer:
Strains encountered here when returning to the third layer: intense pain throughout the body, bleeding from every orifice.
9000①
7000 ~ 12000
The Depths' Fifth Layer:
Strains encountered here when returning to the fourth layer: loss of all senses, confusion, self-harm.
12000 ~ 13000
The Depths' Sixth Layer:
Strains encountered here when returning to the fifth layer: loss of humanity and in some cases death.
14000①
13000 ~ 15500
15000①
16000①
15500 ~ ?
The Depths' Seventh Layer:
Strains encountered here when returning to the sixth layer: certain death.
20000 ~ ???
19000①

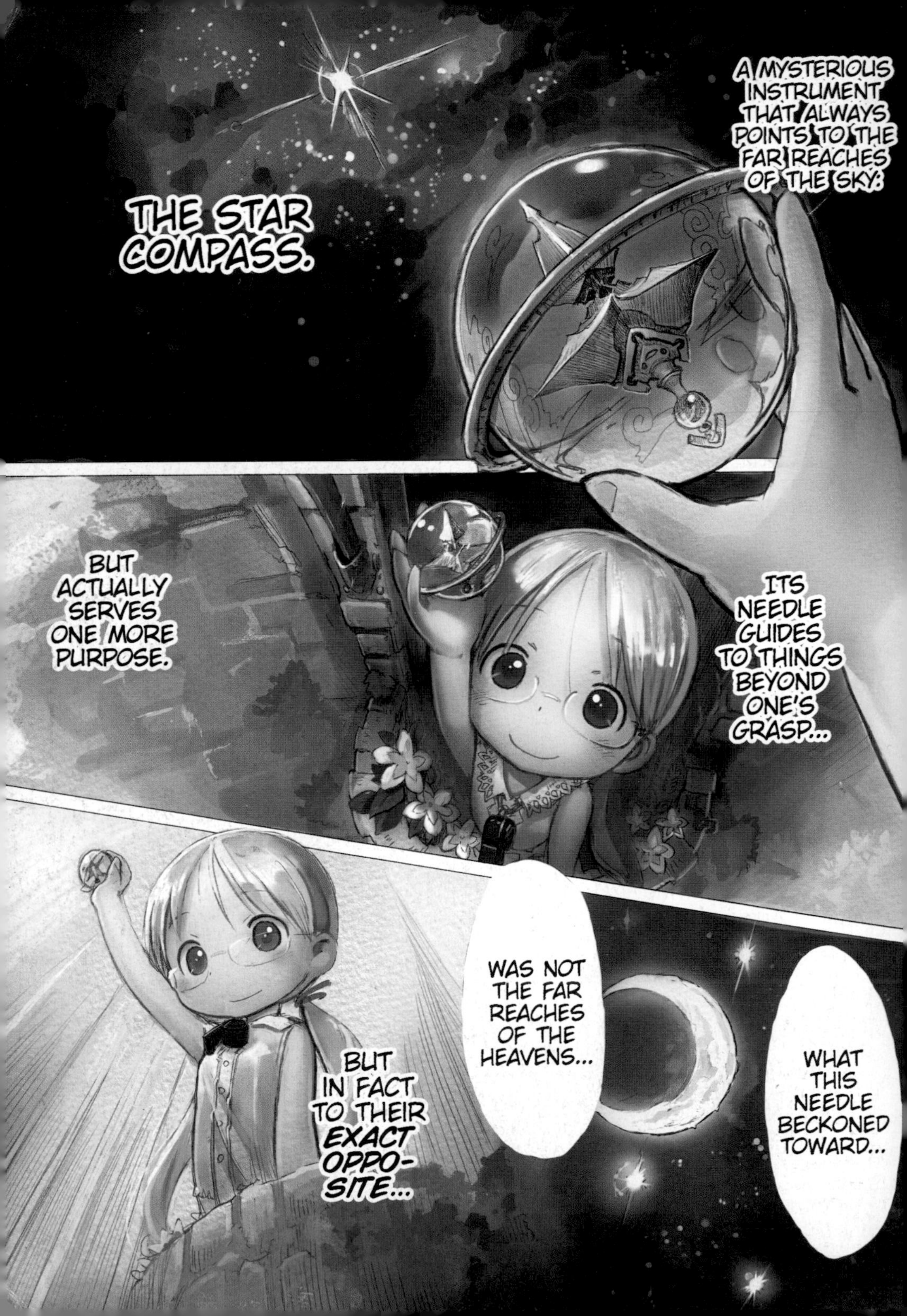
A MYSTERIOUS INSTRUMENT THAT ALWAYS POINTS TO THE FAR REACHES OF THE SKY:
THE STAR COMPASS.
ITS NEEDLE GUIDES TO THINGS BEYOND ONE'S GRASP...
BUT ACTUALLY SERVES ONE MORE PURPOSE.
WHAT THIS NEEDLE BECKONED TOWARD...
WAS NOT THE FAR REACHES OF THE HEAVENS...
BUT IN FACT TO THEIR *EXACT OPPO-SITE*...

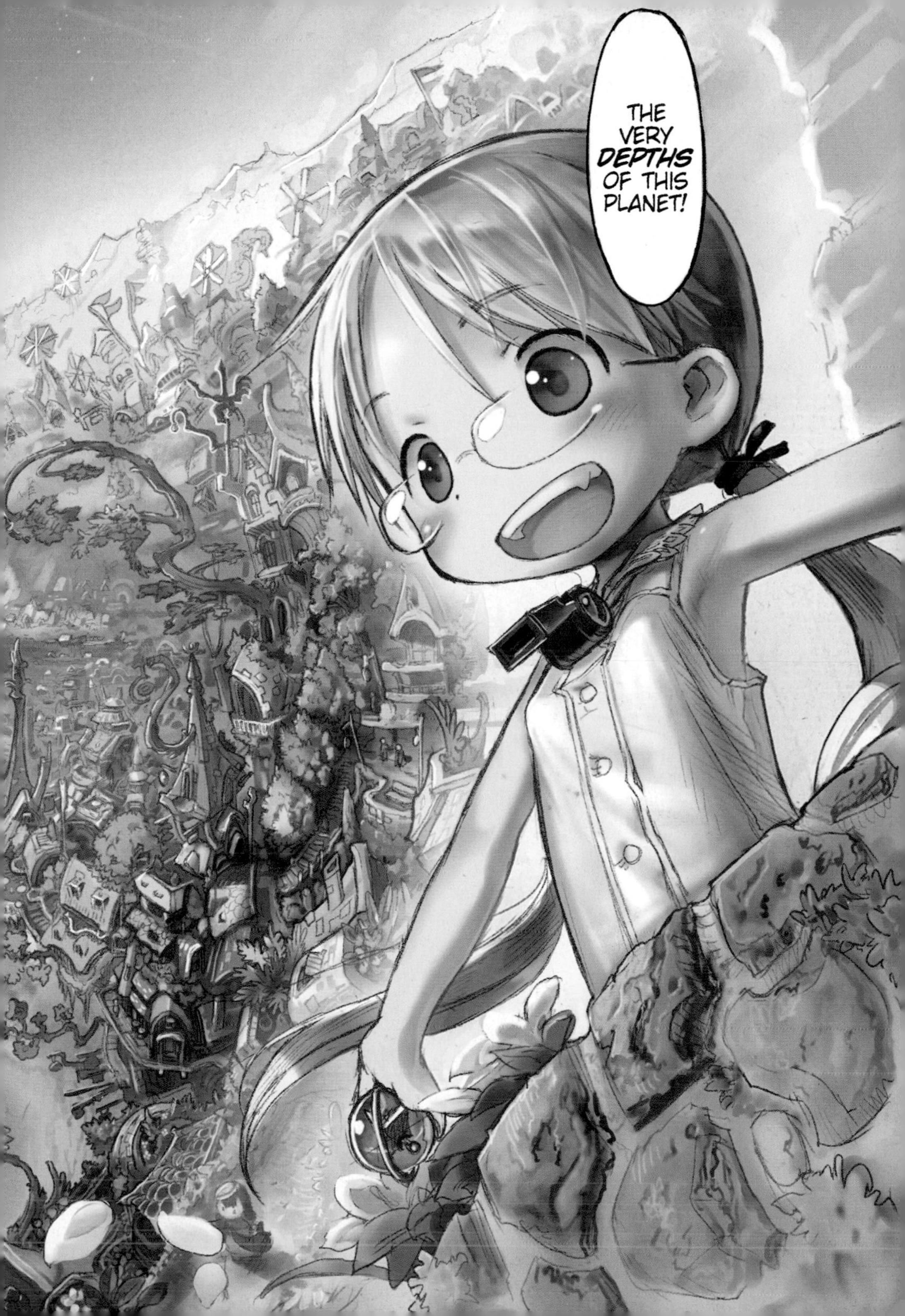
THE VERY DEPTHS OF THIS PLANET!

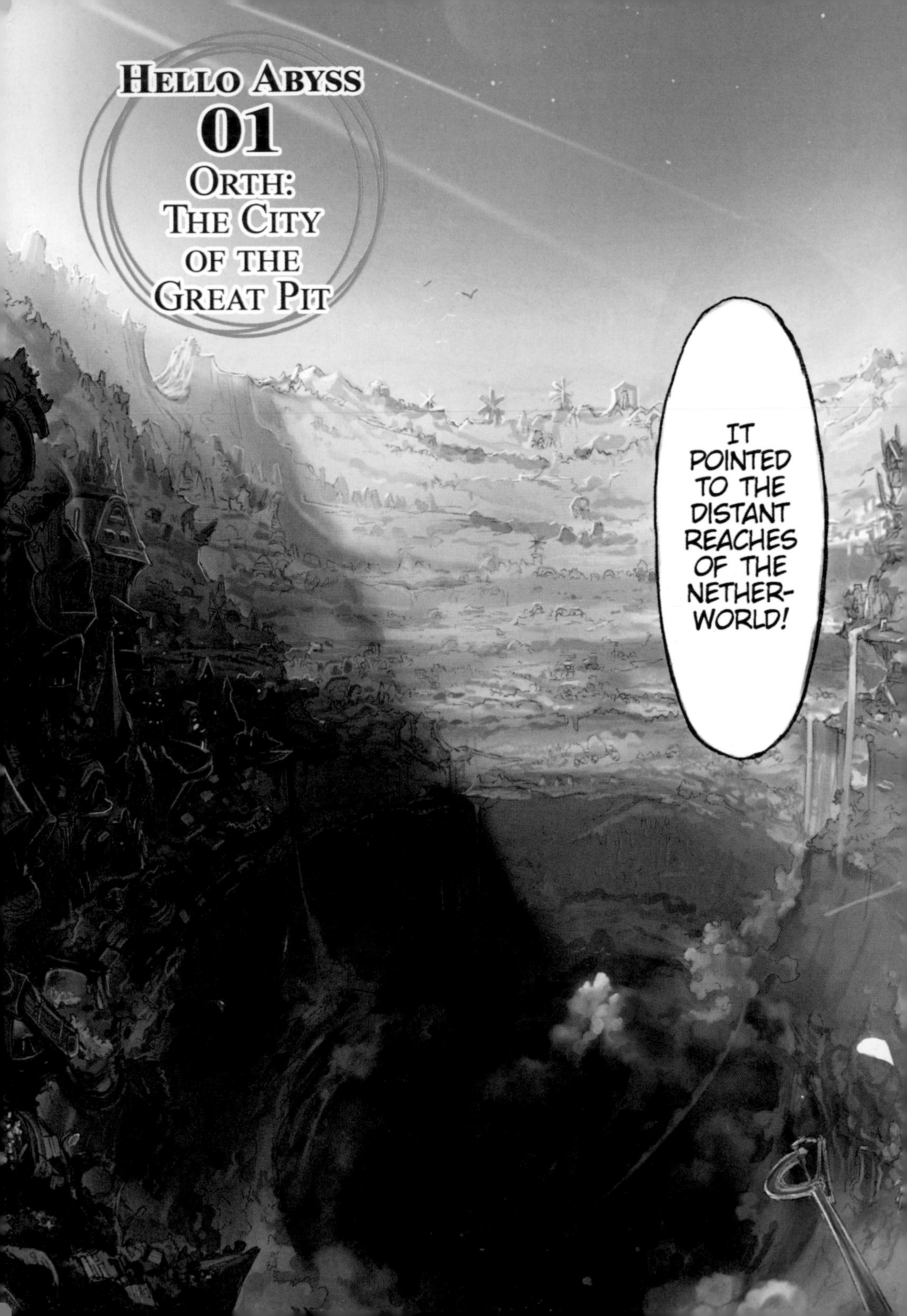
HELLO ABYSS
01
ORTH: THE CITY OF THE GREAT PIT
IT POINTED TO THE DISTANT REACHES OF THE NETHER-WORLD!

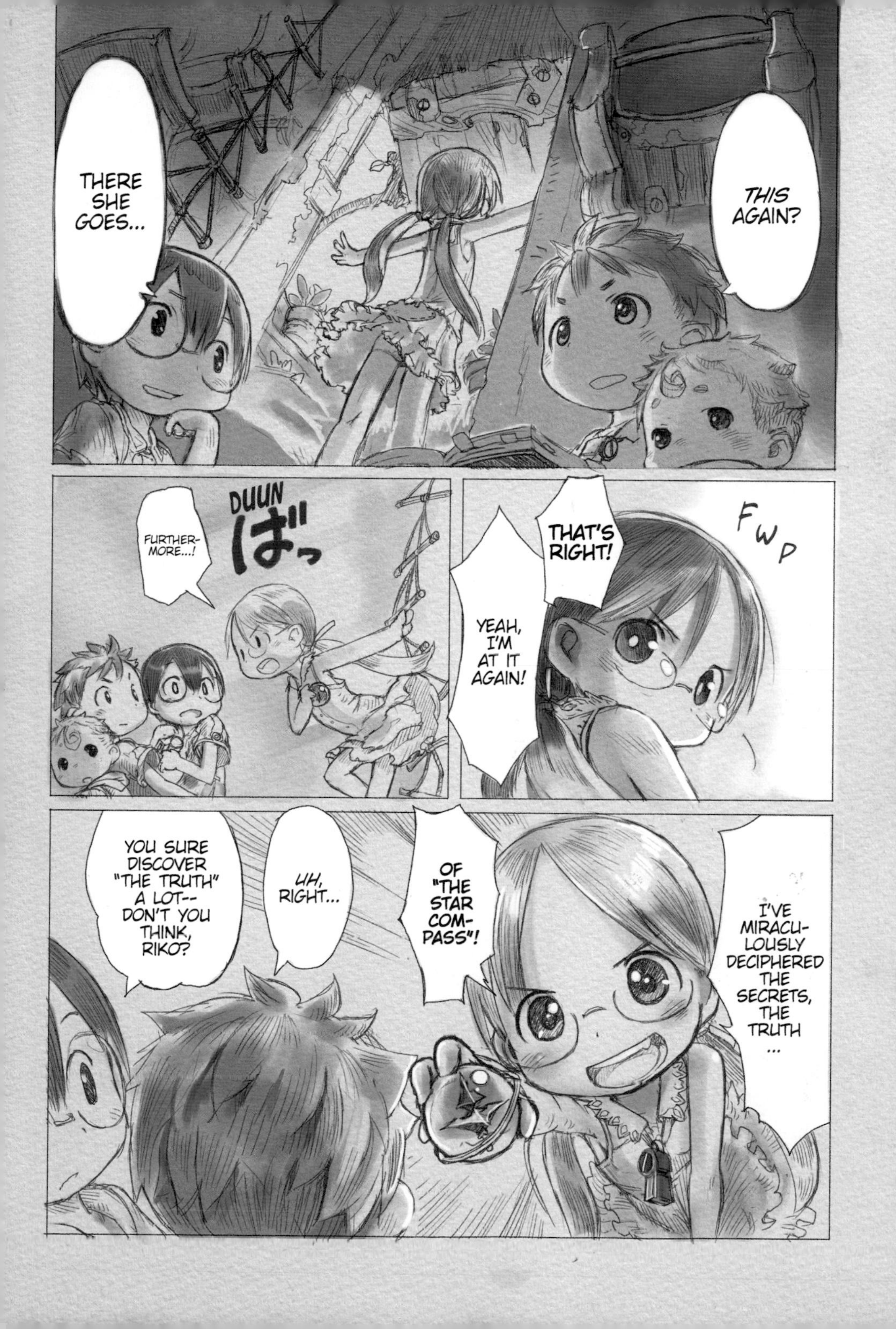
THIS AGAIN?
THERE SHE GOES...
THAT'S RIGHT!
FWP
YEAH, I'M AT IT AGAIN!
DUUN ばっ
FURTHER-MORE...!
I'VE MIRACU-LOUSLY DECIPHERED THE SECRETS, THE TRUTH ...
OF "THE STAR COM-PASS"!
UH, RIGHT...
YOU SURE DISCOVER "THE TRUTH" A LOT-- DON'T YOU THINK, RIKO?

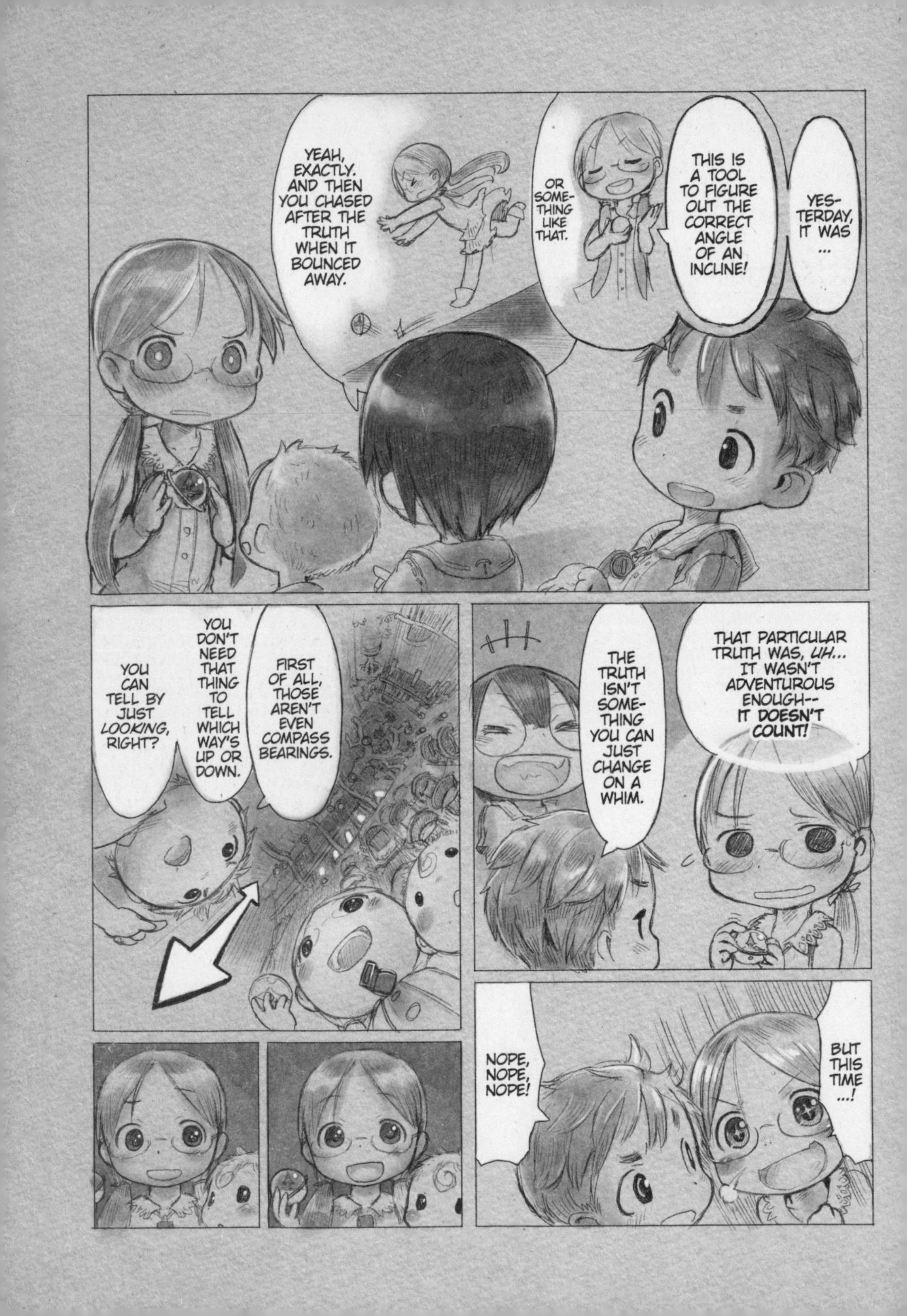
YESTERDAY, IT WAS ...
THIS IS A TOOL TO FIGURE OUT THE CORRECT ANGLE OF AN INCLINE!
OR SOMETHING LIKE THAT.
YEAH, EXACTLY. AND THEN YOU CHASED AFTER THE TRUTH WHEN IT BOUNCED AWAY.
THAT PARTICULAR TRUTH WAS, *UH*... IT WASN'T ADVENTUROUS ENOUGH-- **IT DOESN'T COUNT!**
THE TRUTH ISN'T SOMETHING YOU CAN JUST CHANGE ON A WHIM.
FIRST OF ALL, THOSE AREN'T EVEN COMPASS BEARINGS.
YOU DON'T NEED THAT THING TO TELL WHICH WAY'S UP OR DOWN.
YOU CAN TELL BY JUST *LOOKING*, RIGHT?
BUT THIS TIME ...!
NOPE, NOPE, NOPE!

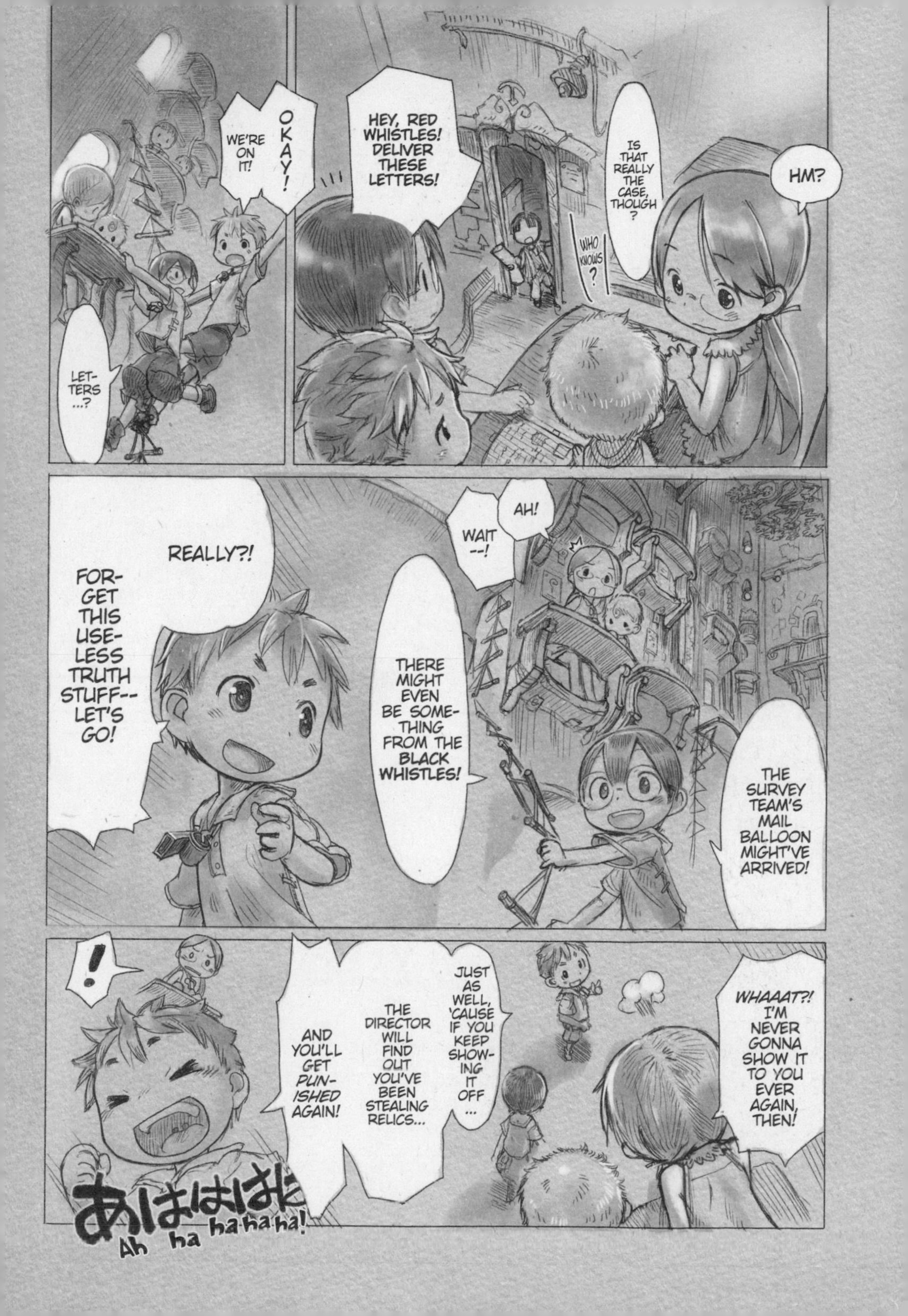
HM?
IS THAT REALLY THE CASE, THOUGH?
WHO KNOWS?
HEY, RED WHISTLES! DELIVER THESE LETTERS!
OKAY!
WE'RE ON IT!
LETTERS...?
AH!
WAIT--!
THE SURVEY TEAM'S MAIL BALLOON MIGHT'VE ARRIVED!
THERE MIGHT EVEN BE SOMETHING FROM THE BLACK WHISTLES!
REALLY?!
FORGET THIS USELESS TRUTH STUFF--LET'S GO!
WHAAAT?! I'M NEVER GONNA SHOW IT TO YOU EVER AGAIN, THEN!
JUST AS WELL, 'CAUSE IF YOU KEEP SHOWING IT OFF...
THE DIRECTOR WILL FIND OUT YOU'VE BEEN STEALING RELICS...
AND YOU'LL GET PUNISHED AGAIN!
!
あははは
Ah ha ha-ha-ha!

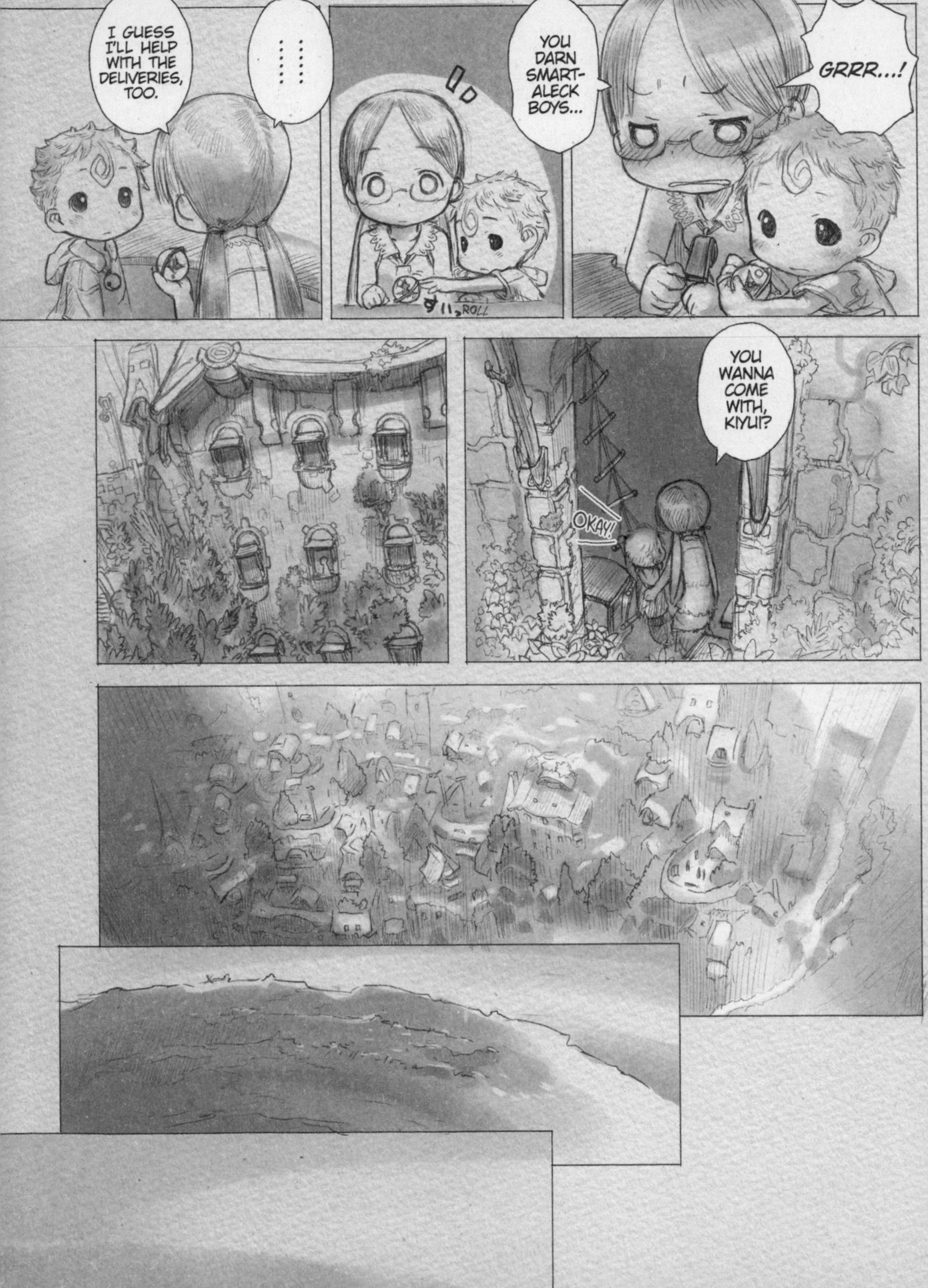
GRRR...!
YOU DARN SMART-ALECK BOYS...
ROLL
......
I GUESS I'LL HELP WITH THE DELIVERIES, TOO.
YOU WANNA COME WITH, KIYUI?
OKAY!

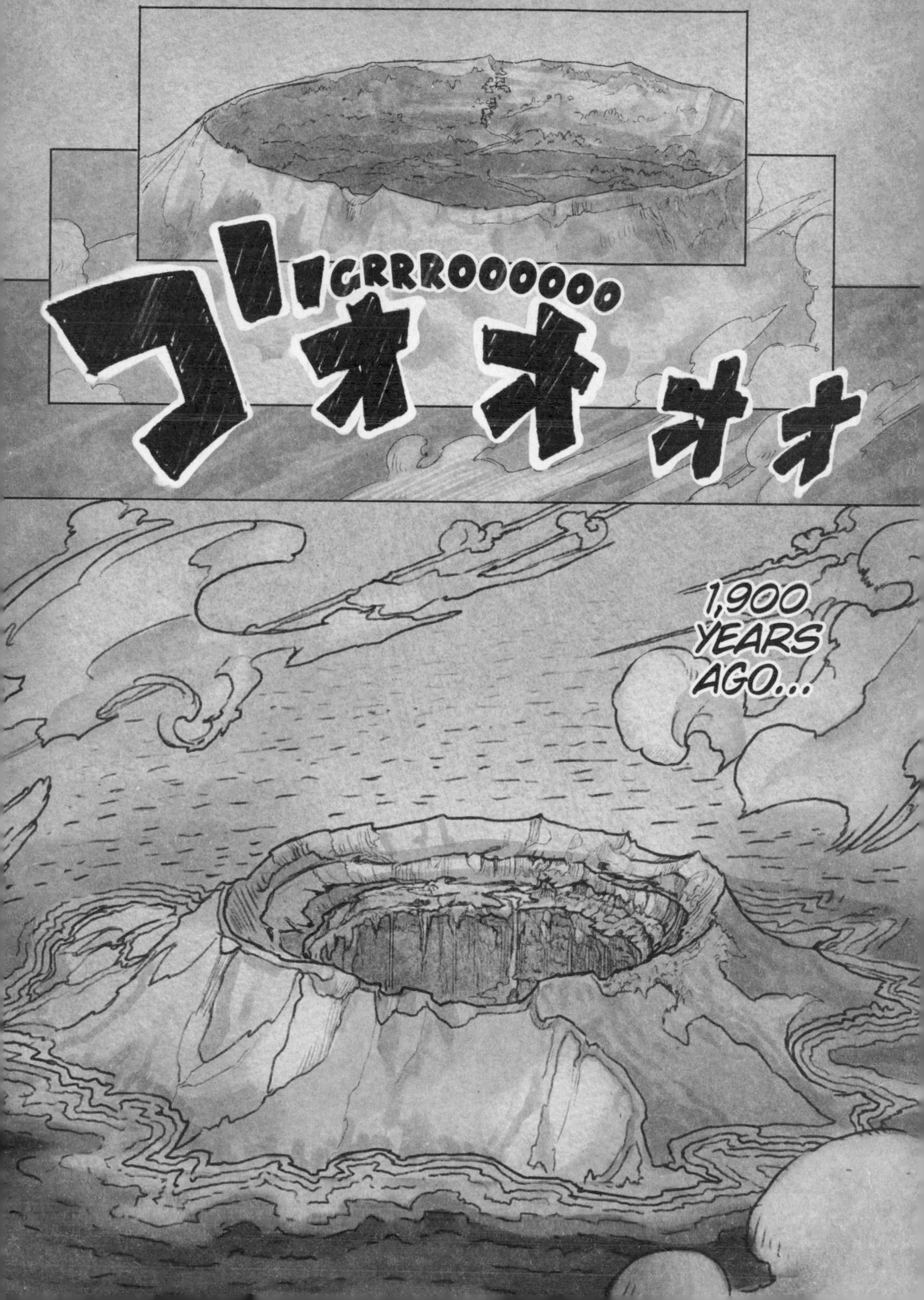
GRRROOOOOO
ゴオオォォ
1,900 YEARS AGO...

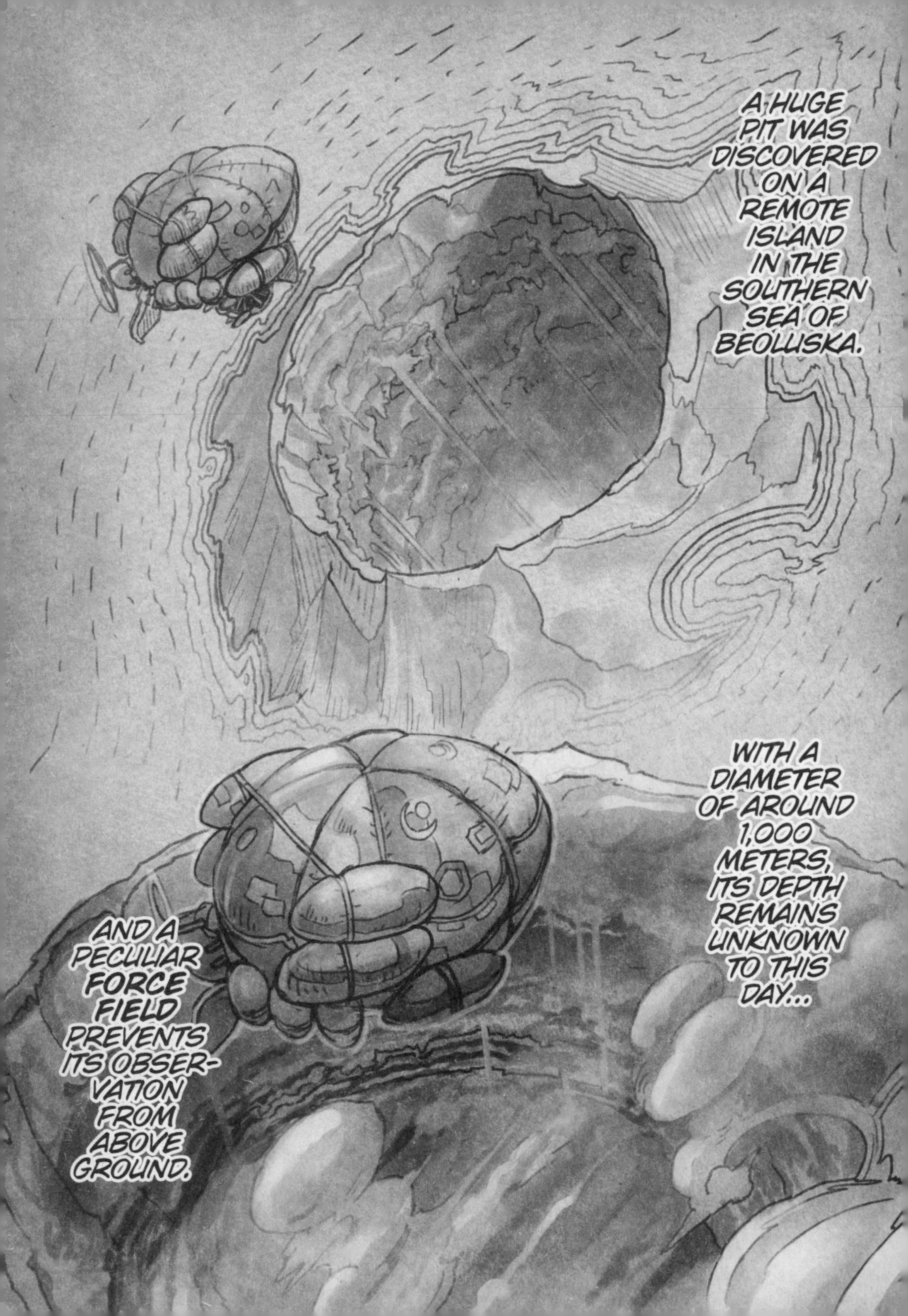
A HUGE PIT WAS DISCOVERED ON A REMOTE ISLAND IN THE SOUTHERN SEA OF BEOLUSKA.
WITH A DIAMETER OF AROUND 1,000 METERS, ITS DEPTH REMAINS UNKNOWN TO THIS DAY...
AND A PECULIAR FORCE FIELD PREVENTS ITS OBSER-VATION FROM ABOVE GROUND.

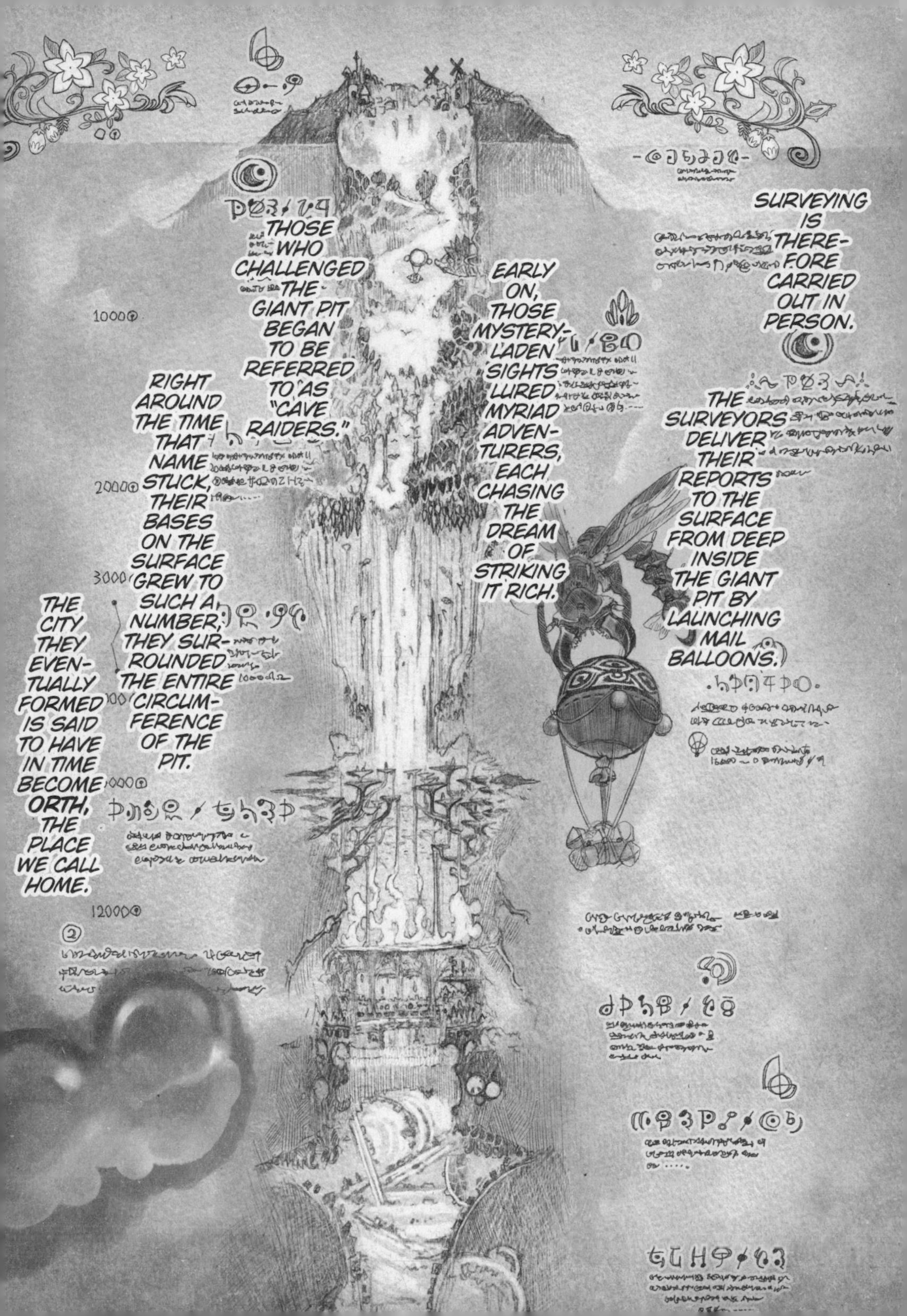
SURVEYING IS THEREFORE CARRIED OUT IN PERSON.
THE SURVEYORS DELIVER THEIR REPORTS TO THE SURFACE FROM DEEP INSIDE THE GIANT PIT BY LAUNCHING MAIL BALLOONS.
EARLY ON, THOSE MYSTERY-LADEN SIGHTS LURED MYRIAD ADVENTURERS, EACH CHASING THE DREAM OF STRIKING IT RICH.
THOSE WHO CHALLENGED THE GIANT PIT BEGAN TO BE REFERRED TO AS "CAVE RAIDERS."
RIGHT AROUND THE TIME THAT NAME STUCK, THEIR BASES ON THE SURFACE GREW TO SUCH A NUMBER, THEY SURROUNDED THE ENTIRE CIRCUMFERENCE OF THE PIT.
THE CITY THEY EVENTUALLY FORMED IS SAID TO HAVE IN TIME BECOME ORTH, THE PLACE WE CALL HOME.

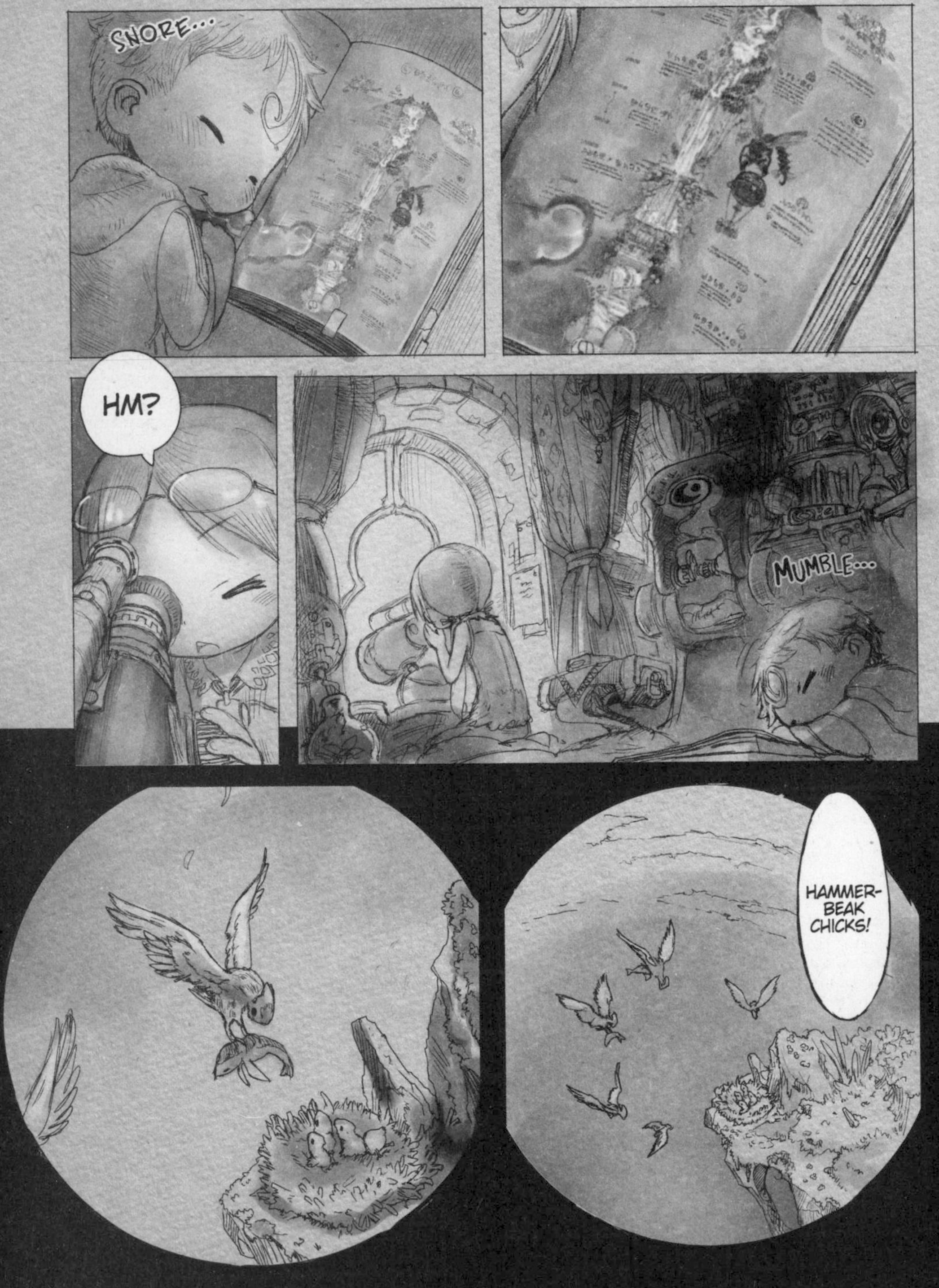
SNORE...
MUMBLE...
HM?
HAMMER-BEAK CHICKS!

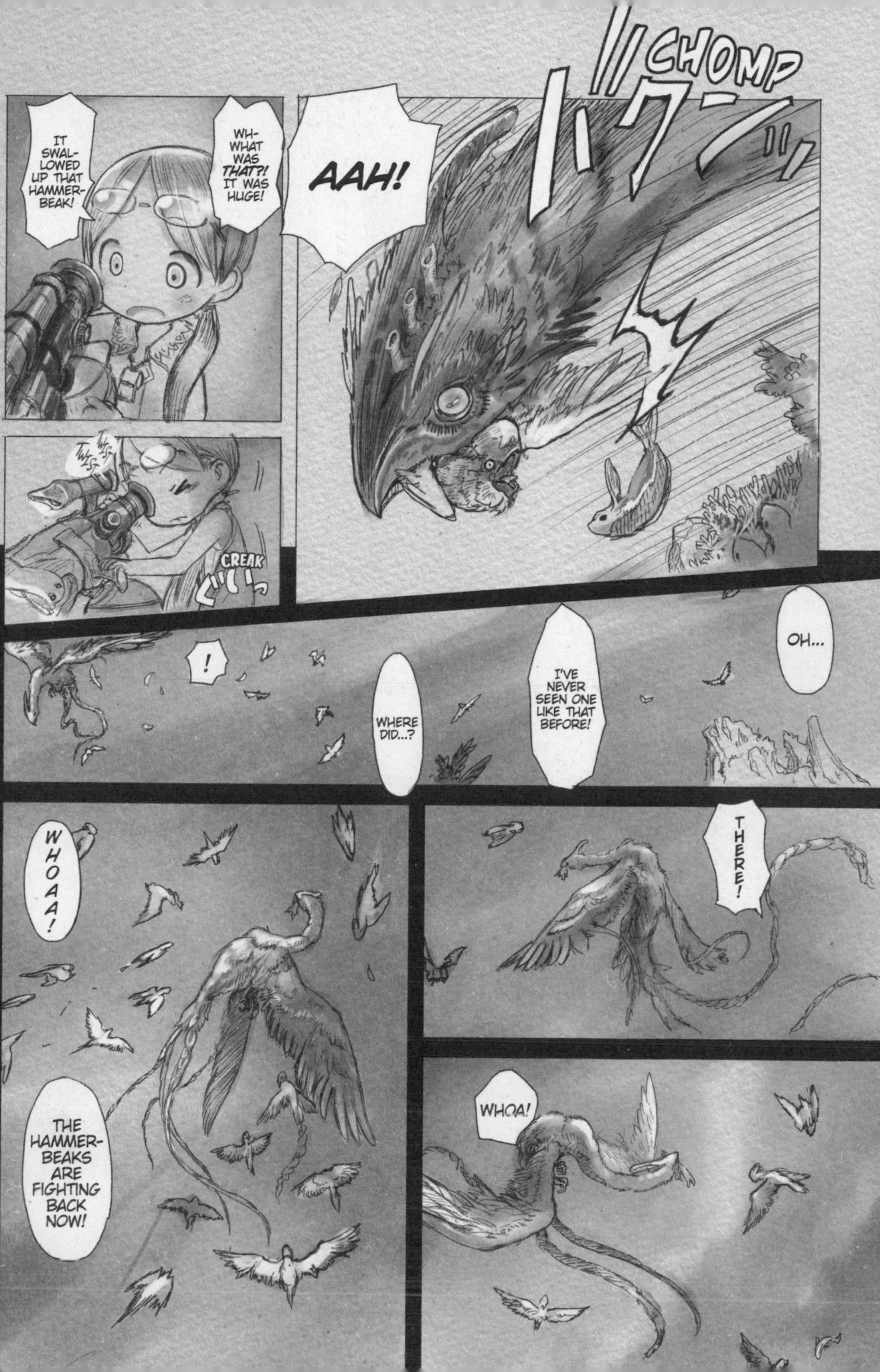
CHOMP
AAH!
WH-WHAT WAS THAT?! IT WAS HUGE!
IT SWALLOWED UP THAT HAMMERBEAK!
TWIST TWIST
CREAK
OH...
I'VE NEVER SEEN ONE LIKE THAT BEFORE!
WHERE DID...?
!
THERE!
WHOA!
WHOAAA!
THE HAMMERBEAKS ARE FIGHTING BACK NOW!

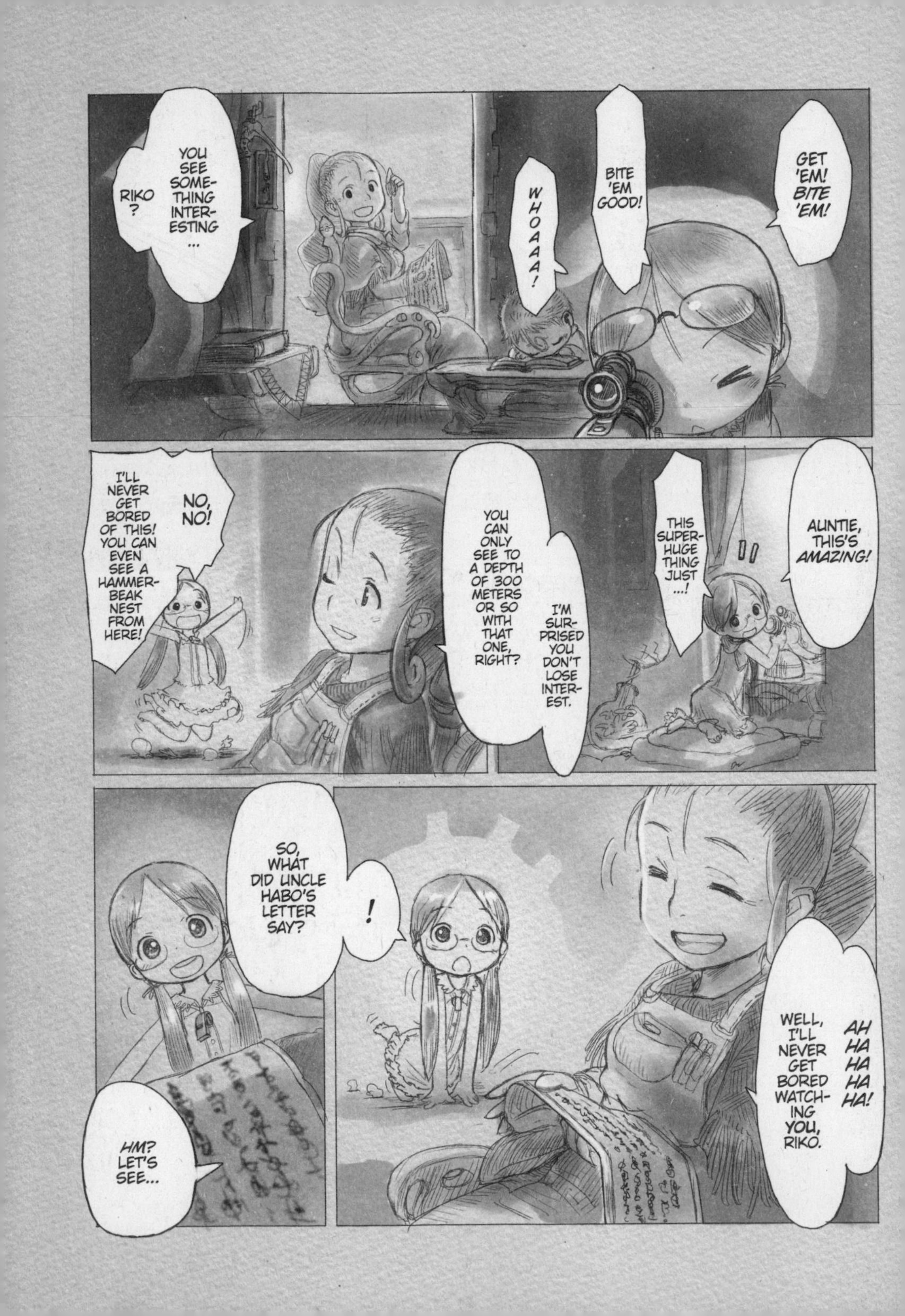
GET 'EM! BITE 'EM!
BITE 'EM GOOD!
WHOAAAA!
YOU SEE SOMETHING INTERESTING...
RIKO?
AUNTIE, THIS'S AMAZING!
THIS SUPER-HUGE THING JUST...!
YOU CAN ONLY SEE TO A DEPTH OF 300 METERS OR SO WITH THAT ONE, RIGHT?
I'M SURPRISED YOU DON'T LOSE INTEREST.
NO, NO!
I'LL NEVER GET BORED OF THIS! YOU CAN EVEN SEE A HAMMERBEAK NEST FROM HERE!
AH HA HA HA HA!
WELL, I'LL NEVER GET BORED WATCHING YOU, RIKO.
!
SO, WHAT DID UNCLE HABO'S LETTER SAY?
HM? LET'S SEE...

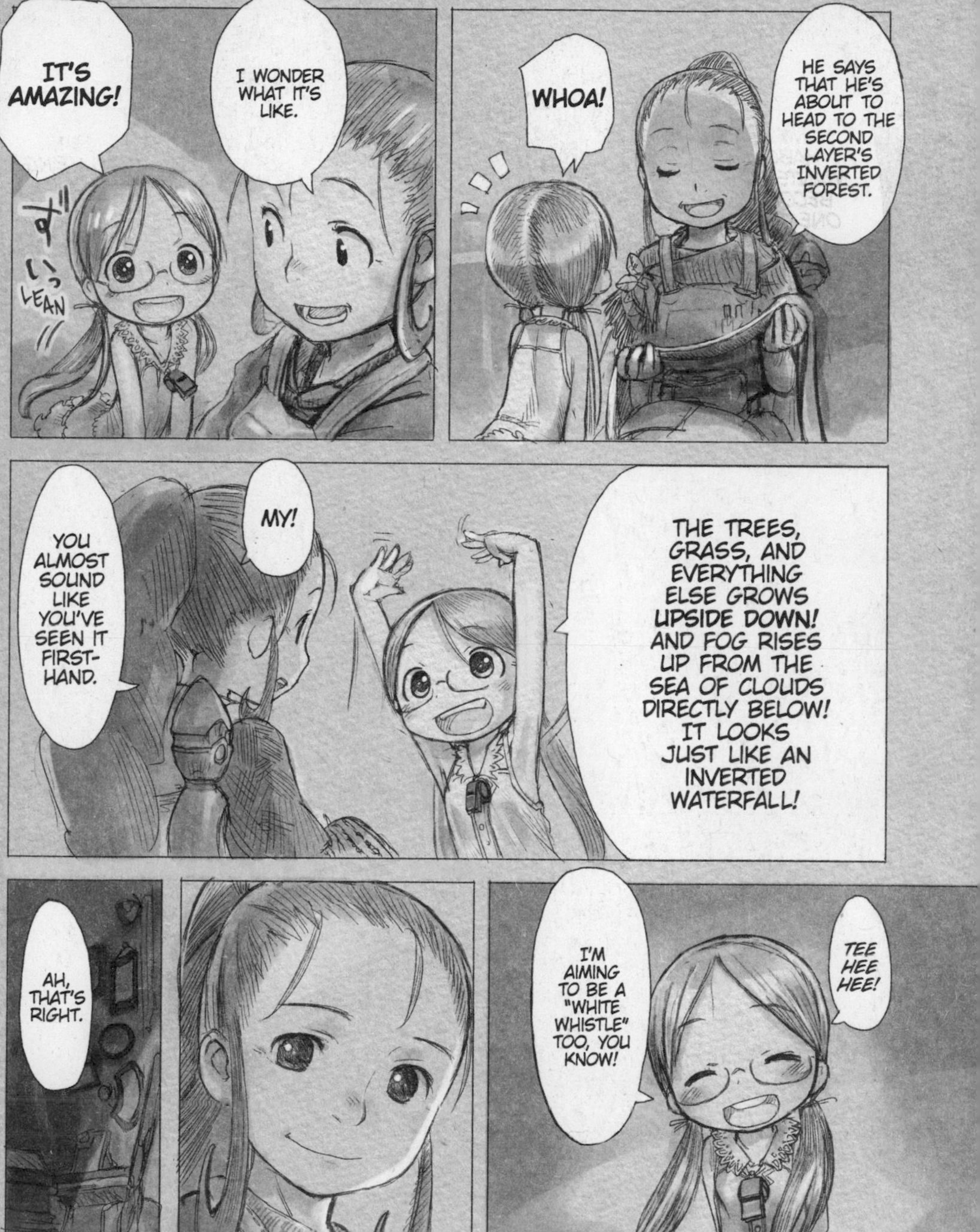
HE SAYS THAT HE'S ABOUT TO HEAD TO THE SECOND LAYER'S INVERTED FOREST.
WHOA!
I WONDER WHAT IT'S LIKE.
IT'S AMAZING!
ずいっ
LEAN
THE TREES, GRASS, AND EVERYTHING ELSE GROWS UPSIDE DOWN! AND FOG RISES UP FROM THE SEA OF CLOUDS DIRECTLY BELOW! IT LOOKS JUST LIKE AN INVERTED WATERFALL!
MY!
YOU ALMOST SOUND LIKE YOU'VE SEEN IT FIRST-HAND.
TEE HEE HEE!
I'M AIMING TO BE A "WHITE WHISTLE" TOO, YOU KNOW!
AH, THAT'S RIGHT.

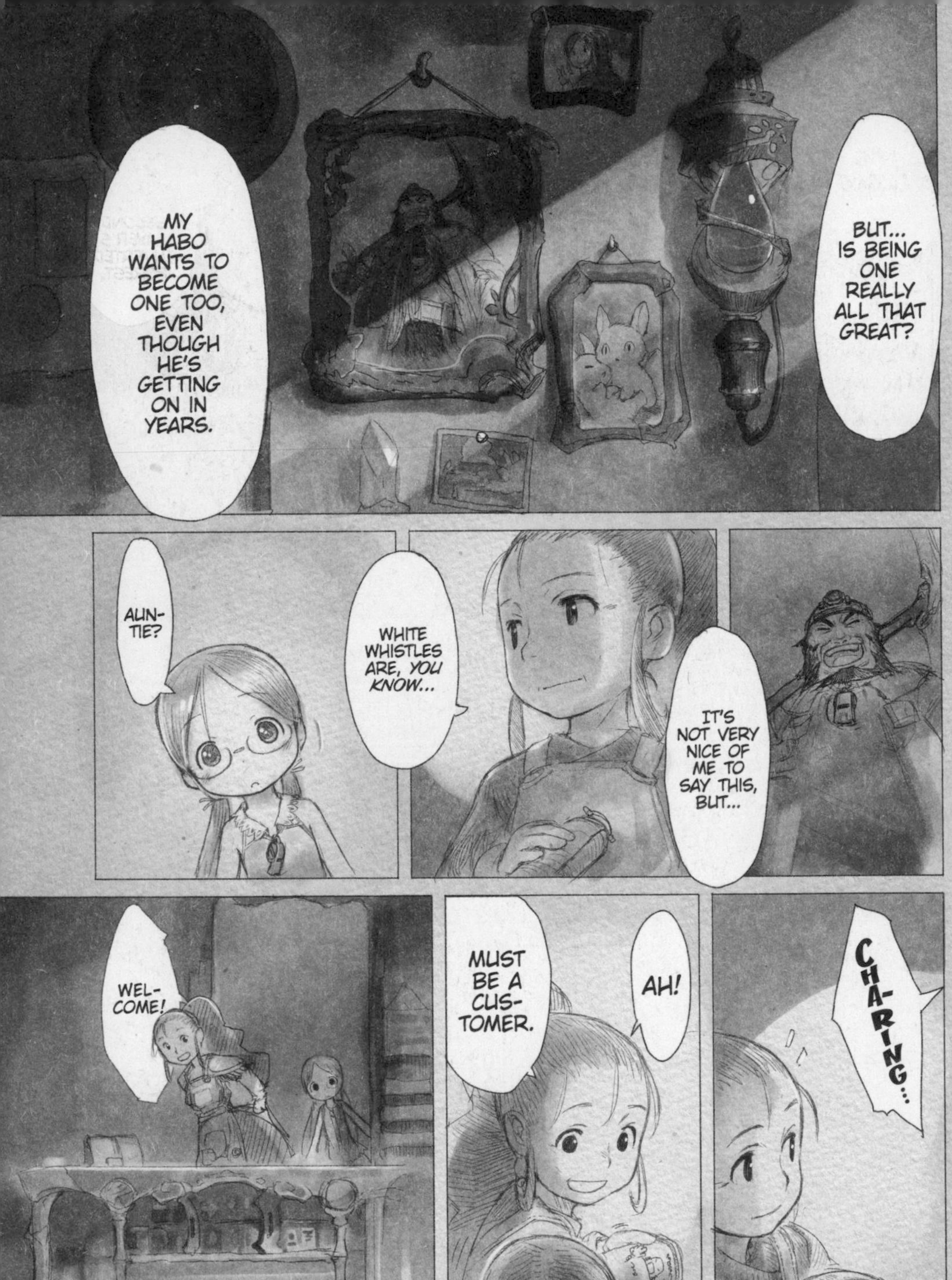
BUT... IS BEING ONE REALLY ALL THAT GREAT?
MY HABO WANTS TO BECOME ONE TOO, EVEN THOUGH HE'S GETTING ON IN YEARS.
IT'S NOT VERY NICE OF ME TO SAY THIS, BUT...
WHITE WHISTLES ARE, YOU KNOW...
AUN-TIE?
CHA-RING...
AH!
MUST BE A CUS-TOMER.
WEL-COME!

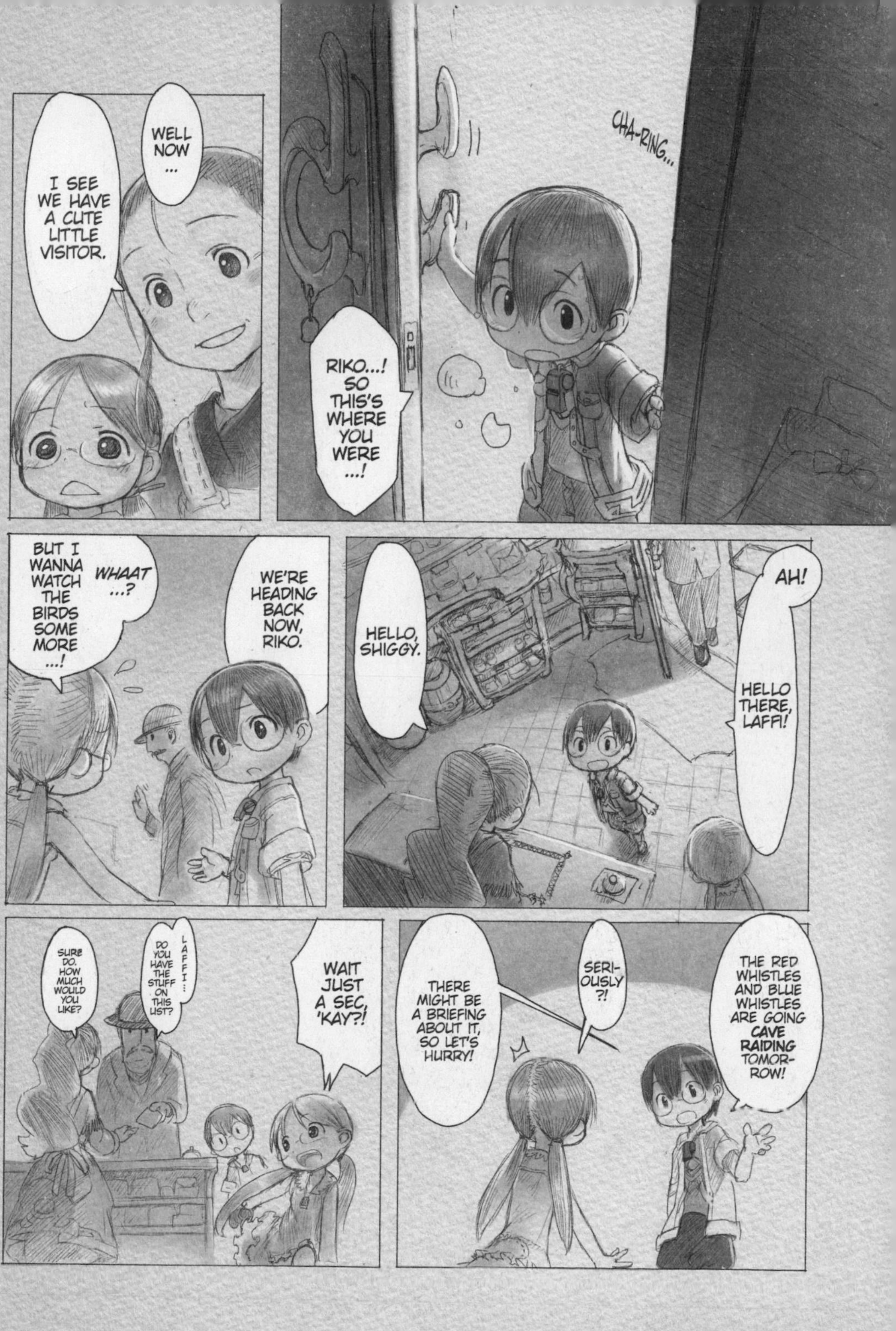
CHA-RING...
RIKO...! SO THIS'S WHERE YOU WERE ...!
WELL NOW ...
I SEE WE HAVE A CUTE LITTLE VISITOR.
AH!
HELLO THERE, LAFFI!
HELLO, SHIGGY.
WE'RE HEADING BACK NOW, RIKO.
WHAAT ...?
BUT I WANNA WATCH THE BIRDS SOME MORE ...!
THE RED WHISTLES AND BLUE WHISTLES ARE GOING CAVE RAIDING TOMORROW!
SERIOUSLY?!
THERE MIGHT BE A BRIEFING ABOUT IT, SO LET'S HURRY!
WAIT JUST A SEC, 'KAY?!
LAFFI... DO YOU HAVE THE STUFF ON THIS LIST?
SURE DO. HOW MUCH WOULD YOU LIKE?

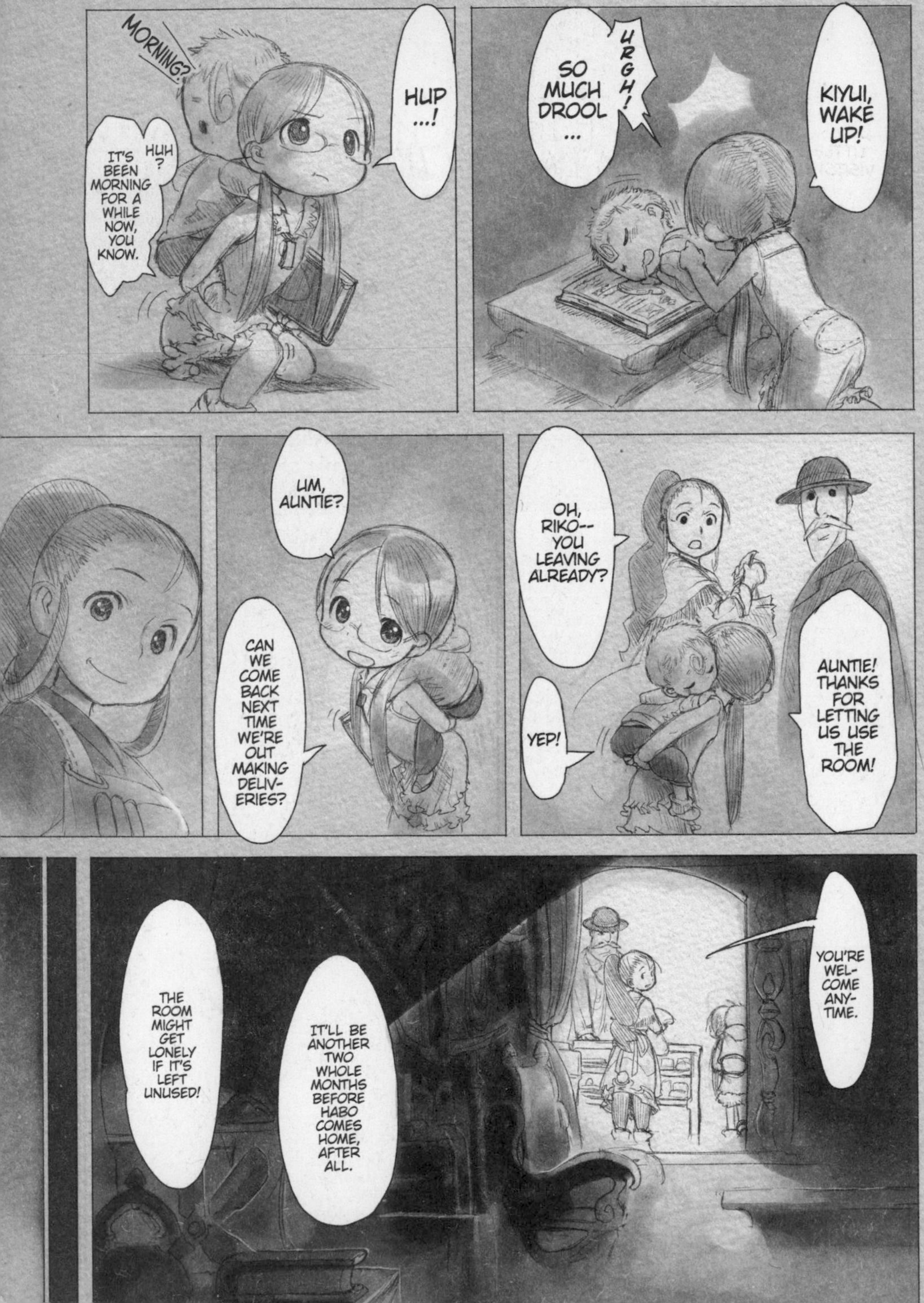
KIYUI, WAKE UP!
URGH!
SO MUCH DROOL ...
HUP ...!
MORNING?
HUH?
IT'S BEEN MORNING FOR A WHILE NOW, YOU KNOW.
AUNTIE! THANKS FOR LETTING US USE THE ROOM!
OH, RIKO-- YOU LEAVING ALREADY?
YEP!
UM, AUNTIE?
CAN WE COME BACK NEXT TIME WE'RE OUT MAKING DELIV- ERIES?
YOU'RE WEL- COME ANY- TIME.
IT'LL BE ANOTHER TWO WHOLE MONTHS BEFORE HABO COMES HOME, AFTER ALL.
THE ROOM MIGHT GET LONELY IF IT'S LEFT UNUSED!

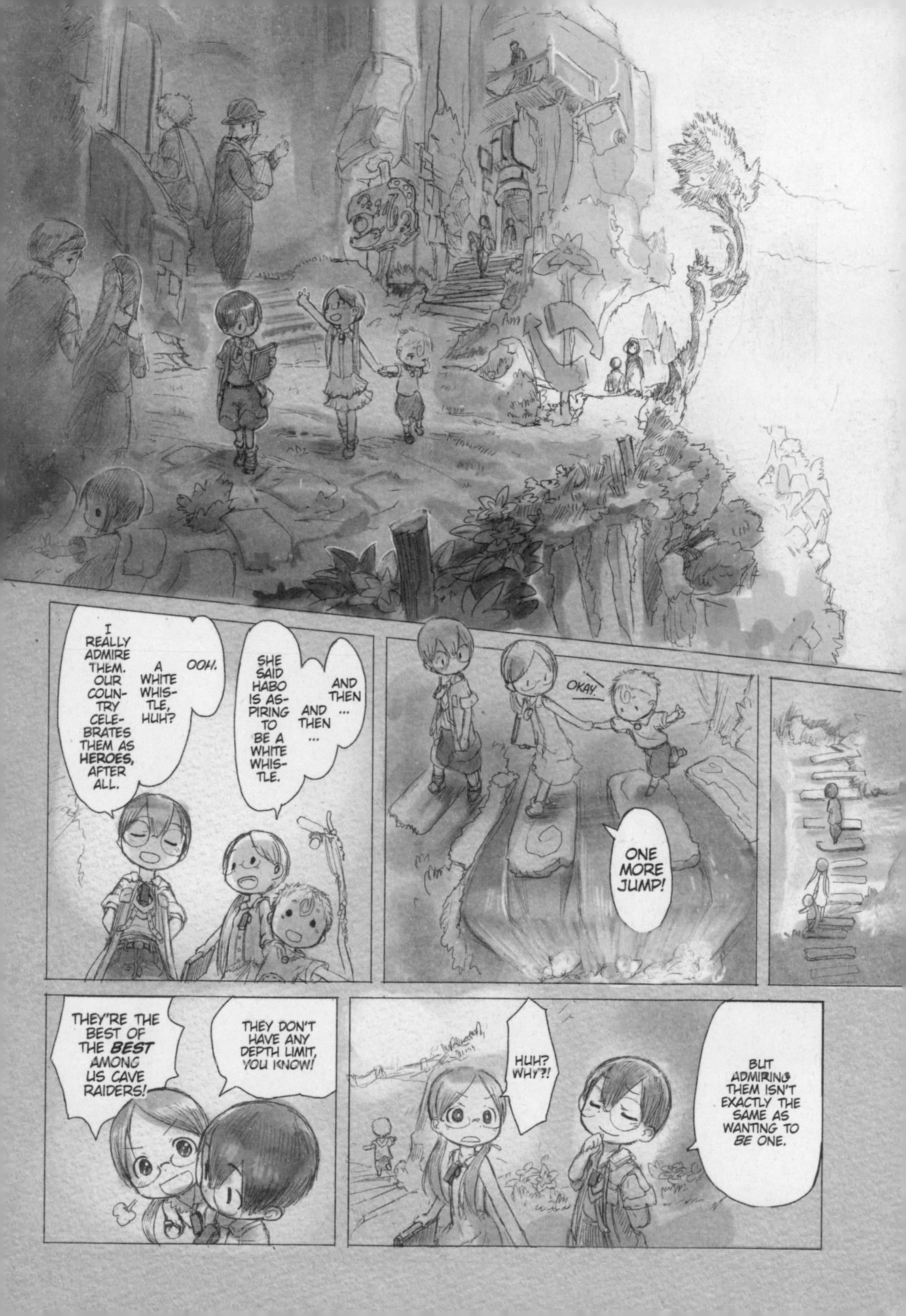
OKAY.
ONE MORE JUMP!
AND THEN ...
AND THEN ...
SHE SAID HABO IS ASPIRING TO BE A WHITE WHISTLE.
OOH.
A WHITE WHISTLE, HUH?
I REALLY ADMIRE THEM. OUR COUNTRY CELEBRATES THEM AS HEROES, AFTER ALL.
BUT ADMIRING THEM ISN'T EXACTLY THE SAME AS WANTING TO BE ONE.
HUH? WHY?!
THEY DON'T HAVE ANY DEPTH LIMIT, YOU KNOW!
THEY'RE THE BEST OF THE BEST AMONG US CAVE RAIDERS!

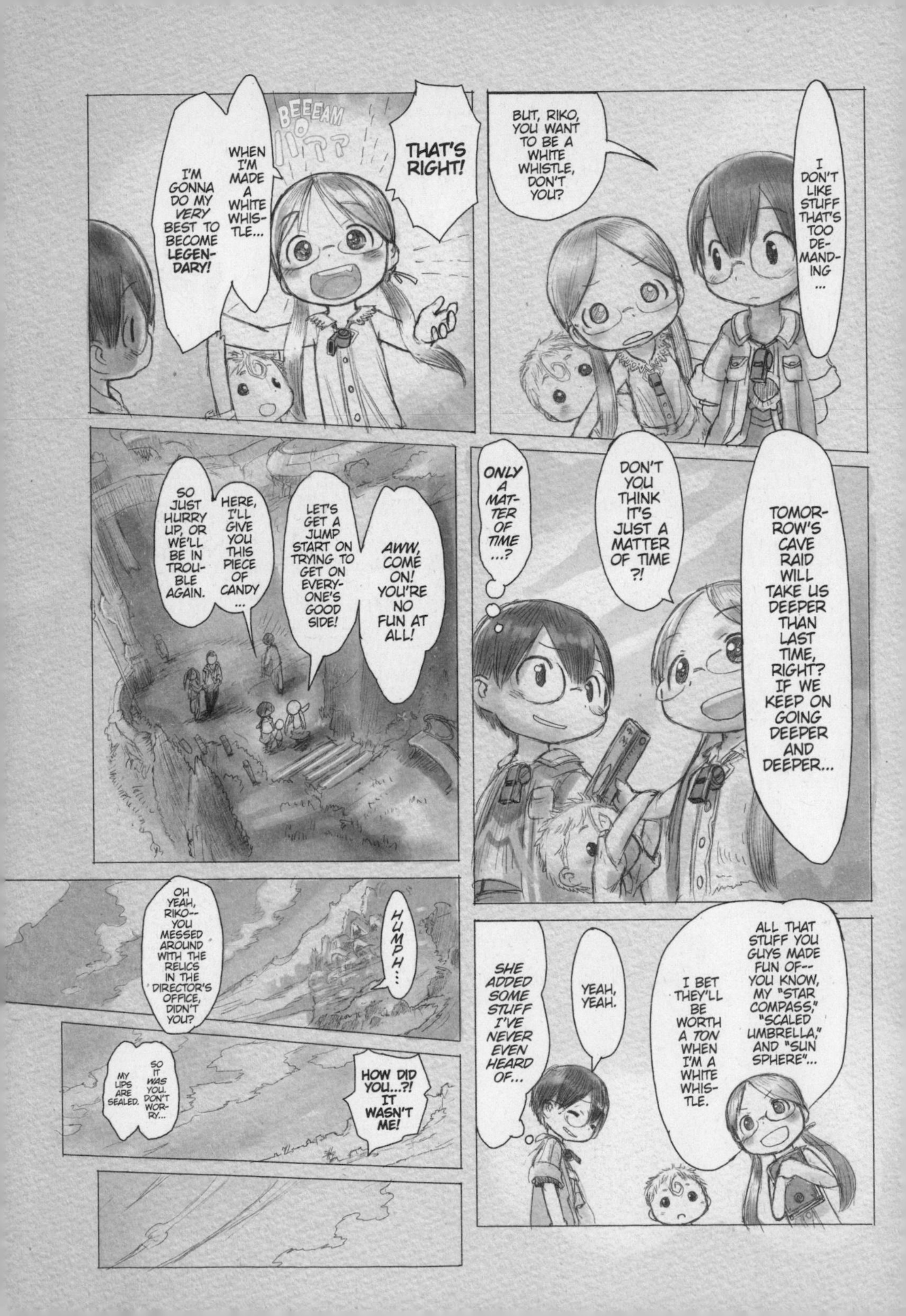
I DON'T LIKE STUFF THAT'S TOO DE-MAND-ING...
BUT, RIKO, YOU WANT TO BE A WHITE WHISTLE, DON'T YOU?
BEEEAM
THAT'S RIGHT!
WHEN I'M MADE A WHITE WHIS-TLE...
I'M GONNA DO MY *VERY* BEST TO BECOME LEGEN-DARY!
TOMOR-ROW'S CAVE RAID WILL TAKE US DEEPER THAN LAST TIME, RIGHT? IF WE KEEP ON GOING DEEPER AND DEEPER...
DON'T YOU THINK IT'S JUST A MATTER OF TIME ?!
ONLY A MAT-TER OF TIME ...?
AWW, COME ON! YOU'RE NO FUN AT ALL!
LET'S GET A JUMP START ON TRYING TO GET ON EVERY-ONE'S GOOD SIDE!
HERE, I'LL GIVE YOU THIS PIECE OF CANDY ...
SO JUST HURRY UP, OR WE'LL BE IN TROU-BLE AGAIN.
ALL THAT STUFF YOU GUYS MADE FUN OF-- YOU KNOW, MY "STAR COMPASS," "SCALED UMBRELLA," AND "SUN SPHERE"...
I BET THEY'LL BE WORTH A *TON* WHEN I'M A WHITE WHIS-TLE.
YEAH, YEAH.
SHE ADDED SOME STUFF I'VE NEVER EVEN HEARD OF...
HUMPH...
OH YEAH, RIKO-- YOU MESSED AROUND WITH THE RELICS IN THE DIRECTOR'S OFFICE, DIDN'T YOU?
HOW DID YOU...?! IT WASN'T ME!
SO IT *WAS* YOU. DON'T WOR-RY...
MY LIPS ARE SEALED.

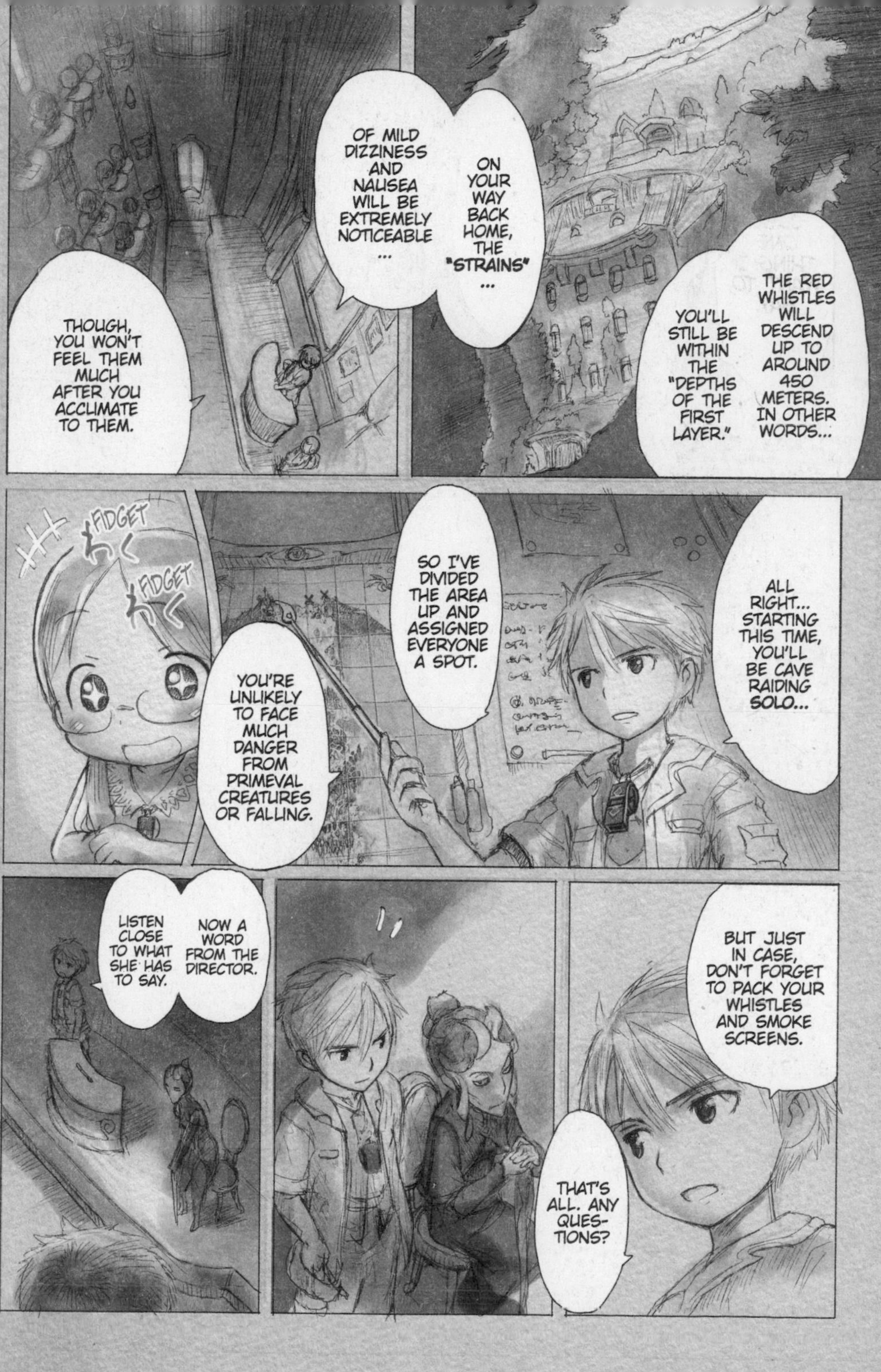
THE RED WHISTLES WILL DESCEND UP TO AROUND 450 METERS. IN OTHER WORDS...
YOU'LL STILL BE WITHIN THE "DEPTHS OF THE FIRST LAYER."
ON YOUR WAY BACK HOME, THE "STRAINS"...
OF MILD DIZZINESS AND NAUSEA WILL BE EXTREMELY NOTICEABLE...
THOUGH, YOU WON'T FEEL THEM MUCH AFTER YOU ACCLIMATE TO THEM.
ALL RIGHT... STARTING THIS TIME, YOU'LL BE CAVE RAIDING SOLO...
SO I'VE DIVIDED THE AREA UP AND ASSIGNED EVERYONE A SPOT.
YOU'RE UNLIKELY TO FACE MUCH DANGER FROM PRIMEVAL CREATURES OR FALLING.
FIDGET
FIDGET
BUT JUST IN CASE, DON'T FORGET TO PACK YOUR WHISTLES AND SMOKE SCREENS.
THAT'S ALL. ANY QUES-TIONS?
NOW A WORD FROM THE DIRECTOR.
LISTEN CLOSE TO WHAT SHE HAS TO SAY.

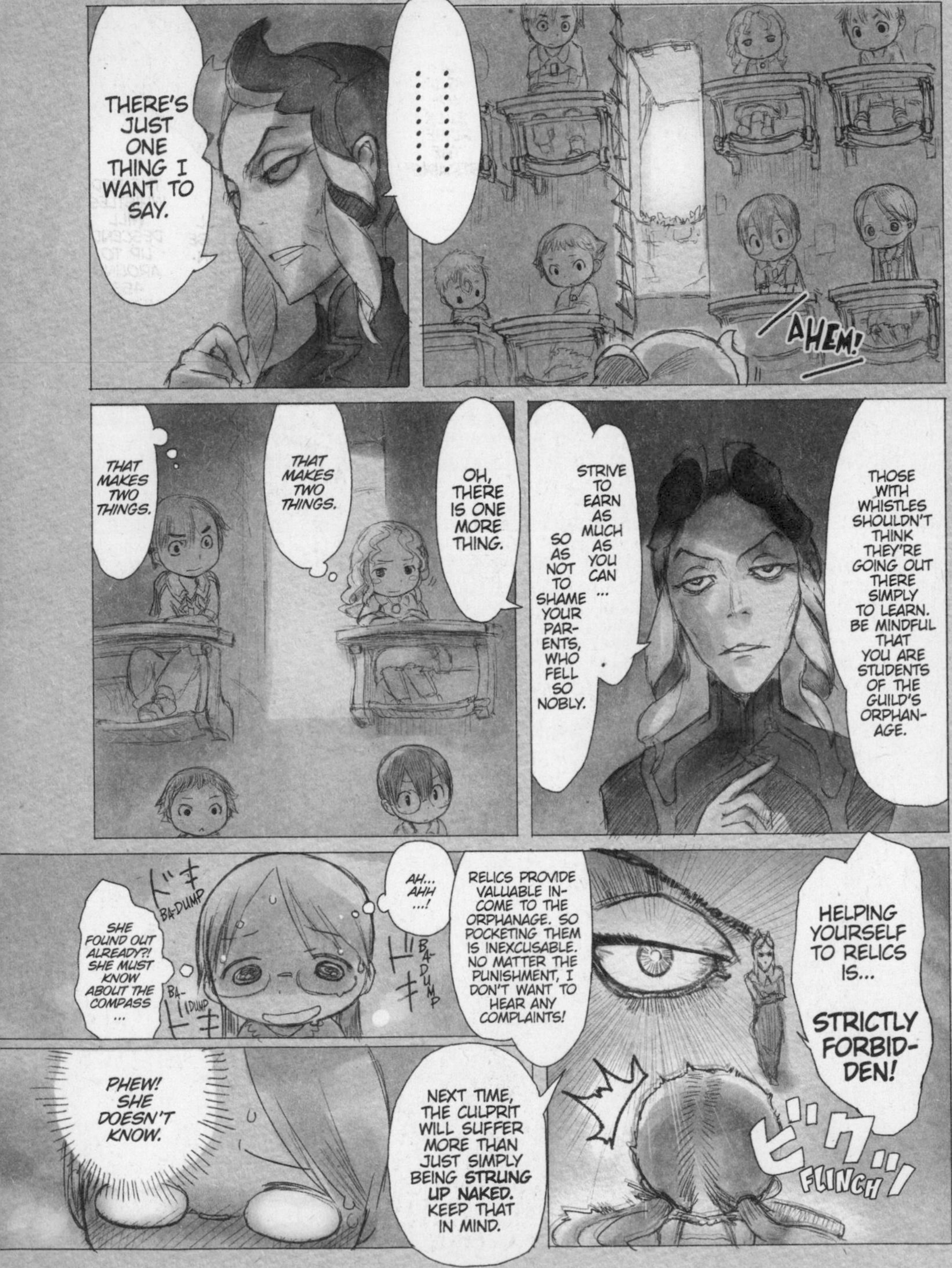
AHEM!
......
THERE'S JUST ONE THING I WANT TO SAY.
THOSE WITH WHISTLES SHOULDN'T THINK THEY'RE GOING OUT THERE SIMPLY TO LEARN. BE MINDFUL THAT YOU ARE STUDENTS OF THE GUILD'S ORPHANAGE.
STRIVE TO EARN AS MUCH AS YOU CAN ... SO AS NOT TO SHAME YOUR PARENTS, WHO FELL SO NOBLY.
OH, THERE IS ONE MORE THING.
THAT MAKES TWO THINGS.
THAT MAKES TWO THINGS.
HELPING YOURSELF TO RELICS IS...
STRICTLY FORBIDDEN!
FLINCH
RELICS PROVIDE VALUABLE INCOME TO THE ORPHANAGE. SO POCKETING THEM IS INEXCUSABLE. NO MATTER THE PUNISHMENT, I DON'T WANT TO HEAR ANY COMPLAINTS!
AH... AHH ...!
BA-DUMP
BA-DUMP
BA-DUMP
SHE FOUND OUT ALREADY?! SHE MUST KNOW ABOUT THE COMPASS ...
NEXT TIME, THE CULPRIT WILL SUFFER MORE THAN JUST SIMPLY BEING STRUNG UP NAKED. KEEP THAT IN MIND.
PHEW! SHE DOESN'T KNOW.

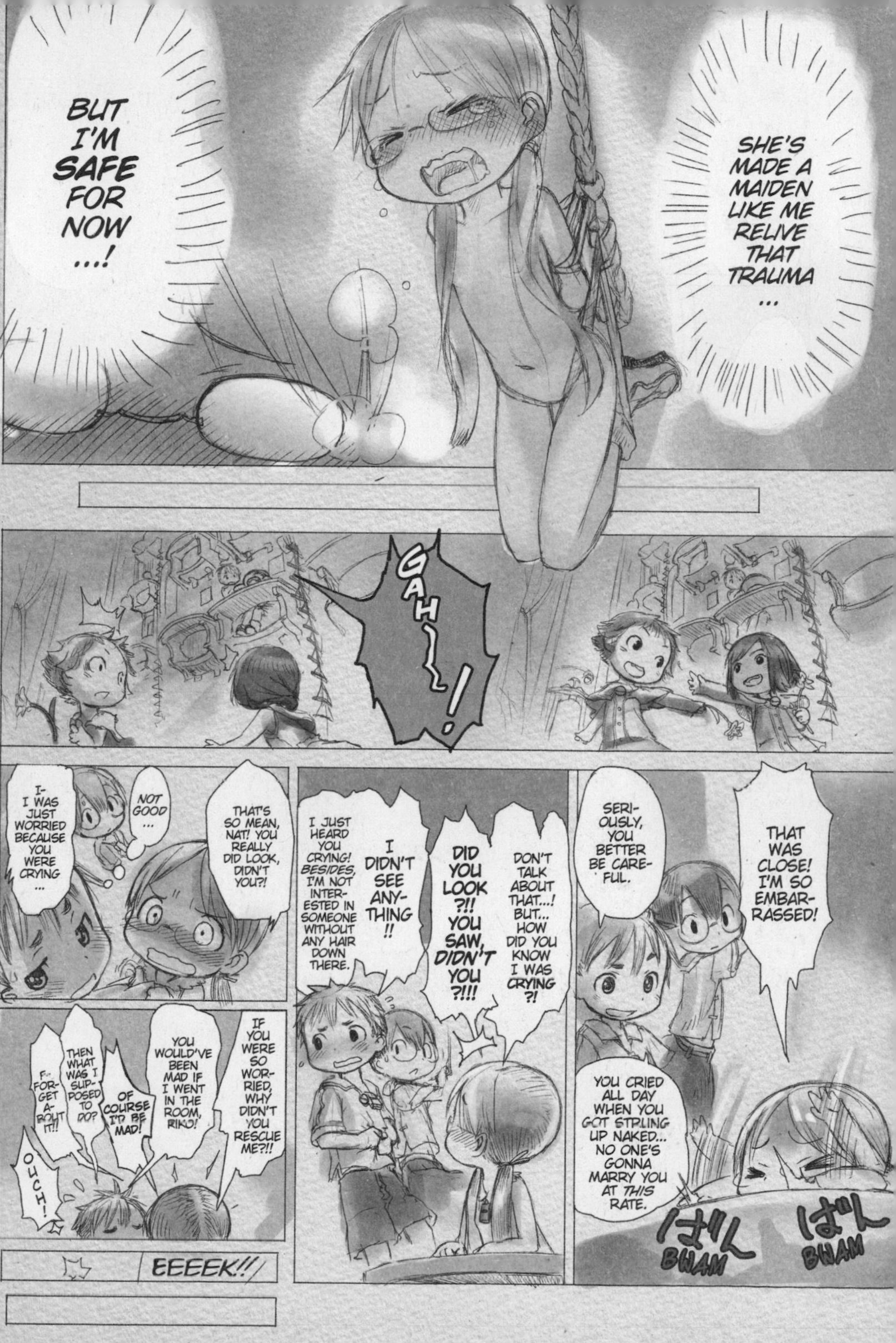
SHE'S MADE A MAIDEN LIKE ME RELIVE THAT TRAUMA...
BUT I'M SAFE FOR NOW...!
GAH~~!
THAT WAS CLOSE! I'M SO EMBARRASSED!
SERIOUSLY, YOU BETTER BE CAREFUL.
YOU CRIED ALL DAY WHEN YOU GOT STRUNG UP NAKED... NO ONE'S GONNA MARRY YOU AT THIS RATE.
ばん BWAM
ばん BWAM
DON'T TALK ABOUT THAT...! BUT... HOW DID YOU KNOW I WAS CRYING?!
DID YOU LOOK?!! YOU SAW, DIDN'T YOU?!!!
I DIDN'T SEE ANYTHING!!
I JUST HEARD YOU CRYING! BESIDES, I'M NOT INTERESTED IN SOMEONE WITHOUT ANY HAIR DOWN THERE.
THAT'S SO MEAN, NAT! YOU REALLY DID LOOK, DIDN'T YOU?!
NOT GOOD...
I- I WAS JUST WORRIED BECAUSE YOU WERE CRYING...
IF YOU WERE SO WORRIED, WHY DIDN'T YOU RESCUE ME?!!
YOU WOULD'VE BEEN MAD IF I WENT IN THE ROOM, RIKO!
OF COURSE I'D BE MAD!
THEN WHAT WAS I SUPPOSED TO DO?
F- FORGET ABOUT IT!!
OUCH!
EEEEK!!

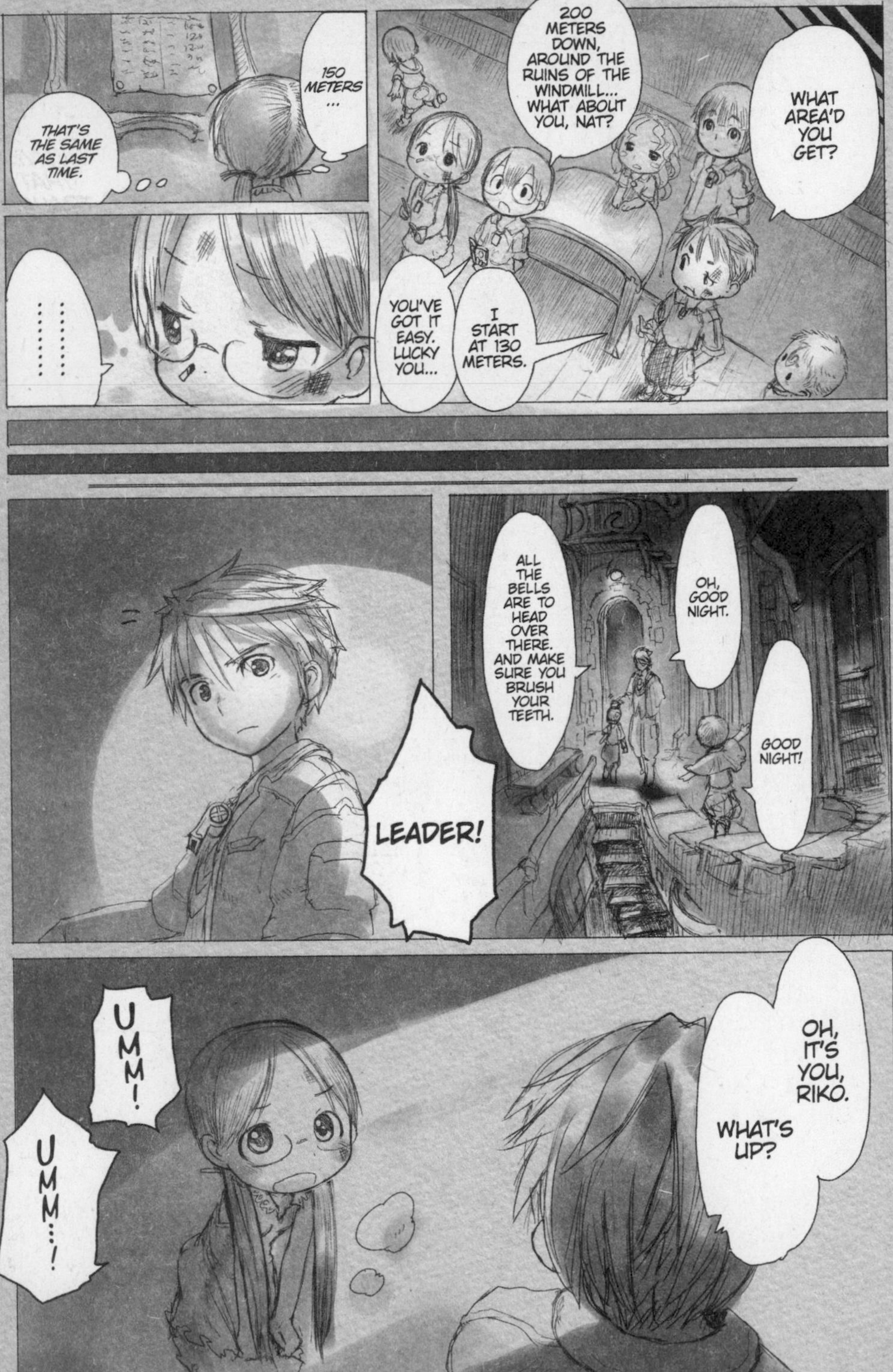
WHAT AREA'D YOU GET?
200 METERS DOWN, AROUND THE RUINS OF THE WINDMILL... WHAT ABOUT YOU, NAT?
I START AT 130 METERS.
YOU'VE GOT IT EASY. LUCKY YOU...
150 METERS...
THAT'S THE SAME AS LAST TIME.
......
OH, GOOD NIGHT.
ALL THE BELLS ARE TO HEAD OVER THERE. AND MAKE SURE YOU BRUSH YOUR TEETH.
GOOD NIGHT!
LEADER!
OH, IT'S YOU, RIKO.
WHAT'S UP?
UMM!
UMM...!

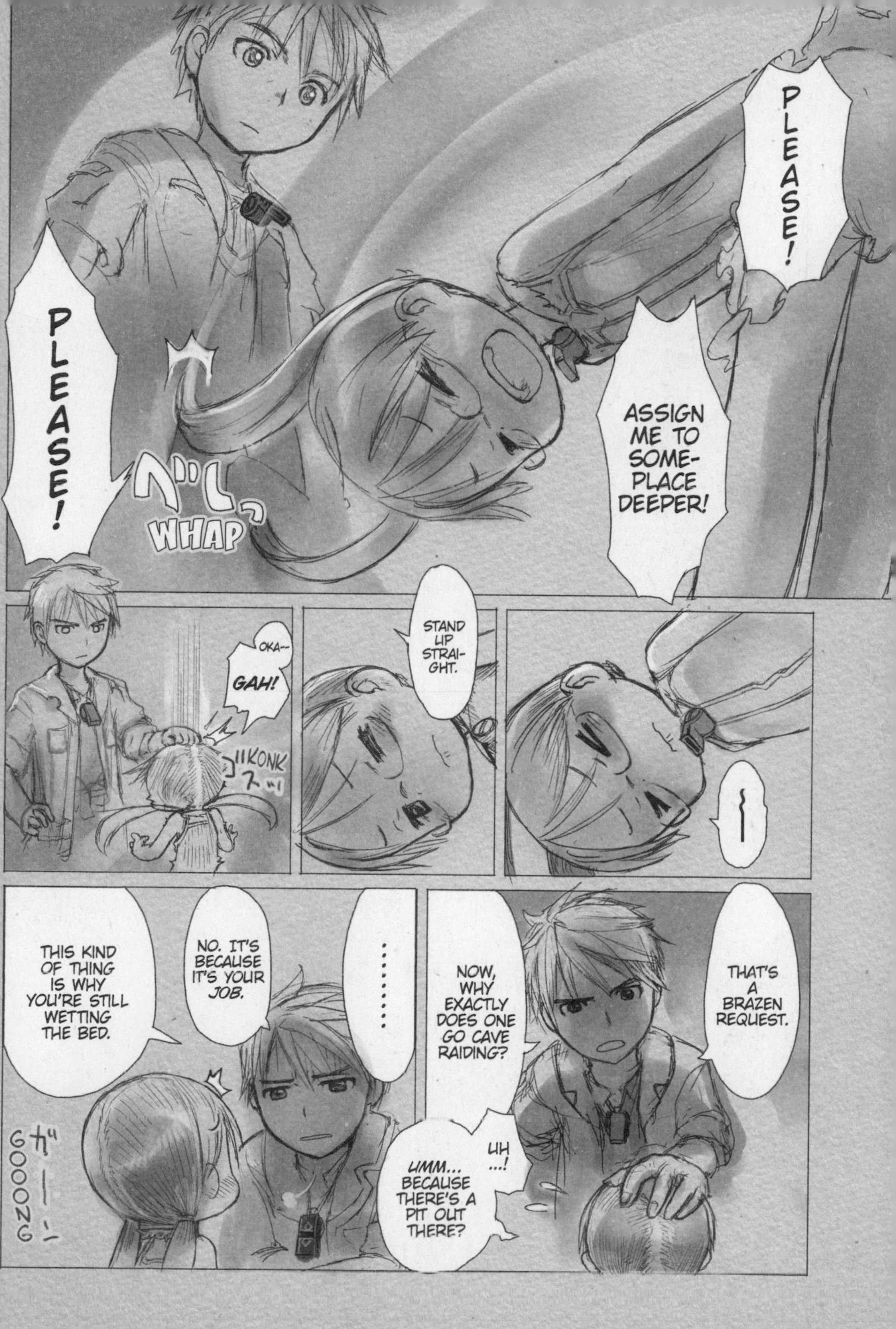
PLEASE!
ASSIGN ME TO SOME-PLACE DEEPER!
PLEASE!
WHAP
—!
STAND UP STRAIGHT.
OKA--
GAH!
KONK
THAT'S A BRAZEN REQUEST.
NOW, WHY EXACTLY DOES ONE GO CAVE RAIDING?
UH ...!
UMM... BECAUSE THERE'S A PIT OUT THERE?
......
NO. IT'S BECAUSE IT'S YOUR JOB.
THIS KIND OF THING IS WHY YOU'RE STILL WETTING THE BED.
GOOOONG

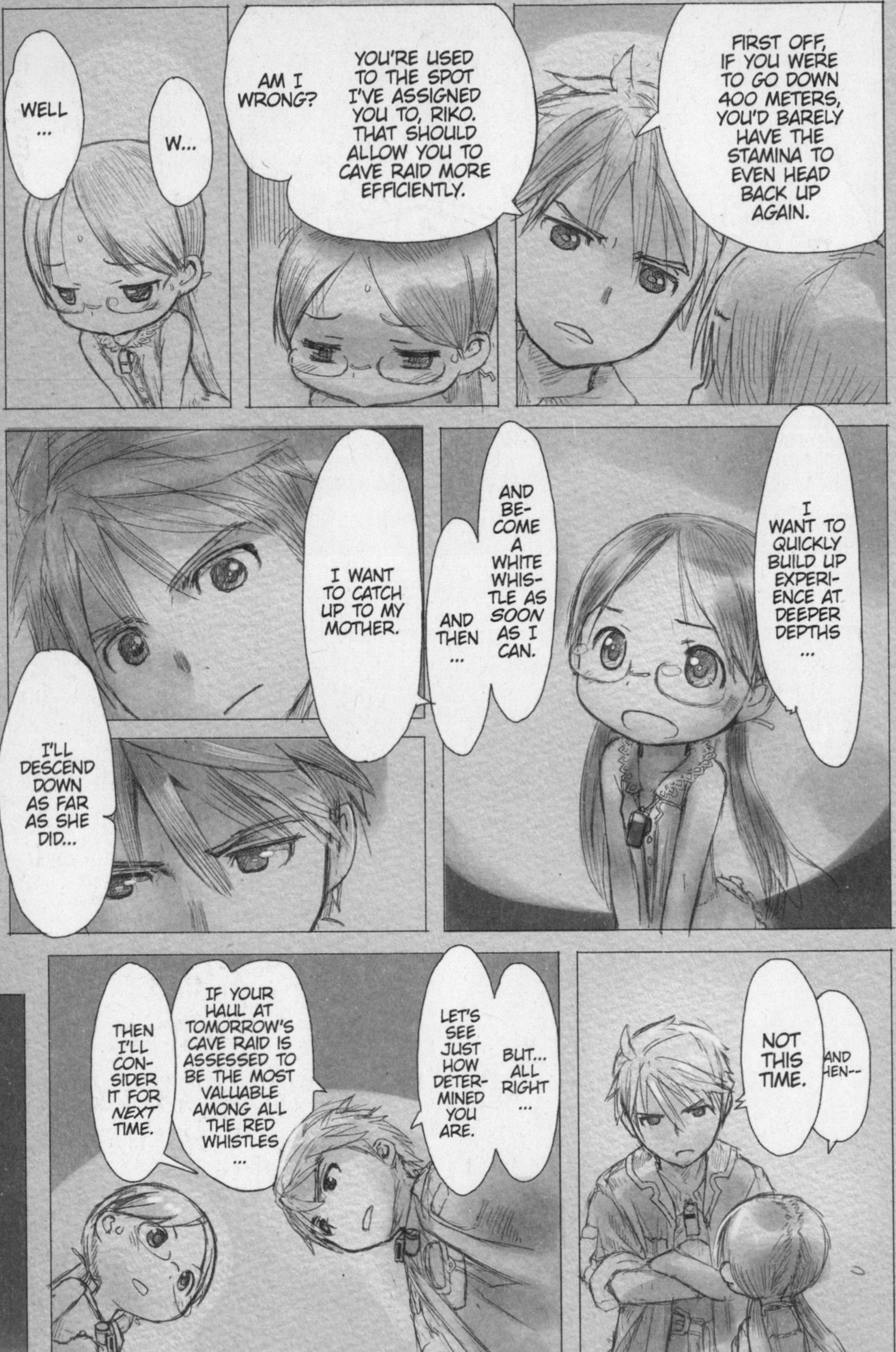
FIRST OFF, IF YOU WERE TO GO DOWN 400 METERS, YOU'D BARELY HAVE THE STAMINA TO EVEN HEAD BACK UP AGAIN.
YOU'RE USED TO THE SPOT I'VE ASSIGNED YOU TO, RIKO. THAT SHOULD ALLOW YOU TO CAVE RAID MORE EFFICIENTLY.
AM I WRONG?
W...
WELL ...
I WANT TO QUICKLY BUILD UP EXPERIENCE AT DEEPER DEPTHS ...
AND BECOME A WHITE WHISTLE AS SOON AS I CAN.
AND THEN ...
I WANT TO CATCH UP TO MY MOTHER.
I'LL DESCEND DOWN AS FAR AS SHE DID...
AND THEN--
NOT THIS TIME.
BUT... ALL RIGHT ...
LET'S SEE JUST HOW DETERMINED YOU ARE.
IF YOUR HAUL AT TOMORROW'S CAVE RAID IS ASSESSED TO BE THE MOST VALUABLE AMONG ALL THE RED WHISTLES ...
THEN I'LL CONSIDER IT FOR *NEXT* TIME.

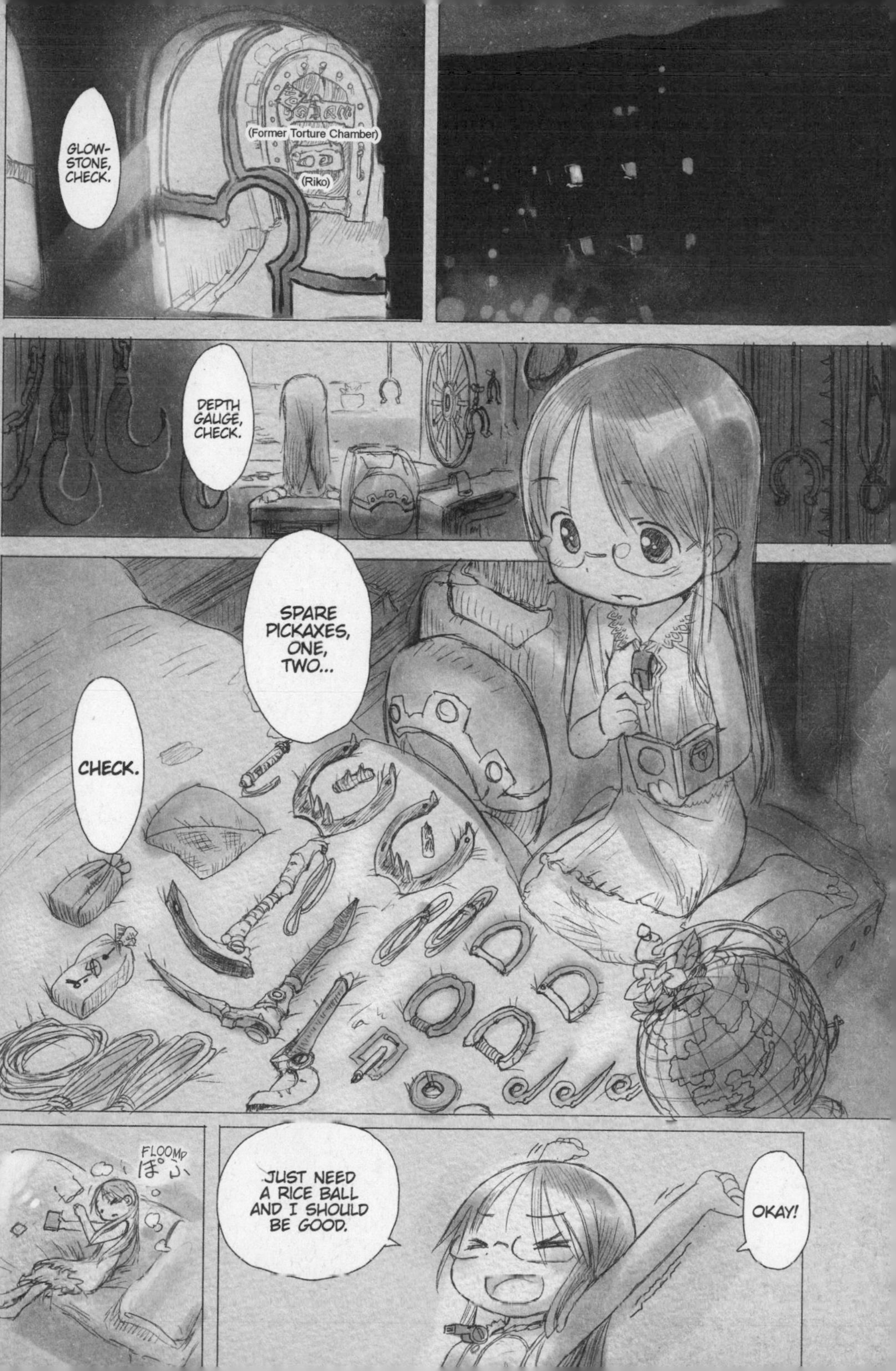
(Former Torture Chamber)
(Riko)
GLOW-STONE, CHECK.
DEPTH GAUGE, CHECK.
SPARE PICKAXES, ONE, TWO...
CHECK.
OKAY!
JUST NEED A RICE BALL AND I SHOULD BE GOOD.
FLOOMP
ぽふ

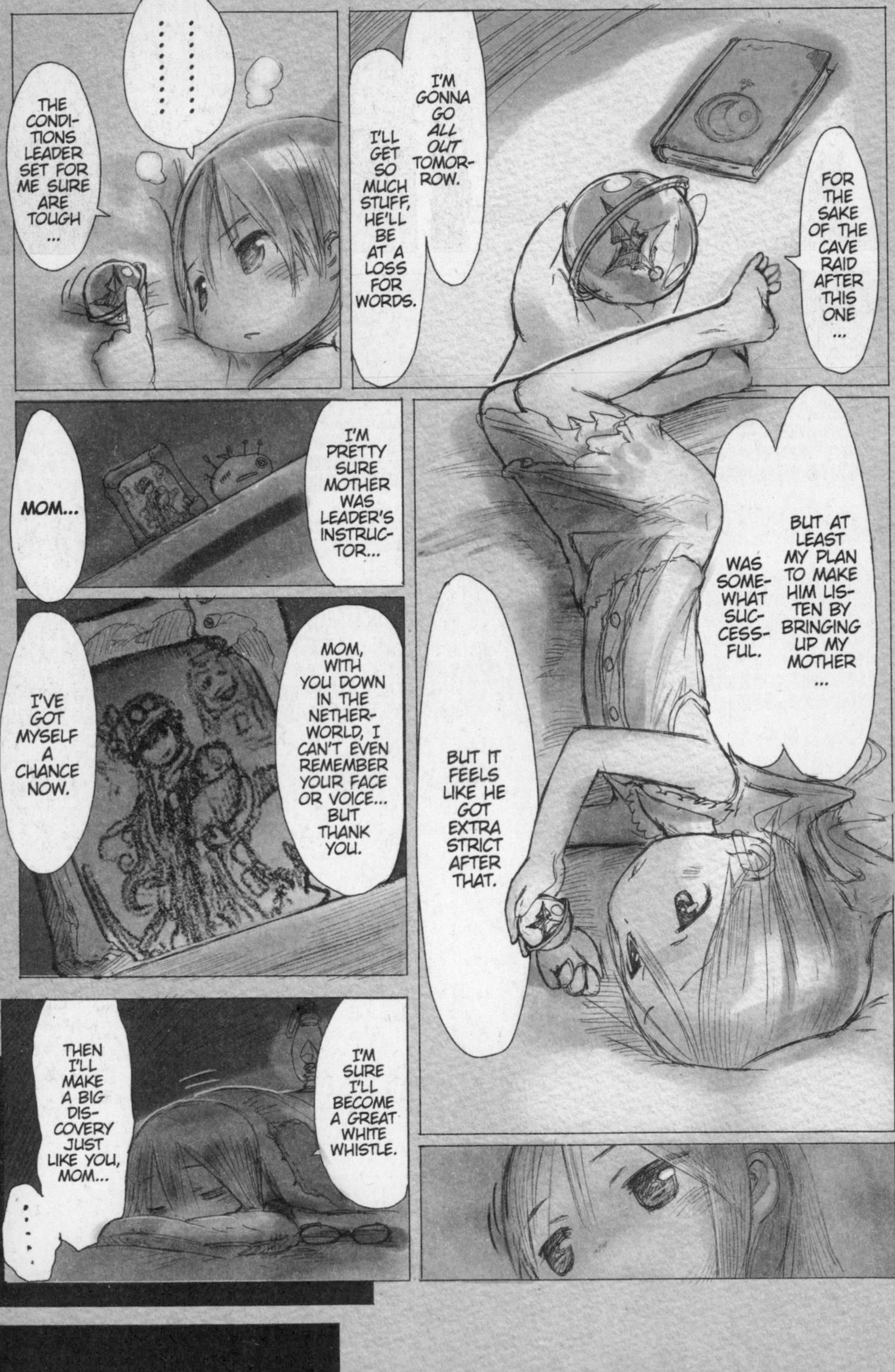
FOR THE SAKE OF THE CAVE RAID AFTER THIS ONE...
I'M GONNA GO ALL OUT TOMORROW.
I'LL GET SO MUCH STUFF, HE'LL BE AT A LOSS FOR WORDS.
......
THE CONDITIONS LEADER SET FOR ME SURE ARE TOUGH...
BUT AT LEAST MY PLAN TO MAKE HIM LISTEN BY BRINGING UP MY MOTHER...
WAS SOMEWHAT SUCCESSFUL.
BUT IT FEELS LIKE HE GOT EXTRA STRICT AFTER THAT.
I'M PRETTY SURE MOTHER WAS LEADER'S INSTRUCTOR...
MOM...
MOM, WITH YOU DOWN IN THE NETHERWORLD, I CAN'T EVEN REMEMBER YOUR FACE OR VOICE... BUT THANK YOU.
I'VE GOT MYSELF A CHANCE NOW.
I'M SURE I'LL BECOME A GREAT WHITE WHISTLE.
THEN I'LL MAKE A BIG DISCOVERY JUST LIKE YOU, MOM...
......

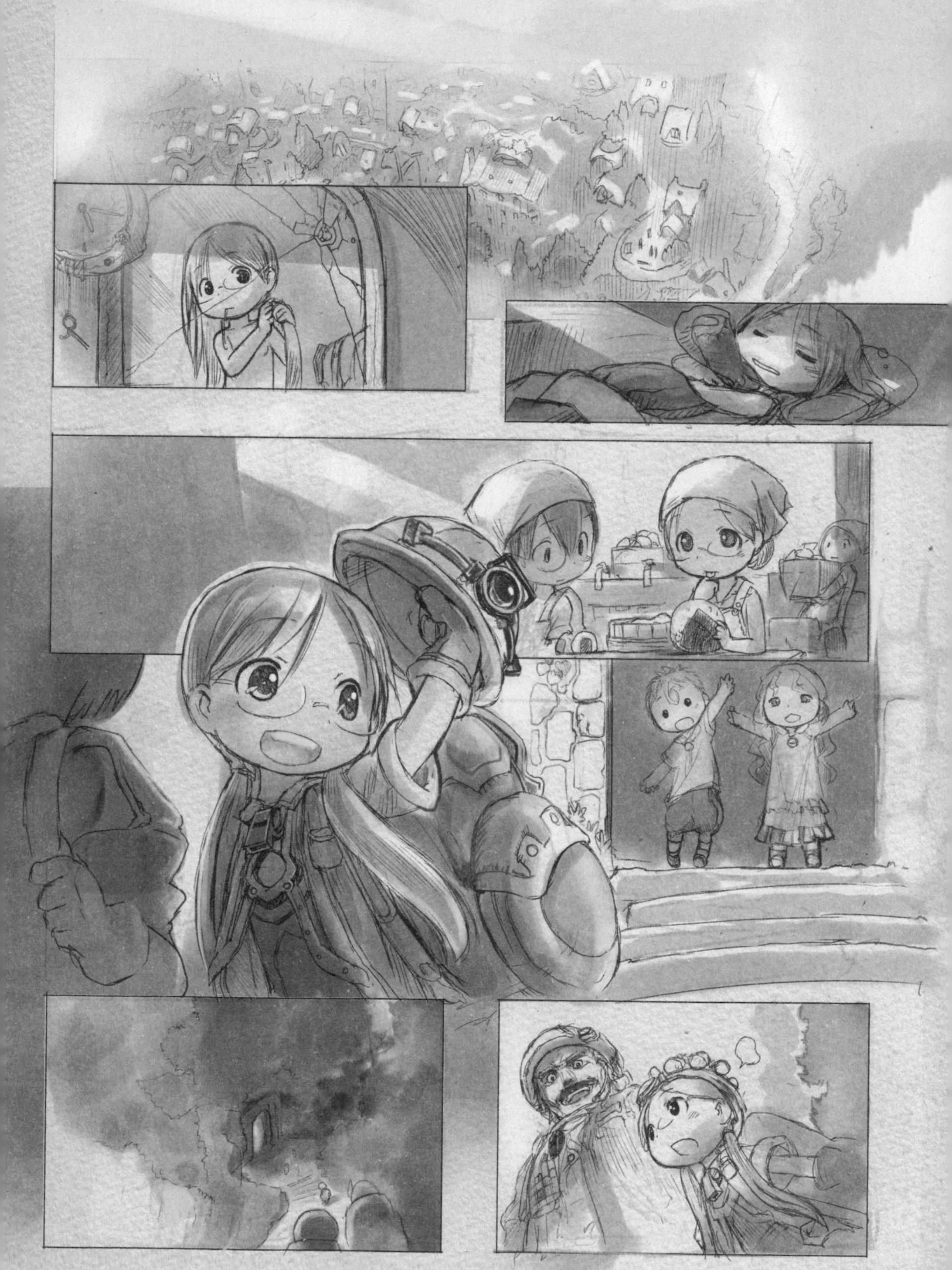

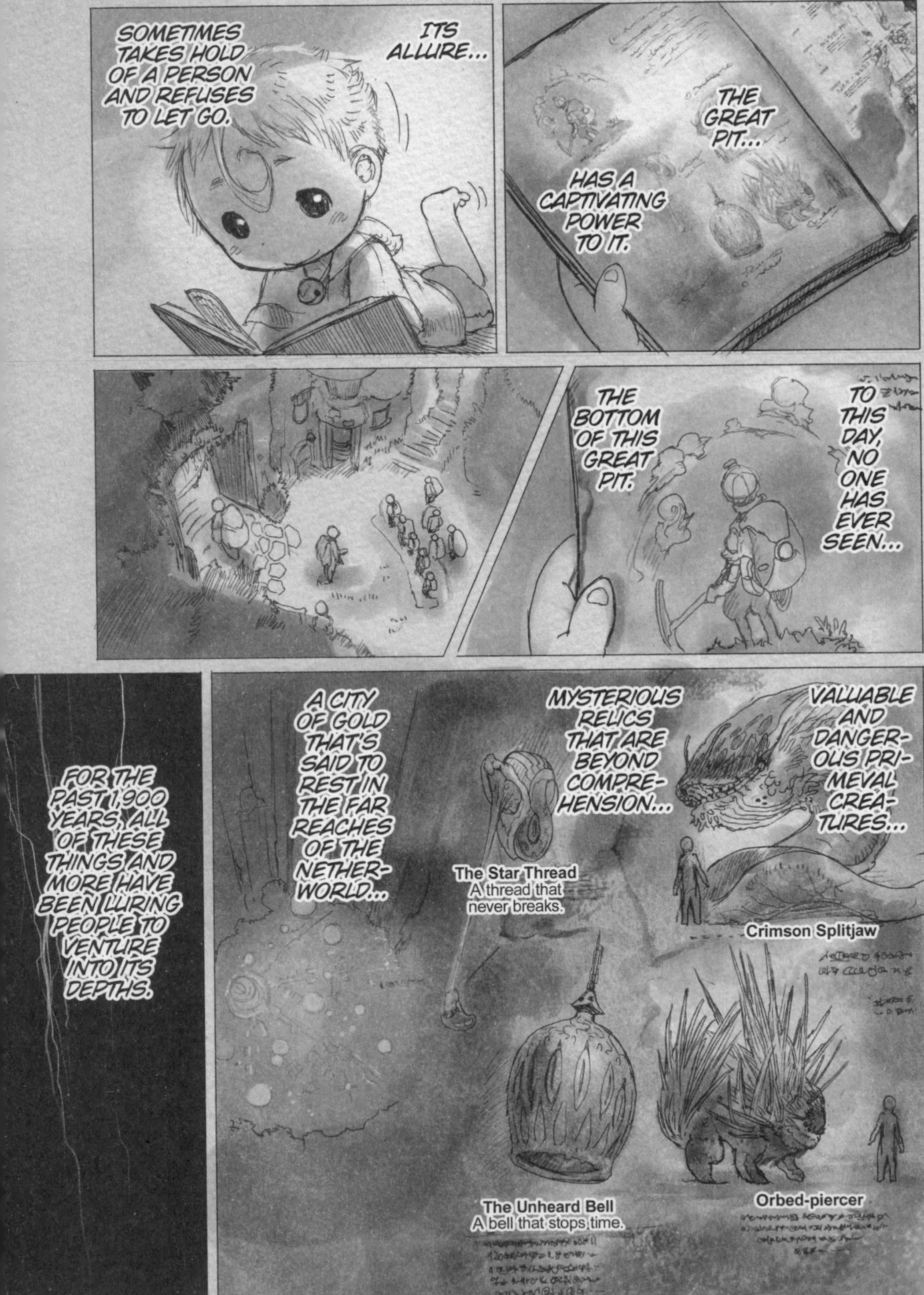
THE GREAT PIT...
HAS A CAPTIVATING POWER TO IT.
ITS ALLURE...
SOMETIMES TAKES HOLD OF A PERSON AND REFUSES TO LET GO.
TO THIS DAY, NO ONE HAS EVER SEEN...
THE BOTTOM OF THIS GREAT PIT.
VALUABLE AND DANGEROUS PRIMEVAL CREATURES...
Crimson Splitjaw
Orbed-piercer
MYSTERIOUS RELICS THAT ARE BEYOND COMPREHENSION...
The Star Thread
A thread that never breaks.
The Unheard Bell
A bell that stops time.
A CITY OF GOLD THAT'S SAID TO REST IN THE FAR REACHES OF THE NETHERWORLD...
FOR THE PAST 1,900 YEARS, ALL OF THESE THINGS AND MORE HAVE BEEN LURING PEOPLE TO VENTURE INTO ITS DEPTHS.

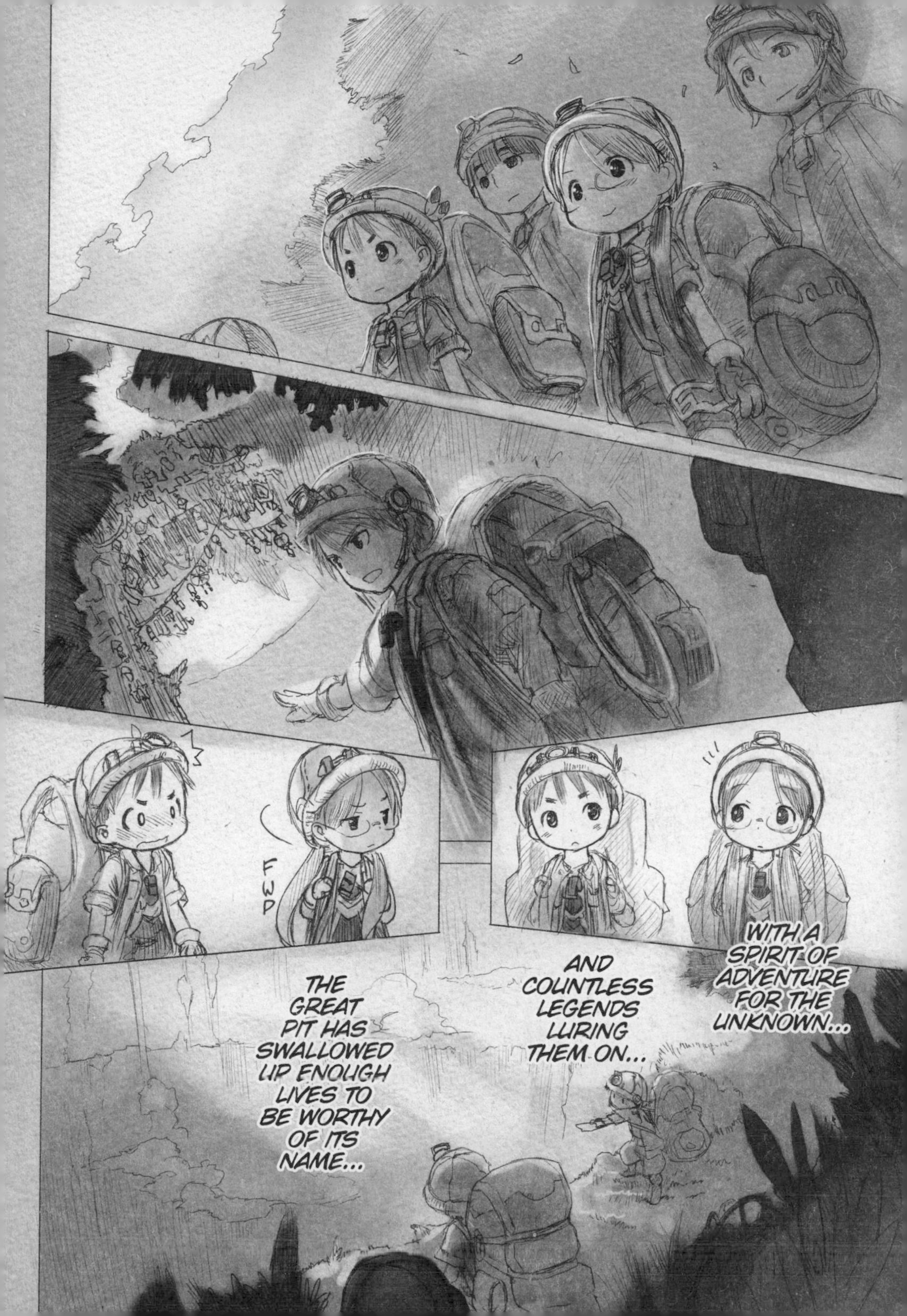
FWP
WITH A SPIRIT OF ADVENTURE FOR THE UNKNOWN...
AND COUNTLESS LEGENDS LURING THEM ON...
THE GREAT PIT HAS SWALLOWED UP ENOUGH LIVES TO BE WORTHY OF ITS NAME...

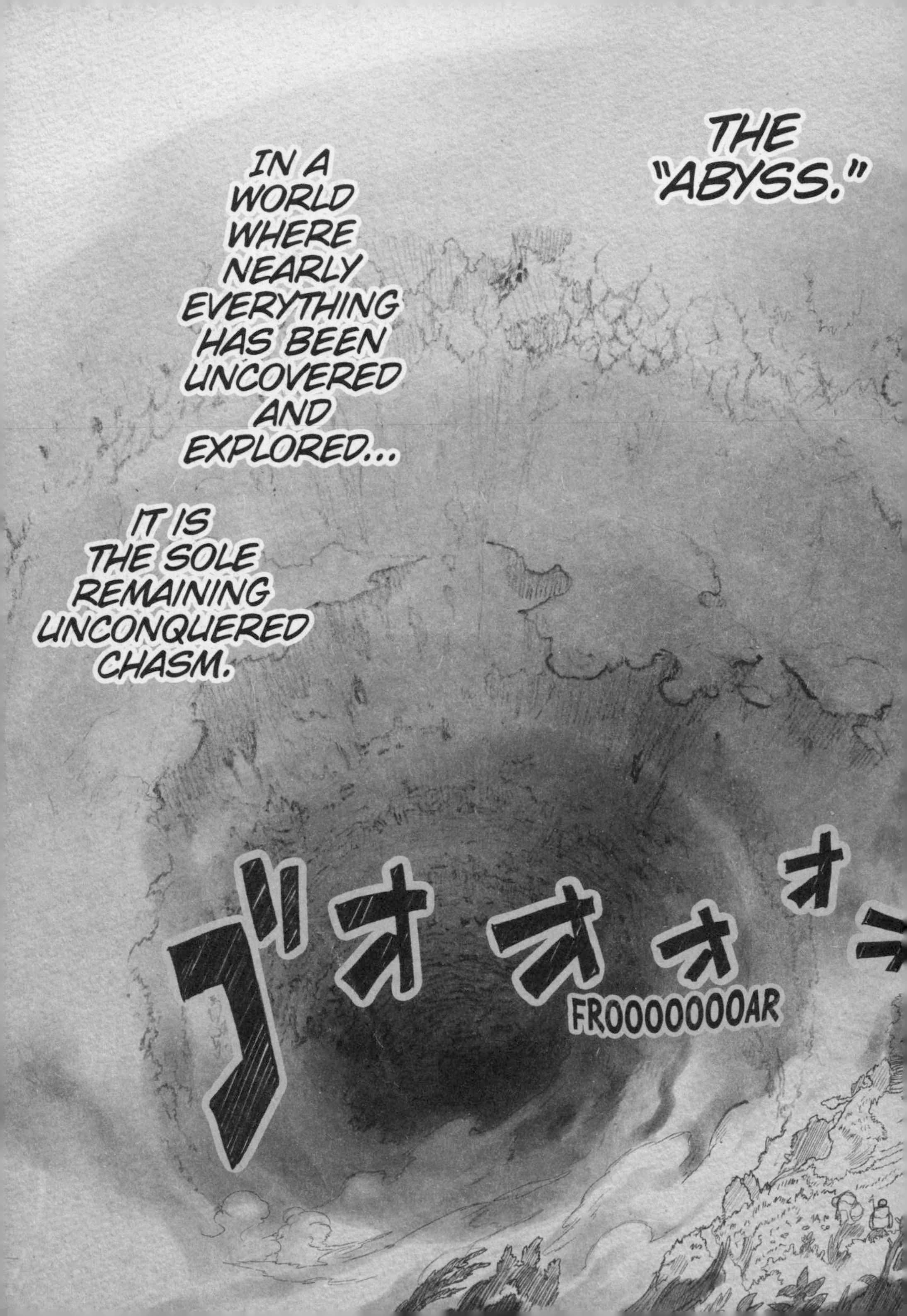
THE "ABYSS."
IN A WORLD WHERE NEARLY EVERYTHING HAS BEEN UNCOVERED AND EXPLORED...
IT IS THE SOLE REMAINING UNCONQUERED CHASM.
ゴオオォォ
FROOOOOOOAR

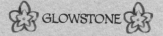

GLOWSTONE

A STONE FOUND IN THE ABYSS.
AFTER BEING POLISHED, IT SHINES BRIGHTLY WHEN
VIBRATIONS OF A CERTAIN FREQUENCY ARE APPLIED
TO IT. CAN BE USED AS AN ARTIFICIAL LIGHT.

A SIMPLE LIST OF THE MECHANISM'S COMPONENTS WOULD BE AS FOLLOWS:
AN IRON CAN AND PLATE, A SEALED GLASS RECEPTACLE,
A PROCESSED TALON CRYSTAL, A WIRE, AND WATER.

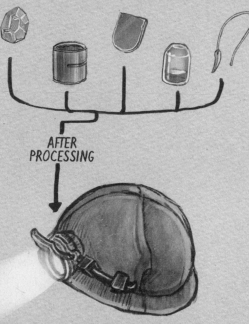

AFTER
PROCESSING

THE LIGHT DOESN'T EMIT HEAT, SO IT'S QUITE STABLE.
HOWEVER, IT EXPLODES FAIRLY EASILY WHEN PRESSURE IS APPLIED TO IT,
SO HANDLE IT WITH CARE.

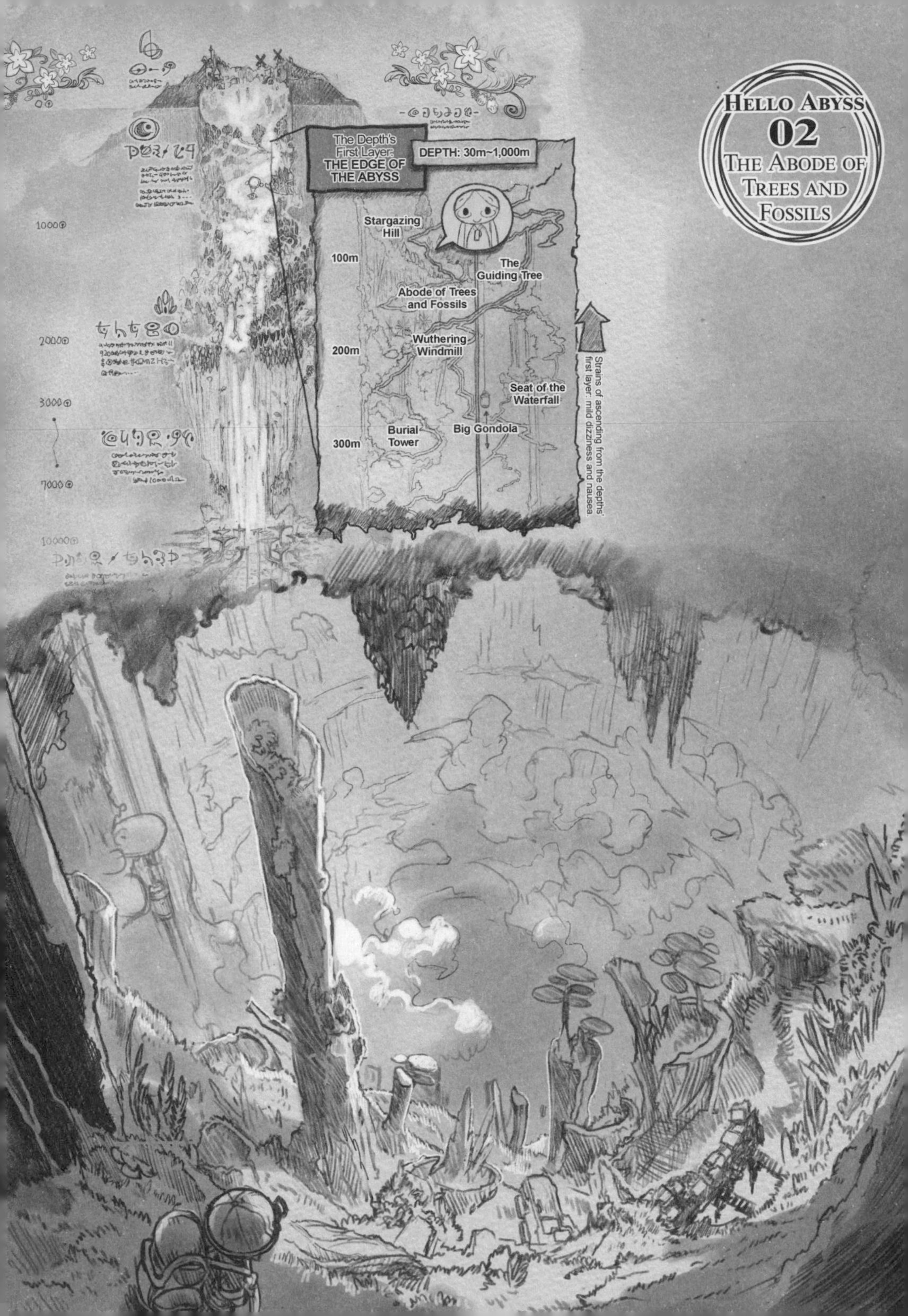
HELLO ABYSS
02
THE ABODE OF TREES AND FOSSILS
The Depth's First Layer:
THE EDGE OF THE ABYSS
DEPTH: 30m~1,000m
Stargazing Hill
100m
The Guiding Tree
Abode of Trees and Fossils
Wuthering Windmill
200m
Seat of the Waterfall
Burial Tower
Big Gondola
300m
Strains of ascending from the depths' first layer: mild dizziness and nausea.
1000
2000
3000
7000
10000

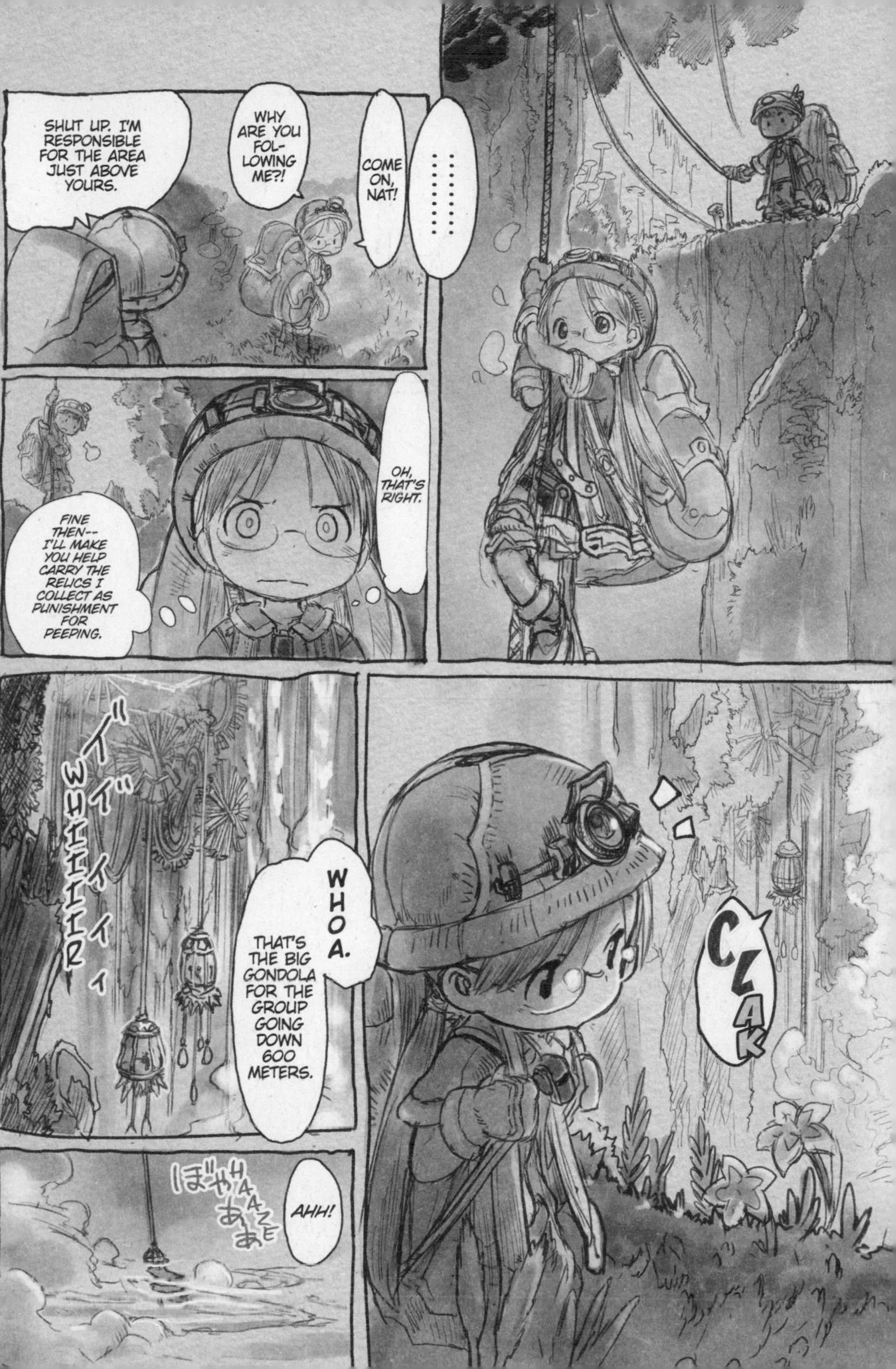

......
COME ON, NAT!
WHY ARE YOU FOL-LOWING ME?!
SHUT UP. I'M RESPONSIBLE FOR THE AREA JUST ABOVE YOURS.
OH, THAT'S RIGHT.
FINE THEN-- I'LL MAKE YOU HELP CARRY THE RELICS I COLLECT AS PUNISHMENT FOR PEEPING.
CLAK
WHOA.
THAT'S THE BIG GONDOLA FOR THE GROUP GOING DOWN 600 METERS.
WHIIIIR
HAAZE
AHH!

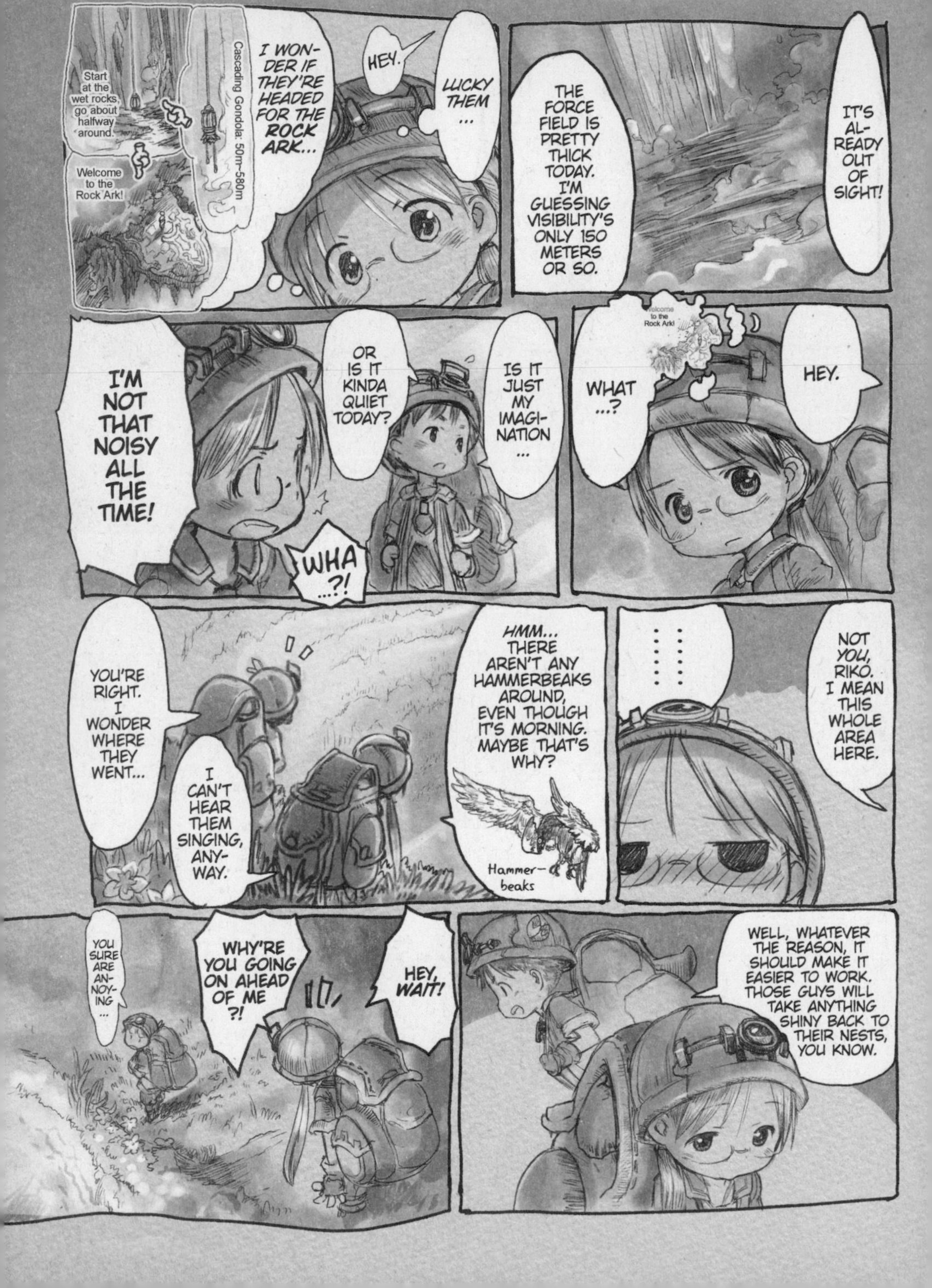
IT'S ALREADY OUT OF SIGHT!
THE FORCE FIELD IS PRETTY THICK TODAY. I'M GUESSING VISIBILITY'S ONLY 150 METERS OR SO.
LUCKY THEM...
HEY.
I WONDER IF THEY'RE HEADED FOR THE ROCK ARK...
Cascading Gondola: 50m-580m
Start at the wet rocks, go about halfway around.
Welcome to the Rock Ark!
HEY.
WHAT...?
Welcome to the Rock Ark!
IS IT JUST MY IMAGINATION...
OR IS IT KINDA QUIET TODAY?
WHA...?!
I'M NOT THAT NOISY ALL THE TIME!
NOT YOU, RIKO. I MEAN THIS WHOLE AREA HERE.
......
HMM... THERE AREN'T ANY HAMMERBEAKS AROUND, EVEN THOUGH IT'S MORNING. MAYBE THAT'S WHY?
Hammer-beaks
I CAN'T HEAR THEM SINGING, ANYWAY.
YOU'RE RIGHT. I WONDER WHERE THEY WENT...
WELL, WHATEVER THE REASON, IT SHOULD MAKE IT EASIER TO WORK. THOSE GUYS WILL TAKE ANYTHING SHINY BACK TO THEIR NESTS, YOU KNOW.
HEY, WAIT!
WHY'RE YOU GOING ON AHEAD OF ME?!
YOU SURE ARE ANNOYING...

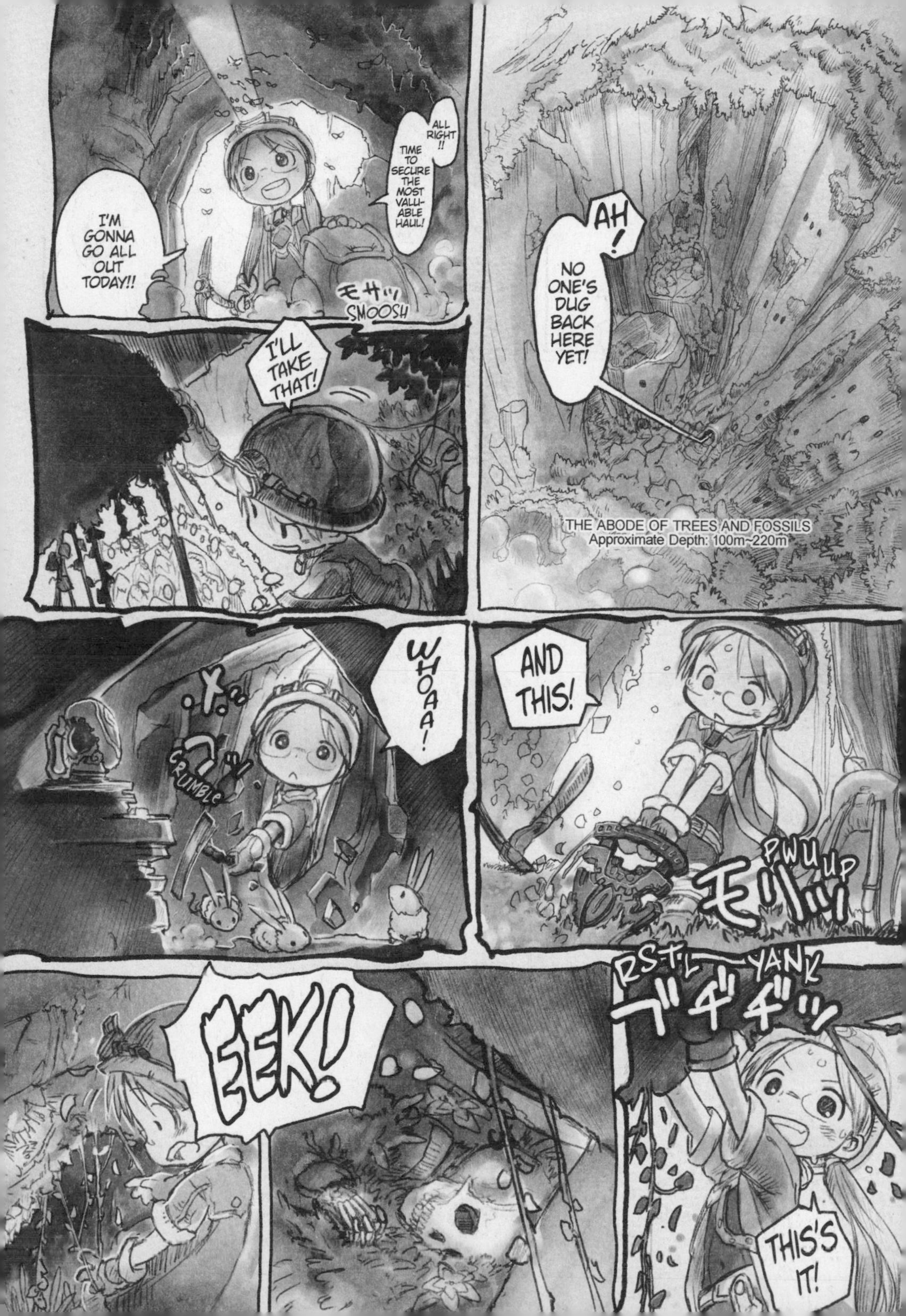
AH!
NO ONE'S DUG BACK HERE YET!
THE ABODE OF TREES AND FOSSILS
Approximate Depth: 100m~220m
ALL RIGHT!!
TIME TO SECURE THE MOST VALU-ABLE HAUL!
I'M GONNA GO ALL OUT TODAY!!
モサッ
SMOOSH
I'LL TAKE THAT!
AND THIS!
PWUUP
WHOAA!
CRUMBLE
RSTL
YANK
THIS'S IT!
EEK!

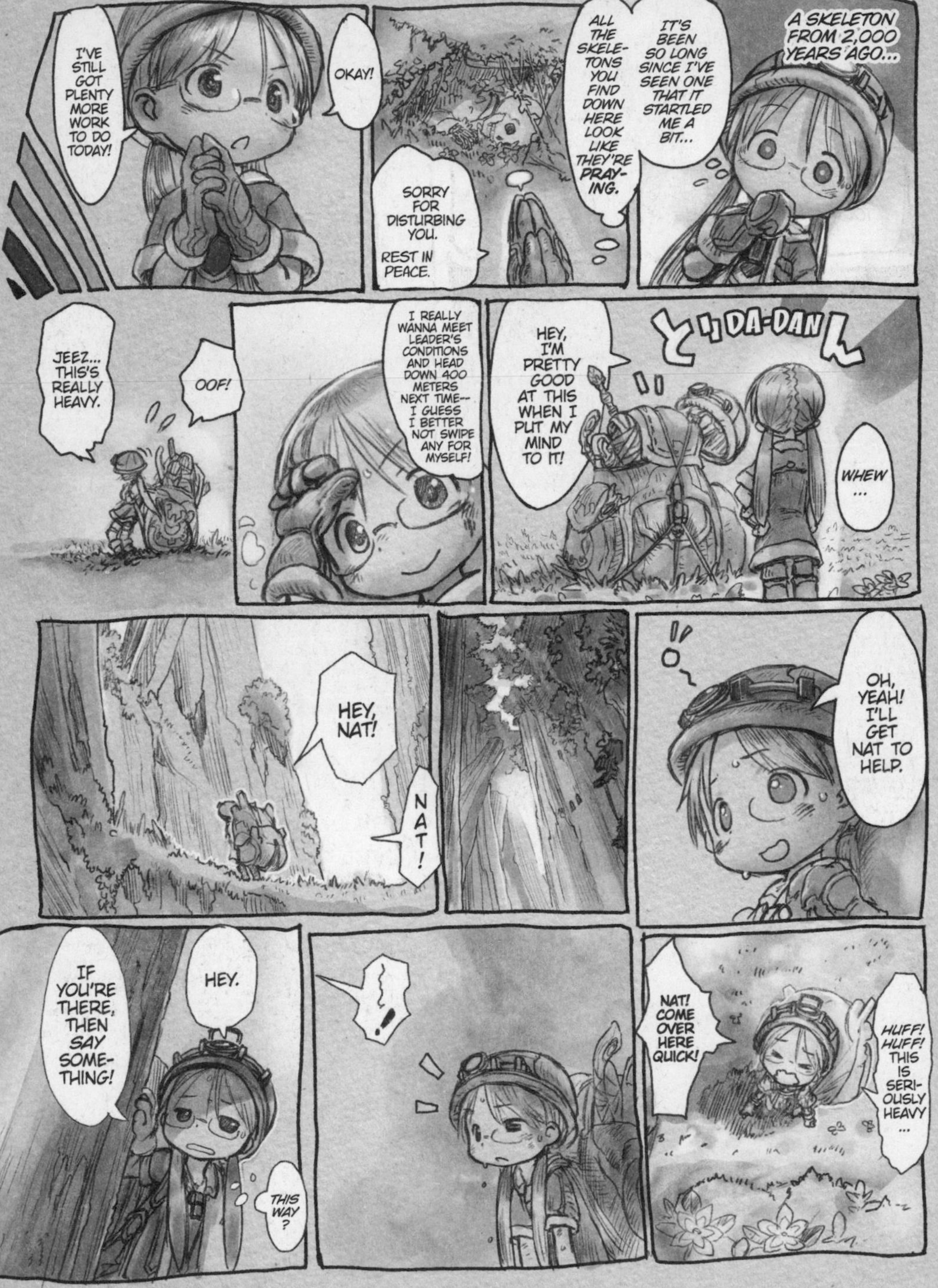
A SKELETON FROM 2,000 YEARS AGO...
IT'S BEEN SO LONG SINCE I'VE SEEN ONE THAT IT STARTLED ME A BIT...
ALL THE SKELETONS YOU FIND DOWN HERE LOOK LIKE THEY'RE PRAYING.
OKAY!
SORRY FOR DISTURBING YOU.
REST IN PEACE.
I'VE STILL GOT PLENTY MORE WORK TO DO TODAY!
DA-DAN
HEY, I'M PRETTY GOOD AT THIS WHEN I PUT MY MIND TO IT!
WHEW...
I REALLY WANNA MEET LEADER'S CONDITIONS AND HEAD DOWN 400 METERS NEXT TIME-- I GUESS I BETTER NOT SWIPE ANY FOR MYSELF!
OOF!
JEEZ... THIS'S REALLY HEAVY.
OH, YEAH! I'LL GET NAT TO HELP.
HEY, NAT!
NAT!
HUFF! HUFF! THIS IS SERIOUSLY HEAVY...
NAT! COME OVER HERE QUICK!
HEY.
IF YOU'RE THERE, THEN SAY SOMETHING!
THIS WAY?

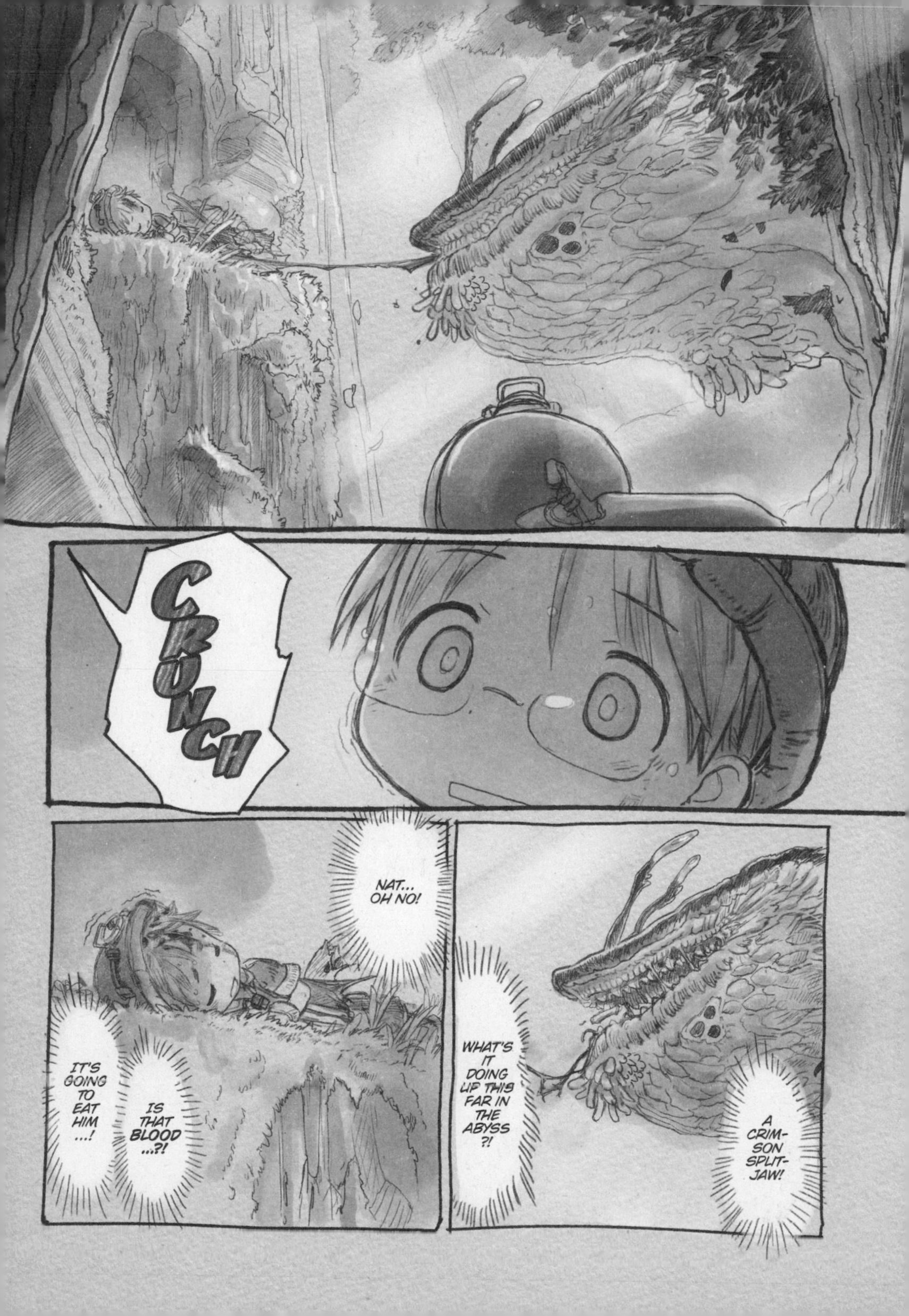
CRUNCH
A CRIMSON SPLIT-JAW!
WHAT'S IT DOING UP THIS FAR IN THE ABYSS?!
NAT... OH NO!
IS THAT BLOOD ...?!
IT'S GOING TO EAT HIM ...!

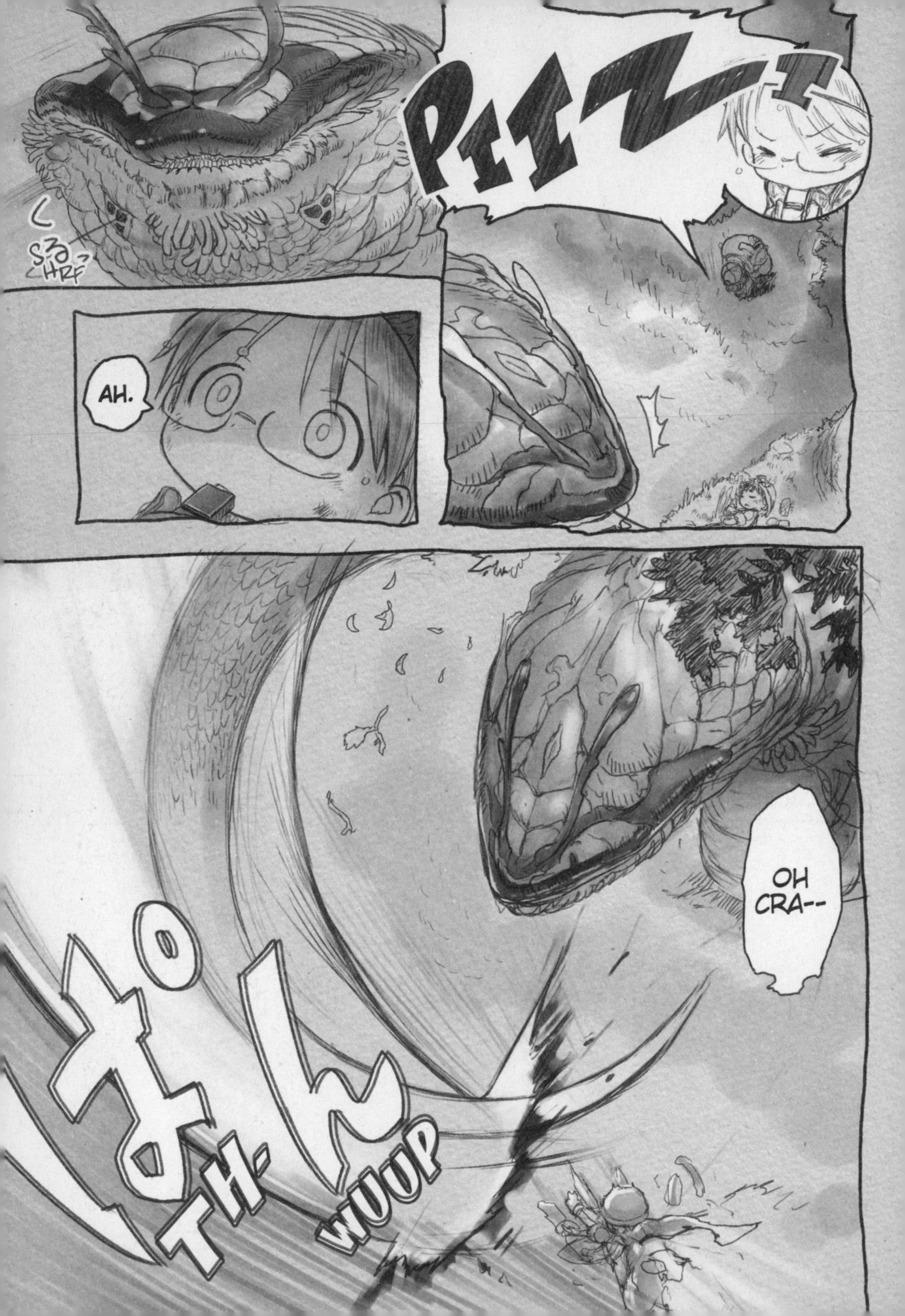
PIIZ--!
HRF
AH.
OH CRA--
TH-WUUP

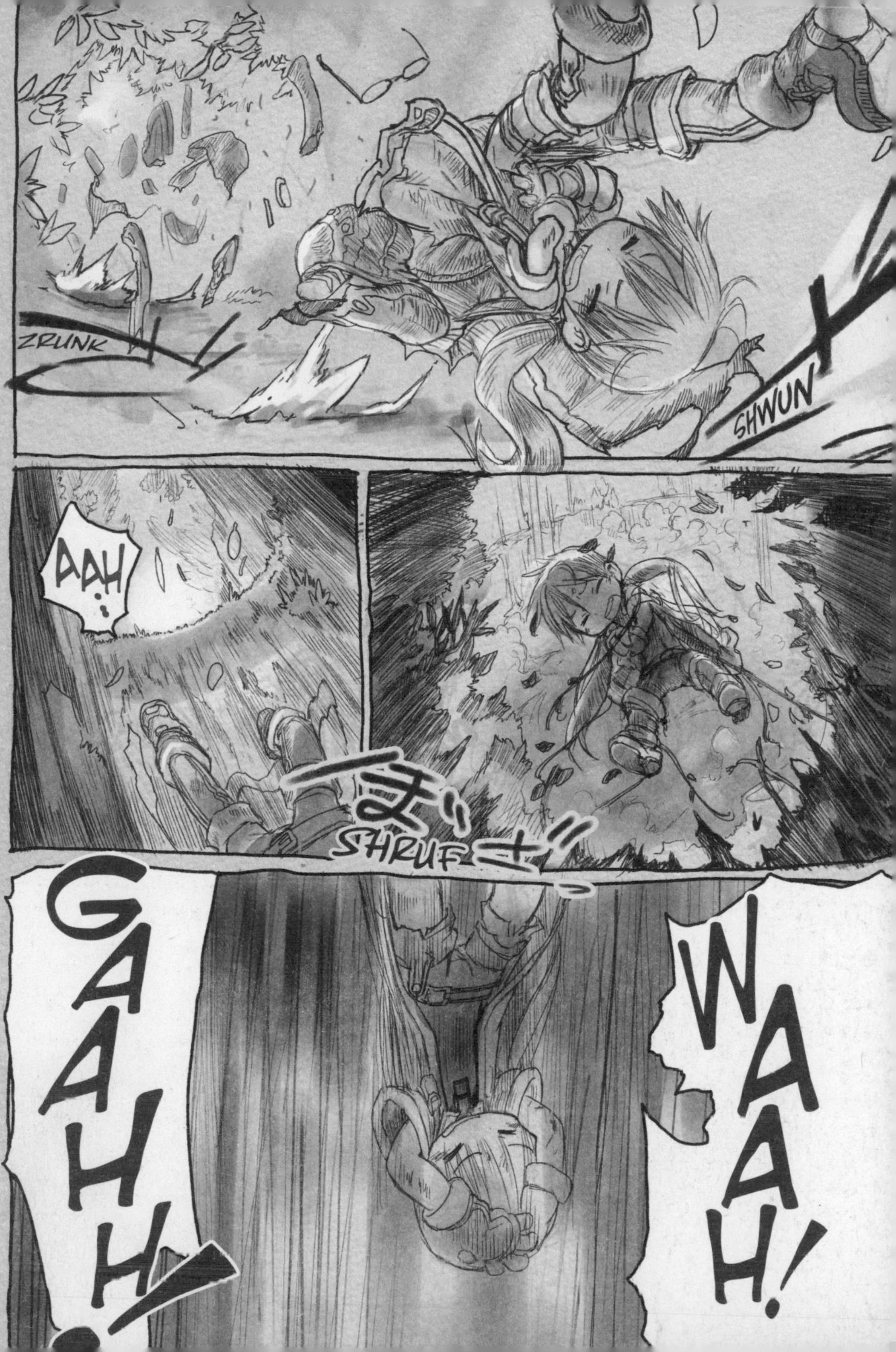
SHWUN
ZRUNK
SHRUF
AAH...
WAAH!
GAAHH!

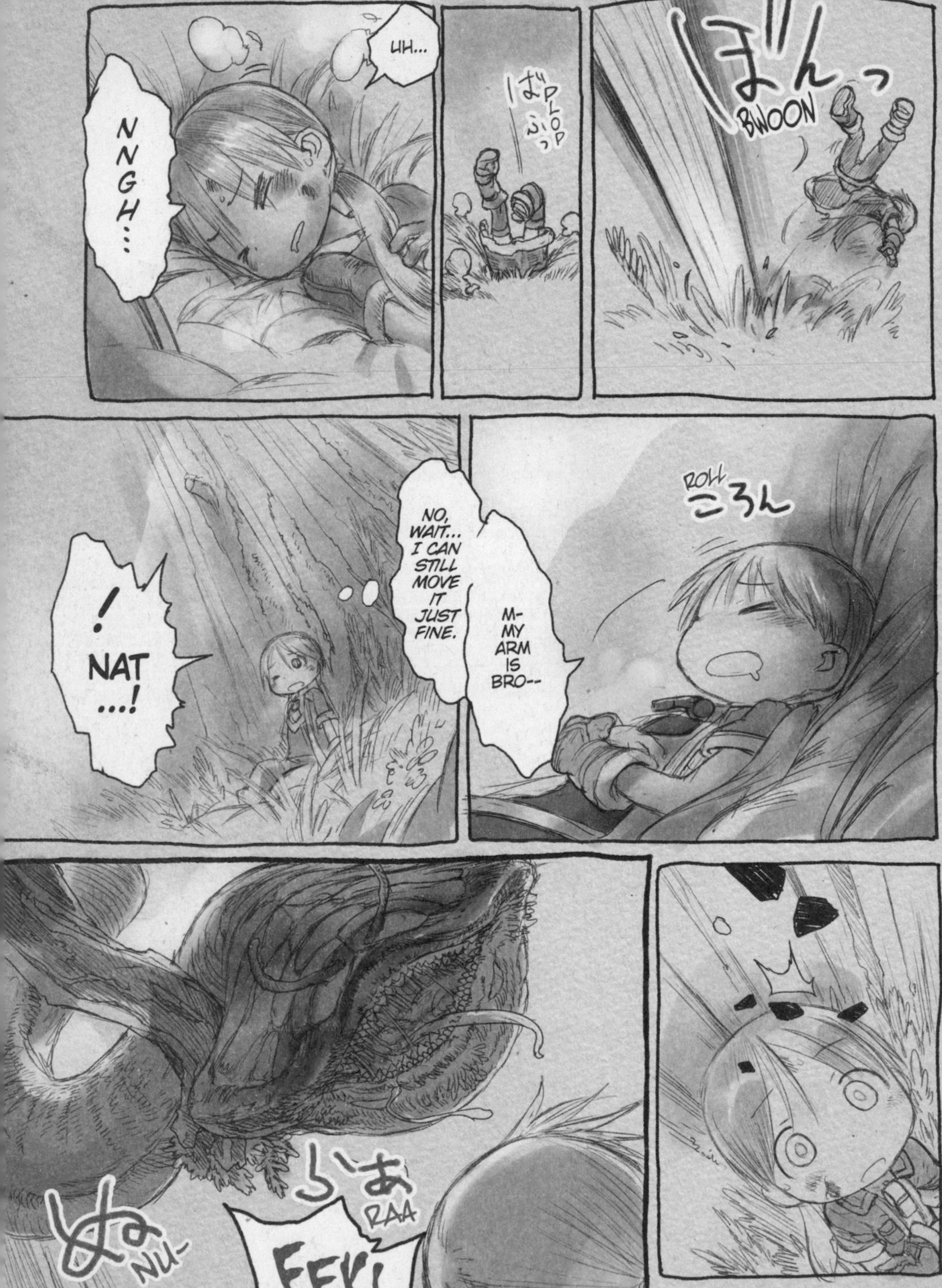
ぼ゛んっ
BWOON
ばふっ
PLOP
UH...
NNGH...
ROLL
ころん
M-MY ARM IS BRO--
NO, WAIT... I CAN STILL MOVE IT JUST FINE.
!
NAT...!
ふぁ
RAA
ぬ
NU-
EEK!

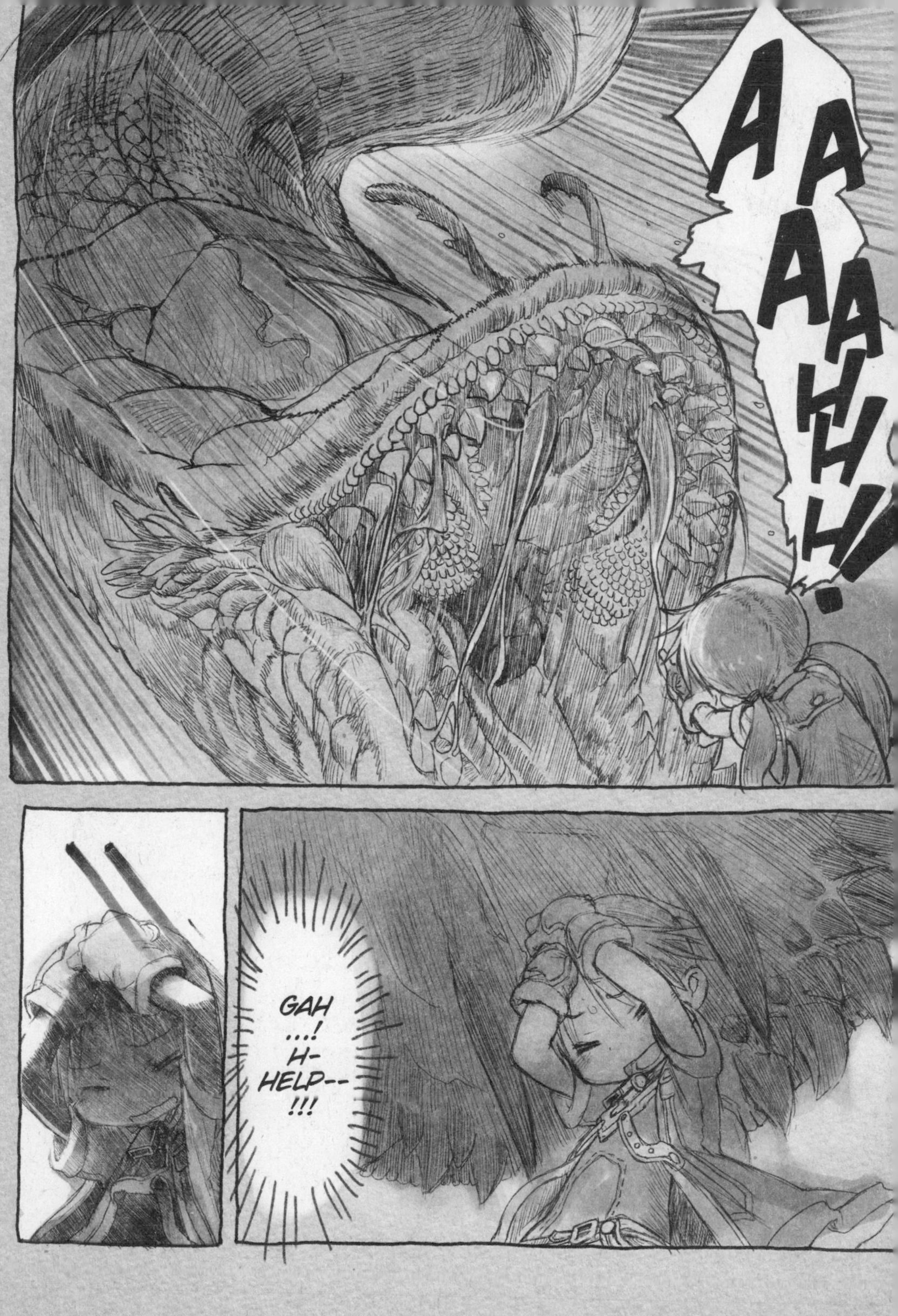
AAAAAHHH!!
GAH ...! H-HELP-- !!!

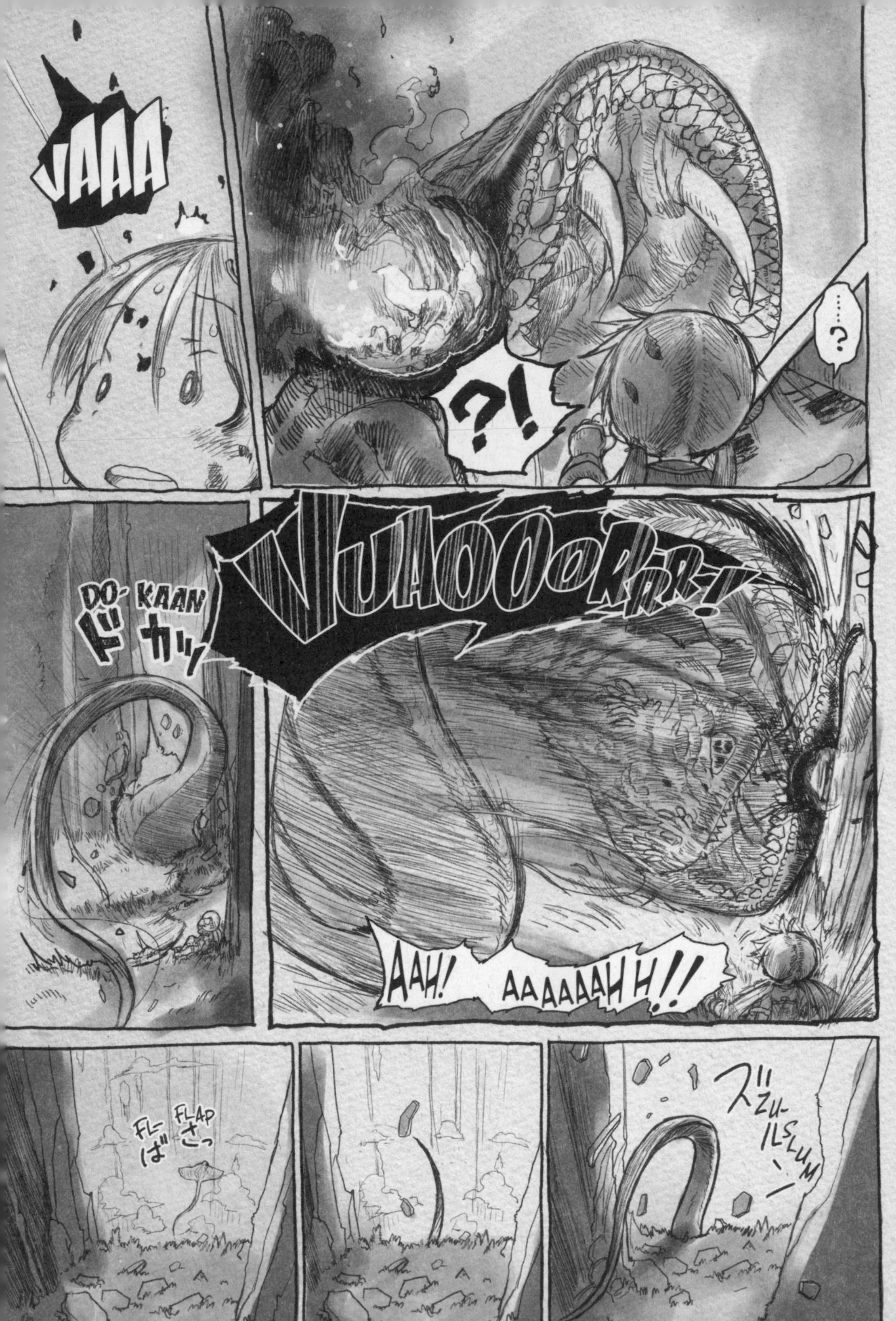

……?
?!
JAAA
VUAOOORRR!
AAH! AAAAAAHH!!
DO-KAAN
ドカッ
ズルルン
ZU-RU-SLUM
FL- FLAP
ばさっ

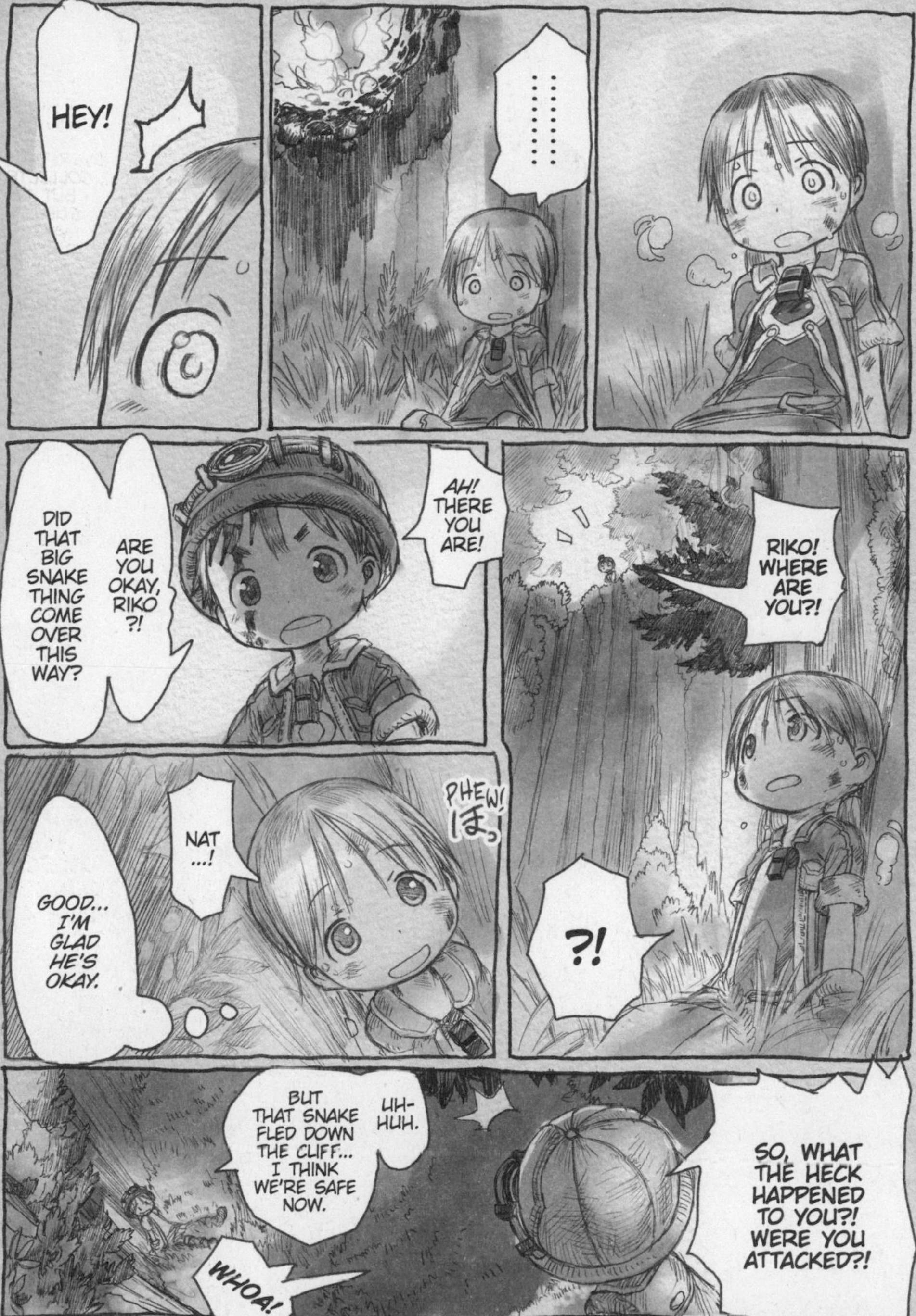
......
HEY!
RIKO! WHERE ARE YOU?!
?!
AH! THERE YOU ARE!
ARE YOU OKAY, RIKO?!
DID THAT BIG SNAKE THING COME OVER THIS WAY?
PHEW! ほっ
NAT ...!
GOOD... I'M GLAD HE'S OKAY.
SO, WHAT THE HECK HAPPENED TO YOU?! WERE YOU ATTACKED?!
UH-HUH.
BUT THAT SNAKE FLED DOWN THE CLIFF... I THINK WE'RE SAFE NOW.
WHOA!

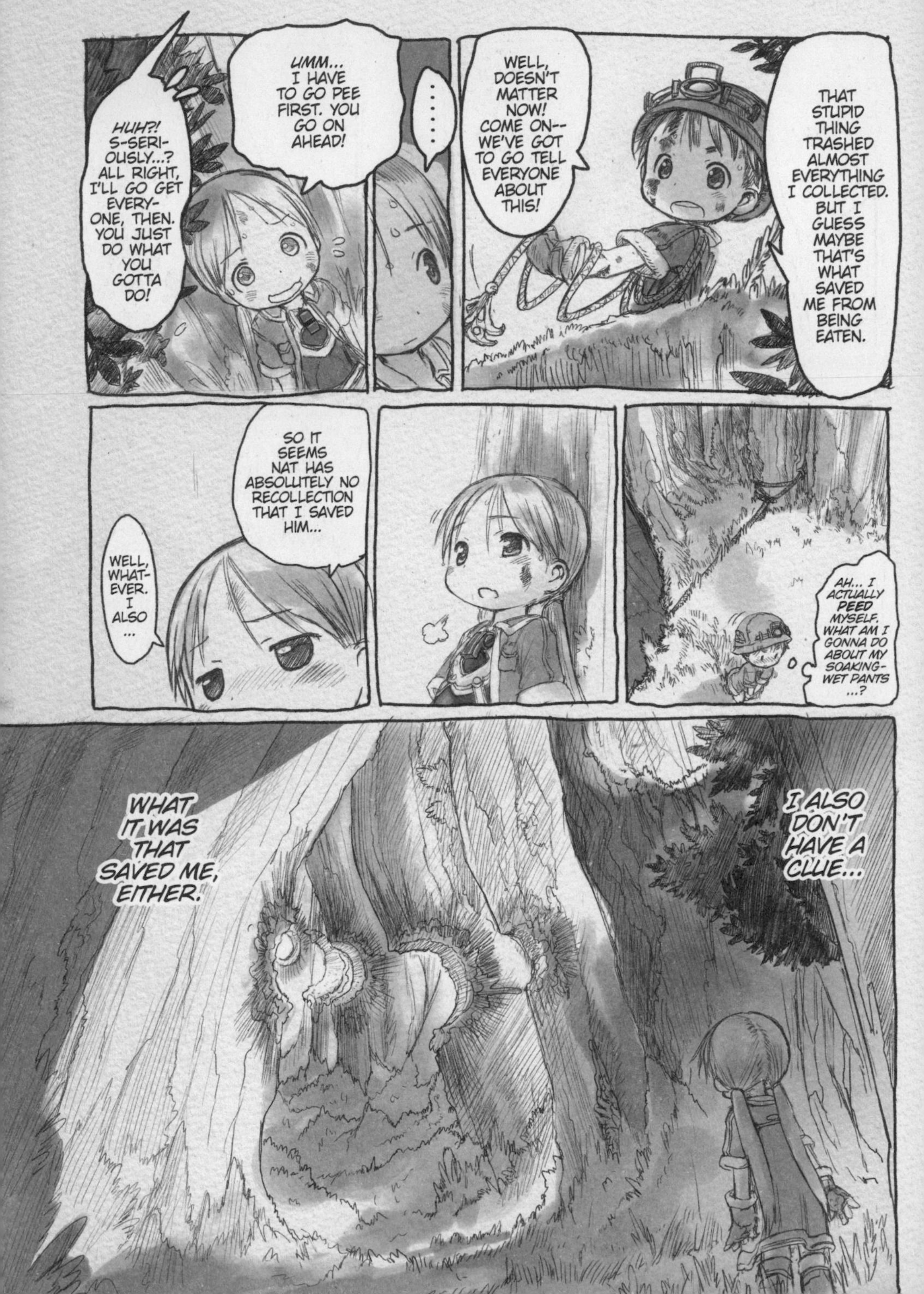
THAT STUPID THING TRASHED ALMOST EVERYTHING I COLLECTED. BUT I GUESS MAYBE THAT'S WHAT SAVED ME FROM BEING EATEN.
WELL, DOESN'T MATTER NOW! COME ON-- WE'VE GOT TO GO TELL EVERYONE ABOUT THIS!
......
UMM... I HAVE TO GO PEE FIRST. YOU GO ON AHEAD!
HUH?! S-SERIOUSLY...? ALL RIGHT, I'LL GO GET EVERYONE, THEN. YOU JUST DO WHAT YOU GOTTA DO!
AH... I ACTUALLY PEED MYSELF. WHAT AM I GONNA DO ABOUT MY SOAKING-WET PANTS ...?
SO IT SEEMS NAT HAS ABSOLUTELY NO RECOLLECTION THAT I SAVED HIM...
WELL, WHATEVER. I ALSO ...
I ALSO DON'T HAVE A CLUE...
WHAT IT WAS THAT SAVED ME, EITHER.

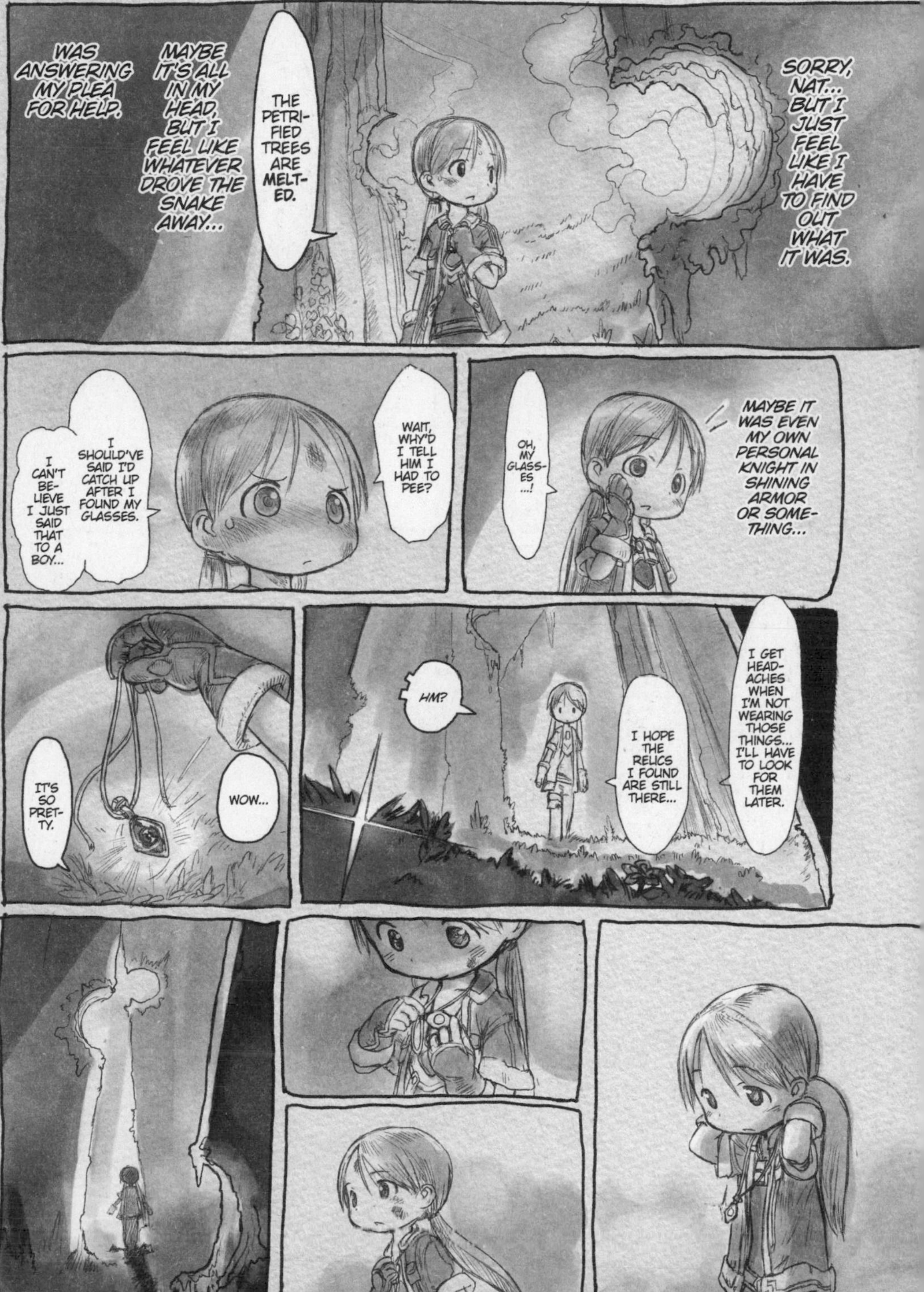
SORRY, NAT... BUT I JUST FEEL LIKE I HAVE TO FIND OUT WHAT IT WAS.
THE PETRIFIED TREES ARE MELTED.
MAYBE IT'S ALL IN MY HEAD, BUT I FEEL LIKE WHATEVER DROVE THE SNAKE AWAY...
WAS ANSWERING MY PLEA FOR HELP.
MAYBE IT WAS EVEN MY OWN PERSONAL KNIGHT IN SHINING ARMOR OR SOMETHING...
OH, MY GLASSES...!
WAIT, WHY'D I TELL HIM I HAD TO PEE?
I SHOULD'VE SAID I'D CATCH UP AFTER I FOUND MY GLASSES.
I CAN'T BELIEVE I JUST SAID THAT TO A BOY...
I GET HEADACHES WHEN I'M NOT WEARING THOSE THINGS... I'LL HAVE TO LOOK FOR THEM LATER.
I HOPE THE RELICS I FOUND ARE STILL THERE...
HM?
WOW...
IT'S SO PRETTY.

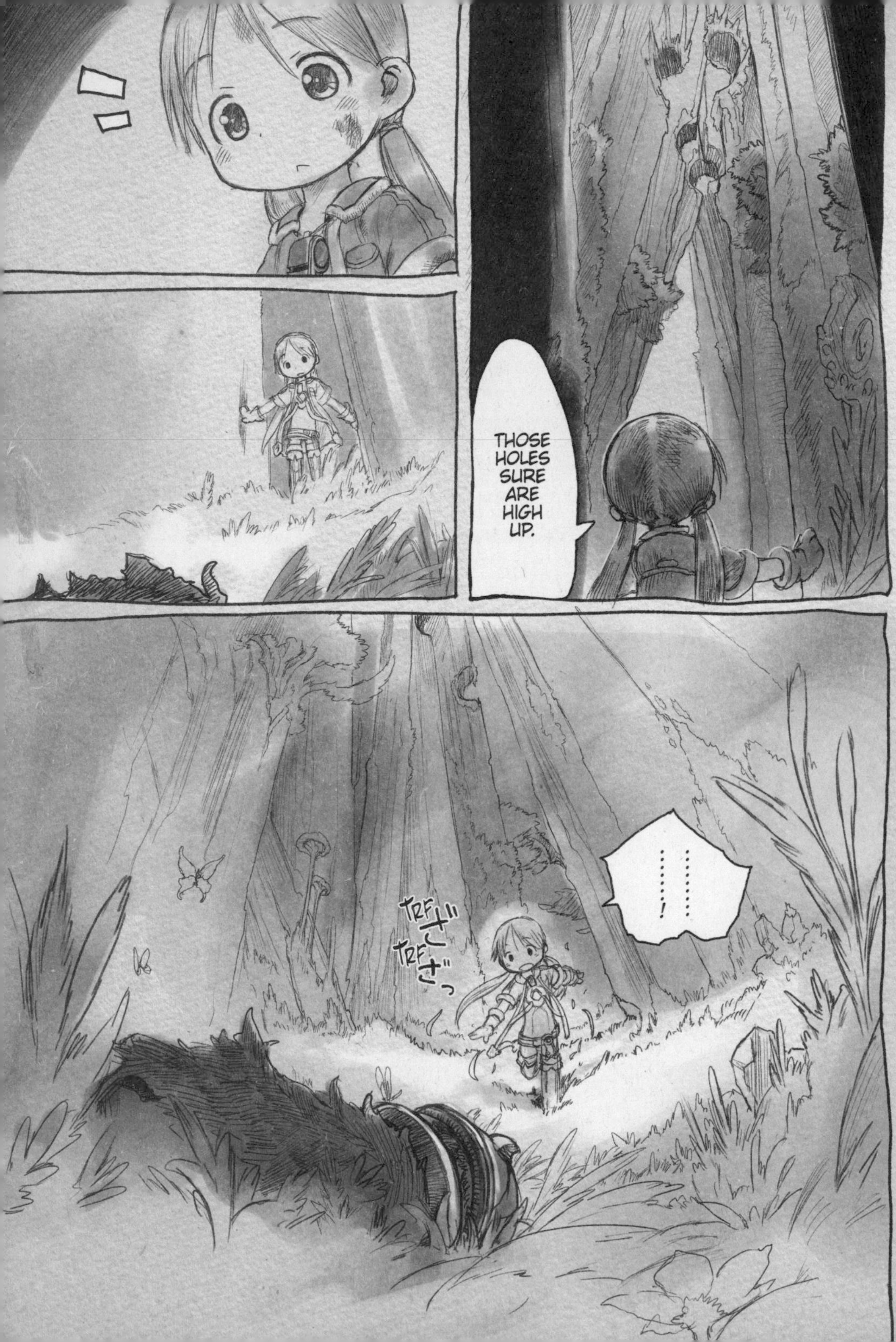
THOSE HOLES SURE ARE HIGH UP.
......!
TRF ざっ TRF ざっ

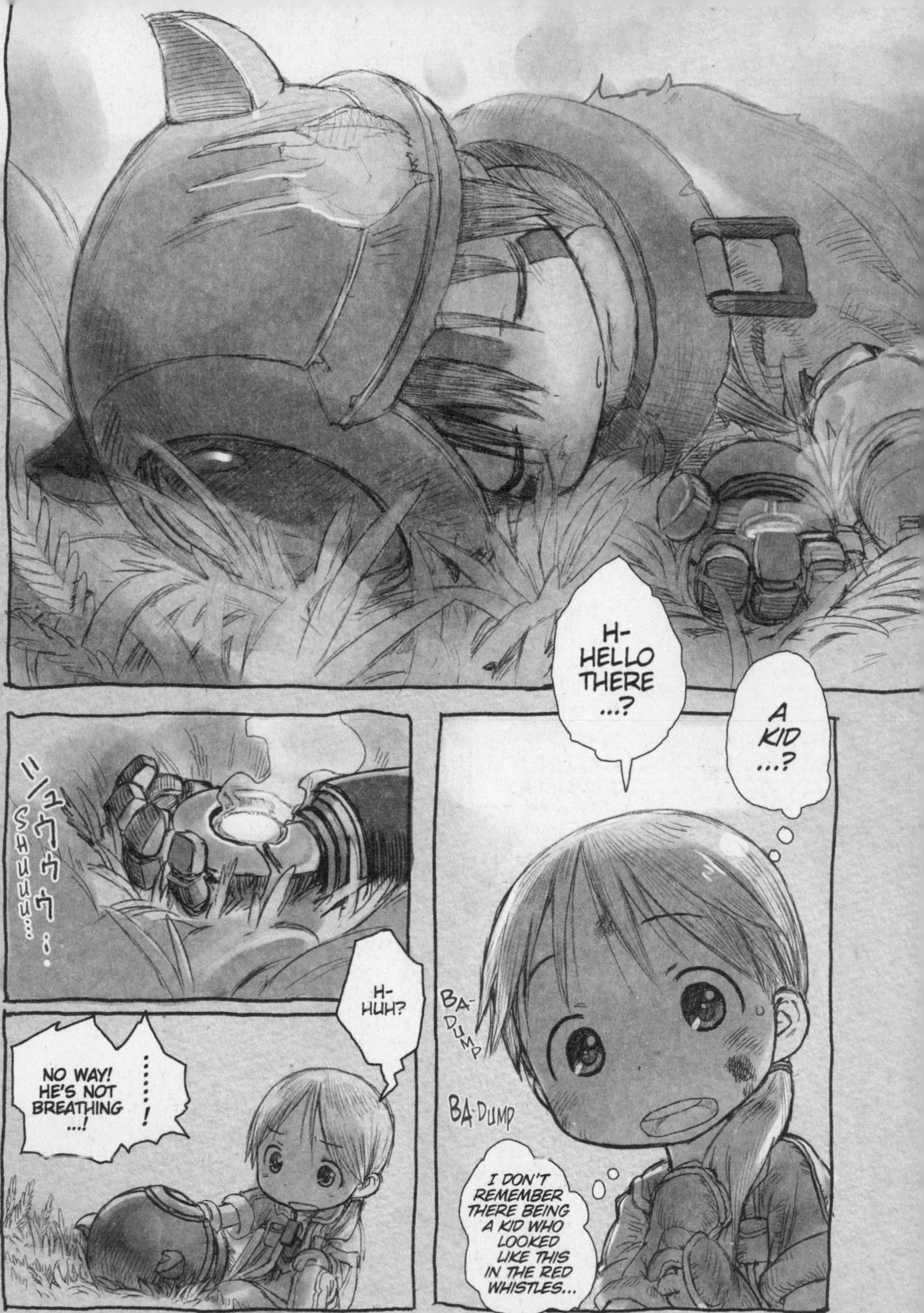
H-HELLO THERE...?
A KID...?
BA-DUMP
BA-DUMP
I DON'T REMEMBER THERE BEING A KID WHO LOOKED LIKE THIS IN THE RED WHISTLES...
シュウウウ…
SHUUUU...
H-HUH?
NO WAY! HE'S NOT BREATHING...!
......!

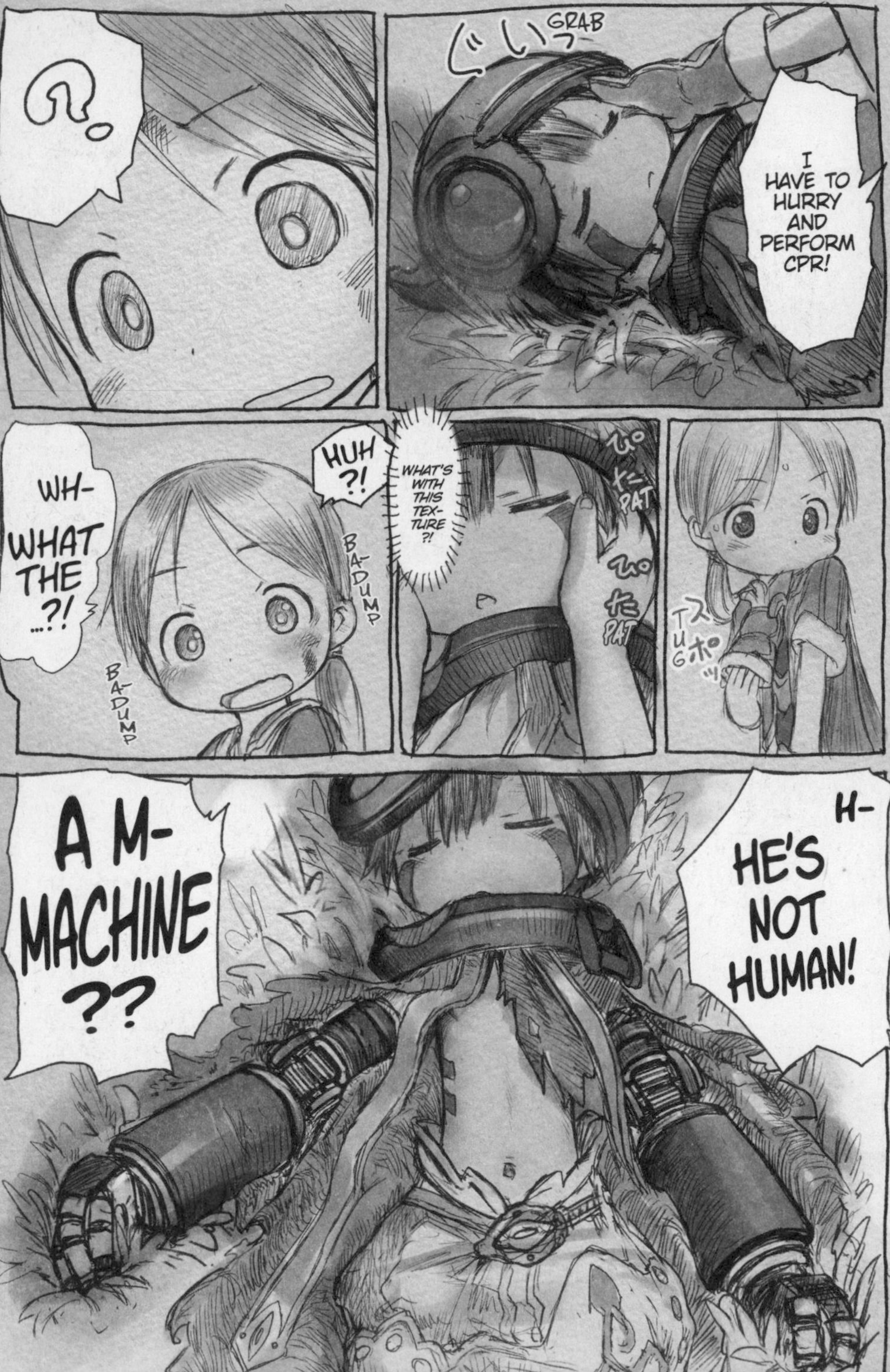

ぐいっ GRAB
I HAVE TO HURRY AND PERFORM CPR!
?
スポッ TUG
ぴた PAT
ぴた PAT
WHAT'S WITH THIS TEX-TURE ?!
HUH ?!
WH- WHAT THE ...?!
BADUMP
BADUMP
H- HE'S NOT HUMAN!
A M- MACHINE ??

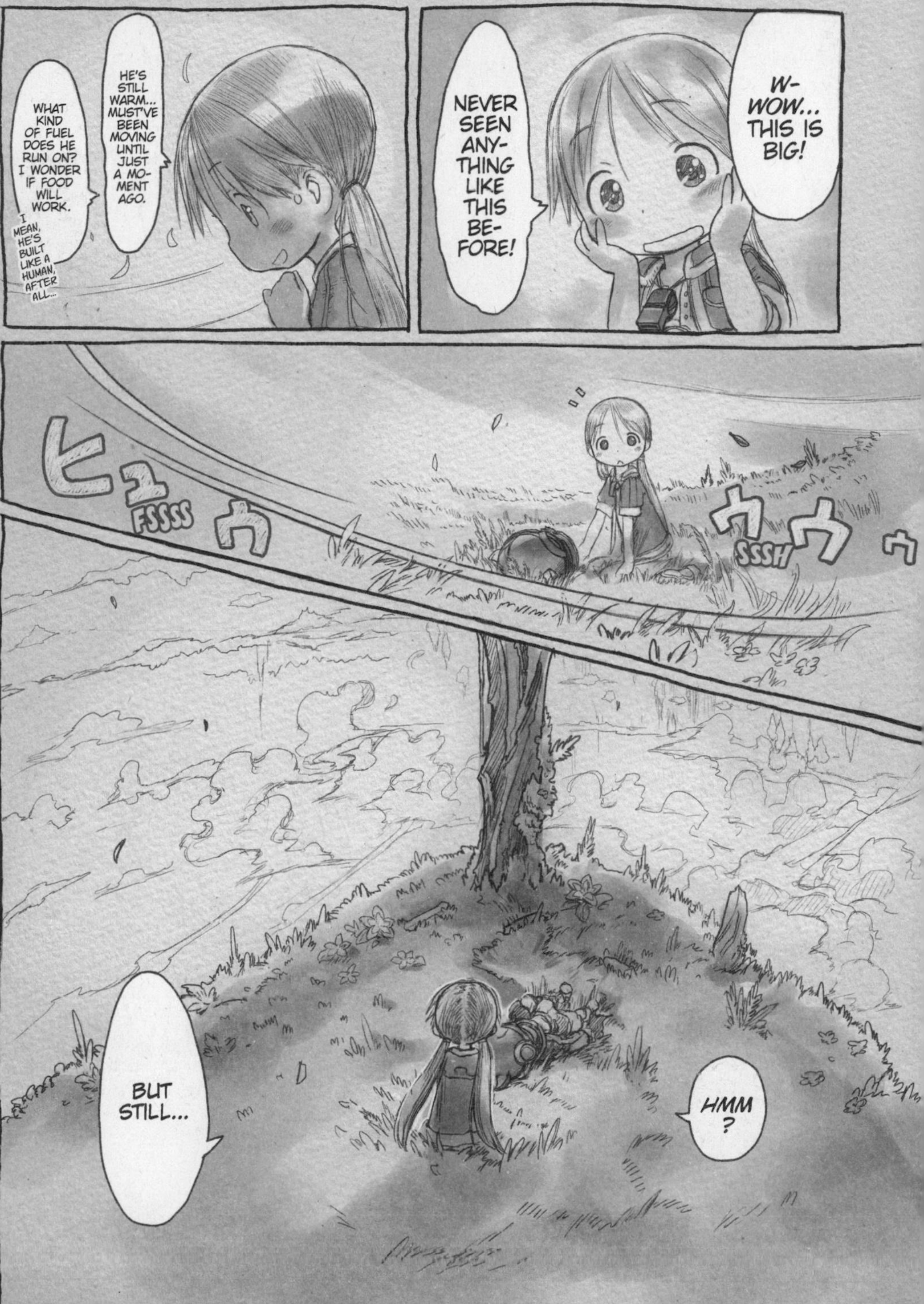
W-WOW... THIS IS BIG!
NEVER SEEN ANYTHING LIKE THIS BEFORE!
HE'S STILL WARM... MUST'VE BEEN MOVING UNTIL JUST A MOMENT AGO.
WHAT KIND OF FUEL DOES HE RUN ON? I WONDER IF FOOD WILL WORK.
I MEAN, HE'S BUILT LIKE A HUMAN, AFTER ALL...
ヒュウ
FSSSS
ウウウウ
SSSH
HMM?
BUT STILL...

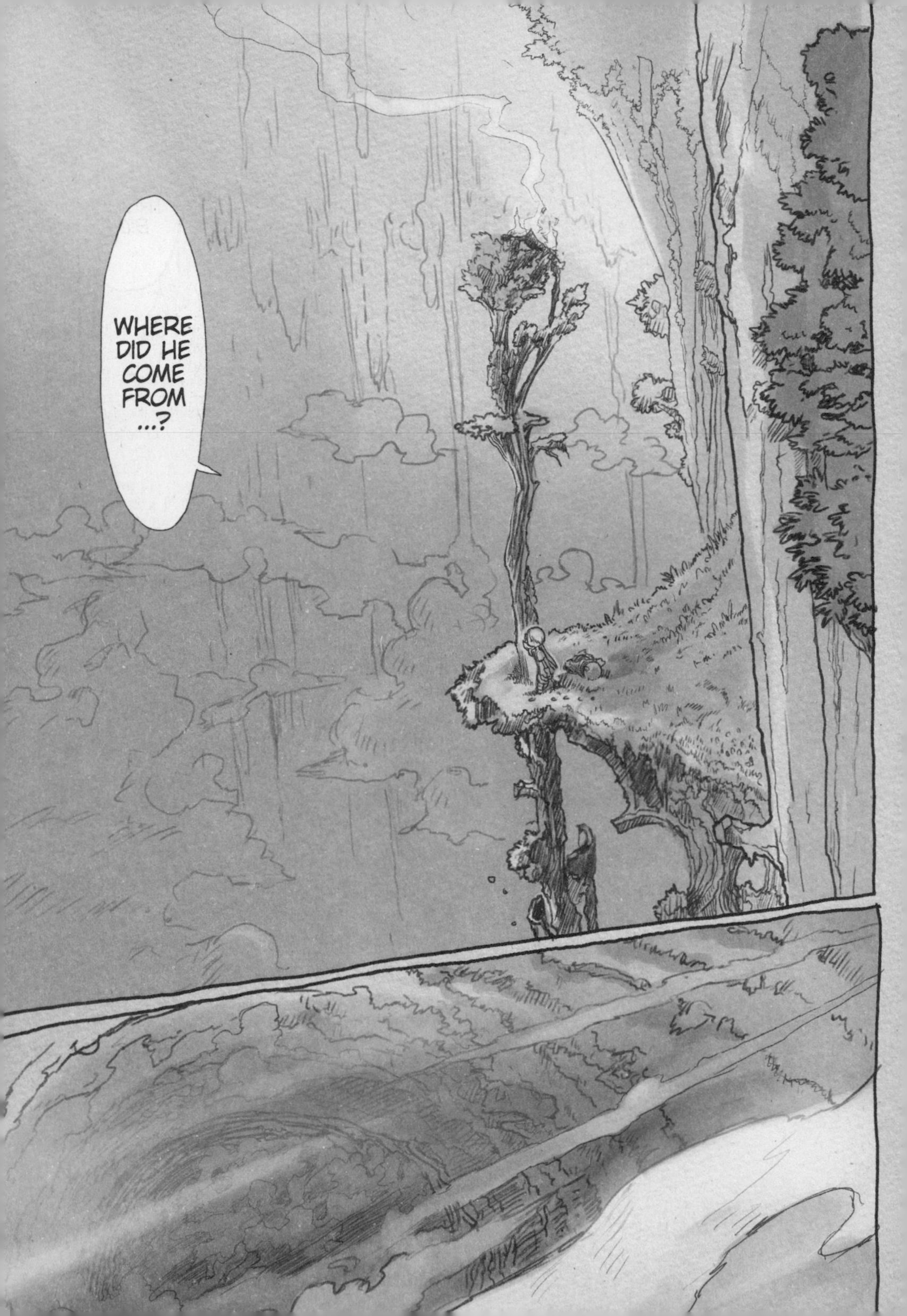
WHERE DID HE COME FROM ...?

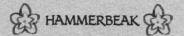
HAMMERBEAK

THESE BIRDS LIVE IN A WIDE AREA RANGING FROM THE
SURFACE ALL THE WAY DOWN TO THE FOURTH LAYER OF THE ABYSS.
THE DEFINING FEATURE OF THIS SPECIES IS THE WAY
ITS BEAK IS FUSED DIRECTLY TO ITS HARD SKULL.
THE WINGSPAN OF AN ADULT CAN EXCEED THREE METERS.

MALES BASH THEIR SKULLS AGAINST EACH OTHER IN DISPUTES.
SPARKS LITERALLY FLY WHEN THEIR HEADS COLLIDE.

THEIR MEAT IS DELICIOUS AND IS TREASURED
AMONG CAVE RAIDERS AS A USEFUL FOOD SOURCE.
THE SKULL OF ONE CAN BE USED AS A FLINT FOR
STARTING FIRES, COOKWARE, OR EVEN AS A CONTAINER.
A SINGLE BIRD CAN PROVIDE BOTH A MEAL AND
THE TOOLS NEEDED TO COOK IT.

THE FEATHERS MAKE
FOR HIGH-QUALITY
KINDLING.

DANGER LEVEL: ★ (INSIGNIFICANT)

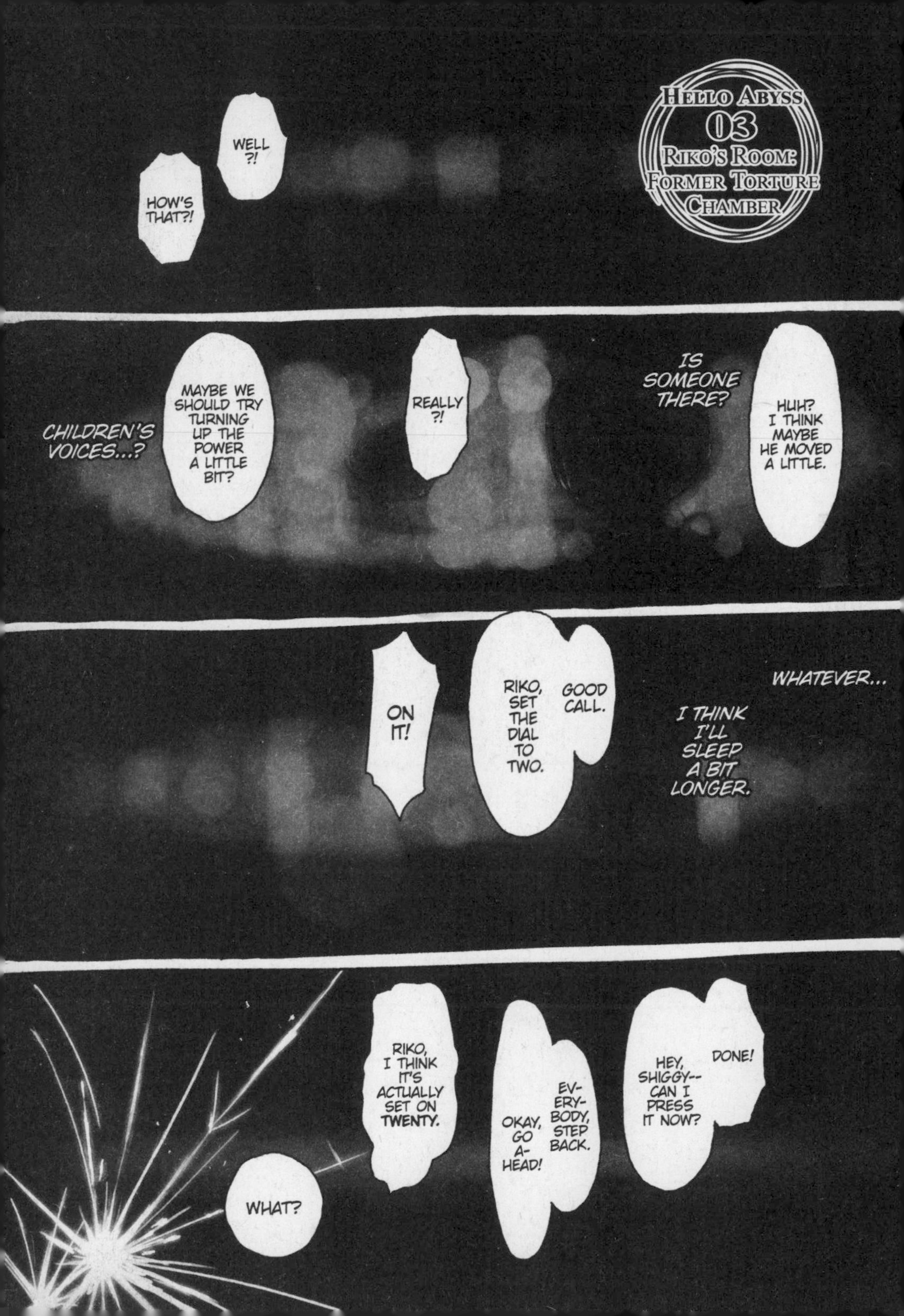
HELLO ABYSS
03
RIKO'S ROOM: FORMER TORTURE CHAMBER
WELL?!
HOW'S THAT?!
HUH? I THINK MAYBE HE MOVED A LITTLE.
IS SOMEONE THERE?
REALLY?!
MAYBE WE SHOULD TRY TURNING UP THE POWER A LITTLE BIT?
CHILDREN'S VOICES...?
WHATEVER...
I THINK I'LL SLEEP A BIT LONGER.
GOOD CALL.
RIKO, SET THE DIAL TO TWO.
ON IT!
DONE!
HEY, SHIGGY-- CAN I PRESS IT NOW?
EVERYBODY, STEP BACK.
OKAY, GO AHEAD!
RIKO, I THINK IT'S ACTUALLY SET ON TWENTY.
WHAT?

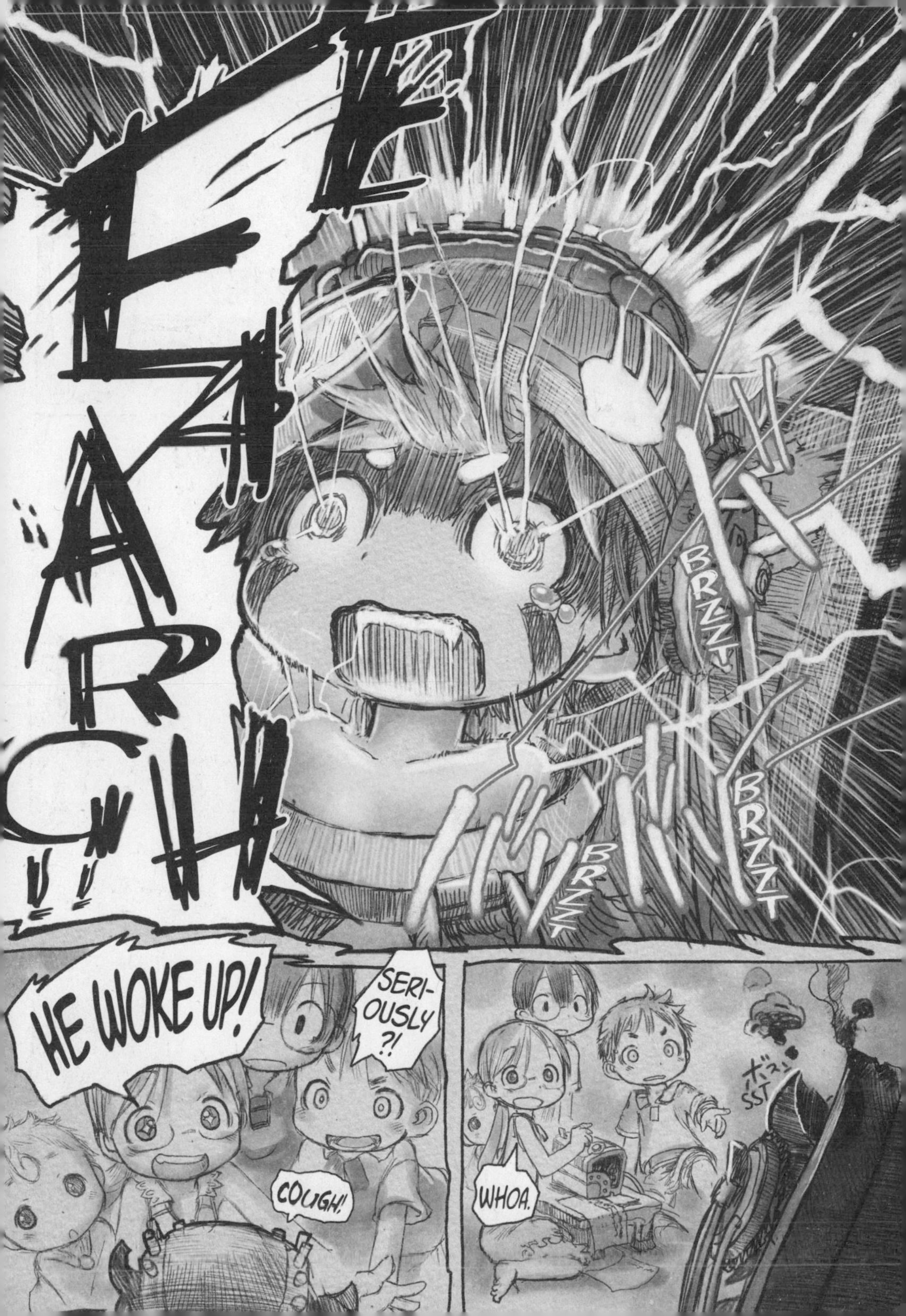
EEAARGH!!
BRZZZT
BRZZZT
BRZZZT
SST
WHOA.
HE WOKE UP!
SERI-OUSLY?!
COUGH!

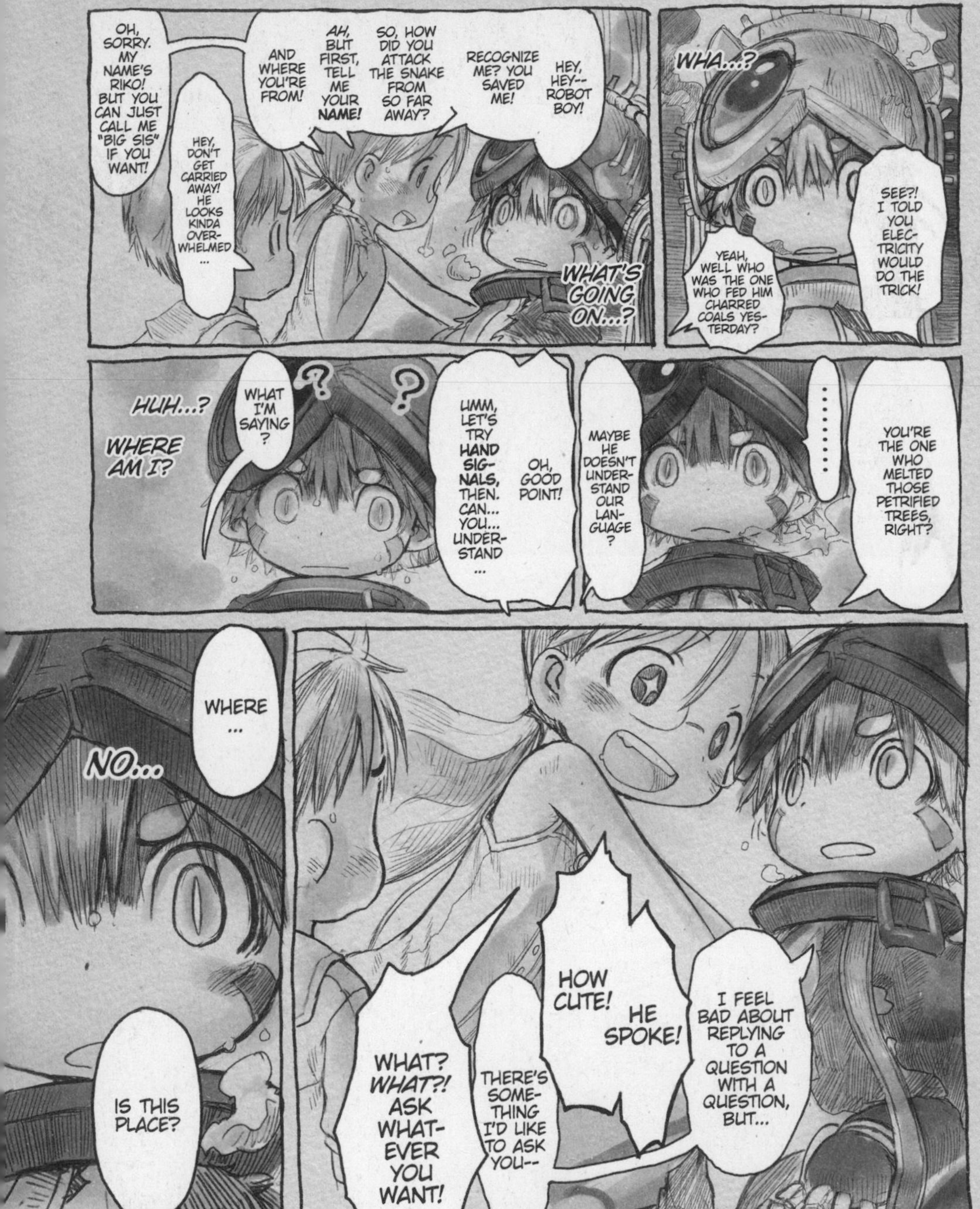
WHA...?
SEE?! I TOLD YOU ELECTRICITY WOULD DO THE TRICK!
YEAH, WELL WHO WAS THE ONE WHO FED HIM CHARRED COALS YESTERDAY?
HEY, HEY-- ROBOT BOY!
RECOGNIZE ME? YOU SAVED ME!
SO, HOW DID YOU ATTACK THE SNAKE FROM SO FAR AWAY?
AH, BUT FIRST, TELL ME YOUR **NAME!**
AND WHERE YOU'RE FROM!
OH, SORRY. MY NAME'S RIKO! BUT YOU CAN JUST CALL ME "BIG SIS" IF YOU WANT!
HEY, DON'T GET CARRIED AWAY! HE LOOKS KINDA OVERWHELMED...
WHAT'S GOING ON...?
YOU'RE THE ONE WHO MELTED THOSE PETRIFIED TREES, RIGHT?
......
MAYBE HE DOESN'T UNDERSTAND OUR LANGUAGE?
OH, GOOD POINT!
UMM, LET'S TRY **HAND SIGNALS,** THEN. CAN... YOU... UNDERSTAND...
WHAT I'M SAYING?
HUH...?
WHERE AM I?
I FEEL BAD ABOUT REPLYING TO A QUESTION WITH A QUESTION, BUT...
HE SPOKE!
HOW CUTE!
THERE'S SOMETHING I'D LIKE TO ASK YOU--
WHAT? *WHAT?!* ASK WHATEVER YOU WANT!
WHERE...
NO...
IS THIS PLACE?

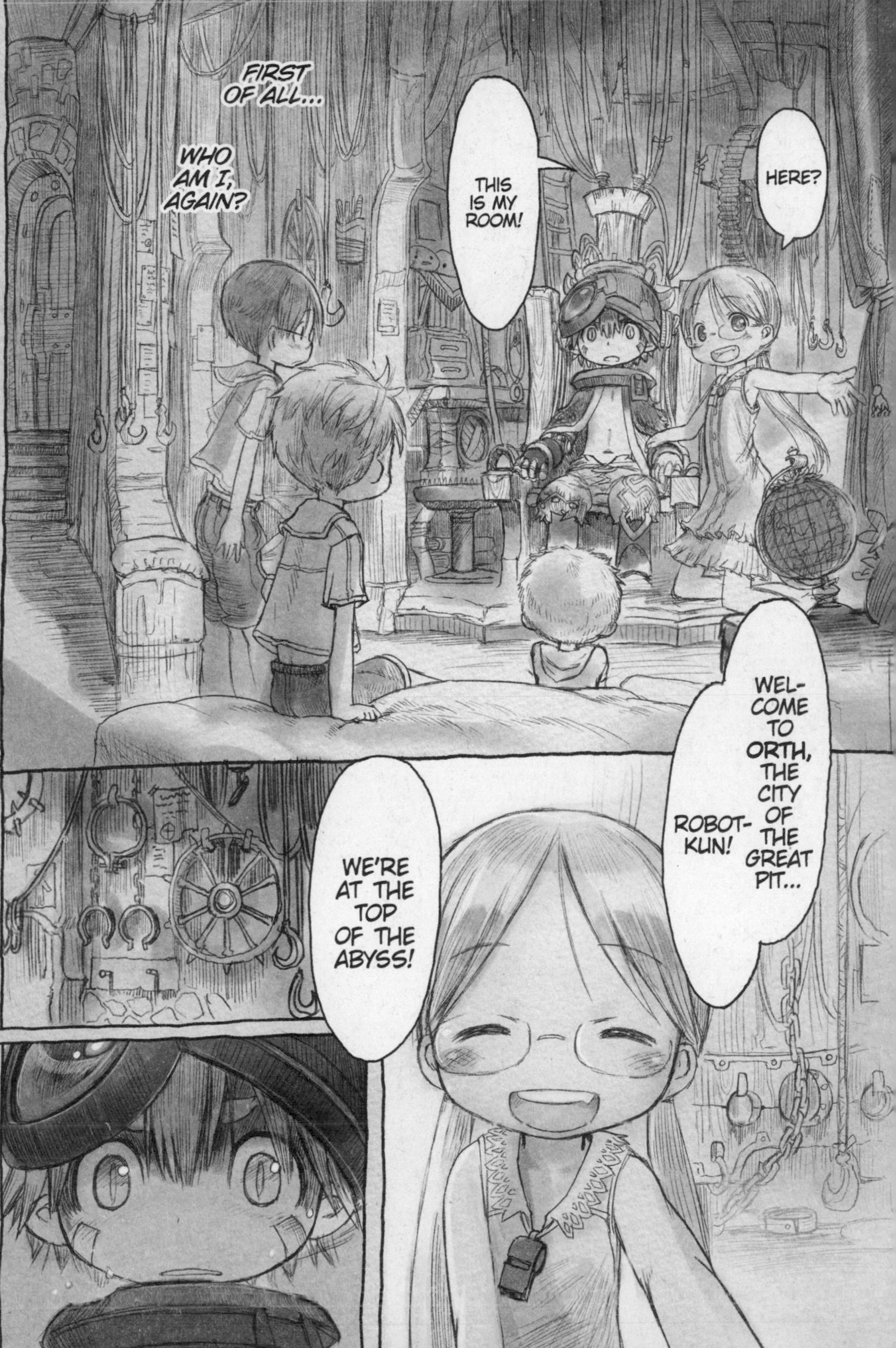
HERE?
THIS IS MY ROOM!
FIRST OF ALL...
WHO AM I, AGAIN?
WEL-COME TO ORTH, THE CITY OF THE GREAT PIT...
ROBOT-KUN!
WE'RE AT THE TOP OF THE ABYSS!

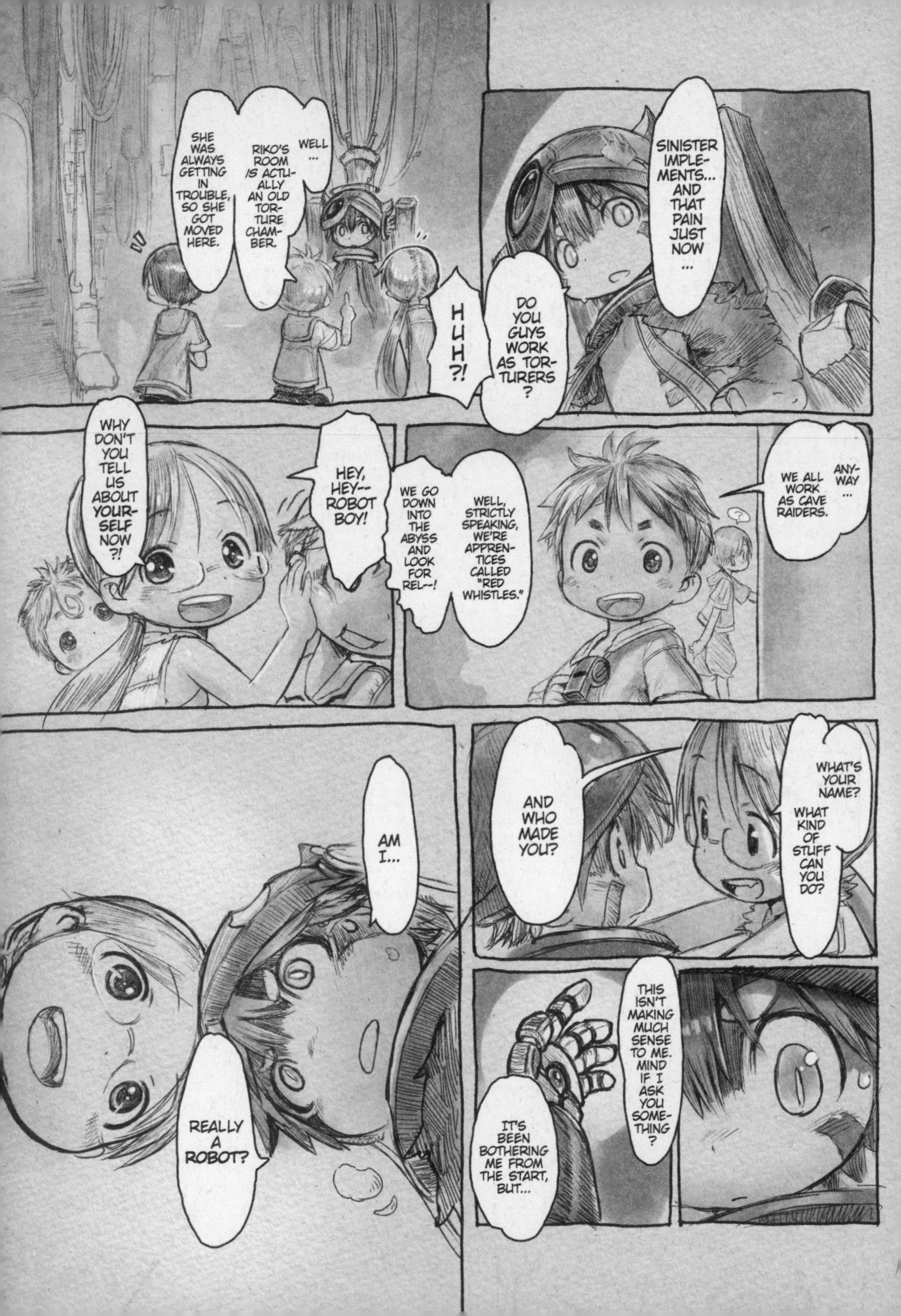
SINISTER IMPLEMENTS... AND THAT PAIN JUST NOW ...
DO YOU GUYS WORK AS TORTURERS?
HUH?!
WELL ...
RIKO'S ROOM IS ACTUALLY AN OLD TORTURE CHAMBER.
SHE WAS ALWAYS GETTING IN TROUBLE, SO SHE GOT MOVED HERE.
ANYWAY ...
WE ALL WORK AS CAVE RAIDERS.
WELL, STRICTLY SPEAKING, WE'RE APPRENTICES CALLED "RED WHISTLES."
WE GO DOWN INTO THE ABYSS AND LOOK FOR REL--!
HEY, HEY-- ROBOT BOY!
WHY DON'T YOU TELL US ABOUT YOURSELF NOW?!
WHAT'S YOUR NAME?
WHAT KIND OF STUFF CAN YOU DO?
AND WHO MADE YOU?
THIS ISN'T MAKING MUCH SENSE TO ME. MIND IF I ASK YOU SOMETHING?
IT'S BEEN BOTHERING ME FROM THE START, BUT...
AM I...
REALLY A ROBOT?

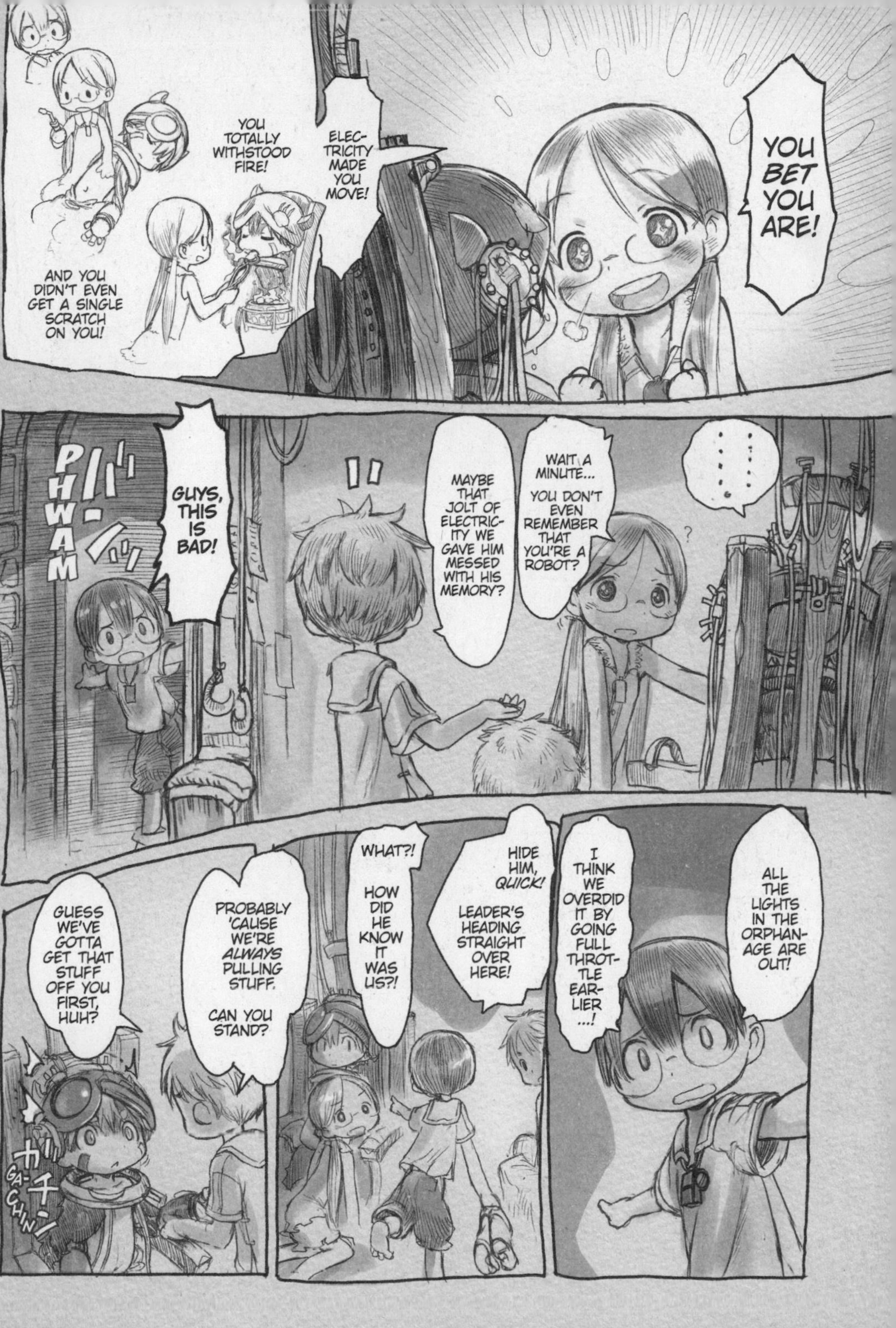
YOU BET YOU ARE!
ELEC-TRICITY MADE YOU MOVE!
YOU TOTALLY WITHSTOOD FIRE!
AND YOU DIDN'T EVEN GET A SINGLE SCRATCH ON YOU!
......
WAIT A MINUTE... YOU DON'T EVEN REMEMBER THAT YOU'RE A ROBOT?
MAYBE THAT JOLT OF ELECTRIC-ITY WE GAVE HIM MESSED WITH HIS MEMORY?
GUYS, THIS IS BAD!
PHWAM
ALL THE LIGHTS IN THE ORPHAN-AGE ARE OUT!
I THINK WE OVERDID IT BY GOING FULL THROT-TLE EAR-LIER ...!
HIDE HIM, QUICK!
LEADER'S HEADING STRAIGHT OVER HERE!
WHAT?!
HOW DID HE KNOW IT WAS US?!
PROBABLY 'CAUSE WE'RE ALWAYS PULLING STUFF.
CAN YOU STAND?
GUESS WE'VE GOTTA GET THAT STUFF OFF YOU FIRST, HUH?
GA-CHIN!

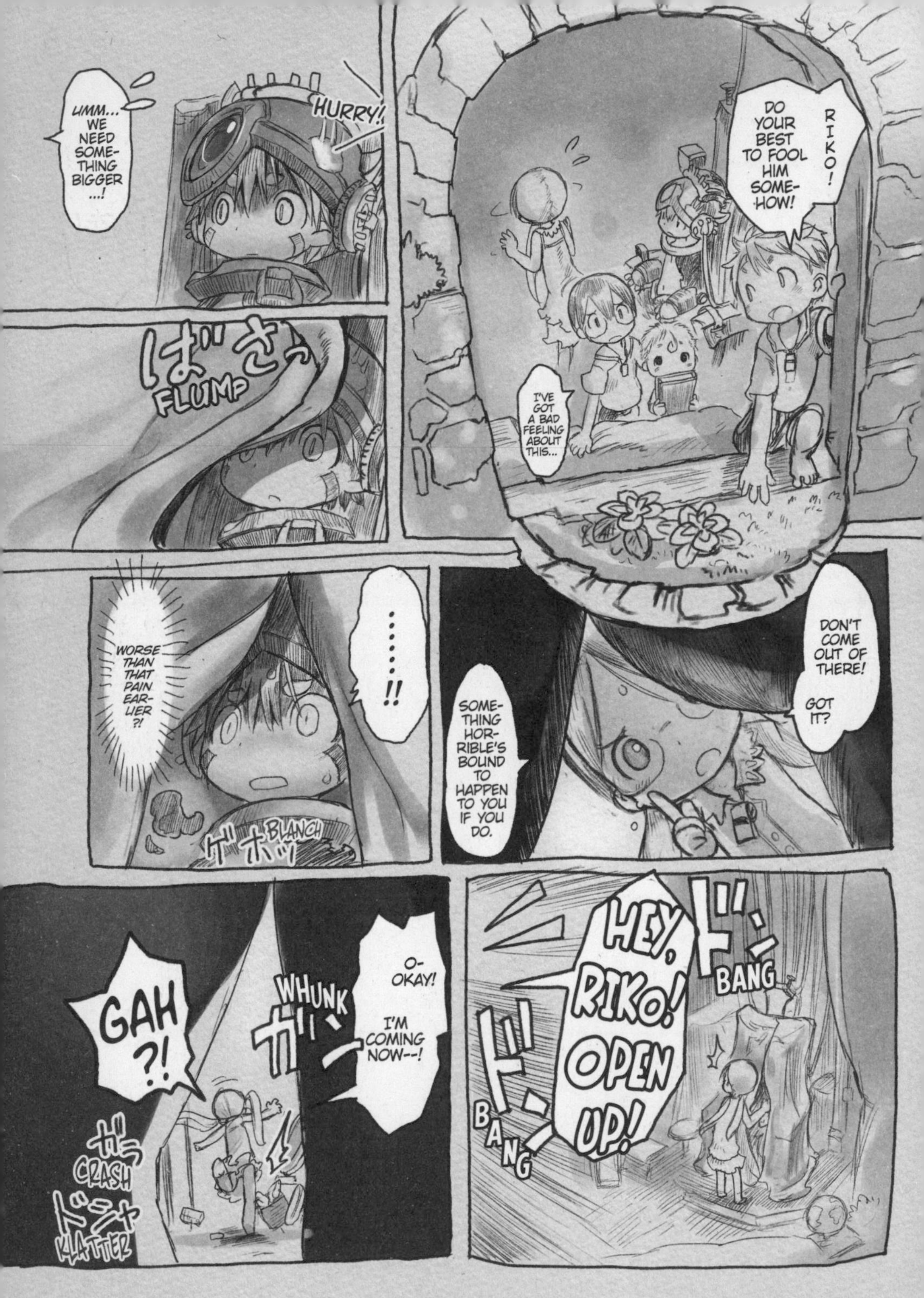
RIKO!
DO YOUR BEST TO FOOL HIM SOME-HOW!
I'VE GOT A BAD FEELING ABOUT THIS...
HURRY!
UMM... WE NEED SOME-THING BIGGER ...!
ばさっ
FLUMP
DON'T COME OUT OF THERE!
GOT IT?
SOME-THING HOR-RIBLE'S BOUND TO HAPPEN TO YOU IF YOU DO.
......!!
WORSE THAN THAT PAIN EAR-LIER?!
ゲホッ
BLANCH
ドン
BANG
HEY, RIKO! OPEN UP!
ドン
BANG
O-OKAY!
I'M COMING NOW--!
ガッ
WHUNK
GAH?!
ガラ
CRASH
ドシャ
KLATTER

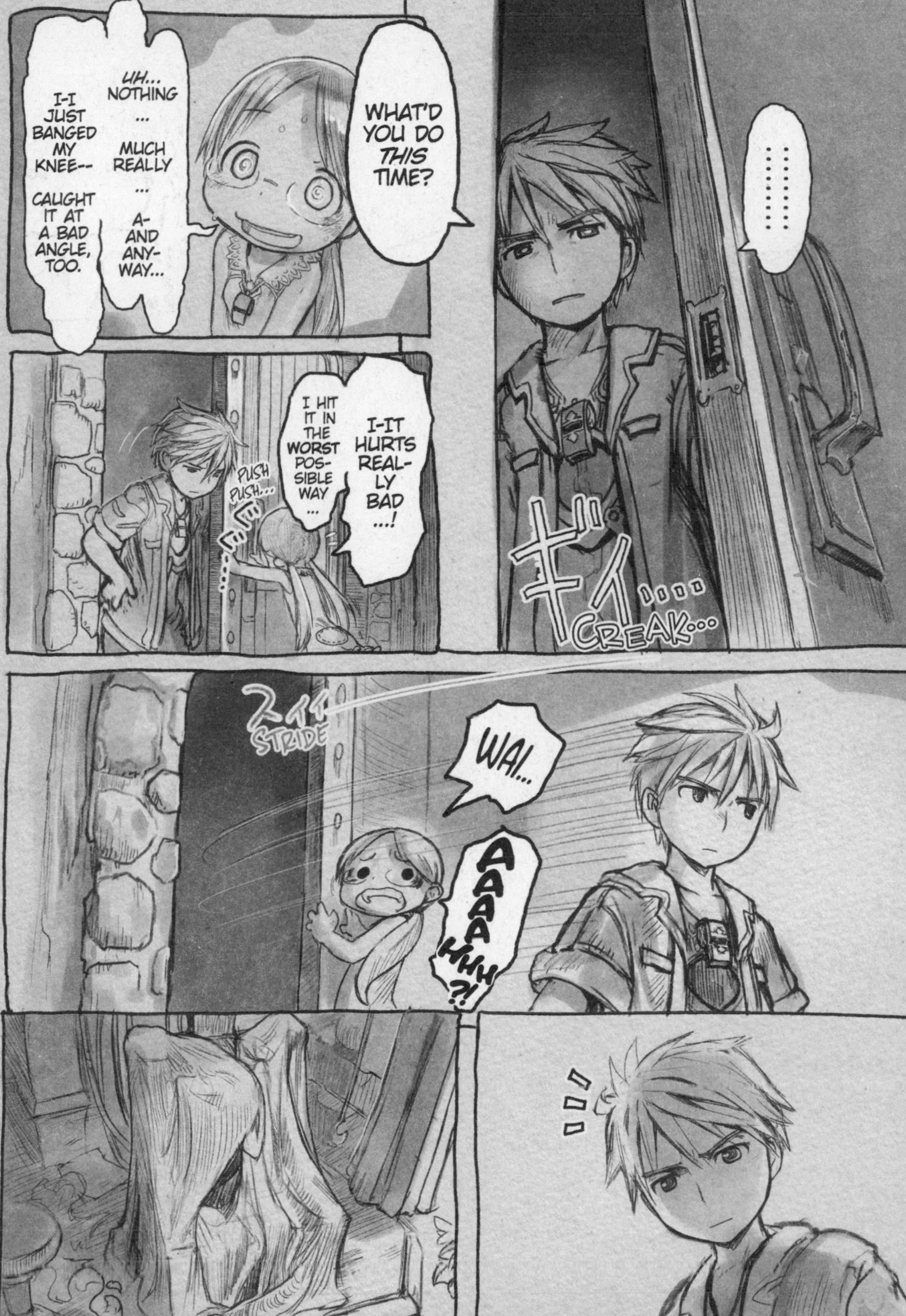
......
ギィ...
CREAK...
WHAT'D YOU DO THIS TIME?
UH... NOTHING ... MUCH REALLY ... A- AND ANYWAY...
I-I JUST BANGED MY KNEE-- CAUGHT IT AT A BAD ANGLE, TOO.
I-IT HURTS REALL-LY BAD ...!
I HIT IT IN THE WORST POS-SIBLE WAY ...
PUSH PUSH...
スイイ
STRIDE
WAI...
AAAAHHH?!

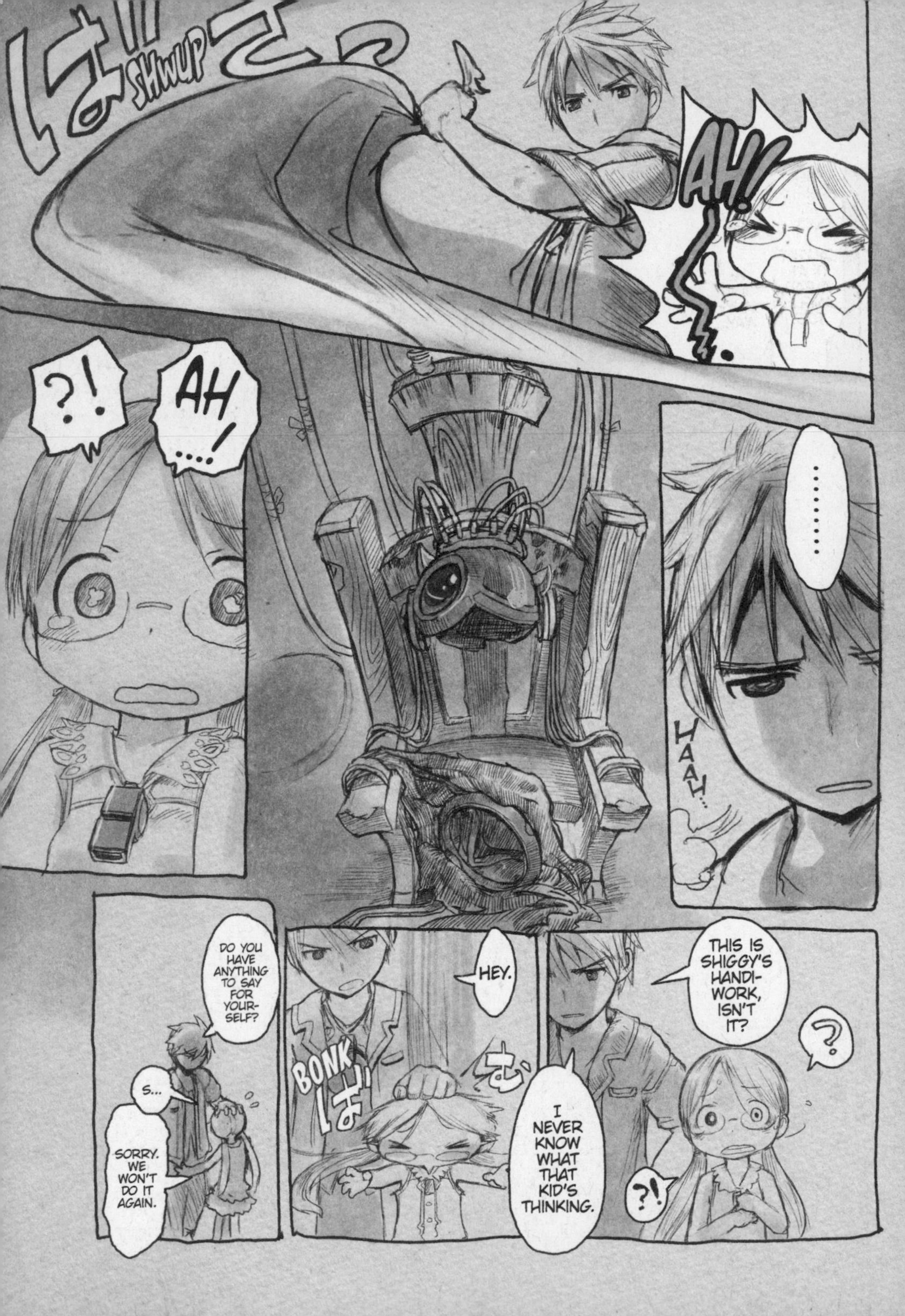
SHWUP
AH!
....
HAAAH...
AH ...!
?!
THIS IS SHIGGY'S HANDI-WORK, ISN'T IT?
?
I NEVER KNOW WHAT THAT KID'S THINKING.
?!
HEY.
BONK
DO YOU HAVE ANYTHING TO SAY FOR YOUR-SELF?
S...
SORRY. WE WON'T DO IT AGAIN.

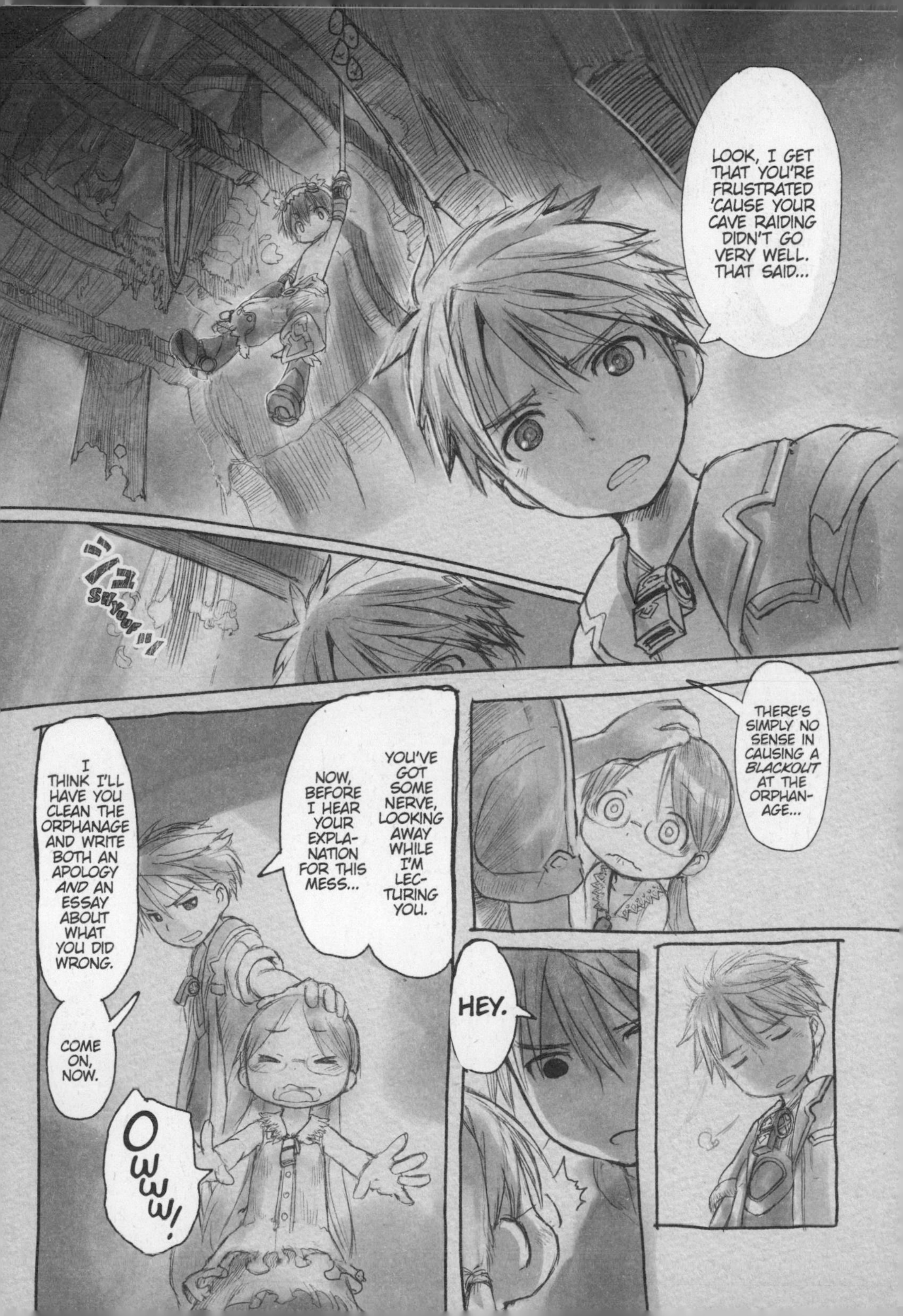
LOOK, I GET THAT YOU'RE FRUSTRATED 'CAUSE YOUR CAVE RAIDING DIDN'T GO VERY WELL. THAT SAID...
シュ
SHYUUF!!
THERE'S SIMPLY NO SENSE IN CAUSING A *BLACKOUT* AT THE ORPHANAGE...
HEY.
YOU'VE GOT SOME NERVE, LOOKING AWAY WHILE I'M LECTURING YOU.
NOW, BEFORE I HEAR YOUR EXPLANATION FOR THIS MESS...
I THINK I'LL HAVE YOU CLEAN THE ORPHANAGE AND WRITE BOTH AN APOLOGY AND AN ESSAY ABOUT WHAT YOU DID WRONG.
COME ON, NOW.
OWW!

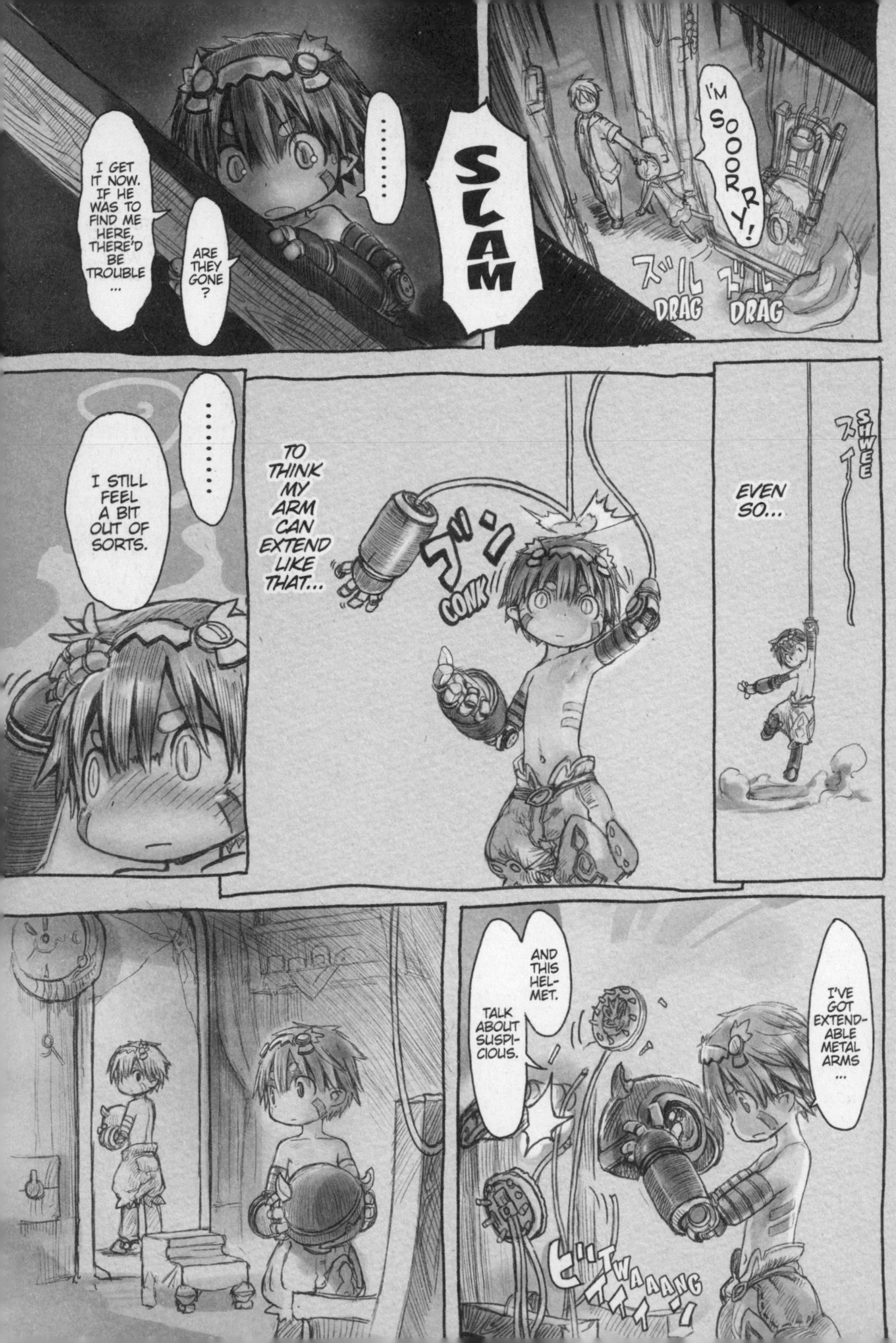
I'M SOOORRY!
DRAG
DRAG
SLAM
......
ARE THEY GONE?
I GET IT NOW. IF HE WAS TO FIND ME HERE, THERE'D BE TROUBLE ...
SHWEE
EVEN SO...
TO THINK MY ARM CAN EXTEND LIKE THAT...
CONK
......
I STILL FEEL A BIT OUT OF SORTS.
I'VE GOT EXTEND-ABLE METAL ARMS ...
AND THIS HEL-MET.
TALK ABOUT SUSPI-CIOUS.
TWAAAANG

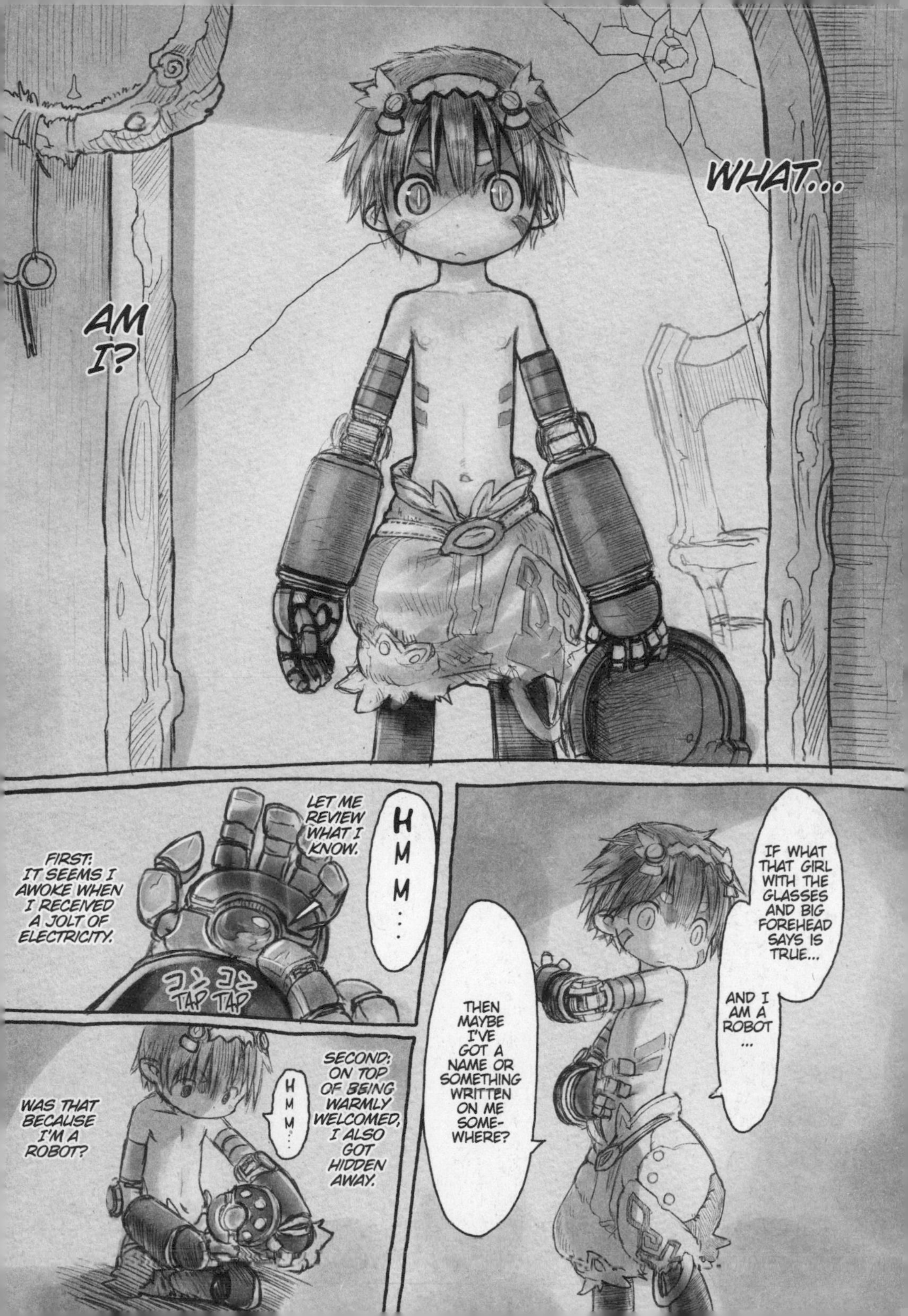
WHAT...
AM I?
IF WHAT THAT GIRL WITH THE GLASSES AND BIG FOREHEAD SAYS IS TRUE...
AND I AM A ROBOT ...
THEN MAYBE I'VE GOT A NAME OR SOMETHING WRITTEN ON ME SOME-WHERE?
HMM...
LET ME REVIEW WHAT I KNOW.
FIRST: IT SEEMS I AWOKE WHEN I RECEIVED A JOLT OF ELECTRICITY.
TAP TAP
HMM...
SECOND: ON TOP OF BEING WARMLY WELCOMED, I ALSO GOT HIDDEN AWAY.
WAS THAT BECAUSE I'M A ROBOT?

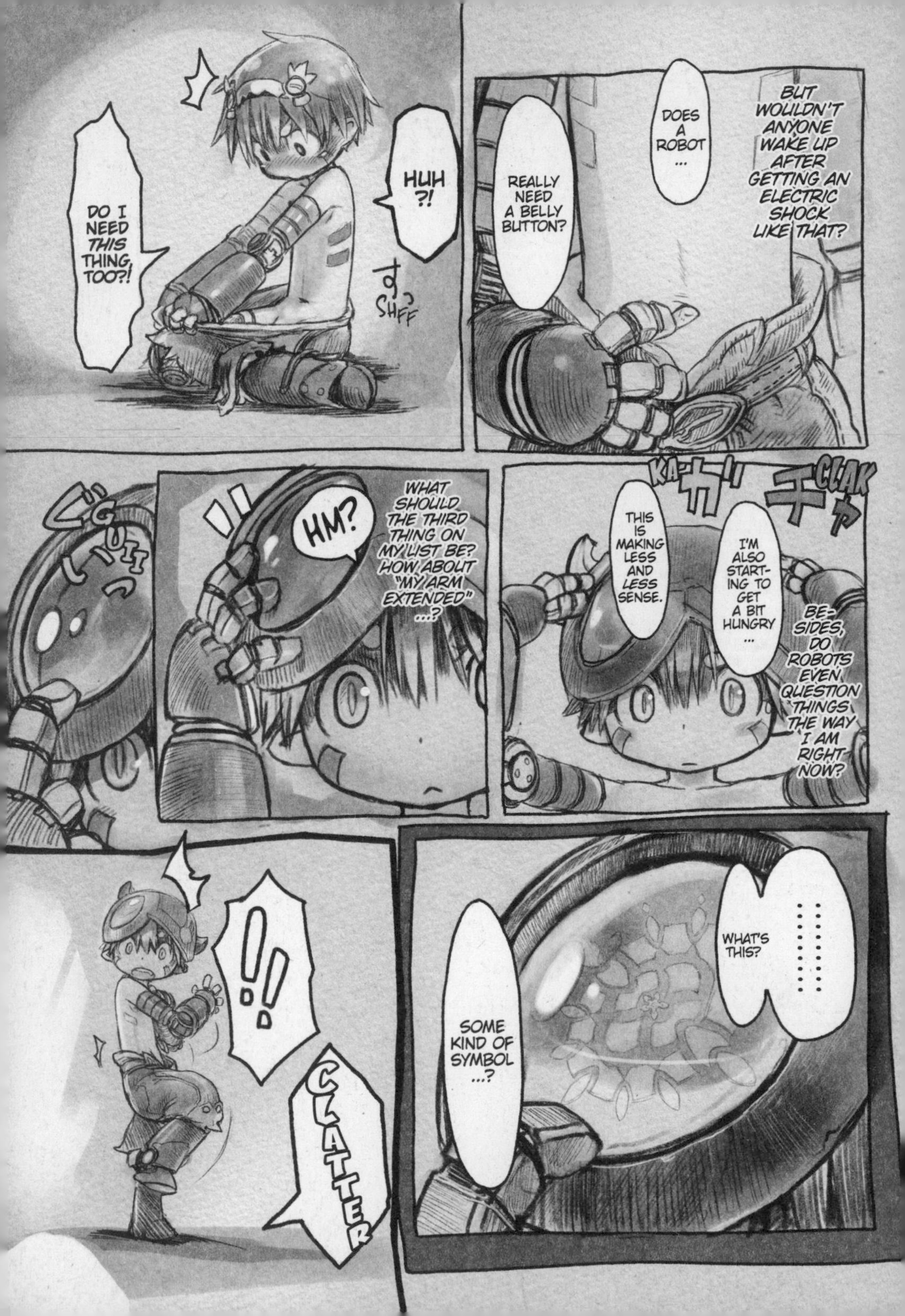
BUT WOULDN'T ANYONE WAKE UP AFTER GETTING AN ELECTRIC SHOCK LIKE THAT?
DOES A ROBOT...
REALLY NEED A BELLY BUTTON?
HUH?!
DO I NEED THIS THING, TOO?!
SHFF
CLAK
KA-
I'M ALSO STARTING TO GET A BIT HUNGRY...
THIS IS MAKING LESS AND LESS SENSE.
BESIDES, DO ROBOTS EVEN QUESTION THINGS THE WAY I AM RIGHT NOW?
WHAT SHOULD THE THIRD THING ON MY LIST BE? HOW ABOUT "MY ARM EXTENDED"...?
HM?
GUII
......
WHAT'S THIS?
SOME KIND OF SYMBOL...?
!!!
CLATTER

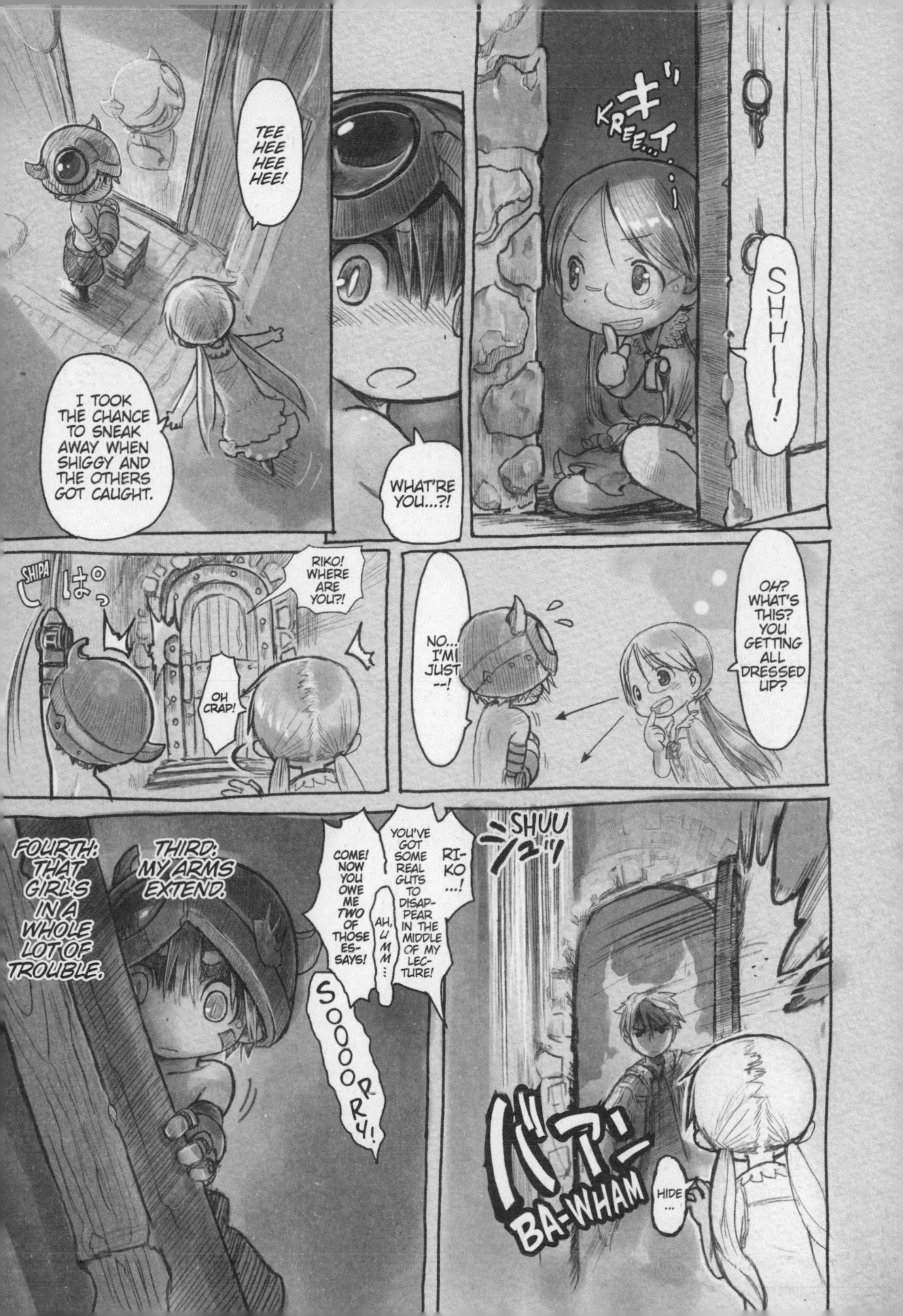
KREE...
SHHH—!
WHAT'RE YOU...?!
TEE HEE HEE HEE!
I TOOK THE CHANCE TO SNEAK AWAY WHEN SHIGGY AND THE OTHERS GOT CAUGHT.
OH? WHAT'S THIS? YOU GETTING ALL DRESSED UP?
NO... I'M JUST --!
RIKO! WHERE ARE YOU?!
SHIPA
OH CRAP!
SHUU
BA-WHAM
HIDE...
RIKO...!
YOU'VE GOT SOME REAL GUTS TO DISAPPEAR IN THE MIDDLE OF MY LECTURE!
AH, UMM...
COME! NOW YOU OWE ME TWO OF THOSE ESSAYS!
SOOOORRY!
THIRD: MY ARMS EXTEND.
FOURTH: THAT GIRL'S IN A WHOLE LOT OF TROUBLE.

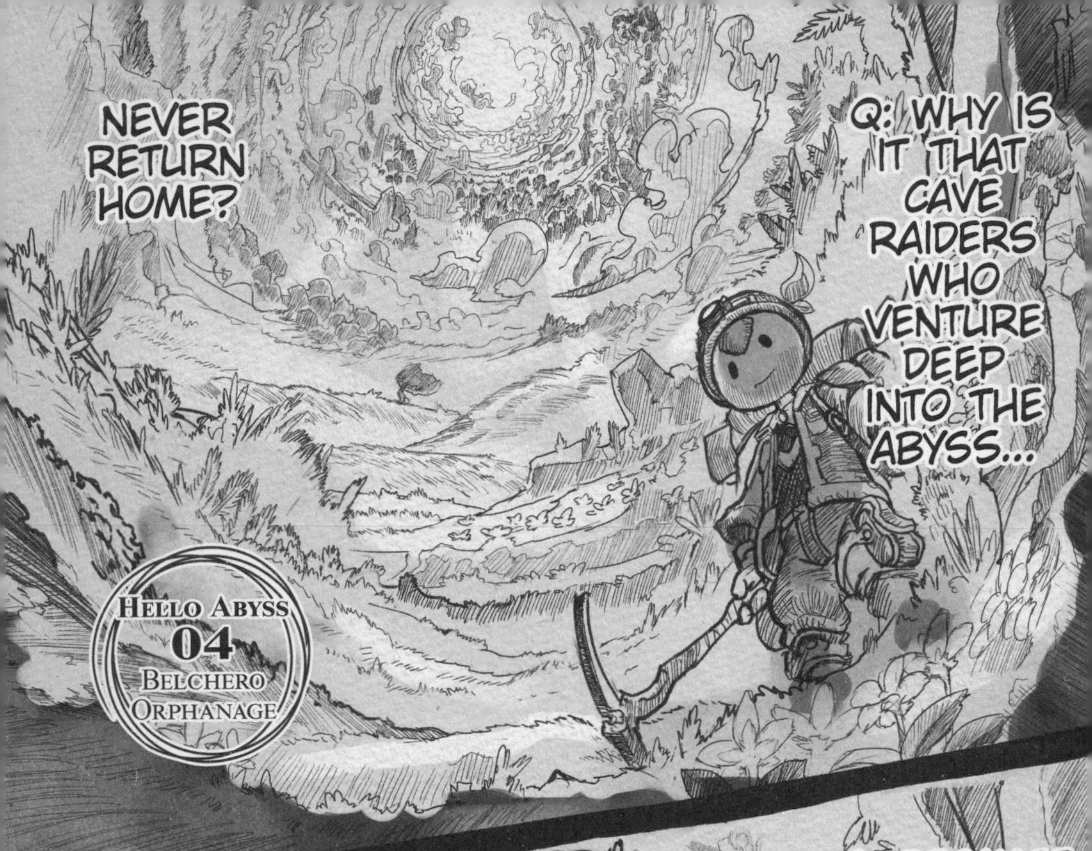
Q: WHY IS IT THAT CAVE RAIDERS WHO VENTURE DEEP INTO THE ABYSS...
NEVER RETURN HOME?
HELLO ABYSS 04 BELCHERO ORPHANAGE
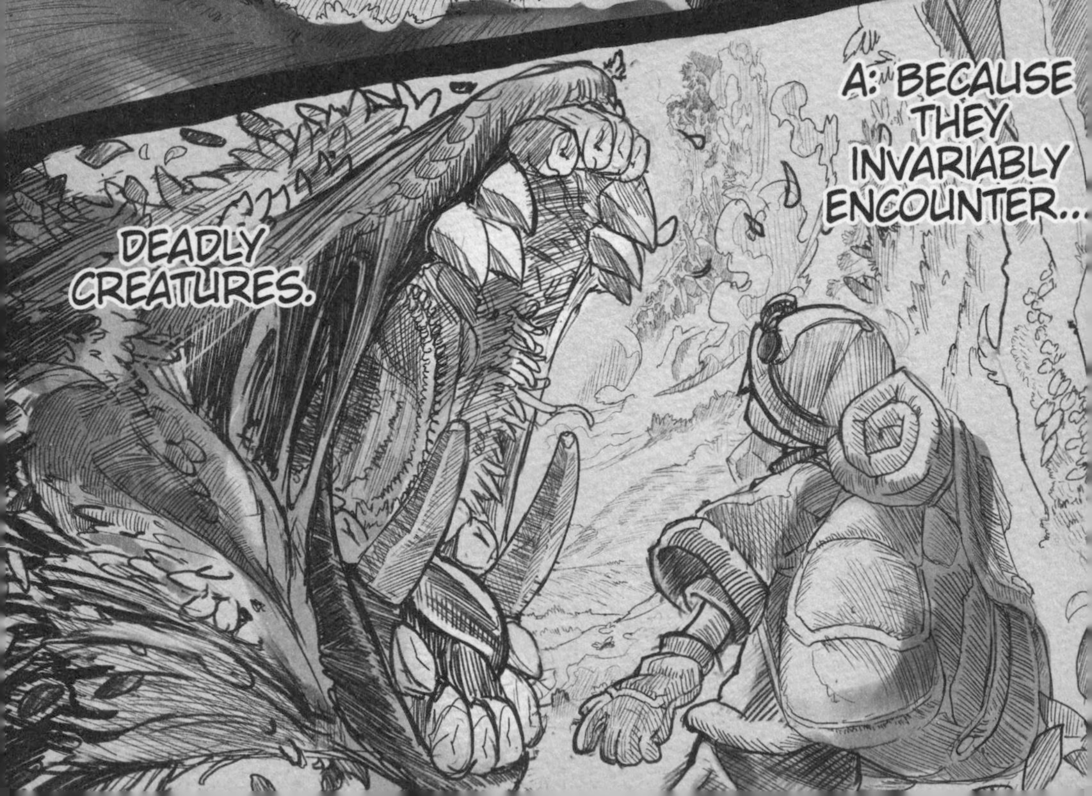
A: BECAUSE THEY INVARIABLY ENCOUNTER...
DEADLY CREATURES.

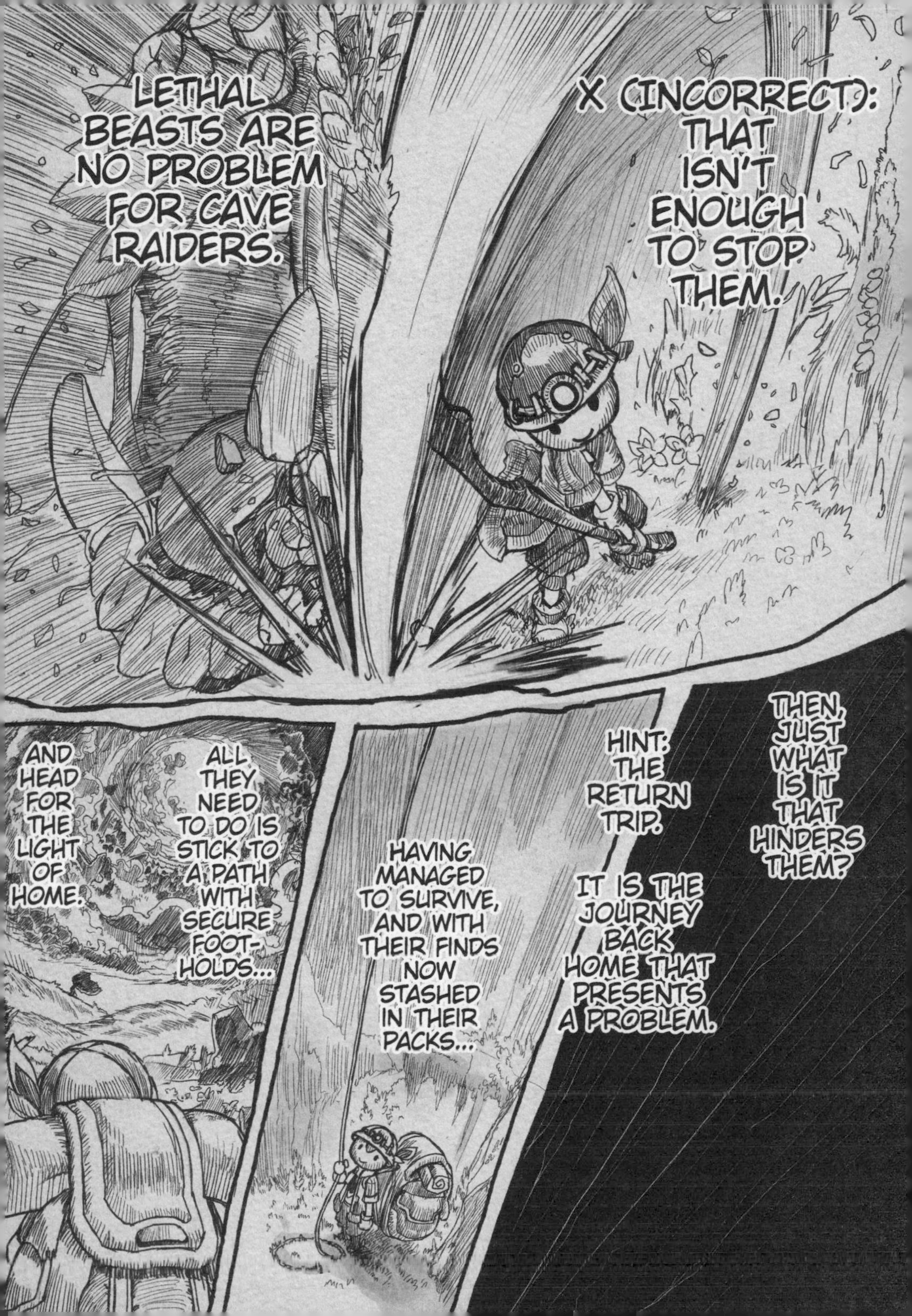
X (INCORRECT): THAT ISN'T ENOUGH TO STOP THEM.
LETHAL BEASTS ARE NO PROBLEM FOR CAVE RAIDERS.
THEN, JUST WHAT IS IT THAT HINDERS THEM?
HINT: THE RETURN TRIP.
IT IS THE JOURNEY BACK HOME THAT PRESENTS A PROBLEM.
HAVING MANAGED TO SURVIVE, AND WITH THEIR FINDS NOW STASHED IN THEIR PACKS...
ALL THEY NEED TO DO IS STICK TO A PATH WITH SECURE FOOT-HOLDS...
AND HEAD FOR THE LIGHT OF HOME.

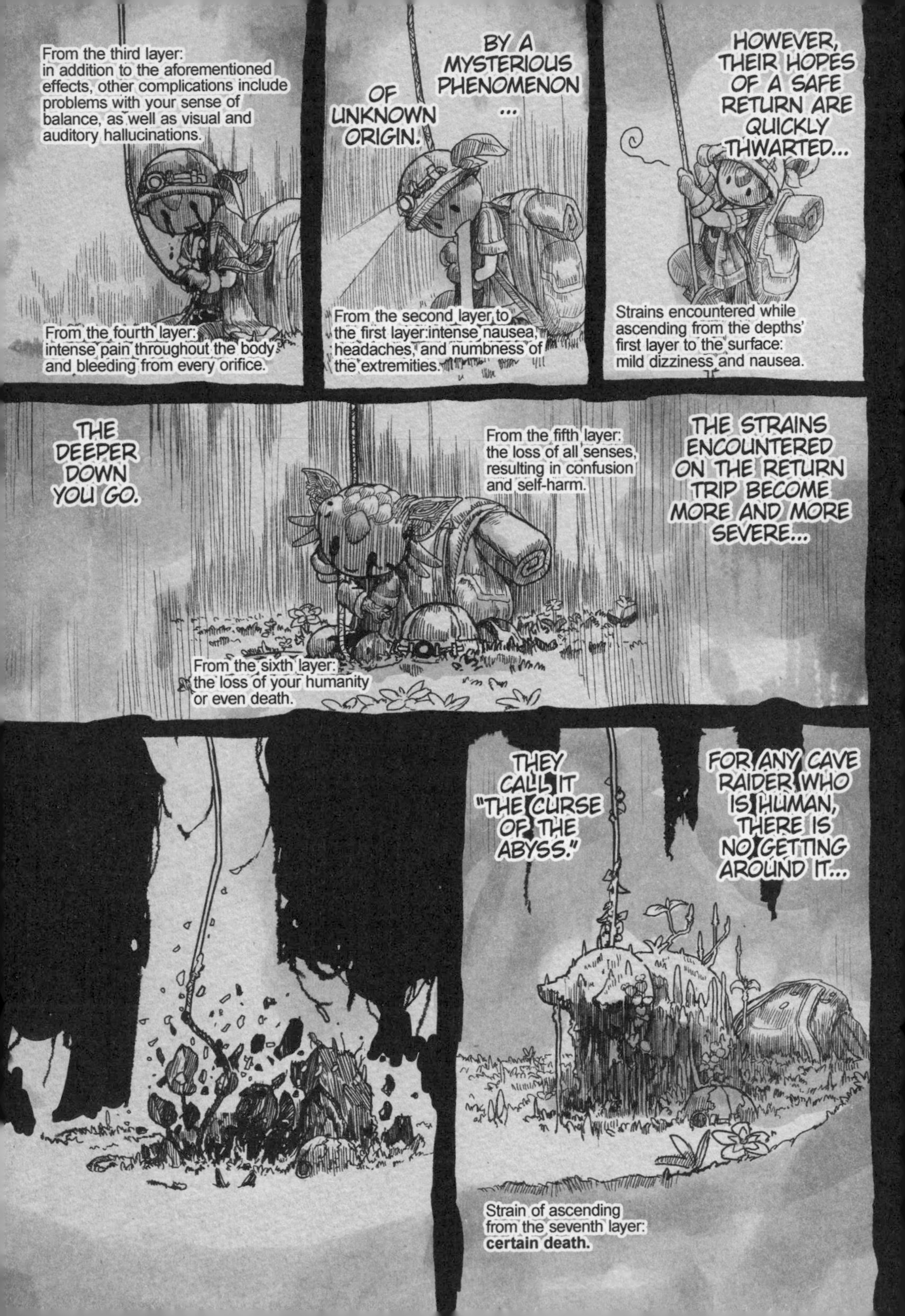
HOWEVER, THEIR HOPES OF A SAFE RETURN ARE QUICKLY THWARTED...
Strains encountered while ascending from the depths' first layer to the surface: mild dizziness and nausea.
BY A MYSTERIOUS PHENOMENON ...
OF UNKNOWN ORIGIN.
From the second layer to the first layer: intense nausea, headaches, and numbness of the extremities.
From the third layer: in addition to the aforementioned effects, other complications include problems with your sense of balance, as well as visual and auditory hallucinations.
From the fourth layer: intense pain throughout the body and bleeding from every orifice.
THE STRAINS ENCOUNTERED ON THE RETURN TRIP BECOME MORE AND MORE SEVERE...
From the fifth layer: the loss of all senses, resulting in confusion and self-harm.
THE DEEPER DOWN YOU GO.
From the sixth layer: the loss of your humanity or even death.
FOR ANY CAVE RAIDER WHO IS HUMAN, THERE IS NO GETTING AROUND IT...
THEY CALL IT "THE CURSE OF THE ABYSS."
Strain of ascending from the seventh layer: **certain death.**

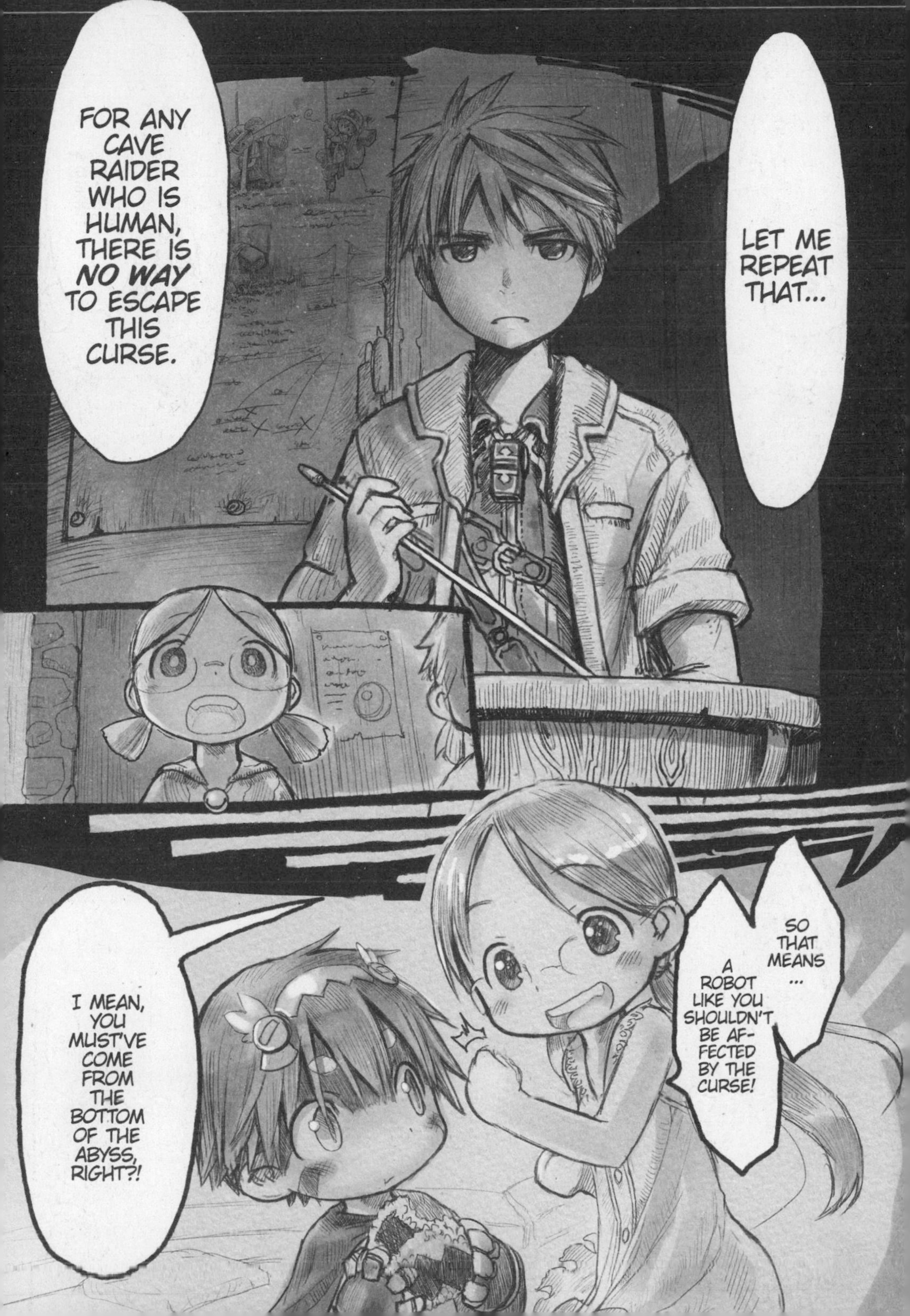
LET ME REPEAT THAT...
FOR ANY CAVE RAIDER WHO IS HUMAN, THERE IS ***NO WAY*** TO ESCAPE THIS CURSE.
SO THAT MEANS...
A ROBOT LIKE YOU SHOULDN'T BE AF-FECTED BY THE CURSE!
I MEAN, YOU MUST'VE COME FROM THE BOTTOM OF THE ABYSS, RIGHT?!

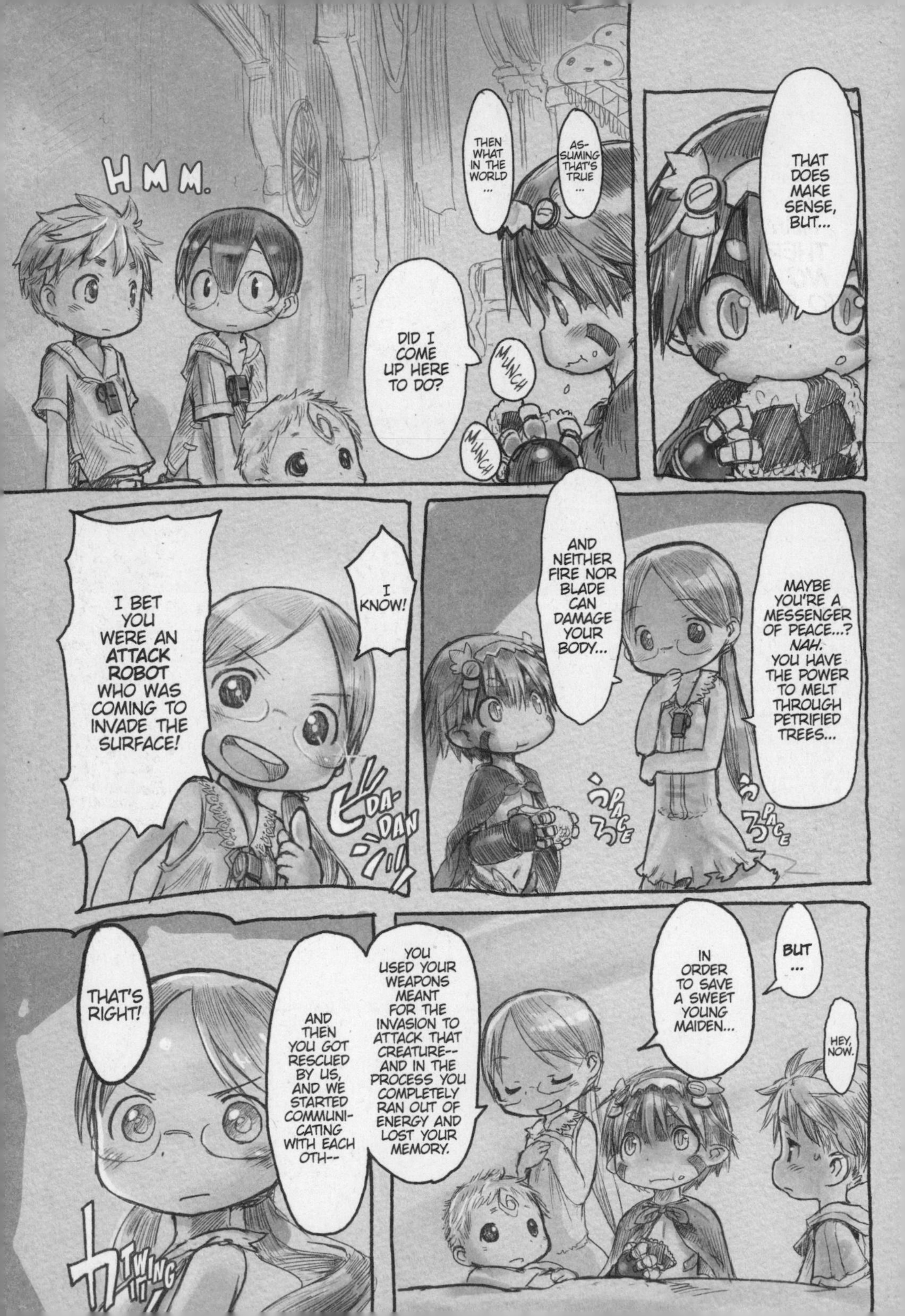
THAT DOES MAKE SENSE, BUT...
AS-SUMING THAT'S TRUE ...
THEN WHAT IN THE WORLD ...
DID I COME UP HERE TO DO?
MUNCH
MUNCH
HMM.
MAYBE YOU'RE A MESSENGER OF PEACE...? NAH. YOU HAVE THE POWER TO MELT THROUGH PETRIFIED TREES...
AND NEITHER FIRE NOR BLADE CAN DAMAGE YOUR BODY...
PACE
PACE
I KNOW!
I BET YOU WERE AN ATTACK ROBOT WHO WAS COMING TO INVADE THE SURFACE!
DA-DAN
BUT ...
IN ORDER TO SAVE A SWEET YOUNG MAIDEN...
YOU USED YOUR WEAPONS MEANT FOR THE INVASION TO ATTACK THAT CREATURE-- AND IN THE PROCESS YOU COMPLETELY RAN OUT OF ENERGY AND LOST YOUR MEMORY.
AND THEN YOU GOT RESCUED BY US, AND WE STARTED COMMUNI-CATING WITH EACH OTH--
HEY, NOW.
THAT'S RIGHT!
TWING

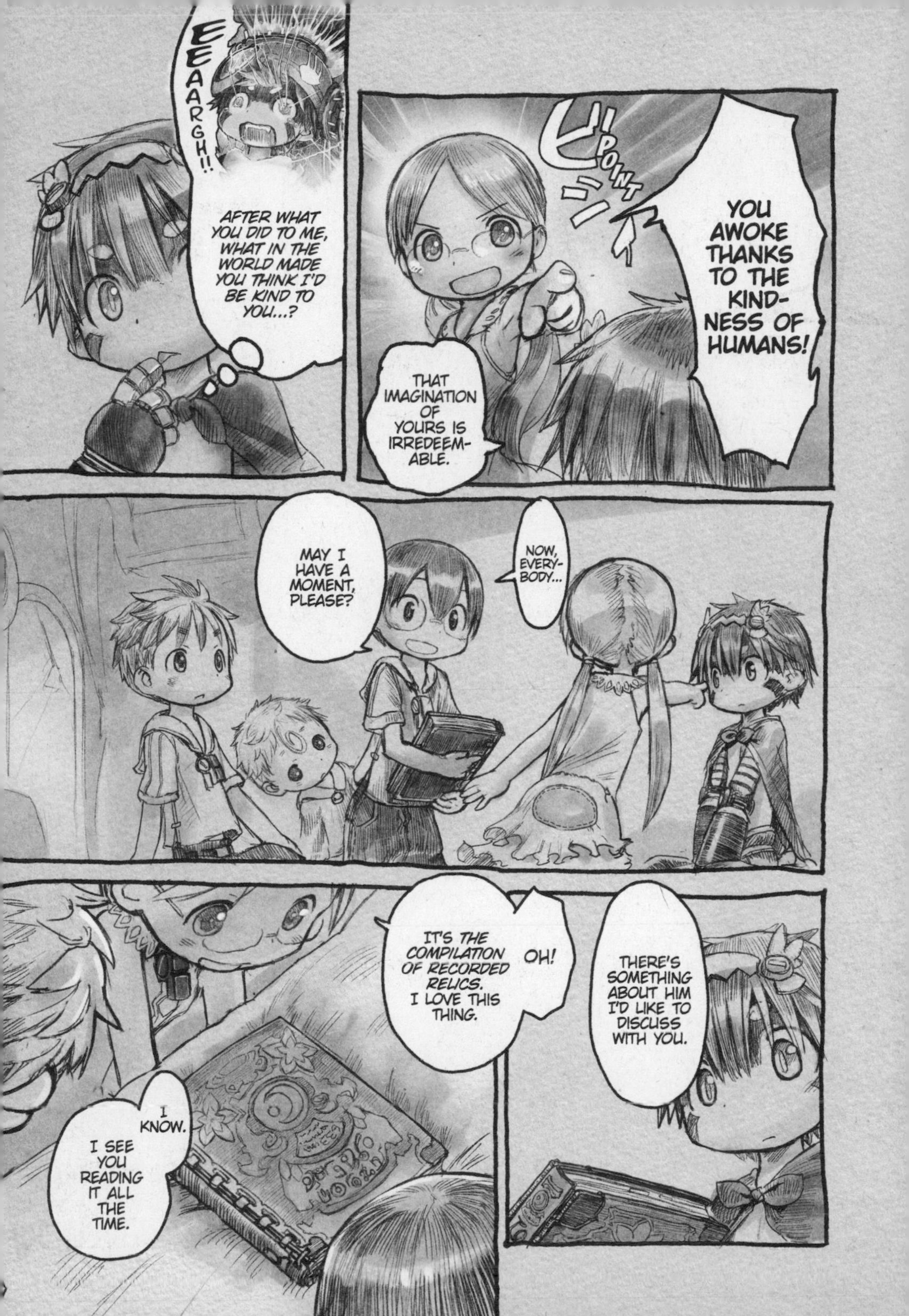
YOU AWOKE THANKS TO THE KINDNESS OF HUMANS!
POINT
THAT IMAGINATION OF YOURS IS IRREDEEMABLE.
EEAARGH!!
AFTER WHAT YOU DID TO ME, WHAT IN THE WORLD MADE YOU THINK I'D BE KIND TO YOU...?
NOW, EVERYBODY...
MAY I HAVE A MOMENT, PLEASE?
THERE'S SOMETHING ABOUT HIM I'D LIKE TO DISCUSS WITH YOU.
OH!
IT'S THE COMPILATION OF RECORDED RELICS. I LOVE THIS THING.
I KNOW. I SEE YOU READING IT ALL THE TIME.

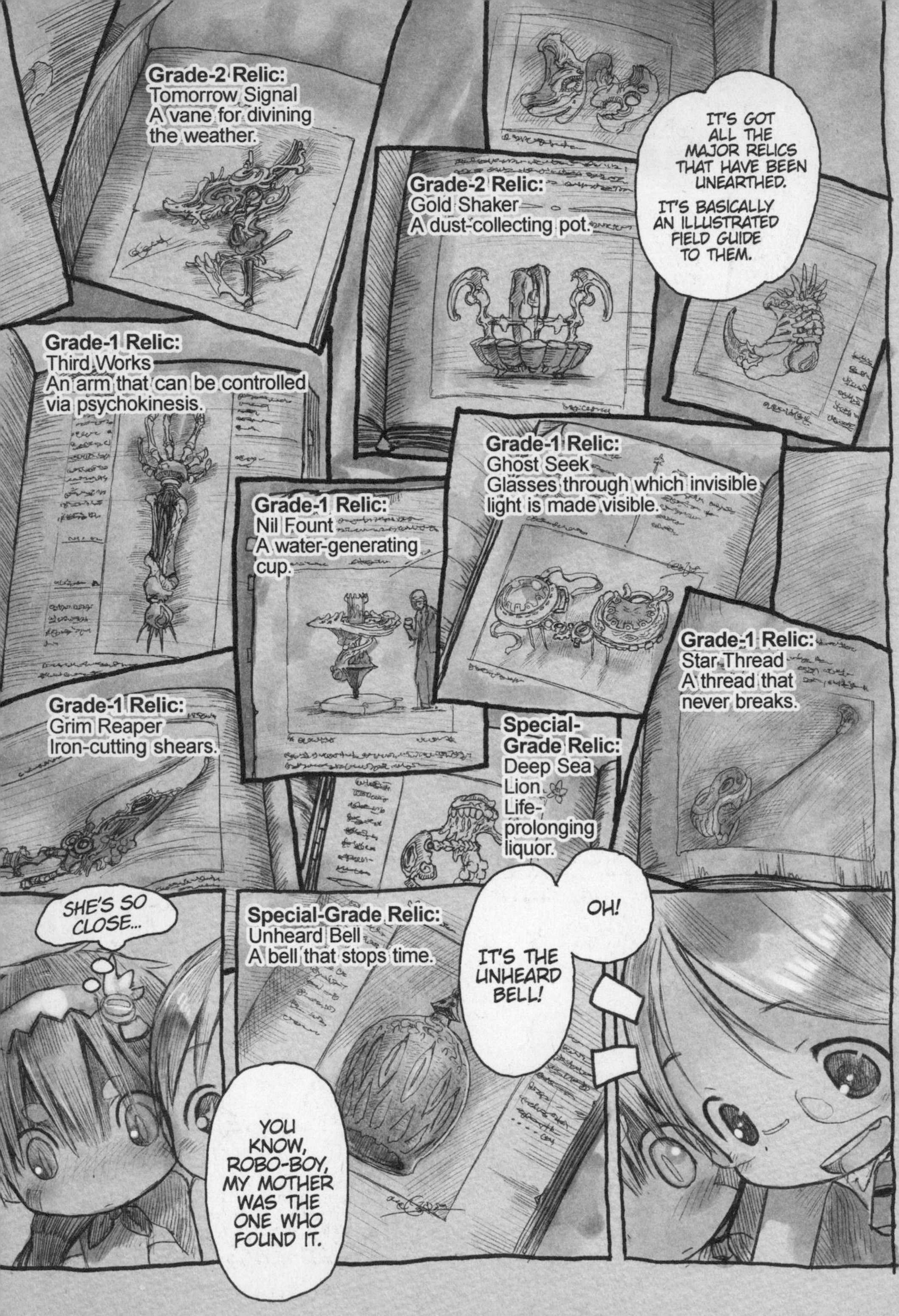
IT'S GOT ALL THE MAJOR RELICS THAT HAVE BEEN UNEARTHED.
IT'S BASICALLY AN ILLUSTRATED FIELD GUIDE TO THEM.
Grade-2 Relic: Gold Shaker A dust-collecting pot.
Grade-2 Relic: Tomorrow Signal A vane for divining the weather.
Grade-1 Relic: Third Works An arm that can be controlled via psychokinesis.
Grade-1 Relic: Ghost Seek Glasses through which invisible light is made visible.
Grade-1 Relic: Nil Fount A water-generating cup.
Grade-1 Relic: Star Thread A thread that never breaks.
Special-Grade Relic: Deep Sea Lion Life-prolonging liquor.
Grade-1 Relic: Grim Reaper Iron-cutting shears.
OH!
IT'S THE UNHEARD BELL!
Special-Grade Relic: Unheard Bell A bell that stops time.
YOU KNOW, ROBO-BOY, MY MOTHER WAS THE ONE WHO FOUND IT.
SHE'S SO CLOSE...

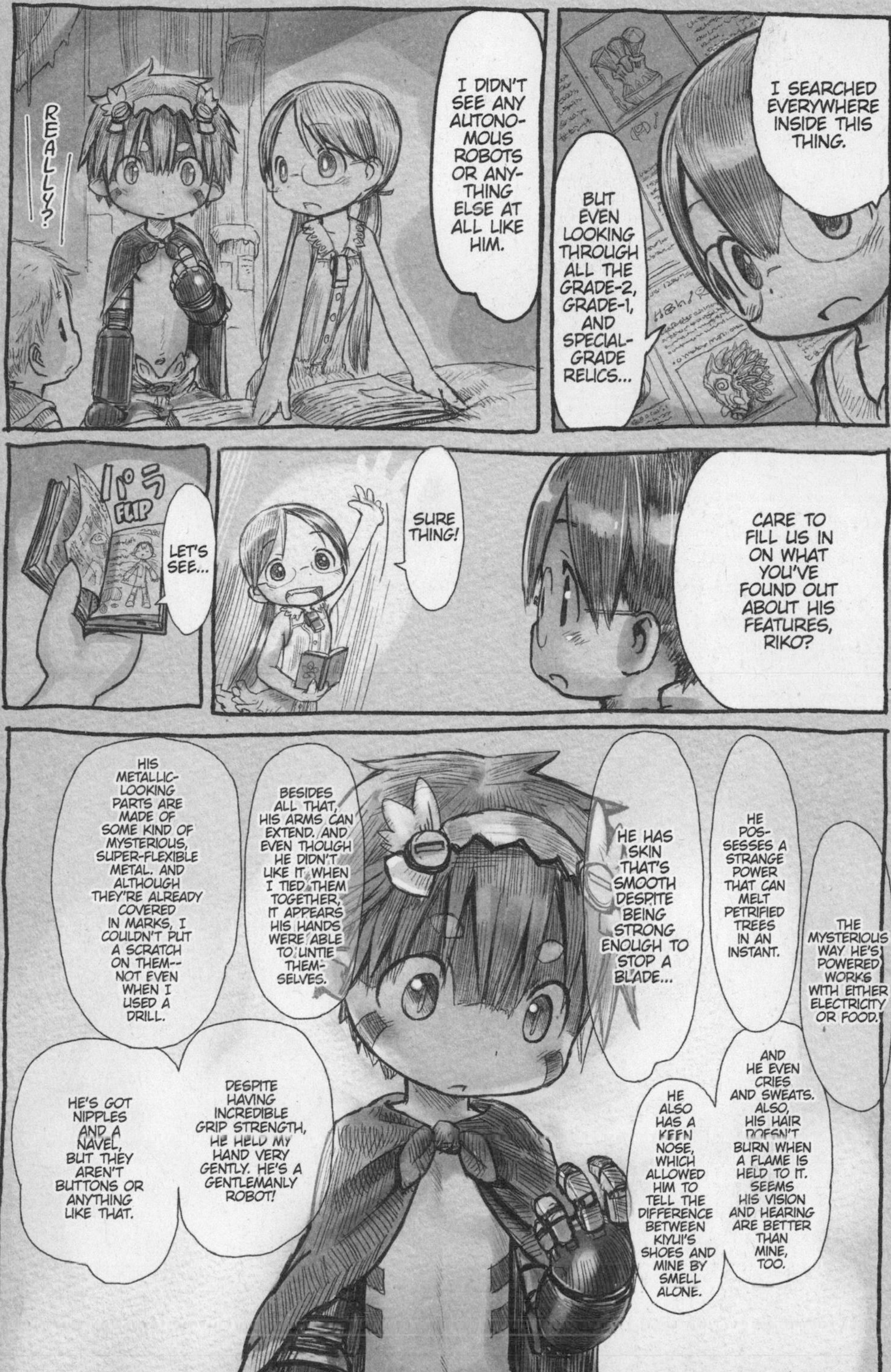
I SEARCHED EVERYWHERE INSIDE THIS THING.
BUT EVEN LOOKING THROUGH ALL THE GRADE-2, GRADE-1, AND SPECIAL-GRADE RELICS...
I DIDN'T SEE ANY AUTONOMOUS ROBOTS OR ANYTHING ELSE AT ALL LIKE HIM.
REALLY?
CARE TO FILL US IN ON WHAT YOU'VE FOUND OUT ABOUT HIS FEATURES, RIKO?
SURE THING!
パラ
FLIP
LET'S SEE...
THE MYSTERIOUS WAY HE'S POWERED WORKS WITH EITHER ELECTRICITY OR FOOD.
HE POSSESSES A STRANGE POWER THAT CAN MELT PETRIFIED TREES IN AN INSTANT.
HE HAS SKIN THAT'S SMOOTH DESPITE BEING STRONG ENOUGH TO STOP A BLADE...
BESIDES ALL THAT, HIS ARMS CAN EXTEND. AND EVEN THOUGH HE DIDN'T LIKE IT WHEN I TIED THEM TOGETHER, IT APPEARS HIS HANDS WERE ABLE TO UNTIE THEMSELVES.
HIS METALLIC-LOOKING PARTS ARE MADE OF SOME KIND OF MYSTERIOUS, SUPER-FLEXIBLE METAL. AND ALTHOUGH THEY'RE ALREADY COVERED IN MARKS, I COULDN'T PUT A SCRATCH ON THEM--NOT EVEN WHEN I USED A DRILL.
AND HE EVEN CRIES AND SWEATS. ALSO, HIS HAIR DOESN'T BURN WHEN A FLAME IS HELD TO IT. SEEMS HIS VISION AND HEARING ARE BETTER THAN MINE, TOO.
HE ALSO HAS A KEEN NOSE, WHICH ALLOWED HIM TO TELL THE DIFFERENCE BETWEEN KIYUI'S SHOES AND MINE BY SMELL ALONE.
DESPITE HAVING INCREDIBLE GRIP STRENGTH, HE HELD MY HAND VERY GENTLY. HE'S A GENTLEMANLY ROBOT!
HE'S GOT NIPPLES AND A NAVEL, BUT THEY AREN'T BUTTONS OR ANYTHING LIKE THAT.

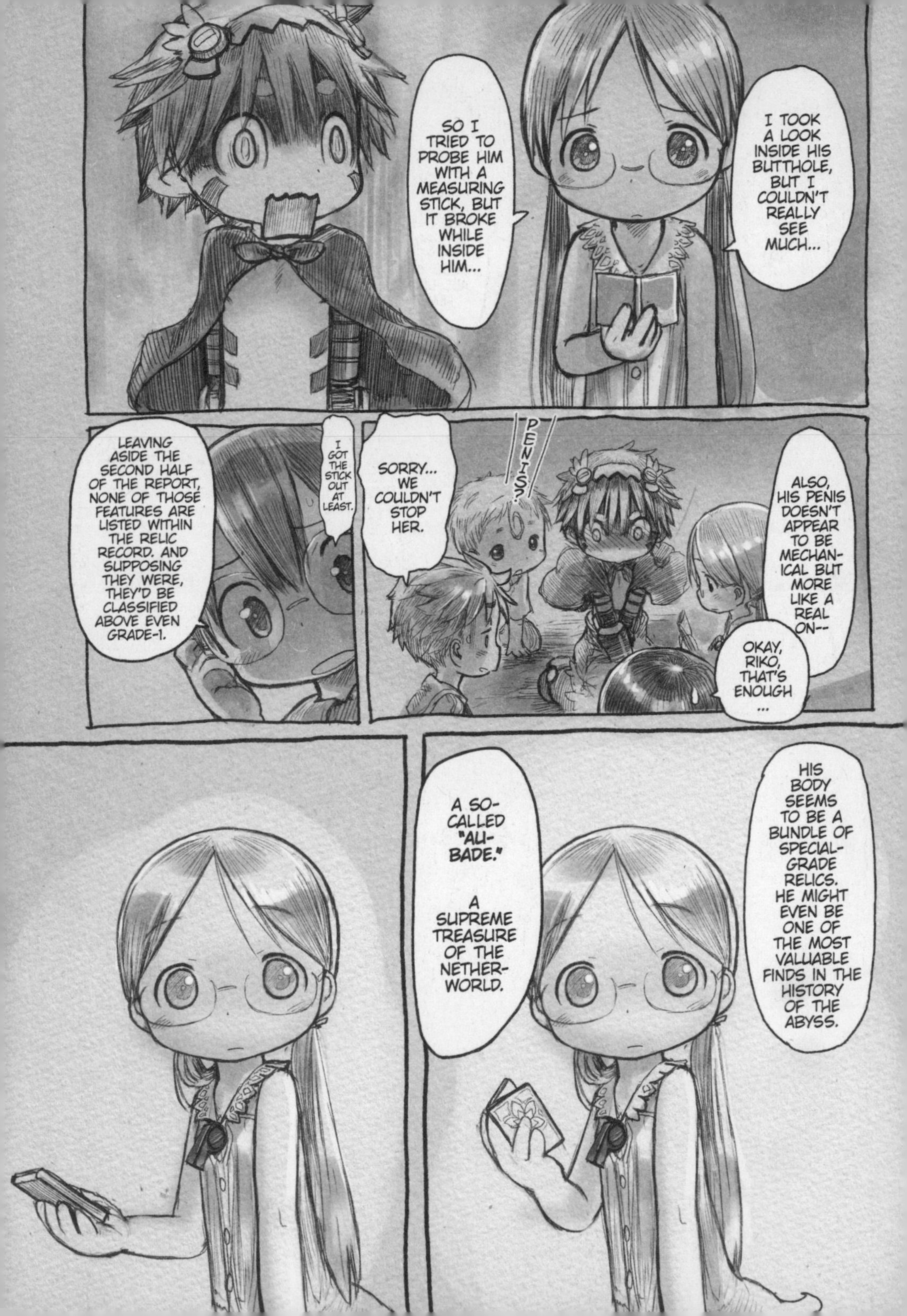
I TOOK A LOOK INSIDE HIS BUTTHOLE, BUT I COULDN'T REALLY SEE MUCH...
SO I TRIED TO PROBE HIM WITH A MEASURING STICK, BUT IT BROKE WHILE INSIDE HIM...
ALSO, HIS PENIS DOESN'T APPEAR TO BE MECHANICAL BUT MORE LIKE A REAL ON--
OKAY, RIKO, THAT'S ENOUGH...
PENIS?
SORRY... WE COULDN'T STOP HER.
I GOT THE STICK OUT AT LEAST.
LEAVING ASIDE THE SECOND HALF OF THE REPORT, NONE OF THOSE FEATURES ARE LISTED WITHIN THE RELIC RECORD. AND SUPPOSING THEY WERE, THEY'D BE CLASSIFIED ABOVE EVEN GRADE-1.
HIS BODY SEEMS TO BE A BUNDLE OF SPECIAL-GRADE RELICS. HE MIGHT EVEN BE ONE OF THE MOST VALUABLE FINDS IN THE HISTORY OF THE ABYSS.
A SO-CALLED "AUBADE."
A SUPREME TREASURE OF THE NETHERWORLD.

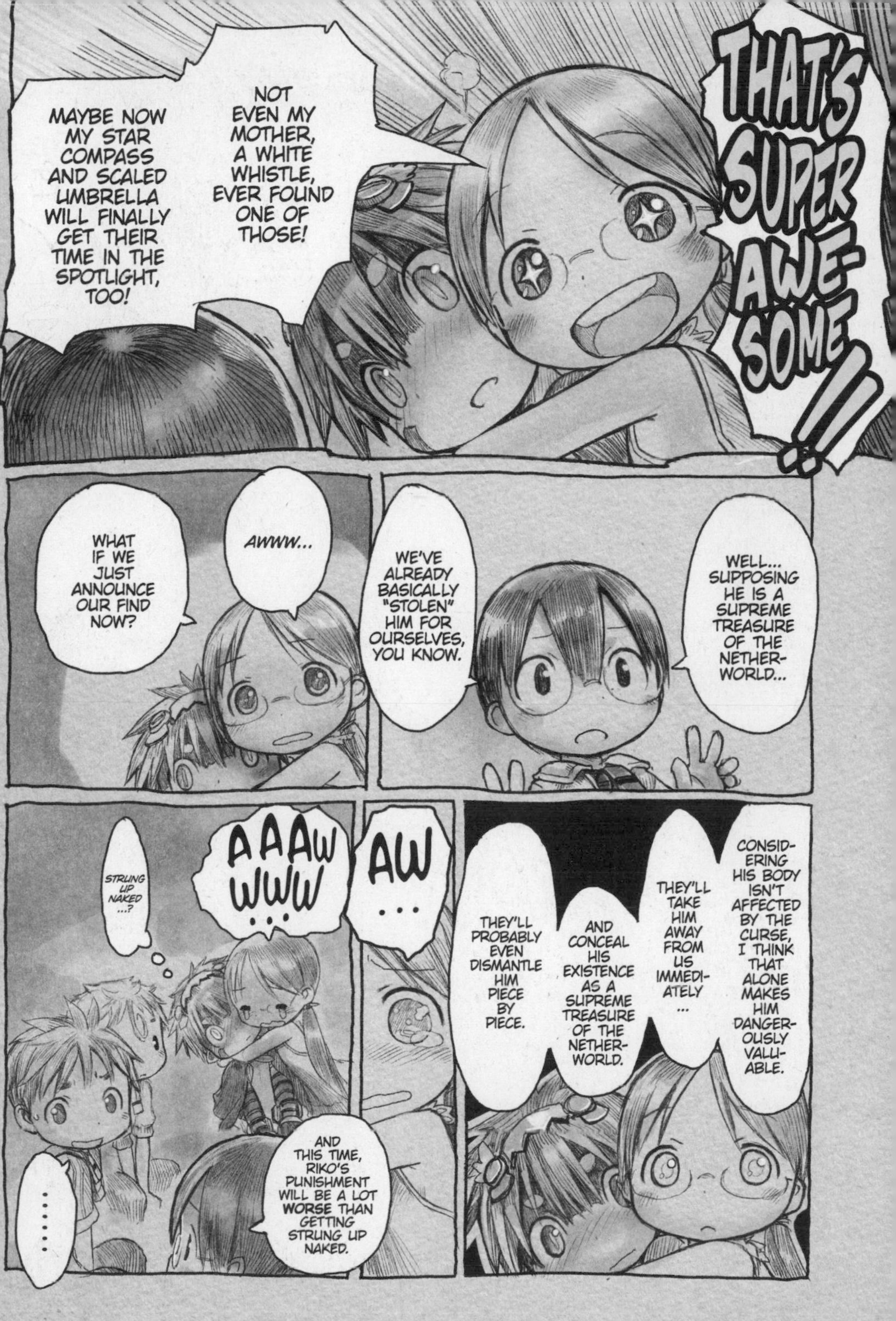
THAT'S SUPER AWE-SOME!!!
NOT EVEN MY MOTHER, A WHITE WHISTLE, EVER FOUND ONE OF THOSE!
MAYBE NOW MY STAR COMPASS AND SCALED UMBRELLA WILL FINALLY GET THEIR TIME IN THE SPOTLIGHT, TOO!
WELL... SUPPOSING HE IS A SUPREME TREASURE OF THE NETHER-WORLD...
WE'VE ALREADY BASICALLY "STOLEN" HIM FOR OURSELVES, YOU KNOW.
AWWW...
WHAT IF WE JUST ANNOUNCE OUR FIND NOW?
CONSID-ERING HIS BODY ISN'T AFFECTED BY THE CURSE, I THINK THAT ALONE MAKES HIM DANGER-OUSLY VALU-ABLE.
THEY'LL TAKE HIM AWAY FROM US IMMEDI-ATELY...
AND CONCEAL HIS EXISTENCE AS A SUPREME TREASURE OF THE NETHER-WORLD.
THEY'LL PROBABLY EVEN DISMANTLE HIM PIECE BY PIECE.
AW...
AND THIS TIME, RIKO'S PUNISHMENT WILL BE A LOT WORSE THAN GETTING STRUNG UP NAKED.
AAAWWWW...
STRUNG UP NAKED...?
......

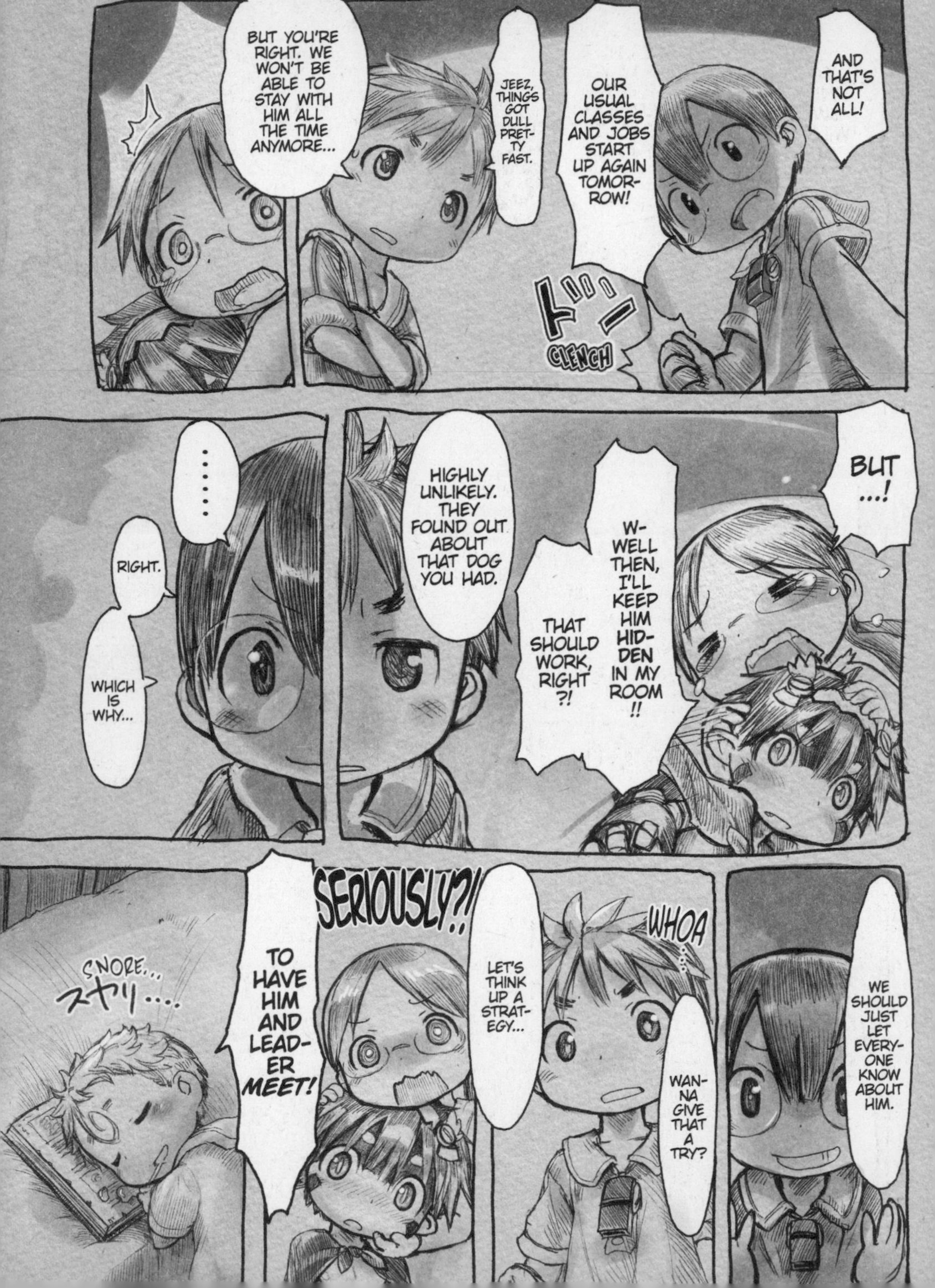
AND THAT'S NOT ALL!
OUR USUAL CLASSES AND JOBS START UP AGAIN TOMORROW!
CLENCH
JEEZ, THINGS GOT DULL PRETTY FAST.
BUT YOU'RE RIGHT. WE WON'T BE ABLE TO STAY WITH HIM ALL THE TIME ANYMORE...
BUT ...!
W-WELL THEN, I'LL KEEP HIM HIDDEN IN MY ROOM !!
THAT SHOULD WORK, RIGHT ?!
HIGHLY UNLIKELY. THEY FOUND OUT ABOUT THAT DOG YOU HAD.
......
RIGHT.
WHICH IS WHY...
WE SHOULD JUST LET EVERYONE KNOW ABOUT HIM.
WHOA...
WANNA GIVE THAT A TRY?
LET'S THINK UP A STRATEGY...
SERIOUSLY?!
TO HAVE HIM AND LEADER MEET!
SNORE...
スヤリ....

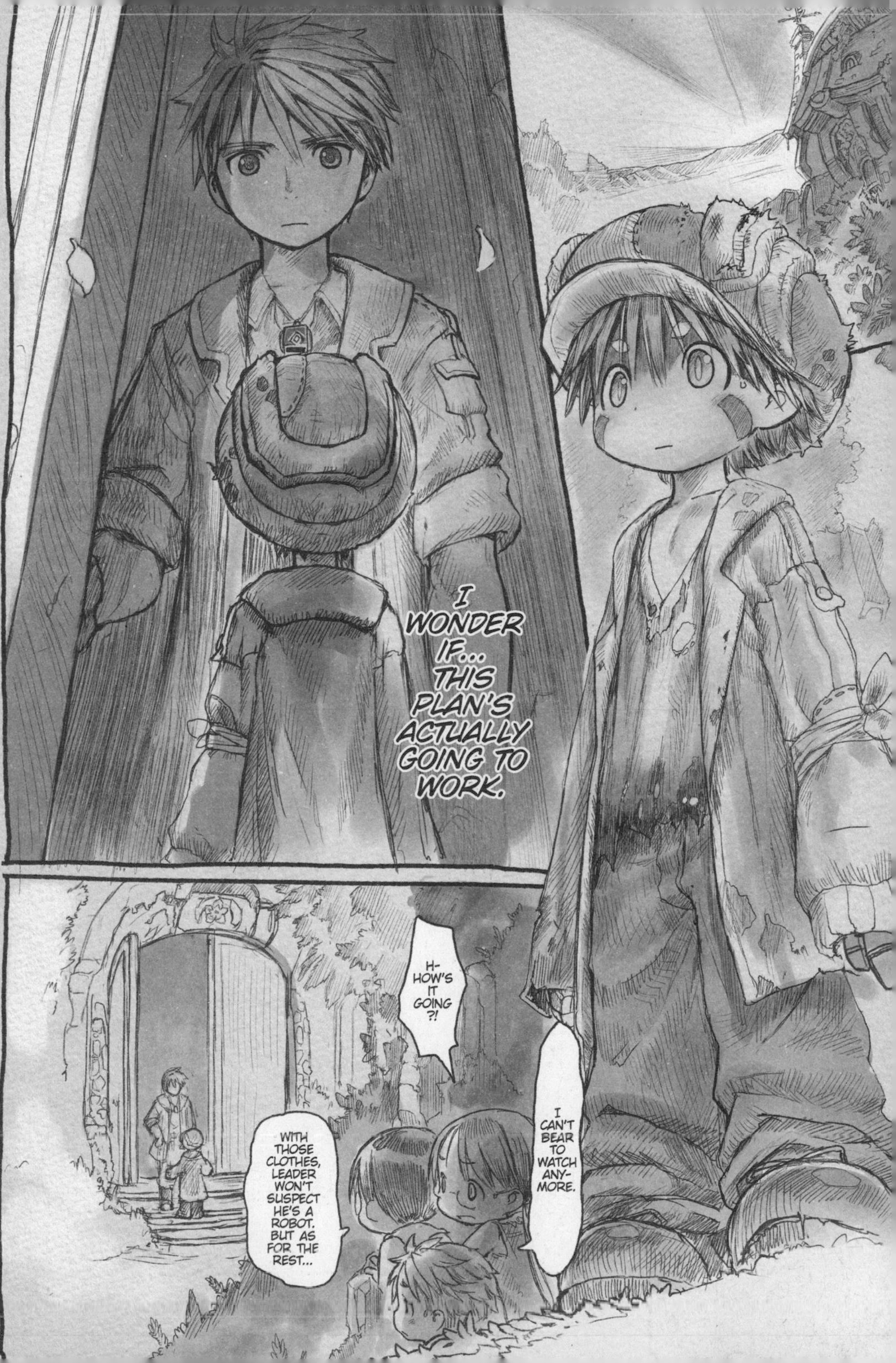
I WONDER IF... THIS PLAN'S ACTUALLY GOING TO WORK.
H-HOW'S IT GOING?!
I CAN'T BEAR TO WATCH ANYMORE.
WITH THOSE CLOTHES, LEADER WON'T SUSPECT HE'S A ROBOT. BUT AS FOR THE REST...

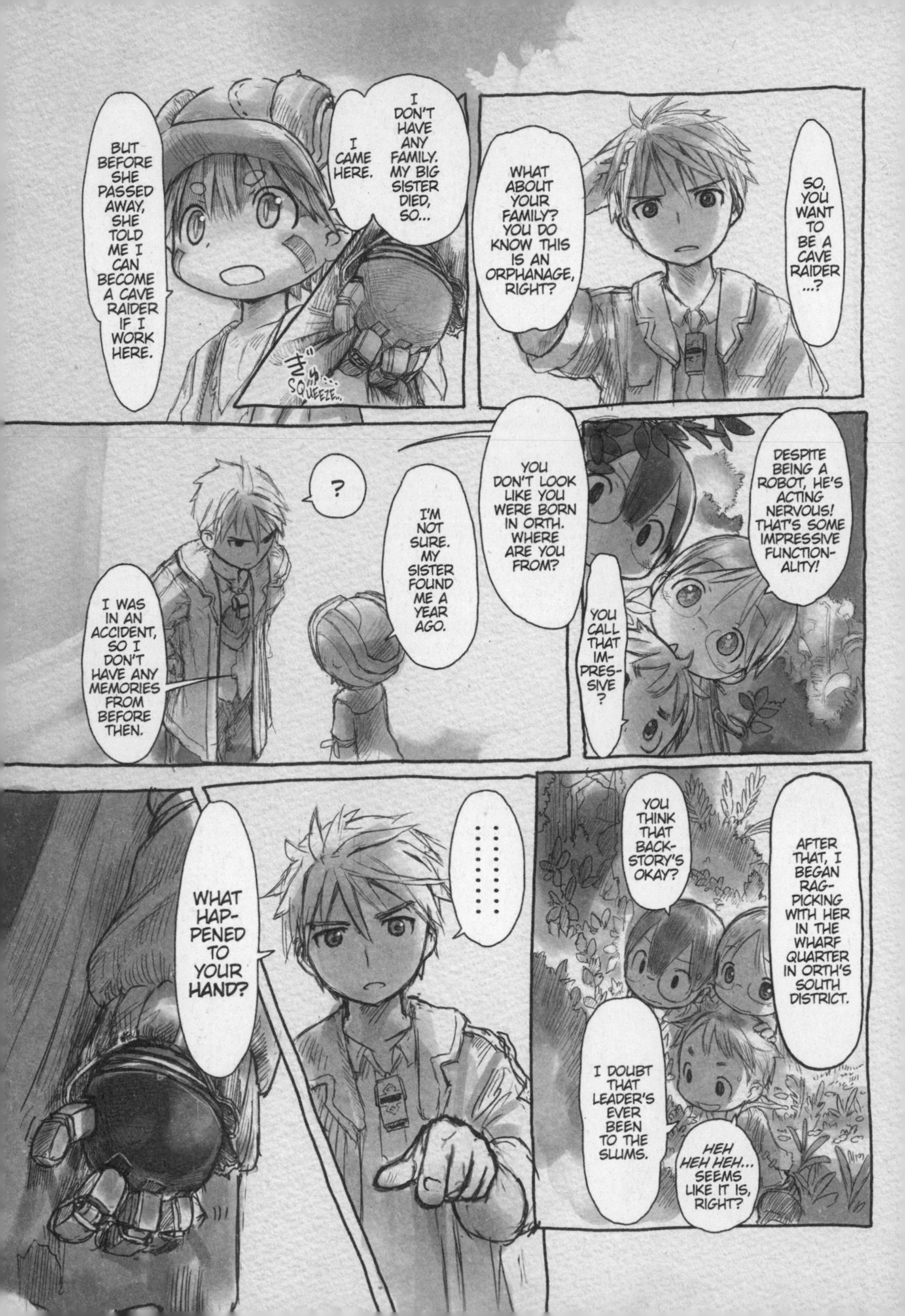
SO, YOU WANT TO BE A CAVE RAIDER...?
WHAT ABOUT YOUR FAMILY? YOU DO KNOW THIS IS AN ORPHANAGE, RIGHT?
I DON'T HAVE ANY FAMILY. MY BIG SISTER DIED, SO...
I CAME HERE.
BUT BEFORE SHE PASSED AWAY, SHE TOLD ME I CAN BECOME A CAVE RAIDER IF I WORK HERE.
SQUEEZE...
DESPITE BEING A ROBOT, HE'S ACTING NERVOUS! THAT'S SOME IMPRESSIVE FUNCTIONALITY!
YOU CALL THAT IMPRESSIVE?
YOU DON'T LOOK LIKE YOU WERE BORN IN ORTH. WHERE ARE YOU FROM?
?
I'M NOT SURE. MY SISTER FOUND ME A YEAR AGO.
I WAS IN AN ACCIDENT, SO I DON'T HAVE ANY MEMORIES FROM BEFORE THEN.
AFTER THAT, I BEGAN RAG-PICKING WITH HER IN THE WHARF QUARTER IN ORTH'S SOUTH DISTRICT.
YOU THINK THAT BACKSTORY'S OKAY?
I DOUBT THAT LEADER'S EVER BEEN TO THE SLUMS.
HEH HEH HEH... SEEMS LIKE IT IS, RIGHT?
......
WHAT HAPPENED TO YOUR HAND?

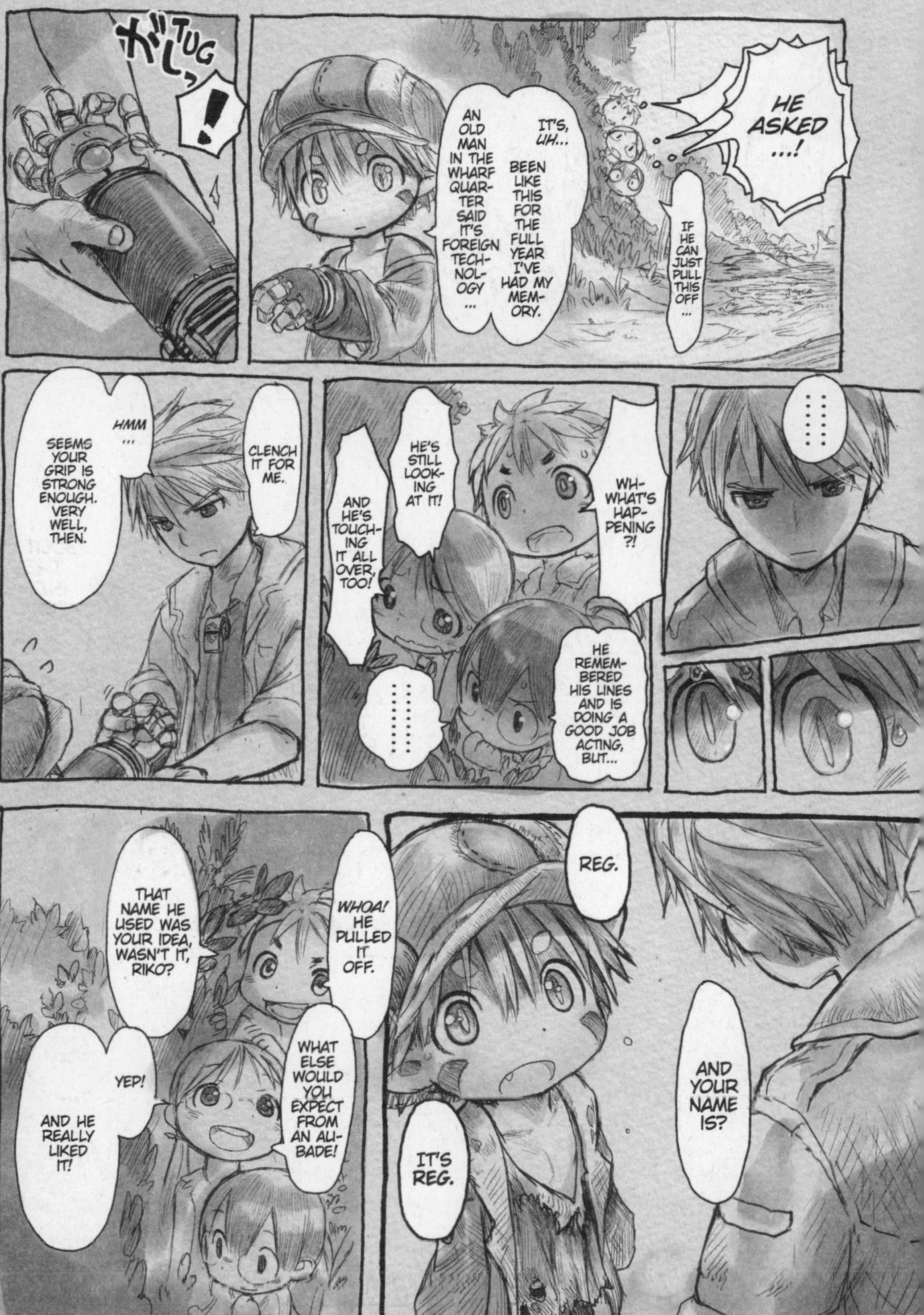
HE ASKED ....!
IF HE CAN JUST PULL THIS OFF ...
IT'S, UH... BEEN LIKE THIS FOR THE FULL YEAR I'VE HAD MY MEMORY.
AN OLD MAN IN THE WHARF QUARTER SAID IT'S FOREIGN TECHNOLOGY ...
!
がしっ TUG
....
WH-WHAT'S HAPPENING?!
HE'S STILL LOOKING AT IT!
AND HE'S TOUCHING IT ALL OVER, TOO!
HE REMEMBERED HIS LINES AND IS DOING A GOOD JOB ACTING, BUT...
......
CLENCH IT FOR ME.
HMM ... SEEMS YOUR GRIP IS STRONG ENOUGH. VERY WELL, THEN.
REG.
AND YOUR NAME IS?
IT'S REG.
WHOA! HE PULLED IT OFF.
THAT NAME HE USED WAS YOUR IDEA, WASN'T IT, RIKO?
WHAT ELSE WOULD YOU EXPECT FROM AN AUBADE!
YEP! AND HE REALLY LIKED IT!

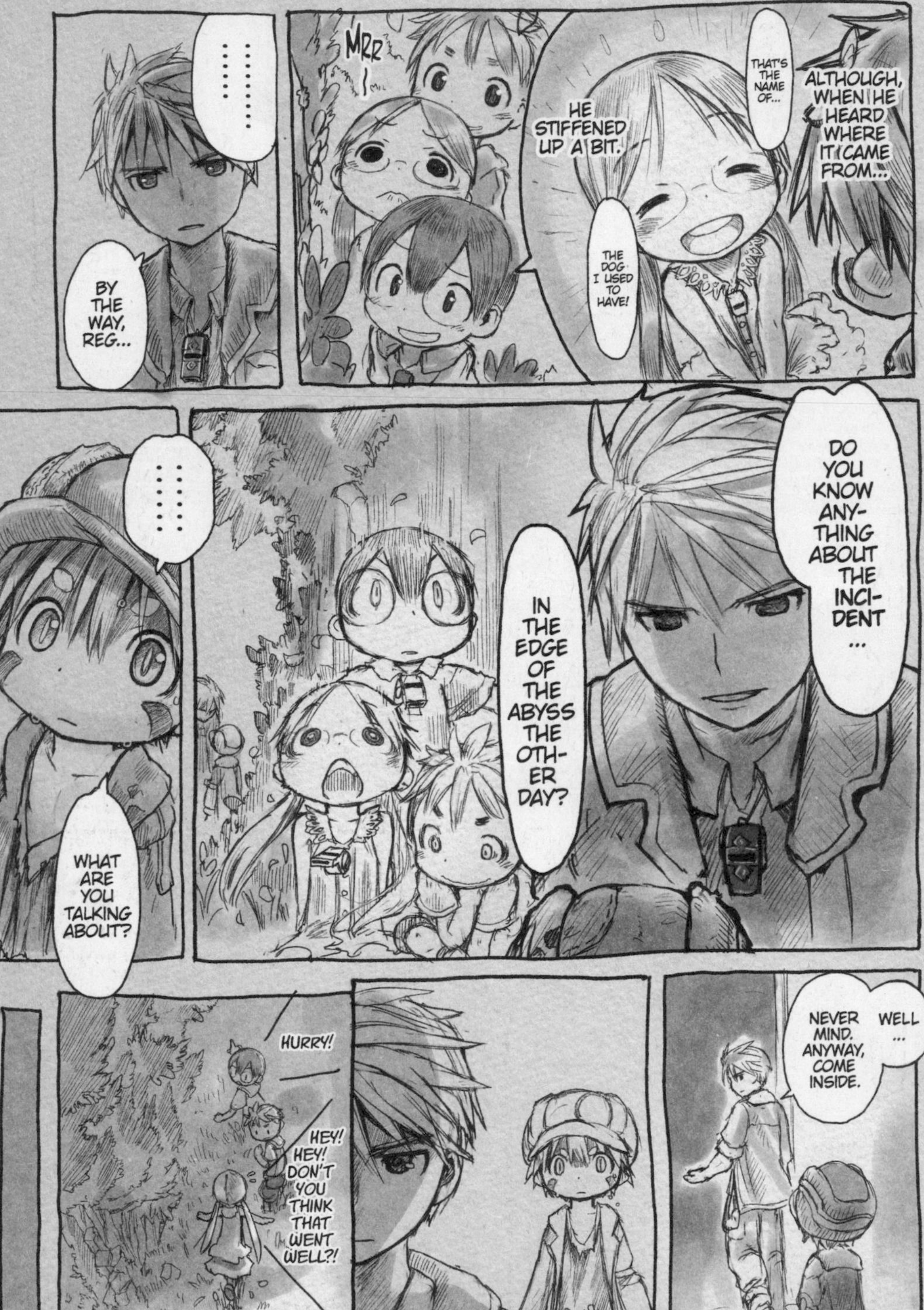
ALTHOUGH, WHEN HE HEARD WHERE IT CAME FROM...
THAT'S THE NAME OF...
HE STIFFENED UP A BIT.
THE DOG I USED TO HAVE!
MRR
......
BY THE WAY, REG...
DO YOU KNOW ANYTHING ABOUT THE INCIDENT...
IN THE EDGE OF THE ABYSS THE OTHER DAY?
......
WHAT ARE YOU TALKING ABOUT?
WELL...
NEVER MIND. ANYWAY, COME INSIDE.
HURRY!
HEY! HEY! DON'T YOU THINK THAT WENT WELL?!

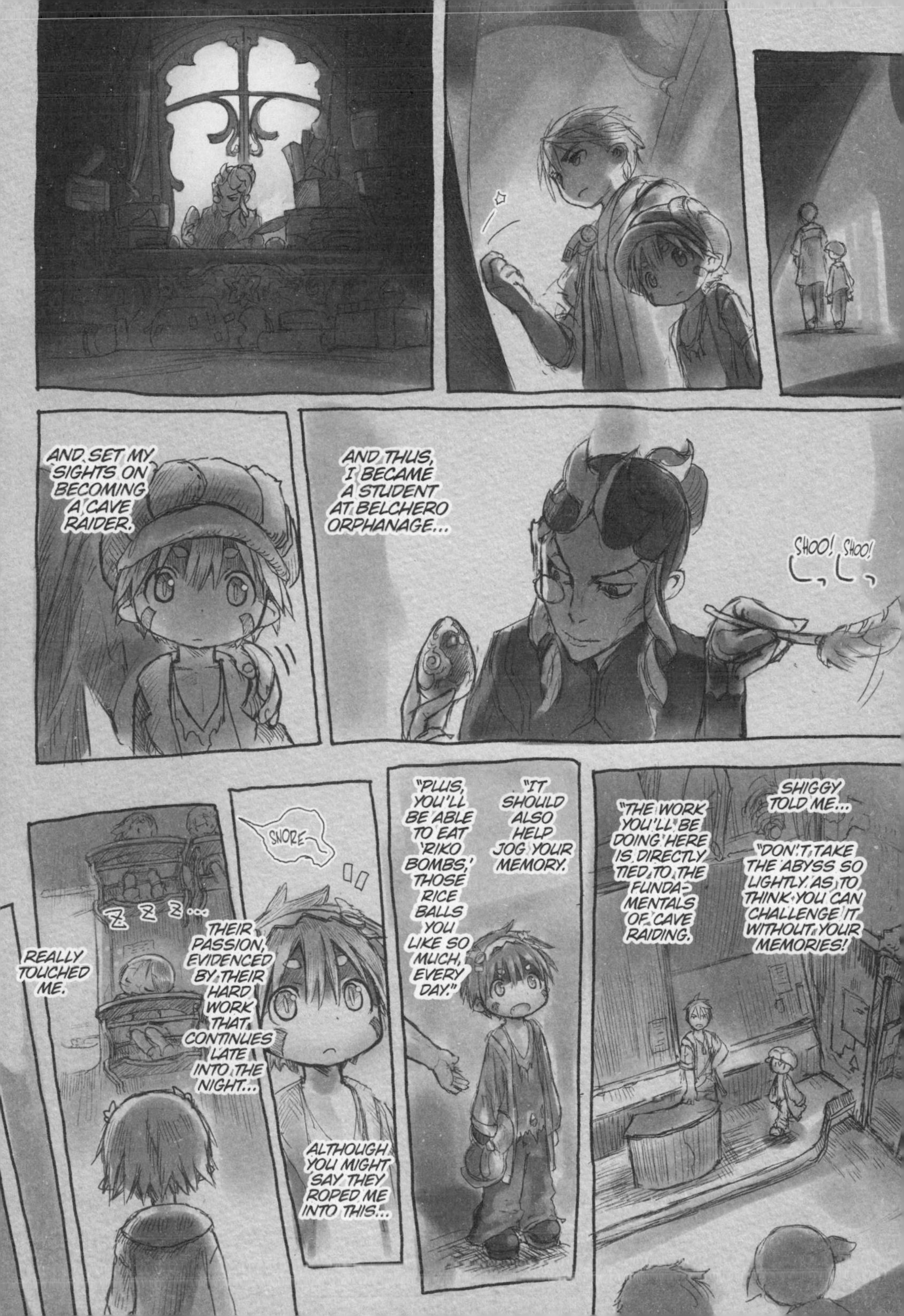
AND THUS, I BECAME A STUDENT AT BELCHERO ORPHANAGE...
SHOO! SHOO!
AND SET MY SIGHTS ON BECOMING A CAVE RAIDER.
SHIGGY TOLD ME...
"DON'T TAKE THE ABYSS SO LIGHTLY AS TO THINK YOU CAN CHALLENGE IT WITHOUT YOUR MEMORIES!
"THE WORK YOU'LL BE DOING HERE IS DIRECTLY TIED TO THE FUNDAMENTALS OF CAVE RAIDING.
"IT SHOULD ALSO HELP JOG YOUR MEMORY.
"PLUS, YOU'LL BE ABLE TO EAT 'RIKO BOMBS,' THOSE RICE BALLS YOU LIKE SO MUCH, EVERY DAY."
SNORE
ALTHOUGH YOU MIGHT SAY THEY ROPED ME INTO THIS...
Z Z Z...
THEIR PASSION, EVIDENCED BY THEIR HARD WORK THAT CONTINUES LATE INTO THE NIGHT...
REALLY TOUCHED ME.

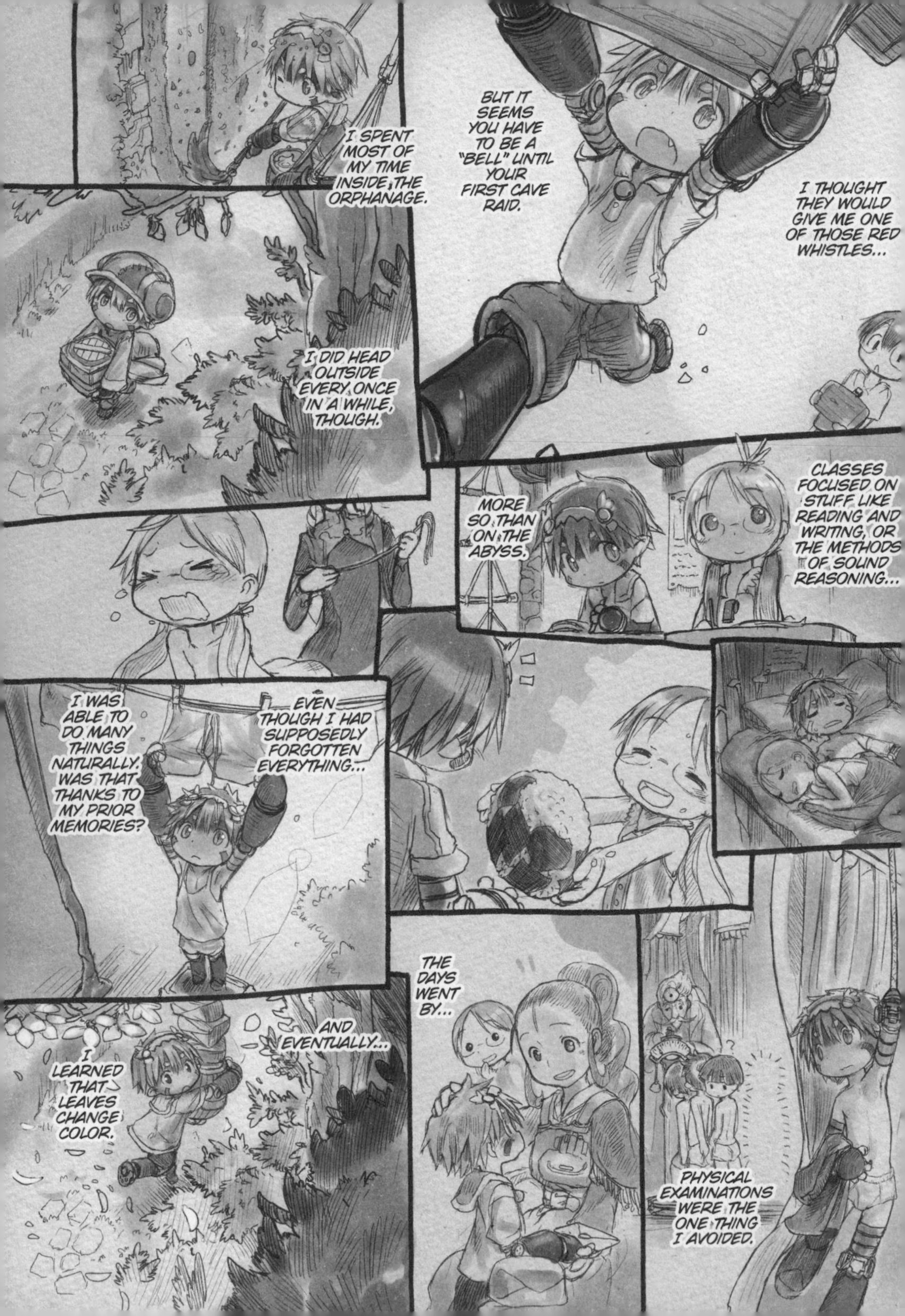
I THOUGHT THEY WOULD GIVE ME ONE OF THOSE RED WHISTLES...
BUT IT SEEMS YOU HAVE TO BE A "BELL" UNTIL YOUR FIRST CAVE RAID.
I SPENT MOST OF MY TIME INSIDE THE ORPHANAGE.
I DID HEAD OUTSIDE EVERY ONCE IN A WHILE, THOUGH.
CLASSES FOCUSED ON STUFF LIKE READING AND WRITING, OR THE METHODS OF SOUND REASONING...
MORE SO THAN ON THE ABYSS.
EVEN THOUGH I HAD SUPPOSEDLY FORGOTTEN EVERYTHING...
I WAS ABLE TO DO MANY THINGS NATURALLY. WAS THAT THANKS TO MY PRIOR MEMORIES?
PHYSICAL EXAMINATIONS WERE THE ONE THING I AVOIDED.
THE DAYS WENT BY...
AND EVENTUALLY...
I LEARNED THAT LEAVES CHANGE COLOR.

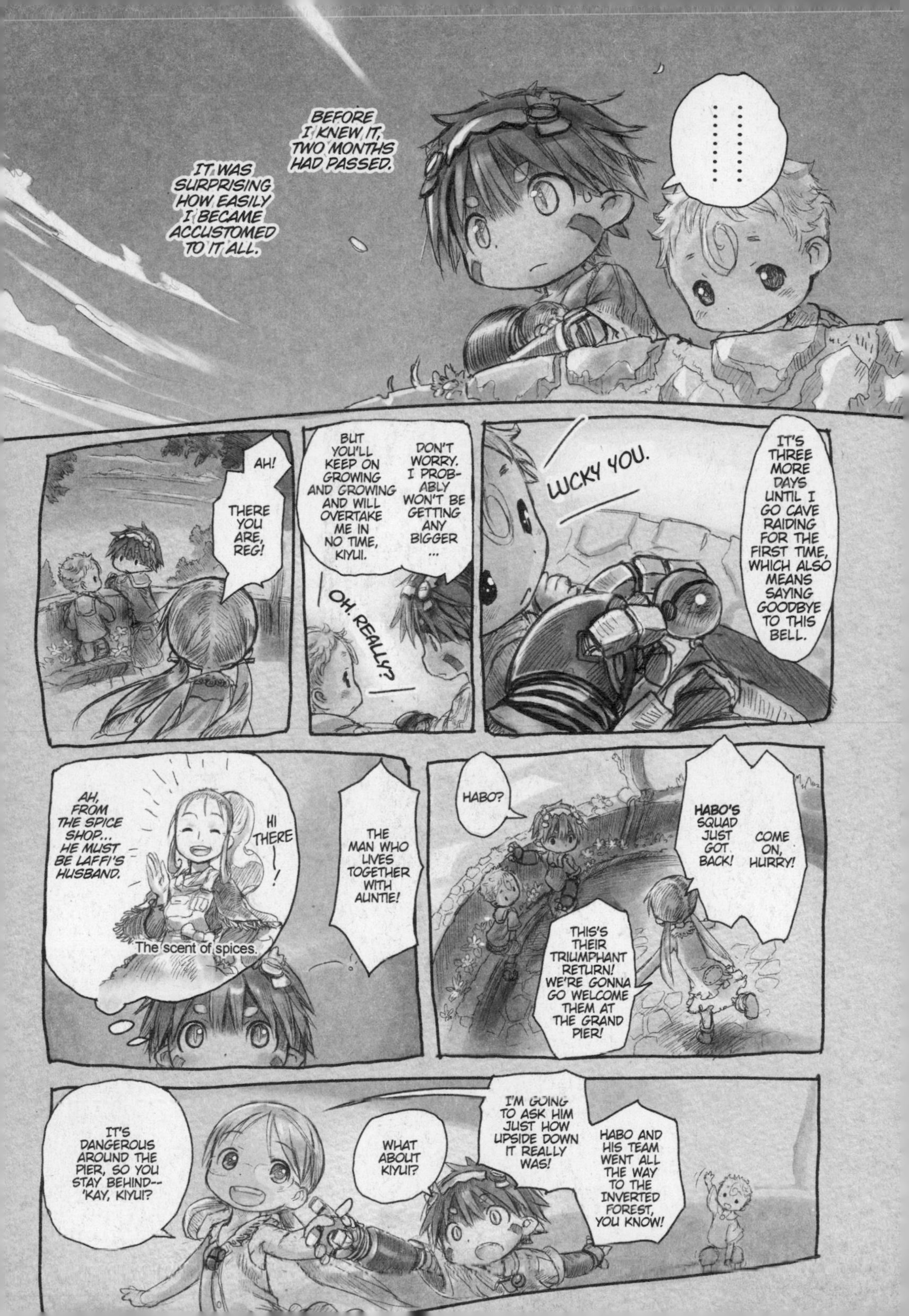
......
BEFORE I KNEW IT, TWO MONTHS HAD PASSED.
IT WAS SURPRISING HOW EASILY I BECAME ACCUSTOMED TO IT ALL.
IT'S THREE MORE DAYS UNTIL I GO CAVE RAIDING FOR THE FIRST TIME, WHICH ALSO MEANS SAYING GOODBYE TO THIS BELL.
LUCKY YOU.
DON'T WORRY. I PROBABLY WON'T BE GETTING ANY BIGGER ...
BUT YOU'LL KEEP ON GROWING AND GROWING AND WILL OVERTAKE ME IN NO TIME, KIYUI.
OH. REALLY?
AH!
THERE YOU ARE, REG!
COME ON, HURRY!
HABO'S SQUAD JUST GOT BACK!
HABO?
THIS'S THEIR TRIUMPHANT RETURN! WE'RE GONNA GO WELCOME THEM AT THE GRAND PIER!
THE MAN WHO LIVES TOGETHER WITH AUNTIE!
HI THERE!
AH, FROM THE SPICE SHOP... HE MUST BE LAFFI'S HUSBAND.
The scent of spices.
HABO AND HIS TEAM WENT ALL THE WAY TO THE INVERTED FOREST, YOU KNOW!
I'M GOING TO ASK HIM JUST HOW UPSIDE DOWN IT REALLY WAS!
WHAT ABOUT KIYUI?
IT'S DANGEROUS AROUND THE PIER, SO YOU STAY BEHIND-- 'KAY, KIYUI?

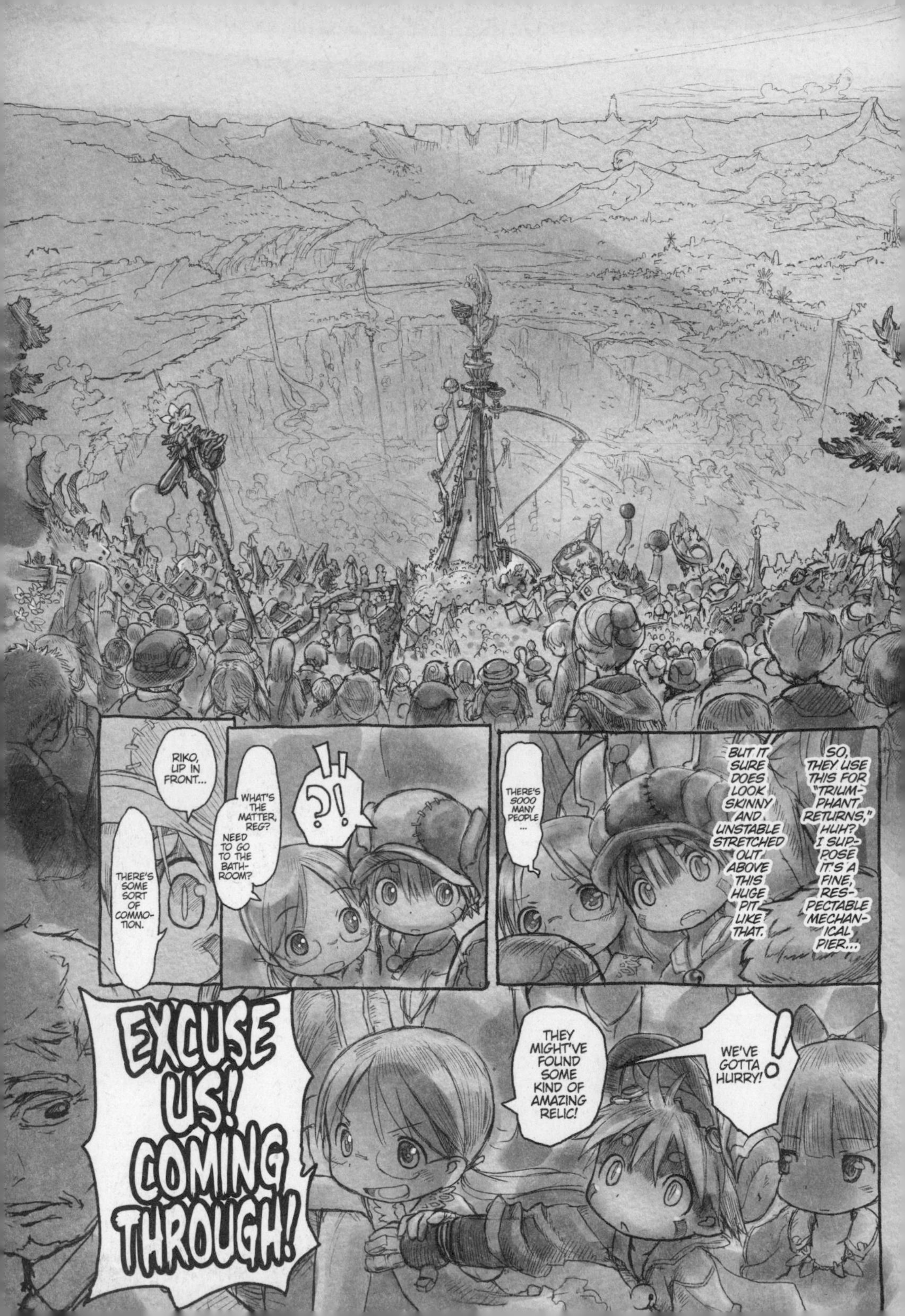
SO, THEY USE THIS FOR "TRIUMPHANT RETURNS," HUH? I SUPPOSE IT'S A FINE, RESPECTABLE MECHANICAL PIER...
BUT IT SURE DOES LOOK SKINNY AND UNSTABLE STRETCHED OUT ABOVE THIS HUGE PIT LIKE THAT.
THERE'S SOOO MANY PEOPLE...
?!
WHAT'S THE MATTER, REG? NEED TO GO TO THE BATHROOM?
RIKO, UP IN FRONT...
THERE'S SOME SORT OF COMMOTION.
!
WE'VE GOTTA HURRY!
THEY MIGHT'VE FOUND SOME KIND OF AMAZING RELIC!
EXCUSE US! COMING THROUGH!

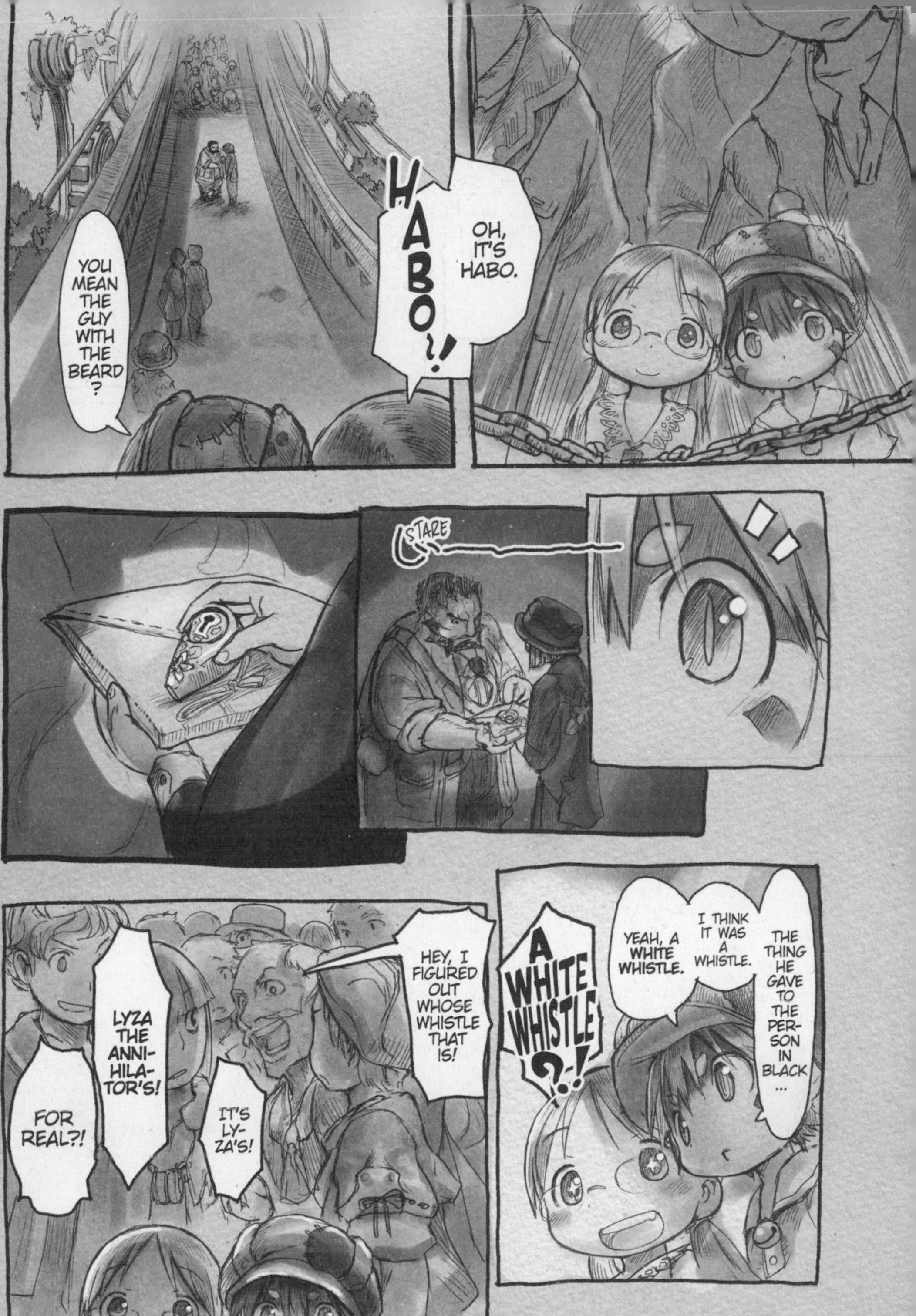
OH, IT'S HABO.
HABO?!
YOU MEAN THE GUY WITH THE BEARD?
STARE
THE THING HE GAVE TO THE PERSON IN BLACK...
I THINK IT WAS A WHISTLE.
YEAH, A WHITE WHISTLE.
A WHITE WHISTLE?!
HEY, I FIGURED OUT WHOSE WHISTLE THAT IS!
LYZA THE ANNIHILATOR'S!
IT'S LYZA'S!
FOR REAL?!

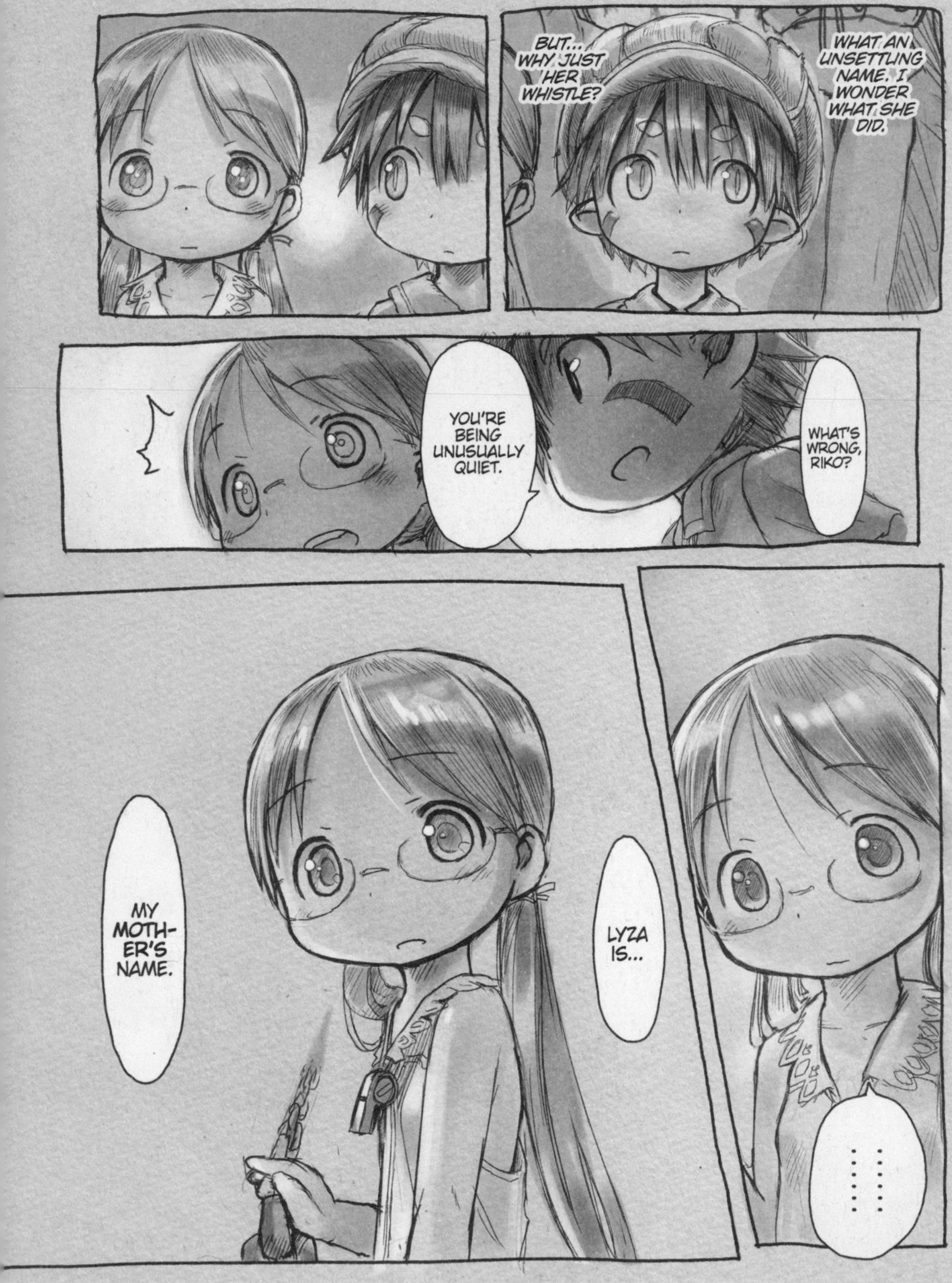
WHAT AN UNSETTLING NAME. I WONDER WHAT SHE DID.
BUT... WHY JUST HER WHISTLE?
WHAT'S WRONG, RIKO?
YOU'RE BEING UNUSUALLY QUIET.
......
LYZA IS...
MY MOTHER'S NAME.

❀ CRIMSON SPLITJAW ❀

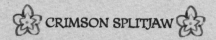

● NOTES FROM A CERTAIN CAVE RAIDER ●

RED, SNAKE-LIKE CREATURES THAT MAKE THEIR HOMES IN THE STEEP CLIFFS OF THE THIRD LAYER. THEY CAN USE THEIR MEMBRANES TO RIDE CURRENTS OF AIR, WHICH ENABLES THEM TO GLIDE ACROSS THE WIDTH OF THE ABYSS IN A FAIRLY STRAIGHT LINE.

IT'S NOT CLEAR IF THEY DO IT FOR NUTRITION OR TO STRENGTHEN THEIR GIZZARDS, BUT THEY ARE FOND OF CONSUMING RELICS AND ORE DEPOSITS. SURELY, THE NUMEROUS TREASURES THEY HAVE SWALLOWED UP LIE RESTING IN THEIR STOMACHS.

ALTHOUGH, WE CAN'T DISCOUNT THE POSSIBILITY THAT THEY'VE BEEN DEFECATED SOMEWHERE.

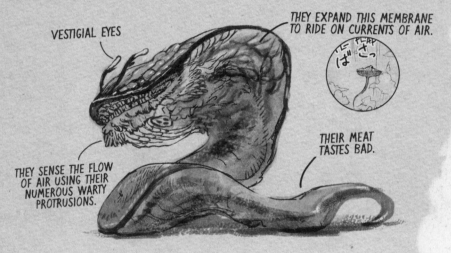

VESTIGIAL EYES

THEY EXPAND THIS MEMBRANE TO RIDE ON CURRENTS OF AIR.

THEY SENSE THE FLOW OF AIR USING THEIR NUMEROUS WARTY PROTRUSIONS.

THEIR MEAT TASTES BAD.

DANGER LEVEL: ★★★★ (DEADLY)

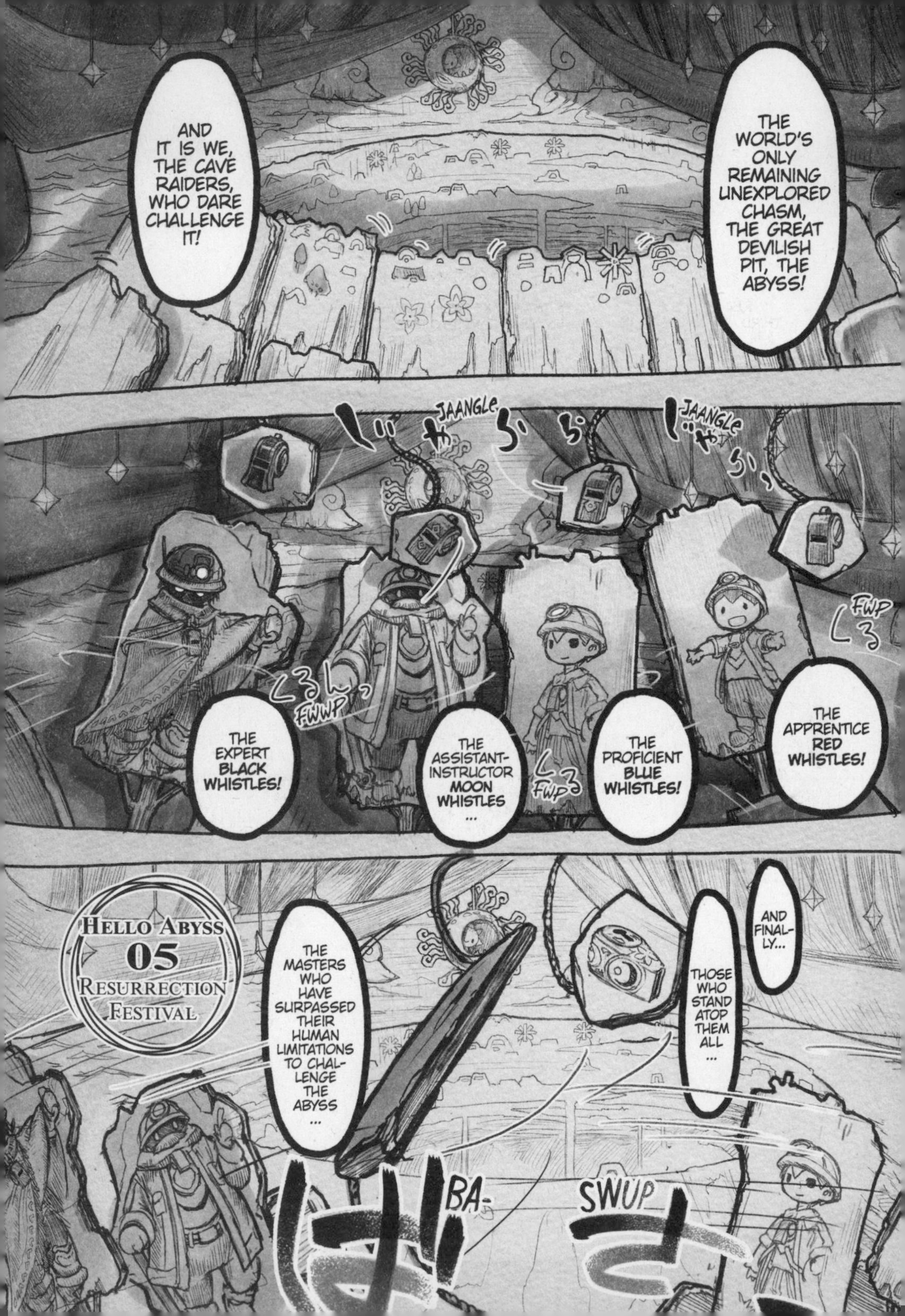
THE WORLD'S ONLY REMAINING UNEXPLORED CHASM, THE GREAT DEVILISH PIT, THE ABYSS!
AND IT IS WE, THE CAVE RAIDERS, WHO DARE CHALLENGE IT!
JAANGLE
JAANGLE
FWP
THE APPRENTICE RED WHISTLES!
THE PROFICIENT BLUE WHISTLES!
FWP
THE ASSISTANT-INSTRUCTOR MOON WHISTLES ...
FWWP
THE EXPERT BLACK WHISTLES!
AND FINALLY...
THOSE WHO STAND ATOP THEM ALL ...
THE MASTERS WHO HAVE SURPASSED THEIR HUMAN LIMITATIONS TO CHALLENGE THE ABYSS ...
HELLO ABYSS 05 RESURRECTION FESTIVAL
SWUP
BA-

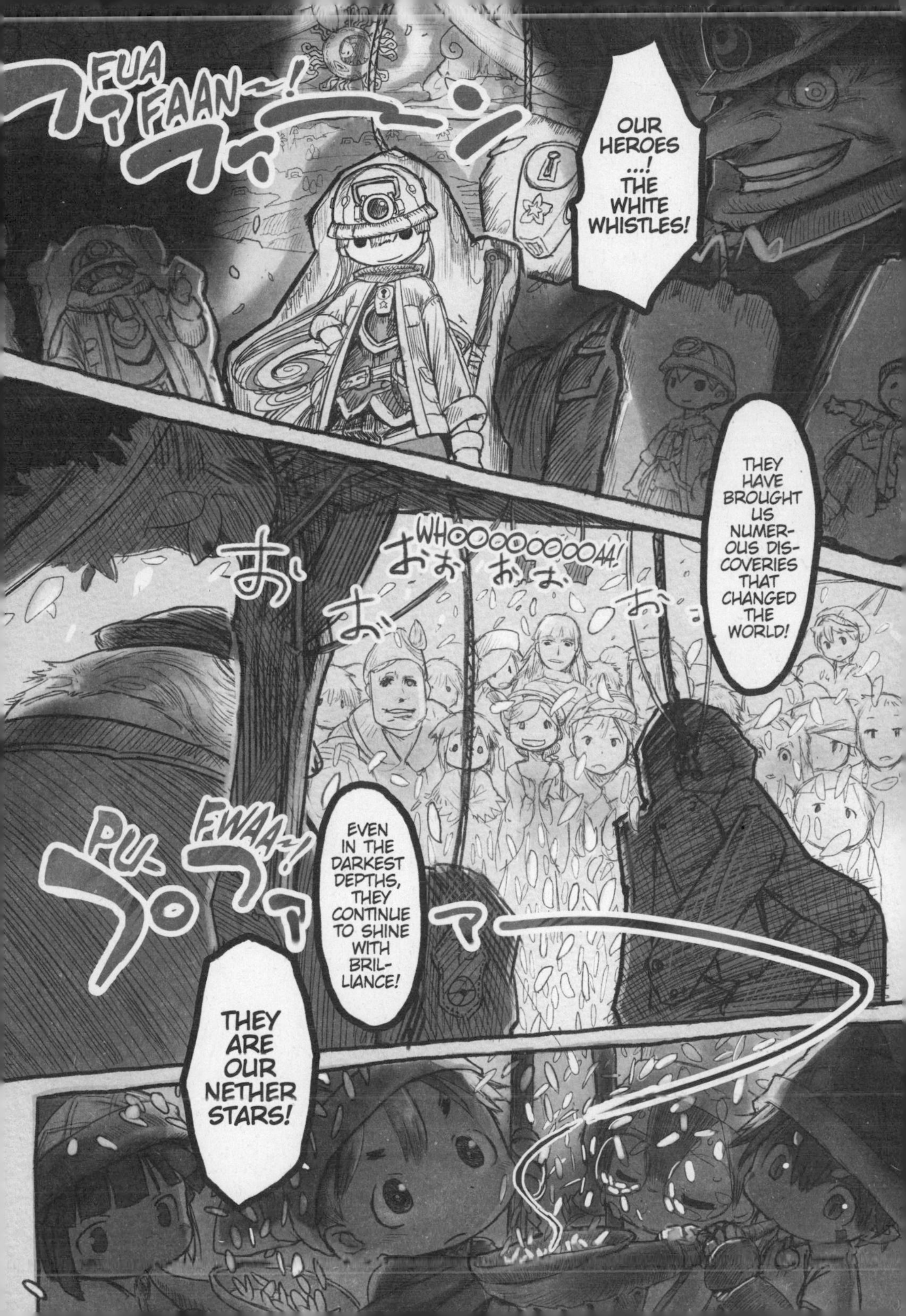
OUR HEROES ...! THE WHITE WHISTLES!
FUA FAAN~!
THEY HAVE BROUGHT US NUMEROUS DISCOVERIES THAT CHANGED THE WORLD!
WHOOOOOOOOOAA!
EVEN IN THE DARKEST DEPTHS, THEY CONTINUE TO SHINE WITH BRILLIANCE!
PU-FWAA~!
THEY ARE OUR NETHER STARS!

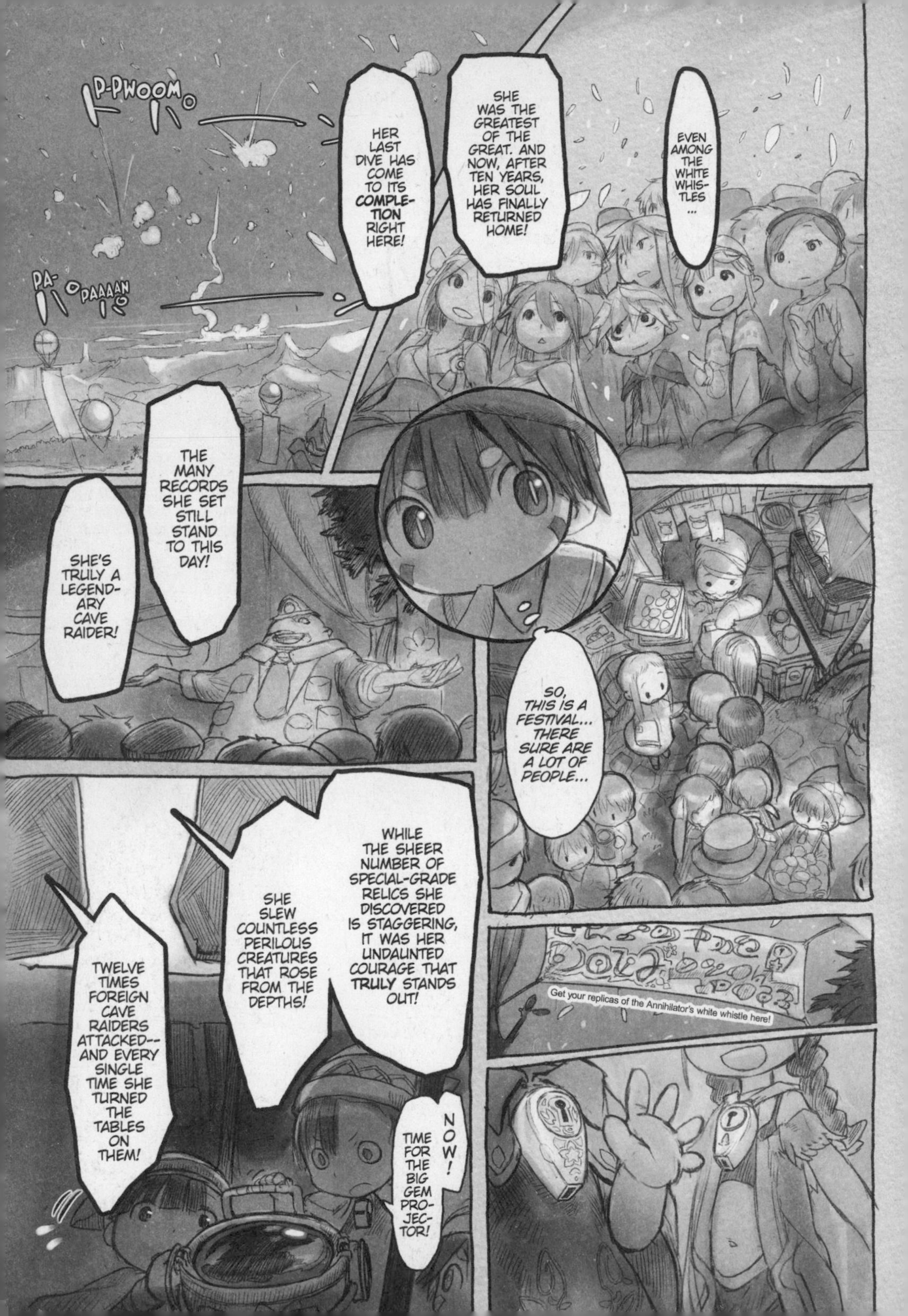
EVEN AMONG THE WHITE WHISTLES...
SHE WAS THE GREATEST OF THE GREAT. AND NOW, AFTER TEN YEARS, HER SOUL HAS FINALLY RETURNED HOME!
HER LAST DIVE HAS COME TO ITS COMPLETION RIGHT HERE!
P-PWOOM
PA-PAAAAN
SO, THIS IS A FESTIVAL... THERE SURE ARE A LOT OF PEOPLE...
THE MANY RECORDS SHE SET STILL STAND TO THIS DAY!
SHE'S TRULY A LEGENDARY CAVE RAIDER!
Get your replicas of the Annihilator's white whistle here!
WHILE THE SHEER NUMBER OF SPECIAL-GRADE RELICS SHE DISCOVERED IS STAGGERING, IT WAS HER UNDAUNTED COURAGE THAT TRULY STANDS OUT!
SHE SLEW COUNTLESS PERILOUS CREATURES THAT ROSE FROM THE DEPTHS!
TWELVE TIMES FOREIGN CAVE RAIDERS ATTACKED--AND EVERY SINGLE TIME SHE TURNED THE TABLES ON THEM!
NOW! TIME FOR THE BIG GEM PROJECTOR!

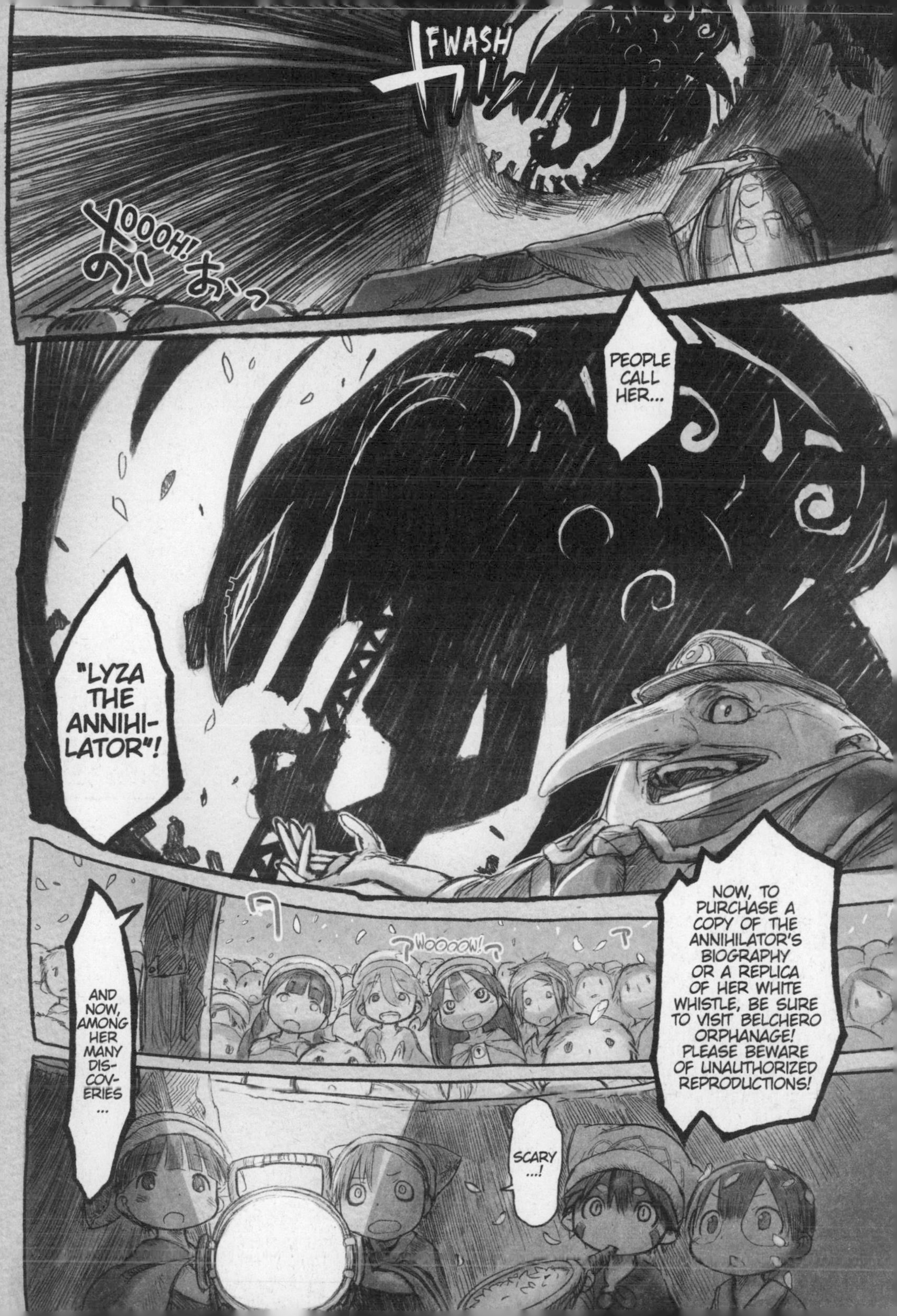
FWASH
OOOH!
PEOPLE CALL HER...
"LYZA THE ANNIHI-LATOR"!
NOW, TO PURCHASE A COPY OF THE ANNIHILATOR'S BIOGRAPHY OR A REPLICA OF HER WHITE WHISTLE, BE SURE TO VISIT BELCHERO ORPHANAGE! PLEASE BEWARE OF UNAUTHORIZED REPRODUCTIONS!
WOOOOW!
AND NOW, AMONG HER MANY DISCOV-ERIES...
SCARY...!

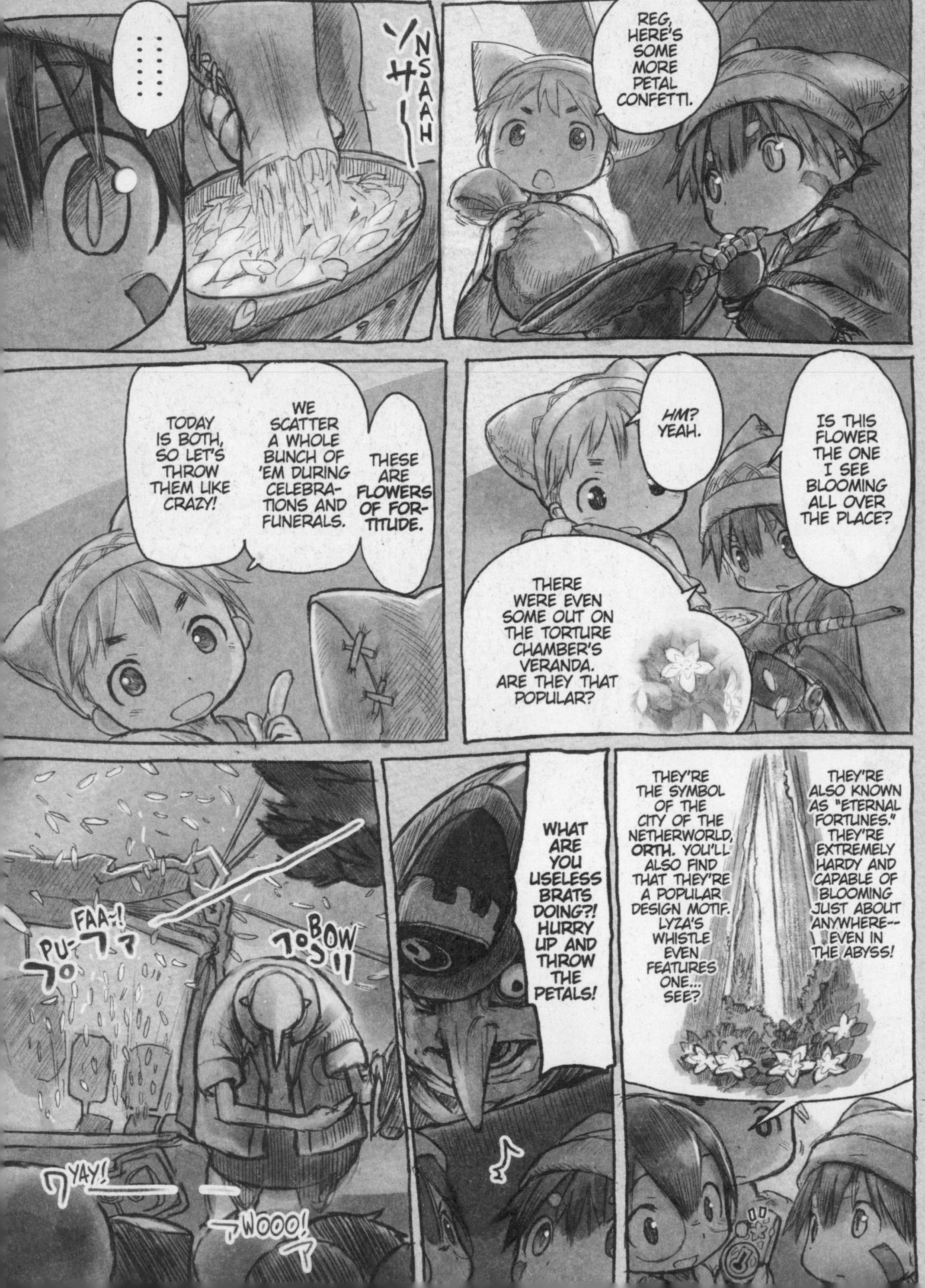

REG, HERE'S SOME MORE PETAL CONFETTI.
NSAAH
......
IS THIS FLOWER THE ONE I SEE BLOOMING ALL OVER THE PLACE?
HM? YEAH.
THERE WERE EVEN SOME OUT ON THE TORTURE CHAMBER'S VERANDA. ARE THEY THAT POPULAR?
THESE ARE FLOWERS OF FORTITUDE.
WE SCATTER A WHOLE BUNCH OF 'EM DURING CELEBRATIONS AND FUNERALS.
TODAY IS BOTH, SO LET'S THROW THEM LIKE CRAZY!
THEY'RE ALSO KNOWN AS "ETERNAL FORTUNES." THEY'RE EXTREMELY HARDY AND CAPABLE OF BLOOMING JUST ABOUT ANYWHERE-- EVEN IN THE ABYSS!
THEY'RE THE SYMBOL OF THE CITY OF THE NETHERWORLD, ORTH. YOU'LL ALSO FIND THAT THEY'RE A POPULAR DESIGN MOTIF. LYZA'S WHISTLE EVEN FEATURES ONE... SEE?
WHAT ARE YOU USELESS BRATS DOING?! HURRY UP AND THROW THE PETALS!
BOW
FAA~!
PU~
YAY!
WOOO!

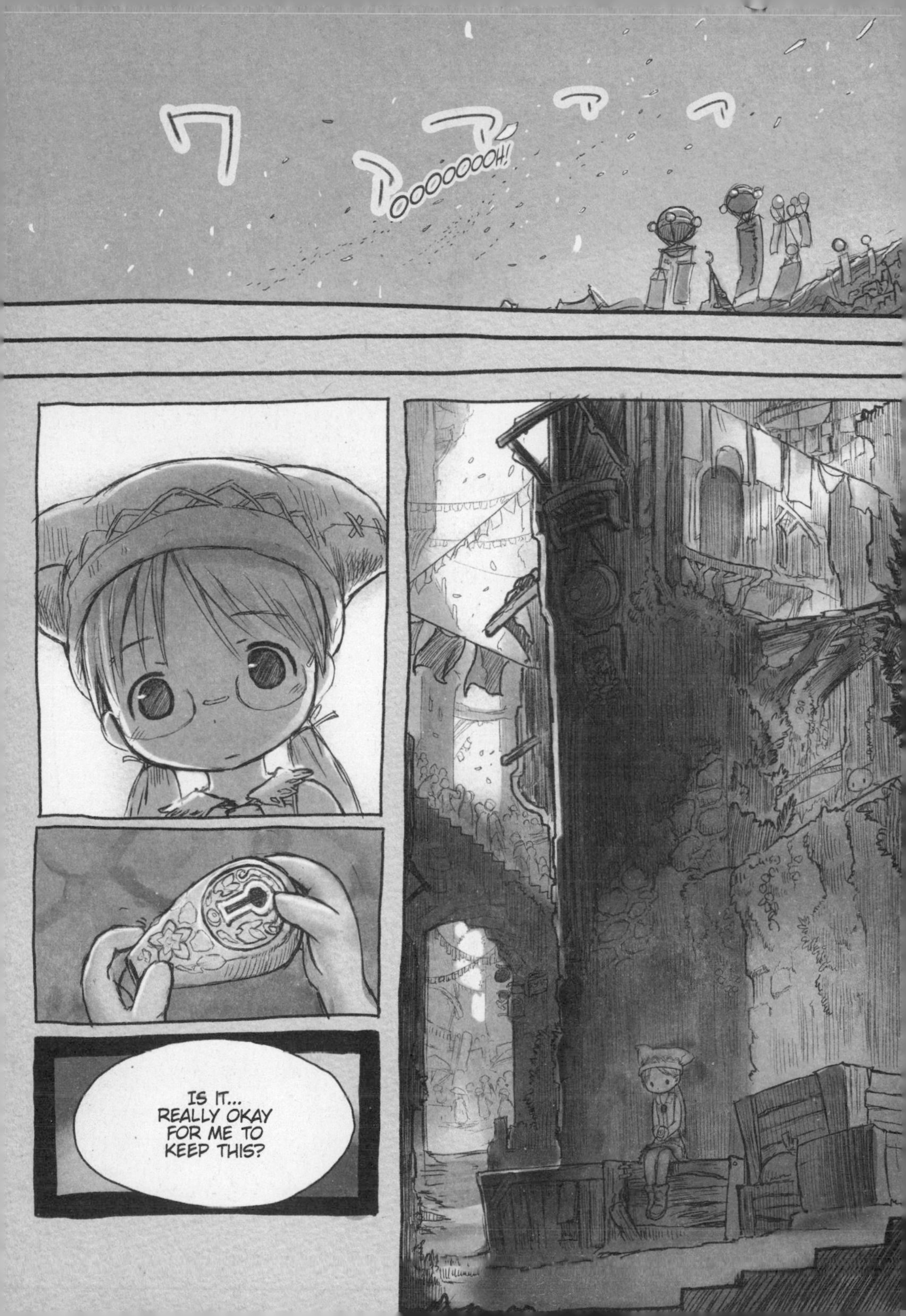
ワァァァ
OOOOOOOOH!
IS IT... REALLY OKAY FOR ME TO KEEP THIS?

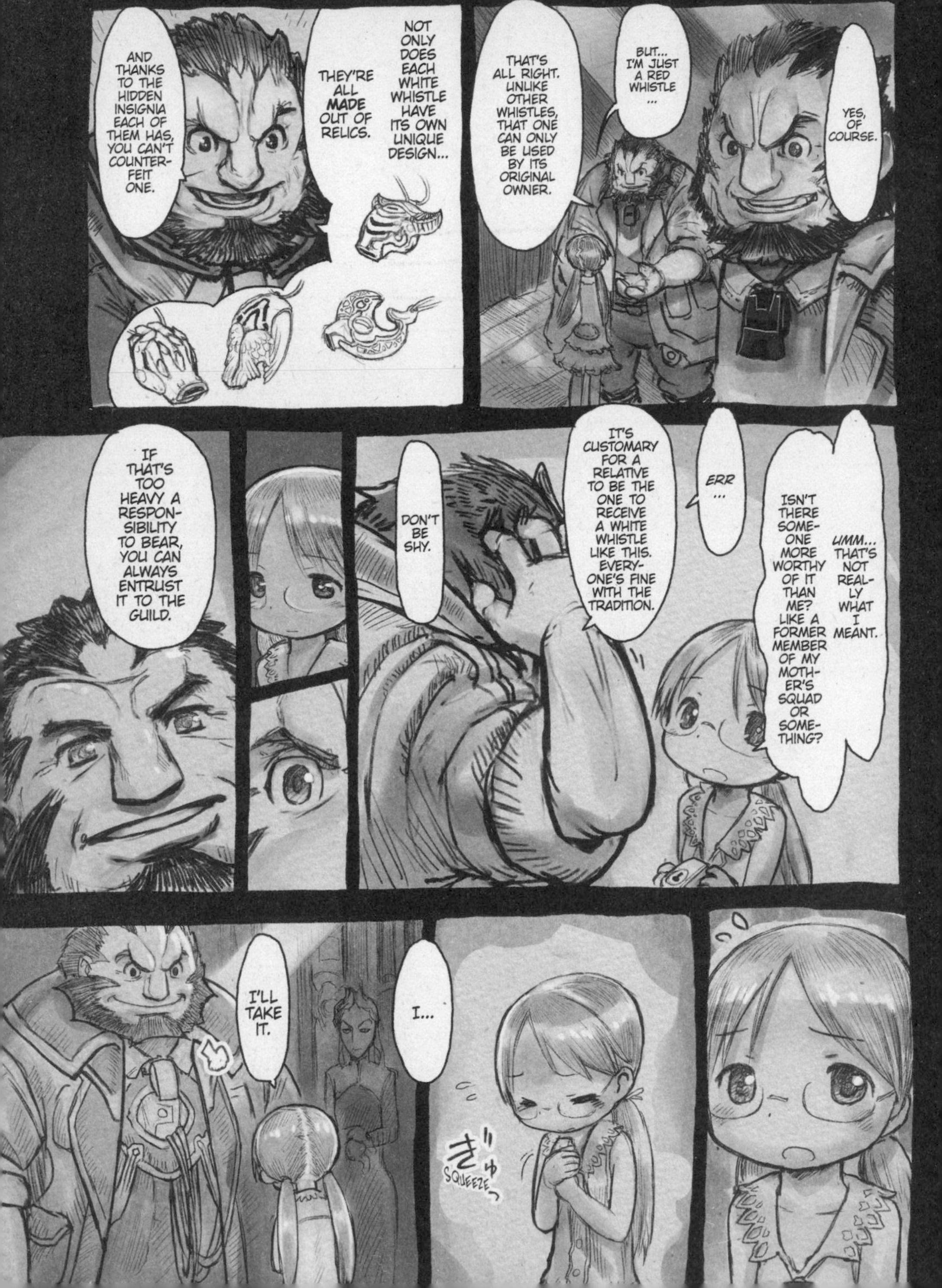
YES, OF COURSE.
BUT... I'M JUST A RED WHISTLE ...
THAT'S ALL RIGHT. UNLIKE OTHER WHISTLES, THAT ONE CAN ONLY BE USED BY ITS ORIGINAL OWNER.
NOT ONLY DOES EACH WHITE WHISTLE HAVE ITS OWN UNIQUE DESIGN...
THEY'RE ALL **MADE** OUT OF RELICS.
AND THANKS TO THE HIDDEN INSIGNIA EACH OF THEM HAS, YOU CAN'T COUNTERFEIT ONE.
UMM... THAT'S NOT REALLY WHAT I MEANT.
ISN'T THERE SOMEONE MORE WORTHY OF IT THAN ME? LIKE A FORMER MEMBER OF MY MOTHER'S SQUAD OR SOMETHING?
ERR ...
IT'S CUSTOMARY FOR A RELATIVE TO BE THE ONE TO RECEIVE A WHITE WHISTLE LIKE THIS. EVERYONE'S FINE WITH THE TRADITION.
DON'T BE SHY.
IF THAT'S TOO HEAVY A RESPONSIBILITY TO BEAR, YOU CAN ALWAYS ENTRUST IT TO THE GUILD.
I...
ぎゅ
SQUEEZE
I'LL TAKE IT.

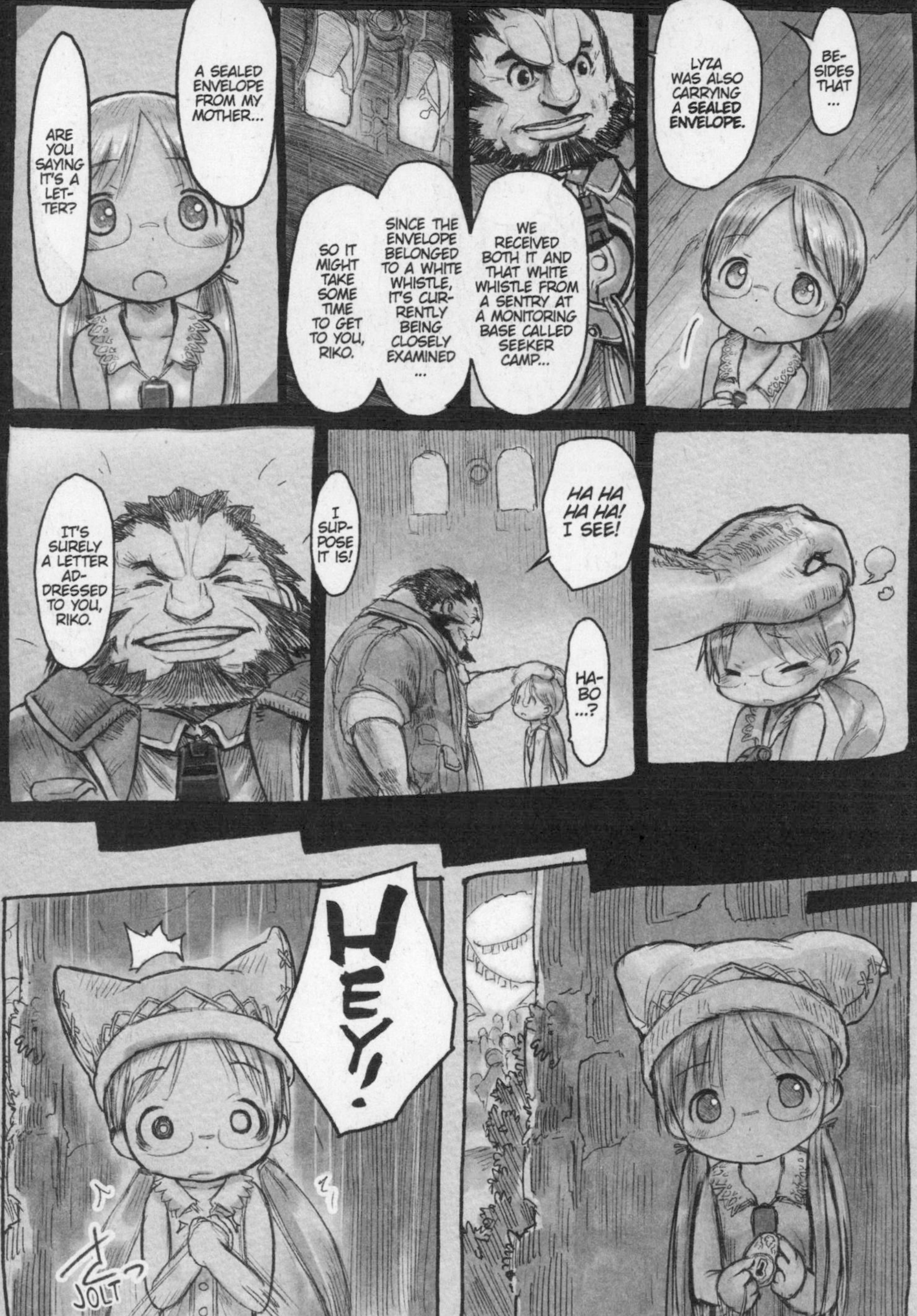
BE-SIDES THAT ...
LYZA WAS ALSO CARRYING A SEALED ENVELOPE.
WE RECEIVED BOTH IT AND THAT WHITE WHISTLE FROM A SENTRY AT A MONITORING BASE CALLED SEEKER CAMP...
SINCE THE ENVELOPE BELONGED TO A WHITE WHISTLE, IT'S CUR-RENTLY BEING CLOSELY EXAMINED ...
SO IT MIGHT TAKE SOME TIME TO GET TO YOU, RIKO.
A SEALED ENVELOPE FROM MY MOTHER...
ARE YOU SAYING IT'S A LET-TER?
HA HA HA HA! I SEE!
I SUP-POSE IT IS!
HA-BO ...?
IT'S SURELY A LETTER AD-DRESSED TO YOU, RIKO.
HEY!!
JOLT

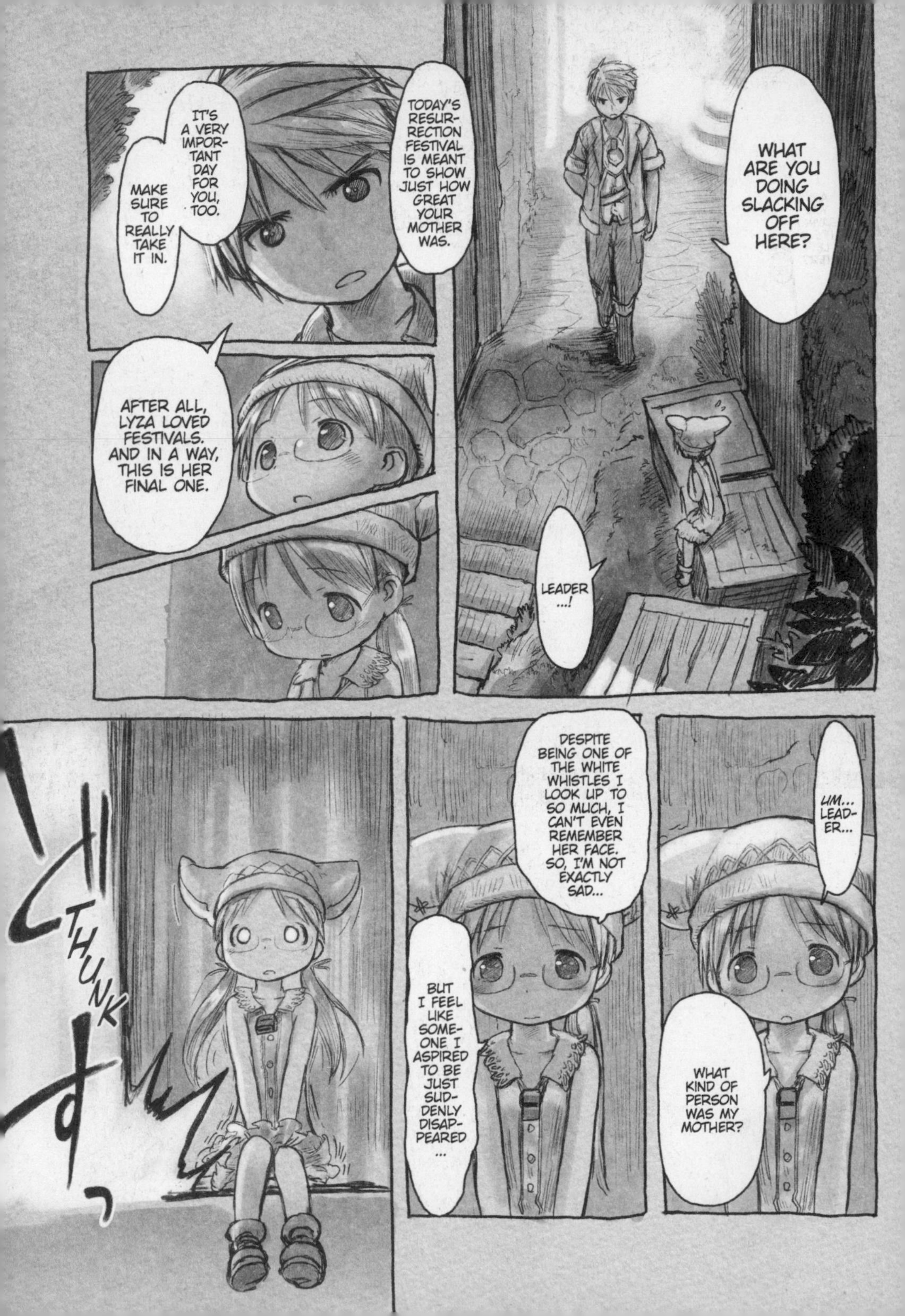
WHAT ARE YOU DOING SLACKING OFF HERE?
LEADER ...!
TODAY'S RESURRECTION FESTIVAL IS MEANT TO SHOW JUST HOW GREAT YOUR MOTHER WAS.
IT'S A VERY IMPORTANT DAY FOR YOU, TOO.
MAKE SURE TO REALLY TAKE IT IN.
AFTER ALL, LYZA LOVED FESTIVALS. AND IN A WAY, THIS IS HER FINAL ONE.
UM... LEADER...
WHAT KIND OF PERSON WAS MY MOTHER?
DESPITE BEING ONE OF THE WHITE WHISTLES I LOOK UP TO SO MUCH, I CAN'T EVEN REMEMBER HER FACE. SO, I'M NOT EXACTLY SAD...
BUT I FEEL LIKE SOMEONE I ASPIRED TO BE JUST SUDDENLY DISAPPEARED...
THUNK

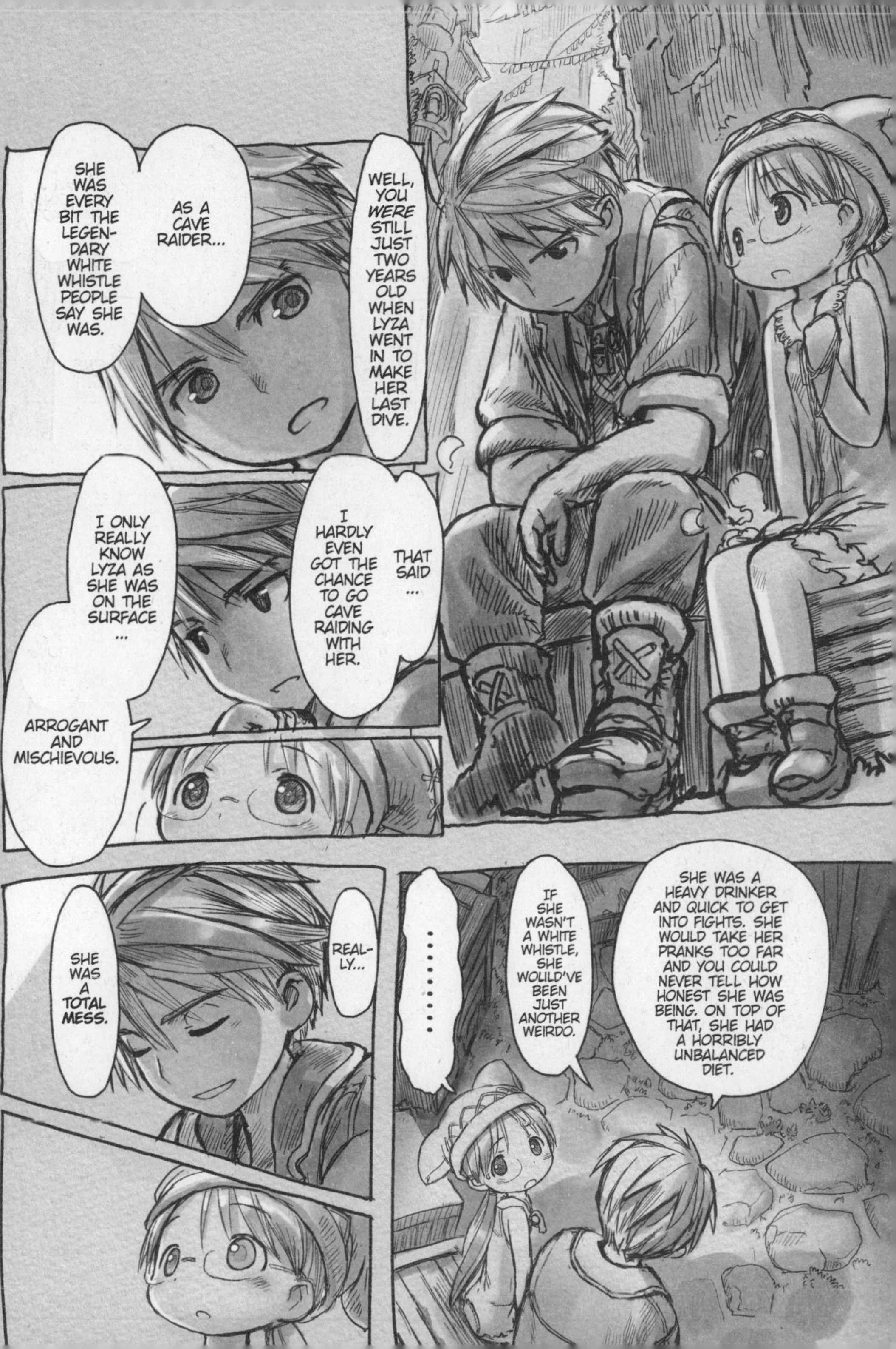
WELL, YOU *WERE* STILL JUST TWO YEARS OLD WHEN LYZA WENT IN TO MAKE HER LAST DIVE.
AS A CAVE RAIDER...
SHE WAS EVERY BIT THE LEGEN-DARY WHITE WHISTLE PEOPLE SAY SHE WAS.
THAT SAID ...
I HARDLY EVEN GOT THE CHANCE TO GO CAVE RAIDING WITH HER.
I ONLY REALLY KNOW LYZA AS SHE WAS ON THE SURFACE ...
ARROGANT AND MISCHIEVOUS.
SHE WAS A HEAVY DRINKER AND QUICK TO GET INTO FIGHTS. SHE WOULD TAKE HER PRANKS TOO FAR AND YOU COULD NEVER TELL HOW HONEST SHE WAS BEING. ON TOP OF THAT, SHE HAD A HORRIBLY UNBALANCED DIET.
IF SHE WASN'T A WHITE WHISTLE, SHE WOULD'VE BEEN JUST ANOTHER WEIRDO.
....
REAL-LY...
SHE WAS A TOTAL MESS.

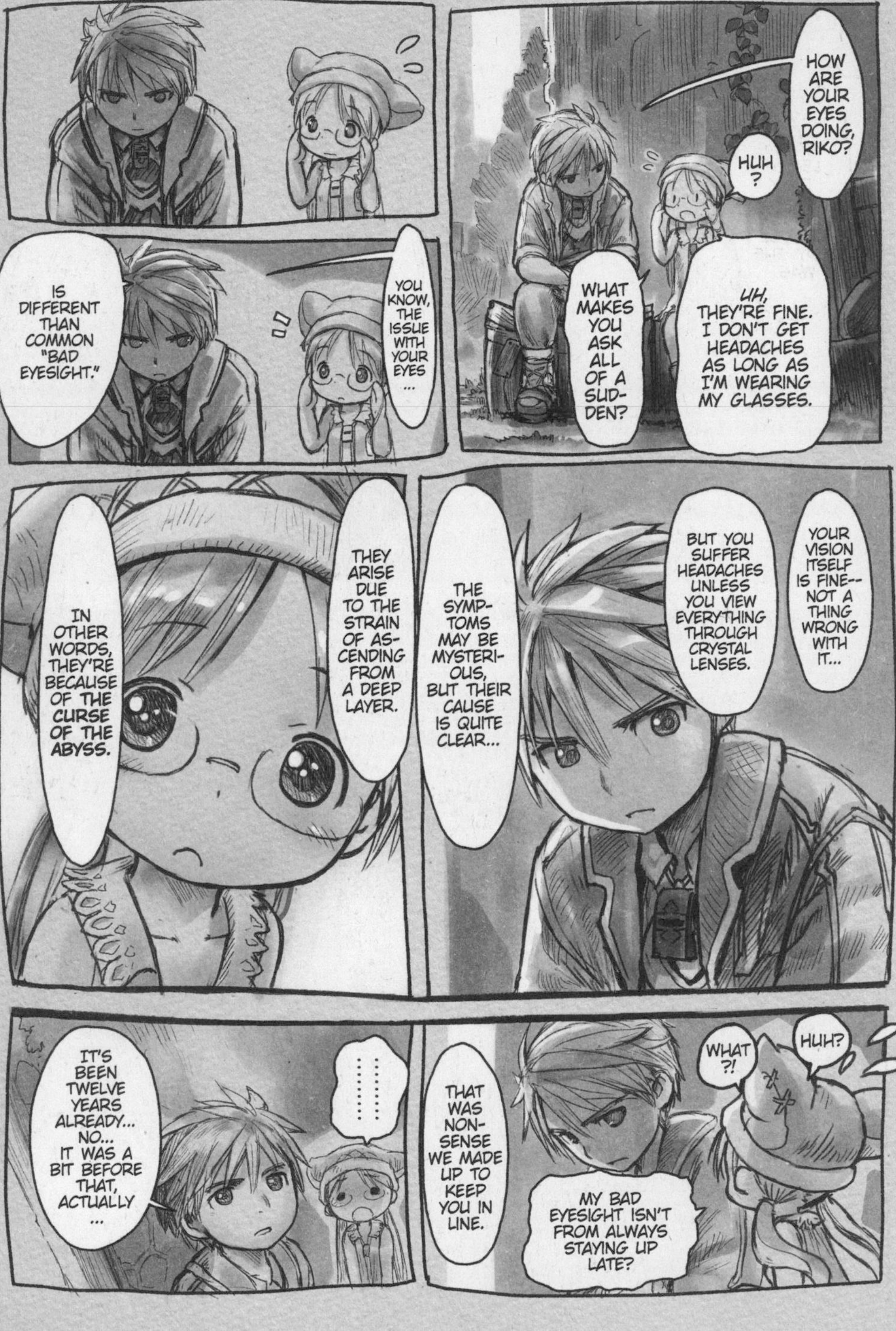
HOW ARE YOUR EYES DOING, RIKO?
HUH?
UH, THEY'RE FINE. I DON'T GET HEADACHES AS LONG AS I'M WEARING MY GLASSES.
WHAT MAKES YOU ASK ALL OF A SUD-DEN?
YOU KNOW, THE ISSUE WITH YOUR EYES ...
IS DIFFERENT THAN COMMON "BAD EYESIGHT."
YOUR VISION ITSELF IS FINE-- NOT A THING WRONG WITH IT...
BUT YOU SUFFER HEADACHES UNLESS YOU VIEW EVERYTHING THROUGH CRYSTAL LENSES.
THE SYMP-TOMS MAY BE MYSTERI-OUS, BUT THEIR CAUSE IS QUITE CLEAR...
THEY ARISE DUE TO THE STRAIN OF AS-CENDING FROM A DEEP LAYER.
IN OTHER WORDS, THEY'RE BECAUSE OF THE CURSE OF THE ABYSS.
HUH?
WHAT ?!
THAT WAS NON-SENSE WE MADE UP TO KEEP YOU IN LINE.
MY BAD EYESIGHT ISN'T FROM ALWAYS STAYING UP LATE?
......
IT'S BEEN TWELVE YEARS ALREADY... NO... IT WAS A BIT BEFORE THAT, ACTUALLY ...

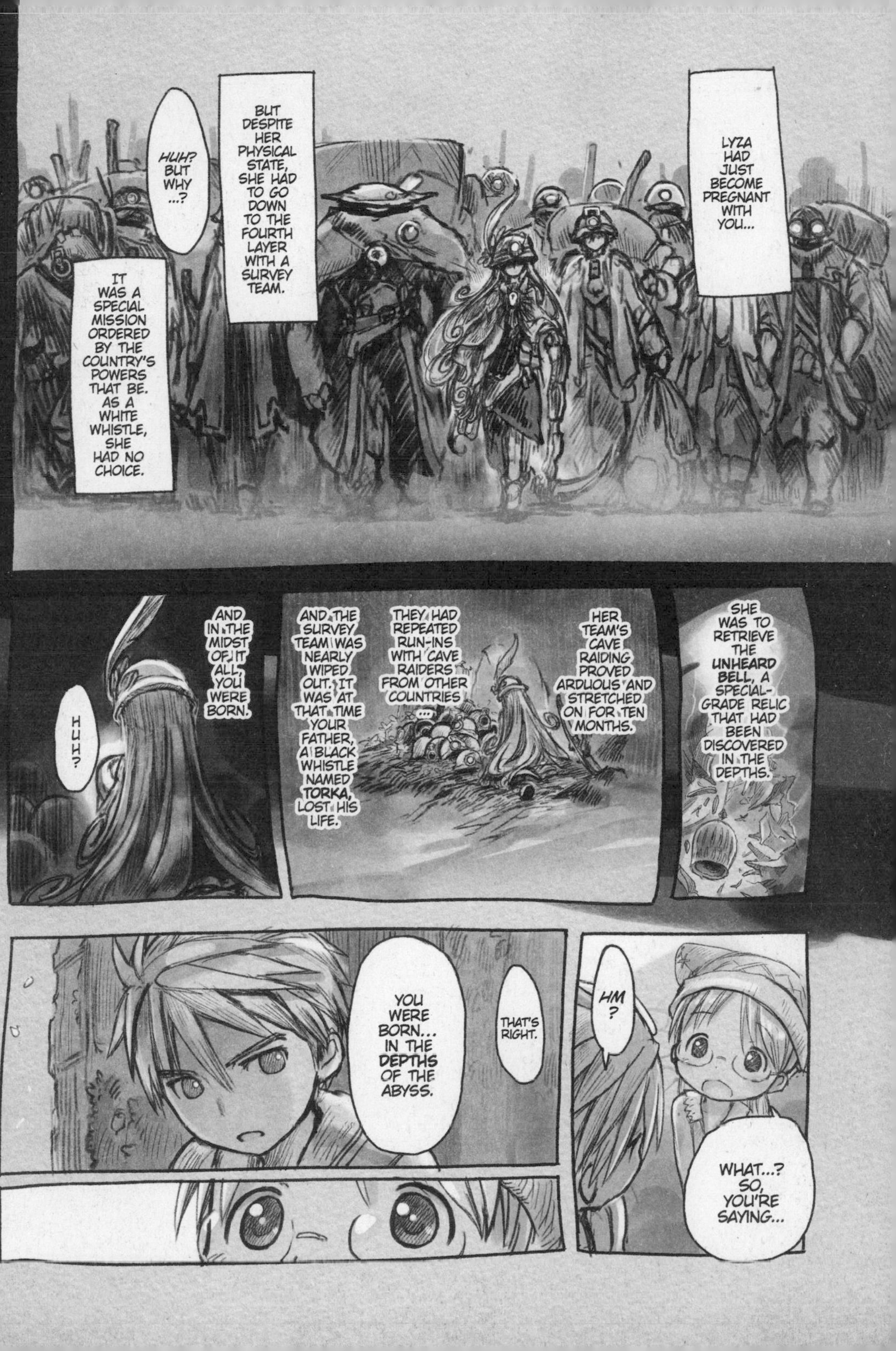
LYZA HAD JUST BECOME PREGNANT WITH YOU...
BUT DESPITE HER PHYSICAL STATE, SHE HAD TO GO DOWN TO THE FOURTH LAYER WITH A SURVEY TEAM.
HUH? BUT WHY ...?
IT WAS A SPECIAL MISSION ORDERED BY THE COUNTRY'S POWERS THAT BE. AS A WHITE WHISTLE, SHE HAD NO CHOICE.
SHE WAS TO RETRIEVE THE UNHEARD BELL, A SPECIAL-GRADE RELIC THAT HAD BEEN DISCOVERED IN THE DEPTHS.
HER TEAM'S CAVE RAIDING PROVED ARDUOUS AND STRETCHED ON FOR TEN MONTHS.
THEY HAD REPEATED RUN-INS WITH CAVE RAIDERS FROM OTHER COUNTRIES ...
AND THE SURVEY TEAM WAS NEARLY WIPED OUT. IT WAS AT THAT TIME YOUR FATHER, A BLACK WHISTLE NAMED TORKA, LOST HIS LIFE.
AND IN THE MIDST OF IT ALL, YOU WERE BORN.
HUH?
HM?
WHAT...? SO, YOU'RE SAYING...
THAT'S RIGHT.
YOU WERE BORN... IN THE DEPTHS OF THE ABYSS.

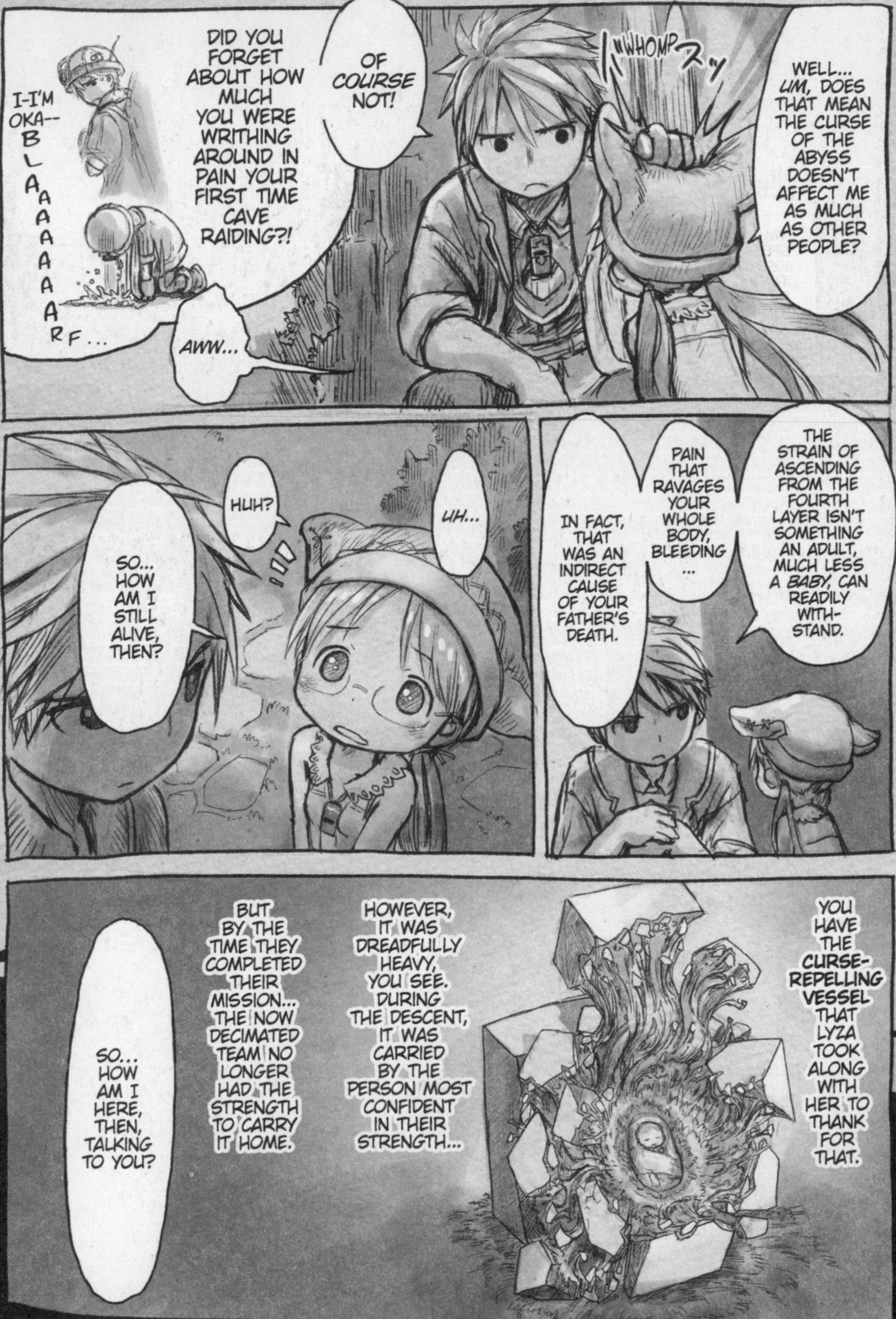
WELL... UM, DOES THAT MEAN THE CURSE OF THE ABYSS DOESN'T AFFECT ME AS MUCH AS OTHER PEOPLE?
WHOMP スッ
OF COURSE NOT!
DID YOU FORGET ABOUT HOW MUCH YOU WERE WRITHING AROUND IN PAIN YOUR FIRST TIME CAVE RAIDING?!
I-I'M OKA--
BLAAAAAAAARF...
AWW...
THE STRAIN OF ASCENDING FROM THE FOURTH LAYER ISN'T SOMETHING AN ADULT, MUCH LESS A BABY, CAN READILY WITH-STAND.
PAIN THAT RAVAGES YOUR WHOLE BODY, BLEEDING...
IN FACT, THAT WAS AN INDIRECT CAUSE OF YOUR FATHER'S DEATH.
UH...
HUH?
SO... HOW AM I STILL ALIVE, THEN?
YOU HAVE THE CURSE-REPELLING VESSEL THAT LYZA TOOK ALONG WITH HER TO THANK FOR THAT.
HOWEVER, IT WAS DREADFULLY HEAVY, YOU SEE. DURING THE DESCENT, IT WAS CARRIED BY THE PERSON MOST CONFIDENT IN THEIR STRENGTH...
BUT BY THE TIME THEY COMPLETED THEIR MISSION... THE NOW DECIMATED TEAM NO LONGER HAD THE STRENGTH TO CARRY IT HOME.
SO... HOW AM I HERE, THEN, TALKING TO YOU?

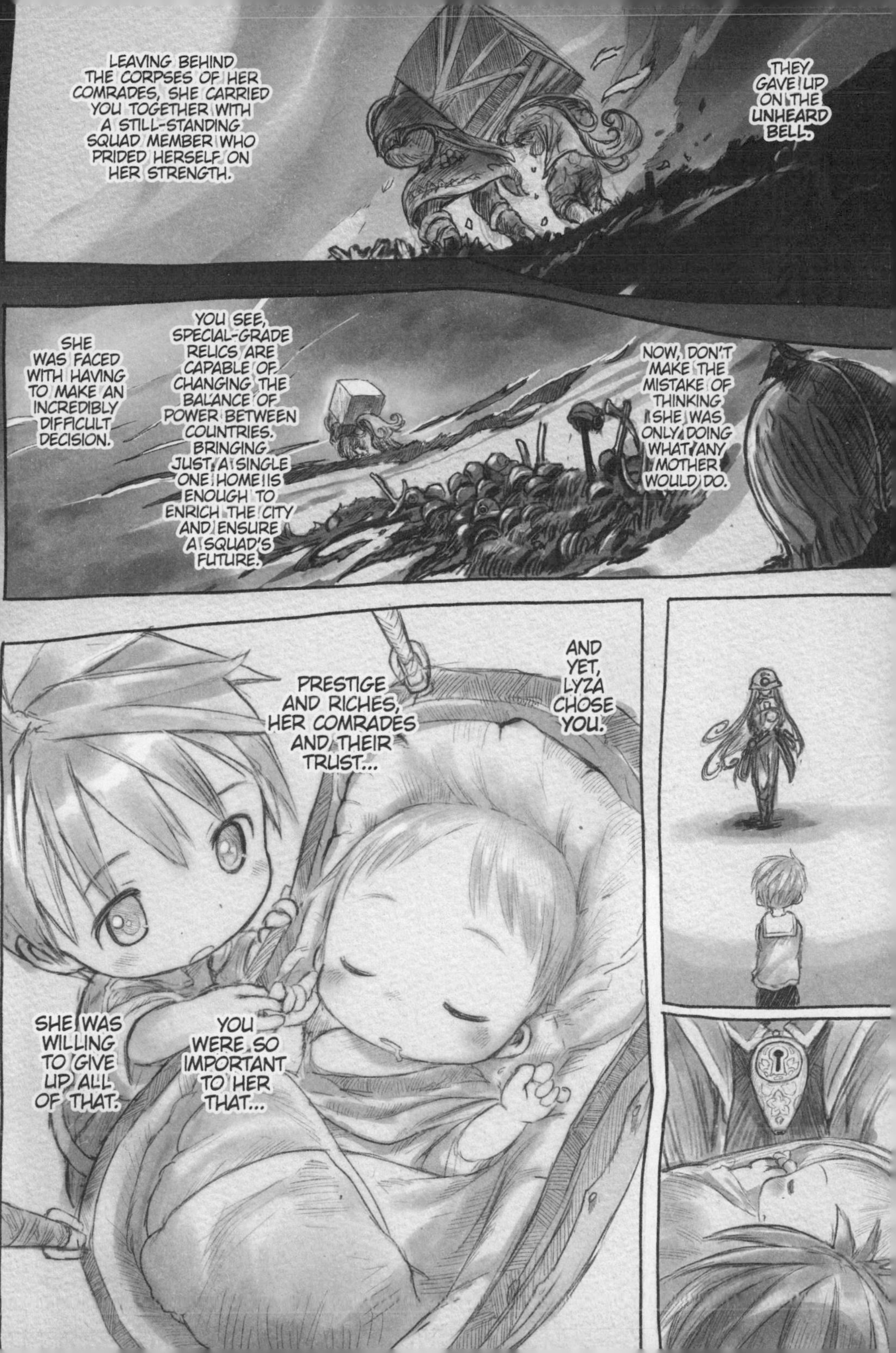
THEY GAVE UP ON THE UNHEARD BELL.
LEAVING BEHIND THE CORPSES OF HER COMRADES, SHE CARRIED YOU TOGETHER WITH A STILL-STANDING SQUAD MEMBER WHO PRIDED HERSELF ON HER STRENGTH.
NOW, DON'T MAKE THE MISTAKE OF THINKING SHE WAS ONLY DOING WHAT ANY MOTHER WOULD DO.
YOU SEE, SPECIAL-GRADE RELICS ARE CAPABLE OF CHANGING THE BALANCE OF POWER BETWEEN COUNTRIES. BRINGING JUST A SINGLE ONE HOME IS ENOUGH TO ENRICH THE CITY AND ENSURE A SQUAD'S FUTURE.
SHE WAS FACED WITH HAVING TO MAKE AN INCREDIBLY DIFFICULT DECISION.
AND YET, LYZA CHOSE YOU.
PRESTIGE AND RICHES, HER COMRADES AND THEIR TRUST...
YOU WERE SO IMPORTANT TO HER THAT...
SHE WAS WILLING TO GIVE UP ALL OF THAT.

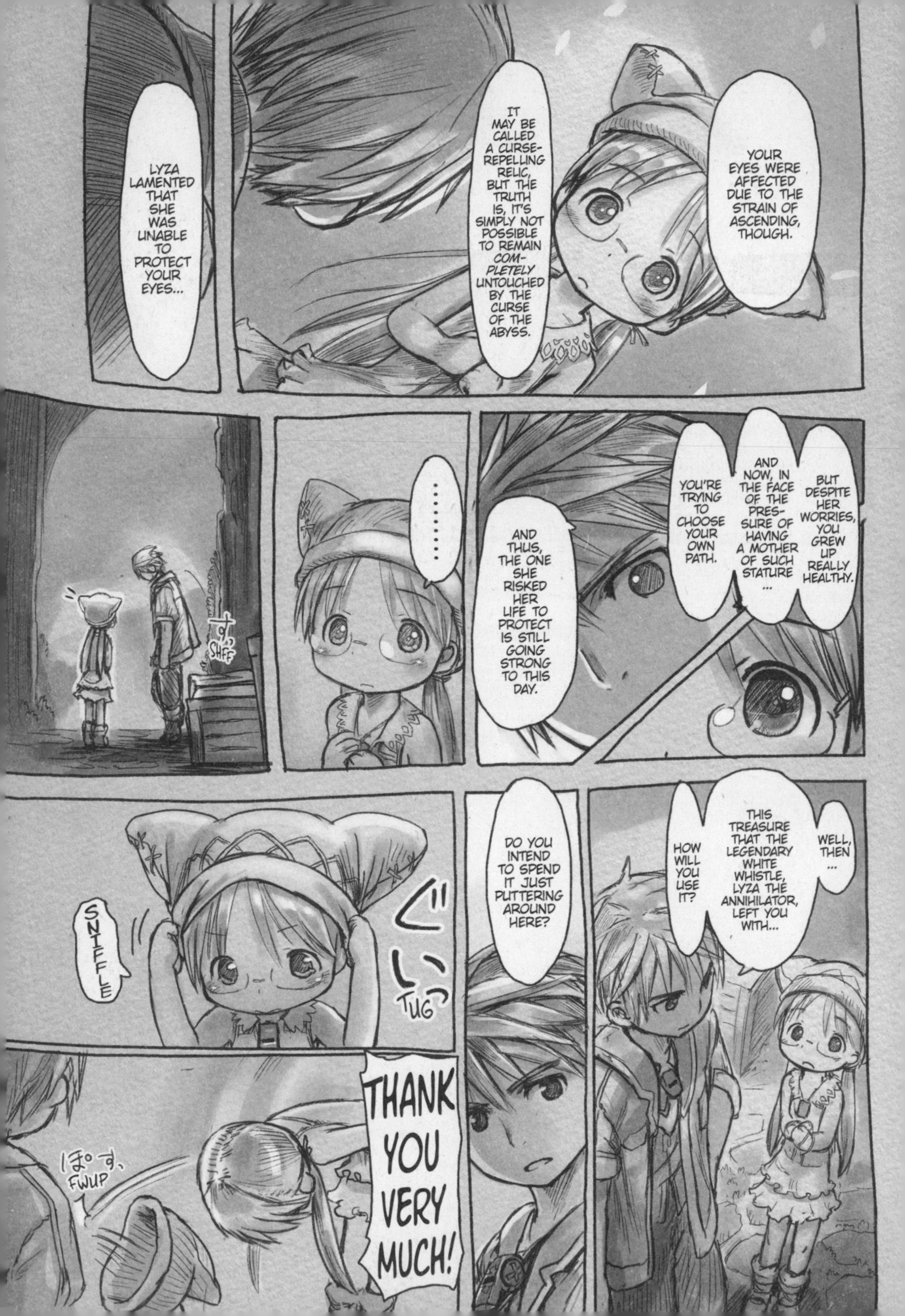
YOUR EYES WERE AFFECTED DUE TO THE STRAIN OF ASCENDING, THOUGH.
IT MAY BE CALLED A CURSE-REPELLING RELIC, BUT THE TRUTH IS, IT'S SIMPLY NOT POSSIBLE TO REMAIN COM-PLETELY UNTOUCHED BY THE CURSE OF THE ABYSS.
LYZA LAMENTED THAT SHE WAS UNABLE TO PROTECT YOUR EYES...
BUT DESPITE HER WORRIES, YOU GREW UP REALLY HEALTHY.
AND NOW, IN THE FACE OF THE PRES-SURE OF HAVING A MOTHER OF SUCH STATURE...
YOU'RE TRYING TO CHOOSE YOUR OWN PATH.
AND THUS, THE ONE SHE RISKED HER LIFE TO PROTECT IS STILL GOING STRONG TO THIS DAY.
....
すっ
SHFF
WELL, THEN...
THIS TREASURE THAT THE LEGENDARY WHITE WHISTLE, LYZA THE ANNIHILATOR, LEFT YOU WITH...
HOW WILL YOU USE IT?
DO YOU INTEND TO SPEND IT JUST PUTTERING AROUND HERE?
ぐいっ
TUG
SNIFFLE
THANK YOU VERY MUCH!
ぼすっ
FWUP

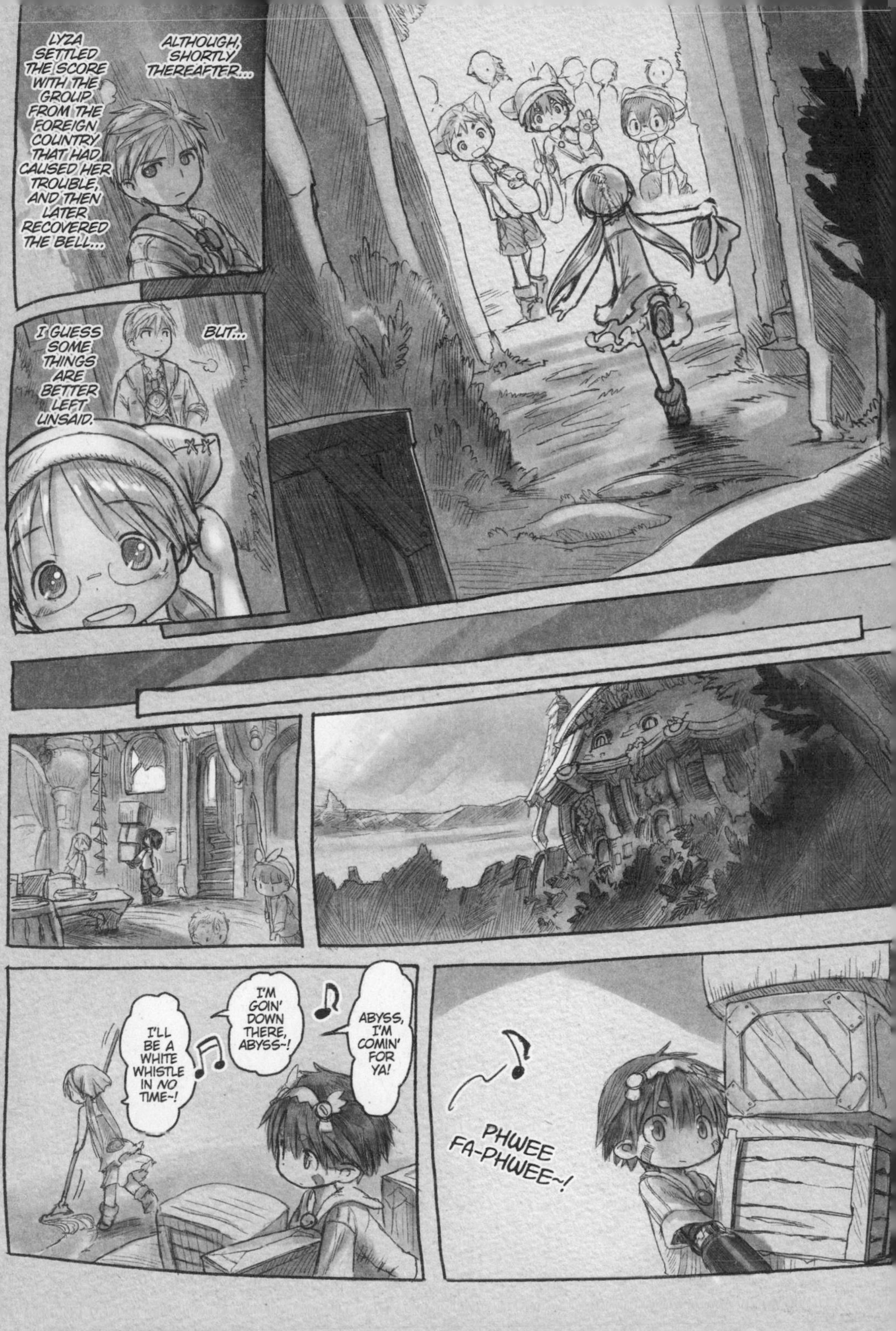
ALTHOUGH, SHORTLY THEREAFTER...
LYZA SETTLED THE SCORE WITH THE GROUP FROM THE FOREIGN COUNTRY THAT HAD CAUSED HER TROUBLE, AND THEN LATER RECOVERED THE BELL...
BUT...
I GUESS SOME THINGS ARE BETTER LEFT UNSAID.
PHWEE FA-PHWEE~!
ABYSS, I'M COMIN' FOR YA!
I'M GOIN' DOWN THERE, ABYSS~!
I'LL BE A WHITE WHISTLE IN NO TIME~!

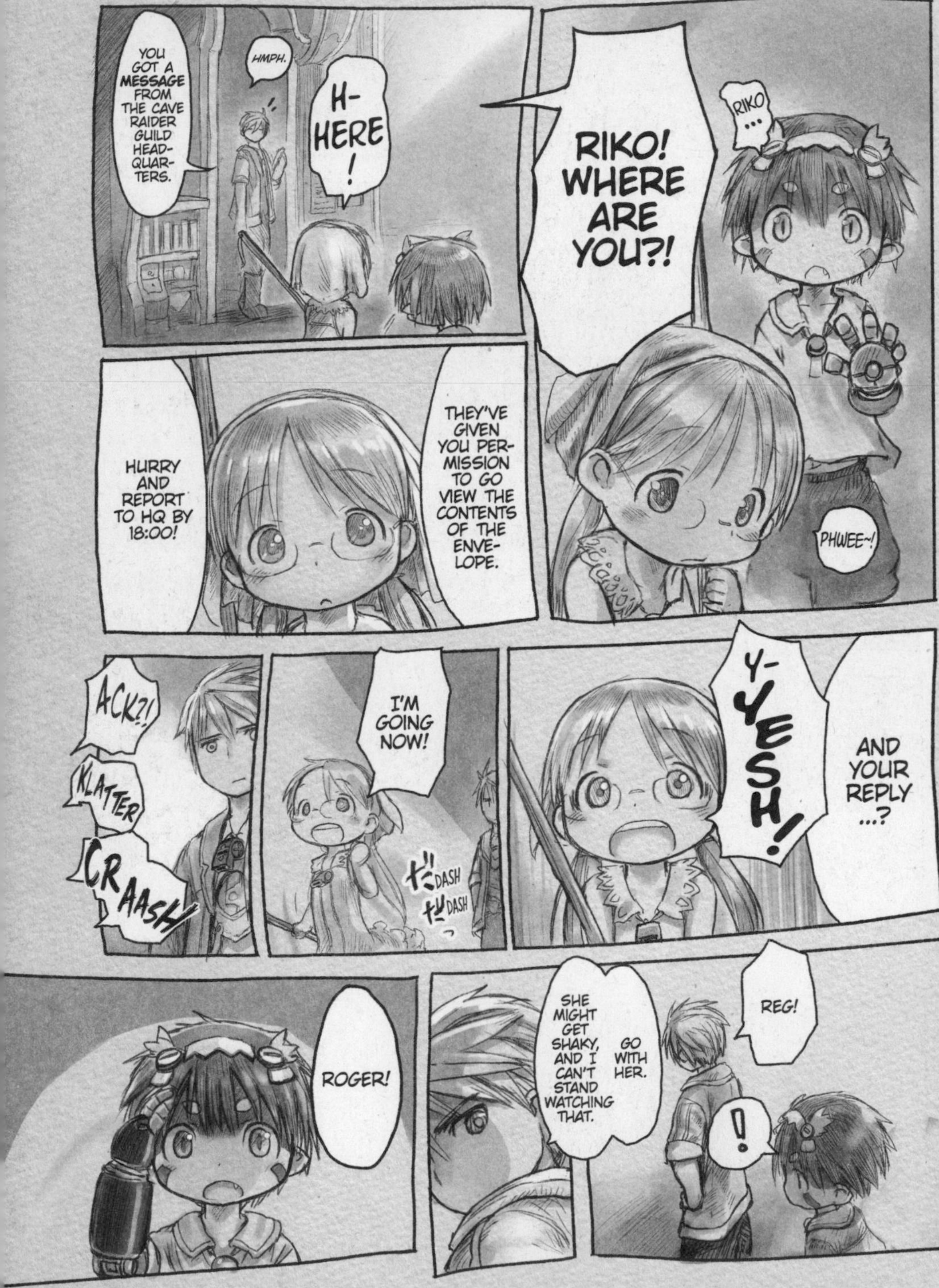
RIKO! WHERE ARE YOU?!
RIKO ...
PHWEE~!
H-HERE!
HMPH.
YOU GOT A MESSAGE FROM THE CAVE RAIDER GUILD HEAD-QUARTERS.
THEY'VE GIVEN YOU PER-MISSION TO GO VIEW THE CONTENTS OF THE ENVE-LOPE.
HURRY AND REPORT TO HQ BY 18:00!
AND YOUR REPLY ...?
Y-YESH!
I'M GOING NOW!
DASH
DASH
ACK?!
KLATTER
CRAASH
REG!
!
GO WITH HER.
SHE MIGHT GET SHAKY, AND I CAN'T STAND WATCHING THAT.
ROGER!

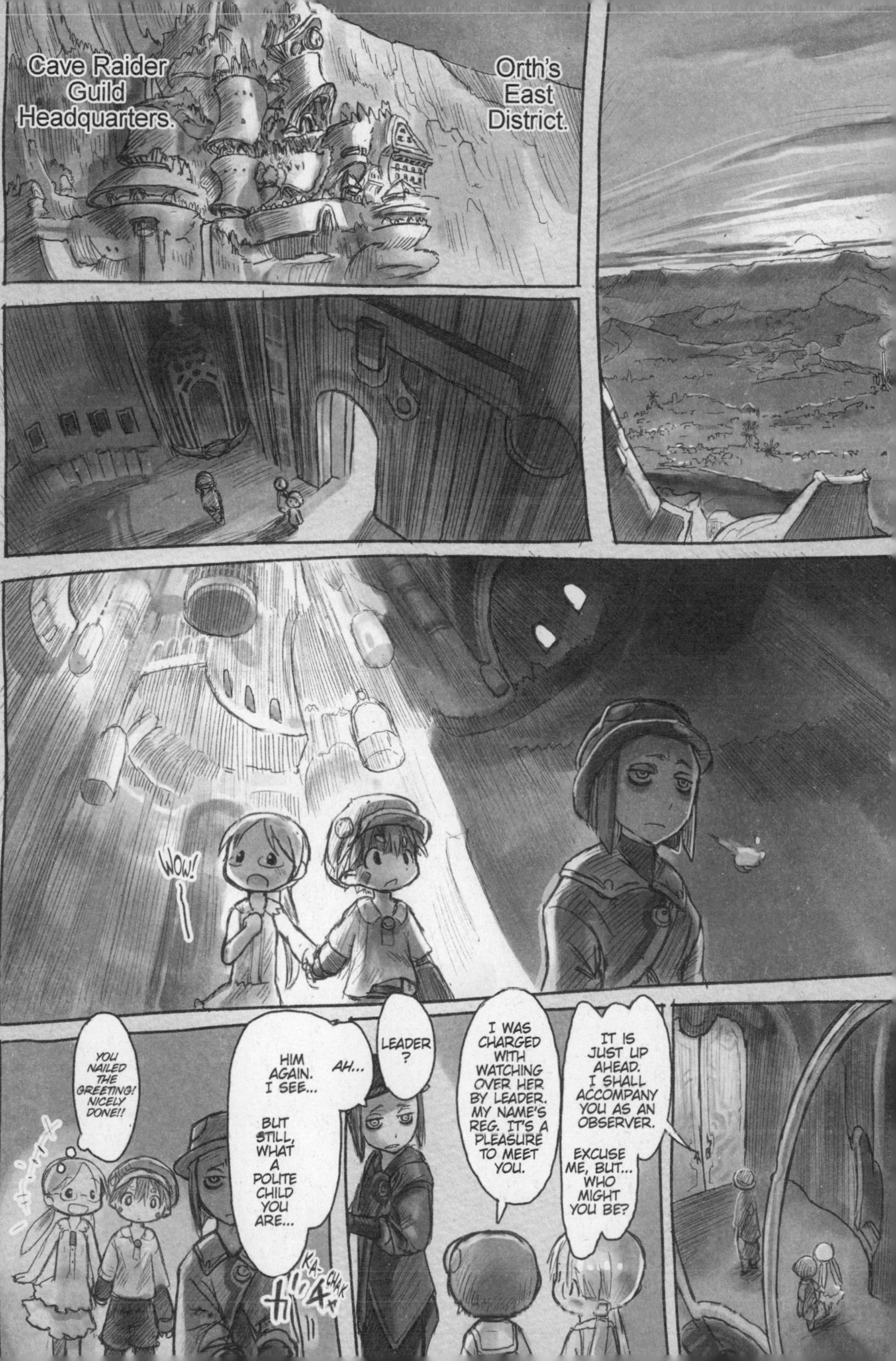
Orth's East District.
Cave Raider Guild Headquarters.
WOW!
IT IS JUST UP AHEAD. I SHALL ACCOMPANY YOU AS AN OBSERVER.
EXCUSE ME, BUT... WHO MIGHT YOU BE?
I WAS CHARGED WITH WATCHING OVER HER BY LEADER. MY NAME'S REG. IT'S A PLEASURE TO MEET YOU.
LEADER?
AH...
HIM AGAIN. I SEE...
BUT STILL, WHAT A POLITE CHILD YOU ARE...
KA-CHAK
YOU NAILED THE GREETING! NICELY DONE!!

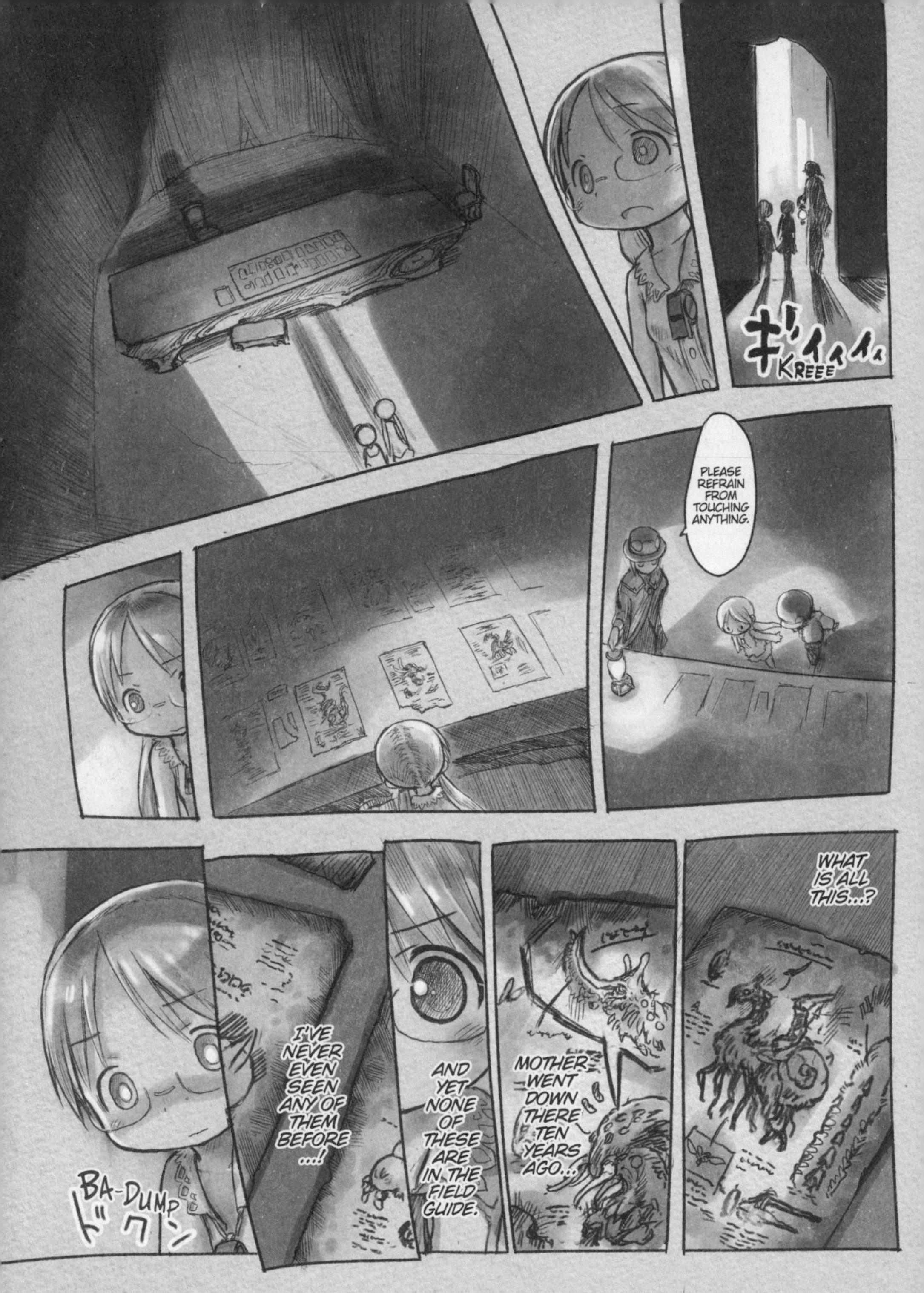
ギイイイ
KREEE
PLEASE REFRAIN FROM TOUCHING ANYTHING.
WHAT IS ALL THIS...?
MOTHER WENT DOWN THERE TEN YEARS AGO...
AND YET NONE OF THESE ARE IN THE FIELD GUIDE.
I'VE NEVER EVEN SEEN ANY OF THEM BEFORE...!
BA-DUMP
ドクン

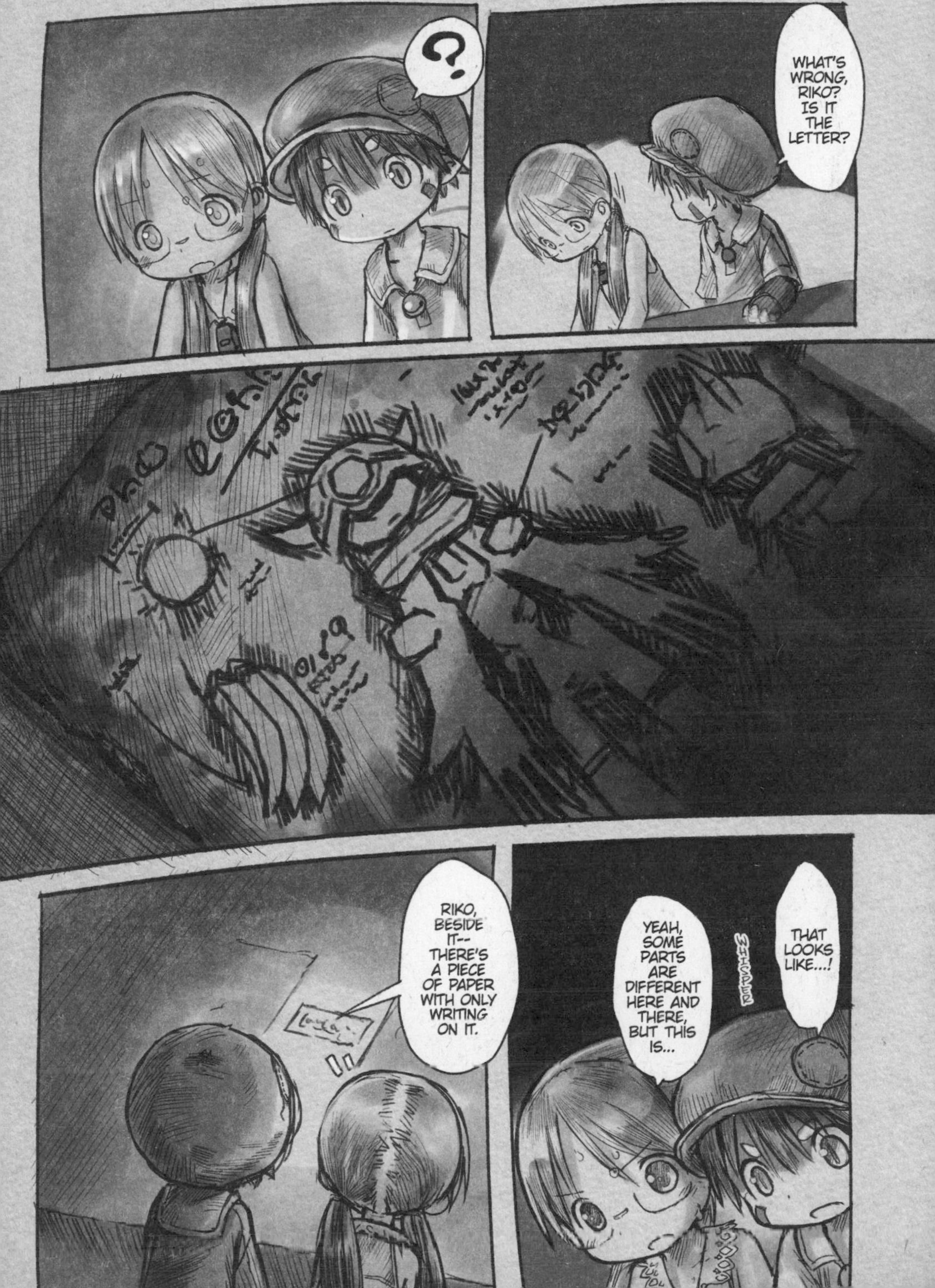
WHAT'S WRONG, RIKO? IS IT THE LETTER?
?
THAT LOOKS LIKE...!
WHISPER
YEAH, SOME PARTS ARE DIFFERENT HERE AND THERE, BUT THIS IS...
RIKO, BESIDE IT-- THERE'S A PIECE OF PAPER WITH ONLY WRITING ON IT.
!!

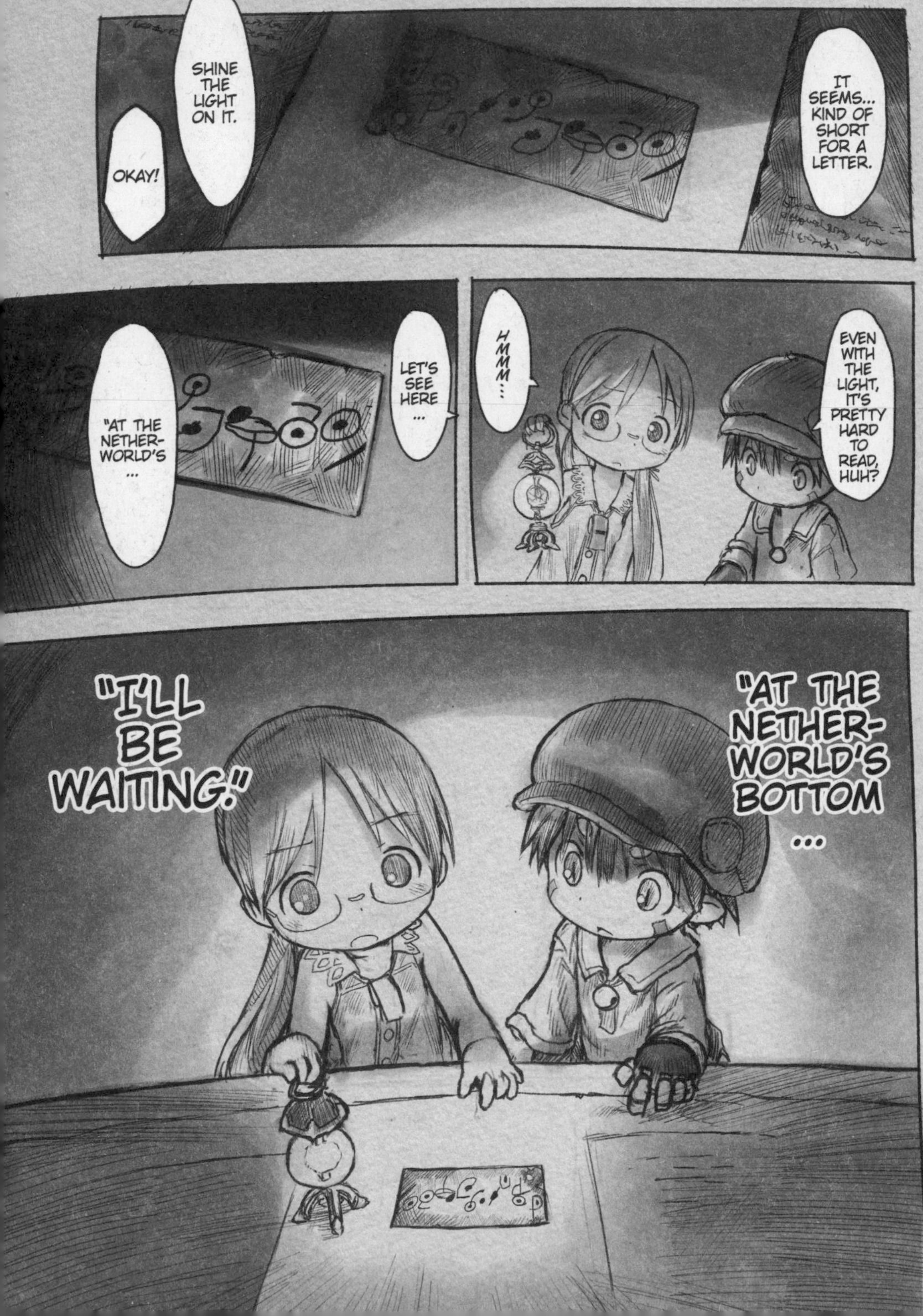
IT SEEMS... KIND OF SHORT FOR A LETTER.
SHINE THE LIGHT ON IT.
OKAY!
EVEN WITH THE LIGHT, IT'S PRETTY HARD TO READ, HUH?
HMMM...
LET'S SEE HERE...
"AT THE NETHER-WORLD'S...
"AT THE NETHER-WORLD'S BOTTOM...
"I'LL BE WAITING."

"THE FLOWER OF FORTITUDE"

 ## ETERNAL FORTUNE

THIS PLANT TAKES ROOT IN ANY ENVIRONMENT.
A FAST-GROWING SPECIES, IT BLOOMS--
AND SUBSEQUENTLY RELEASES ITS SEEDS--
ALL THROUGHOUT THE YEAR.

THEY TEND TO PRODUCE LARGER, WHITER FLOWERS THE COLDER THE REGION
THEY GROW IN IS. IT HAS BEEN DESIGNATED THE "OFFICIAL CITY FLOWER" OF
ORTH DUE TO THE GOOD LUCK INHERENT WITH THIS FORTITUDE.

CULTIVATED ALL AROUND THE CITY, THE FLOWER HAS BECOME PART OF THE LOCAL SCENERY.

IN ORTH, IT IS CUSTOMARY TO SHOWER THE ABYSS WITH THESE
FLOWERS DURING CELEBRATIONS AND OCCASIONS OF MOURNING.

THE PLANT IS A COMMON SIGHT EVEN IN THE ABYSS.
SINCE ITS ROOTS AND SEEDS CAN EASILY BE OBTAINED THERE, THEY
MAKE FOR HANDY COOKING INGREDIENTS AND SEASONINGS.

ETERNAL FORTUNES DON'T FAVOR ANY PARTICULAR PLACE TO BLOOM.

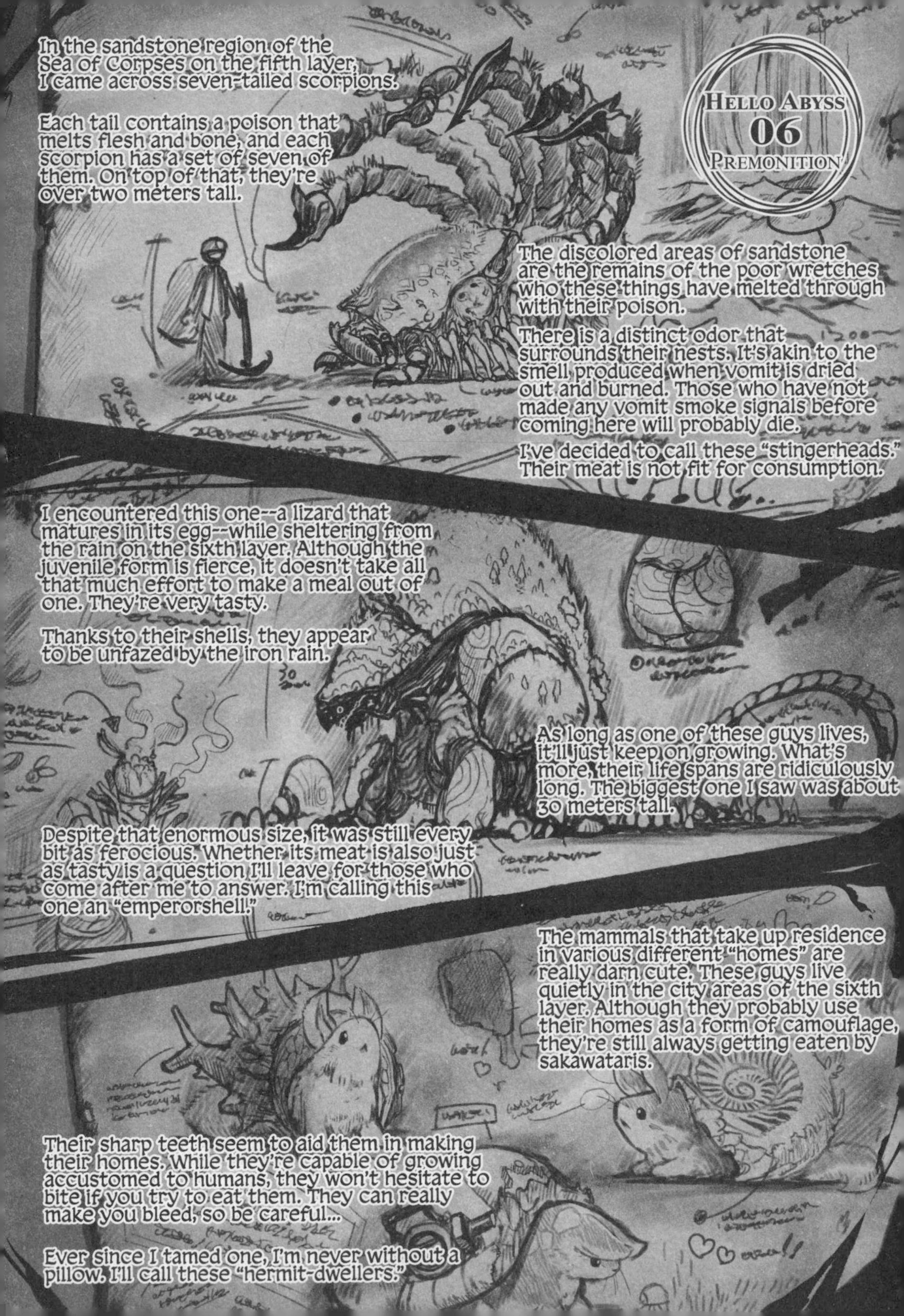
HELLO ABYSS 06 PREMONITION
In the sandstone region of the Sea of Corpses on the fifth layer, I came across seven-tailed scorpions.
Each tail contains a poison that melts flesh and bone, and each scorpion has a set of seven of them. On top of that, they're over two meters tall.
The discolored areas of sandstone are the remains of the poor wretches who these things have melted through with their poison.
There is a distinct odor that surrounds their nests. It's akin to the smell produced when vomit is dried out and burned. Those who have not made any vomit smoke signals before coming here will probably die.
I've decided to call these "stingerheads." Their meat is not fit for consumption.
I encountered this one--a lizard that matures in its egg--while sheltering from the rain on the sixth layer. Although the juvenile form is fierce, it doesn't take all that much effort to make a meal out of one. They're very tasty.
Thanks to their shells, they appear to be unfazed by the iron rain.
As long as one of these guys lives, it'll just keep on growing. What's more, their life spans are ridiculously long. The biggest one I saw was about 30 meters tall.
Despite that enormous size, it was still every bit as ferocious. Whether its meat is also just as tasty is a question I'll leave for those who come after me to answer. I'm calling this one an "emperorshell."
The mammals that take up residence in various different "homes" are really darn cute. These guys live quietly in the city areas of the sixth layer. Although they probably use their homes as a form of camouflage, they're still always getting eaten by sakawataris.
Their sharp teeth seem to aid them in making their homes. While they're capable of growing accustomed to humans, they won't hesitate to bite if you try to eat them. They can really make you bleed, so be careful...
Ever since I tamed one, I'm never without a pillow. I'll call these "hermit-dwellers."

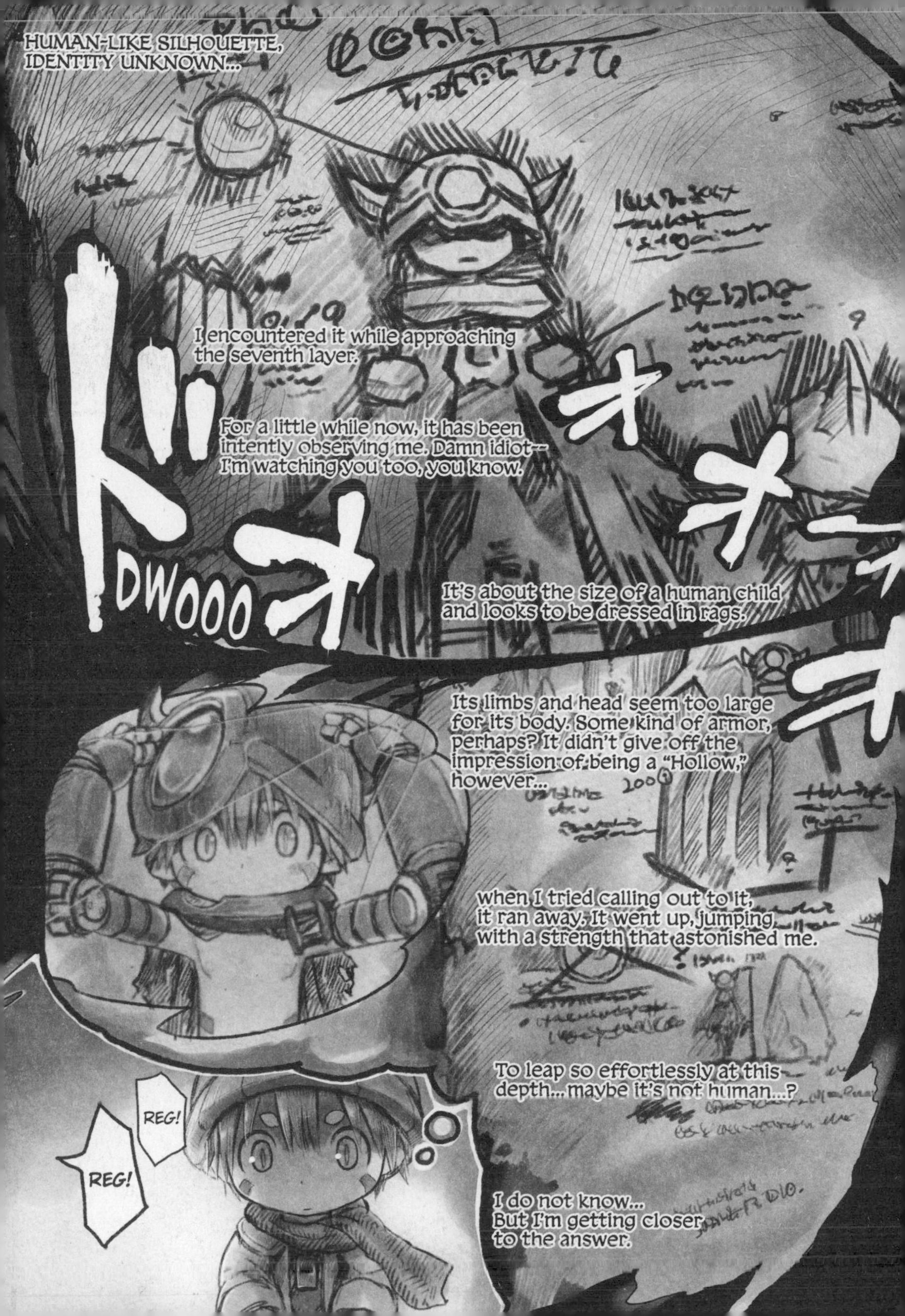
HUMAN-LIKE SILHOUETTE, IDENTITY UNKNOWN...
I encountered it while approaching the seventh layer.
For a little while now, it has been intently observing me. Damn idiot-- I'm watching you too, you know.
ドオオオオ
DWOOO
It's about the size of a human child and looks to be dressed in rags.
Its limbs and head seem too large for its body. Some kind of armor, perhaps? It didn't give off the impression of being a "Hollow," however...
when I tried calling out to it, it ran away. It went up, jumping with a strength that astonished me.
To leap so effortlessly at this depth... maybe it's not human...?
REG!
REG!
I do not know... But I'm getting closer to the answer.

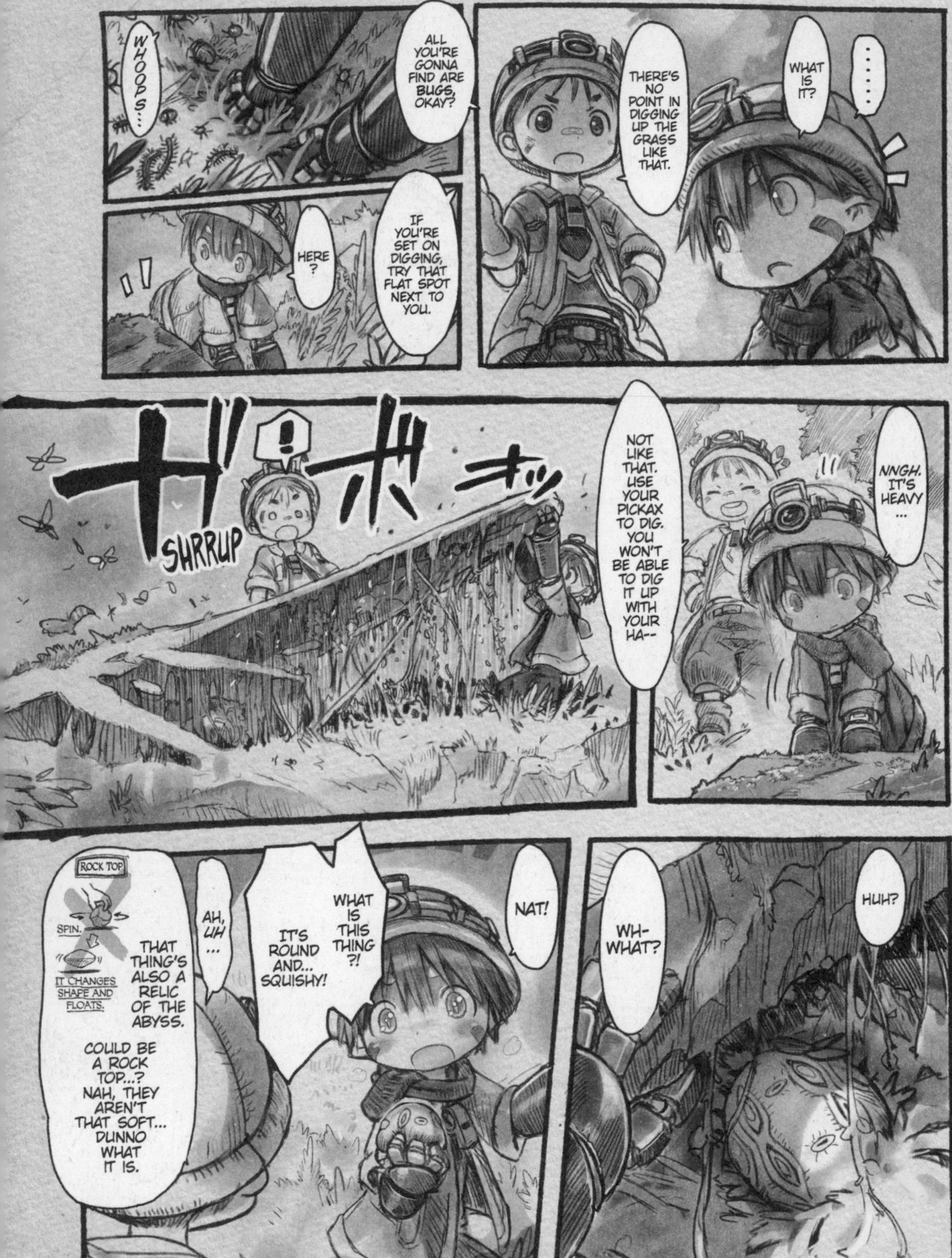
......
WHAT IS IT?
THERE'S NO POINT IN DIGGING UP THE GRASS LIKE THAT.
ALL YOU'RE GONNA FIND ARE BUGS, OKAY?
WHOOPS...
IF YOU'RE SET ON DIGGING, TRY THAT FLAT SPOT NEXT TO YOU.
HERE?
NNGH. IT'S HEAVY...
NOT LIKE THAT. USE YOUR PICKAX TO DIG. YOU WON'T BE ABLE TO DIG IT UP WITH YOUR HA--
キッ
ザボ
!
SHRRUP
HUH?
WH-WHAT?
NAT!
WHAT IS THIS THING?!
IT'S ROUND AND... SQUISHY!
AH, UH...
THAT THING'S ALSO A RELIC OF THE ABYSS.
COULD BE A ROCK TOP...? NAH, THEY AREN'T THAT SOFT... DUNNO WHAT IT IS.
ROCK TOP
SPIN.
IT CHANGES SHAPE AND FLOATS.

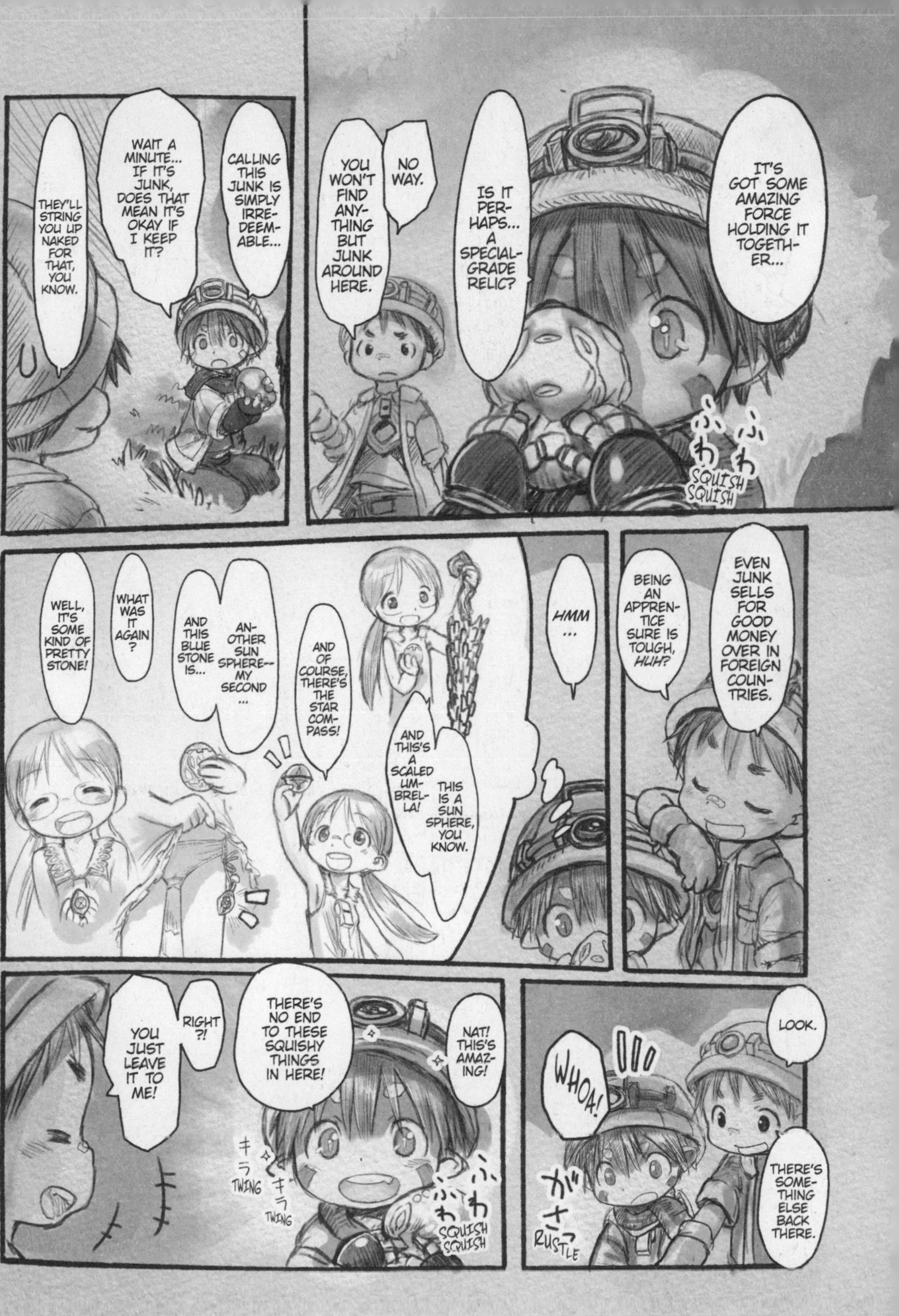
IT'S GOT SOME AMAZING FORCE HOLDING IT TOGETHER...
IS IT PERHAPS... A SPECIAL-GRADE RELIC?
NO WAY.
YOU WON'T FIND ANYTHING BUT JUNK AROUND HERE.
ふわ ふわ
SQUISH SQUISH
CALLING THIS JUNK IS SIMPLY IRREDEEMABLE...
WAIT A MINUTE... IF IT'S JUNK, DOES THAT MEAN IT'S OKAY IF I KEEP IT?
THEY'LL STRING YOU UP NAKED FOR THAT, YOU KNOW.
EVEN JUNK SELLS FOR GOOD MONEY OVER IN FOREIGN COUNTRIES.
BEING AN APPRENTICE SURE IS TOUGH, *HUH?*
HMM...
AND OF COURSE, THERE'S THE STAR COMPASS!
ANOTHER SUN SPHERE-- MY SECOND...
AND THIS BLUE STONE IS...
WHAT WAS IT AGAIN?
WELL, IT'S SOME KIND OF PRETTY STONE!
AND THIS'S A SCALED UMBRELLA!
THIS IS A SUN SPHERE, YOU KNOW.
LOOK.
WHOA!
THERE'S SOMETHING ELSE BACK THERE.
がさっ
RUSTLE
NAT! THIS'S AMAZING!
THERE'S NO END TO THESE SQUISHY THINGS IN HERE!
RIGHT?!
YOU JUST LEAVE IT TO ME!
キラ キラ
TWING TWING
ふわ ふわ
SQUISH SQUISH

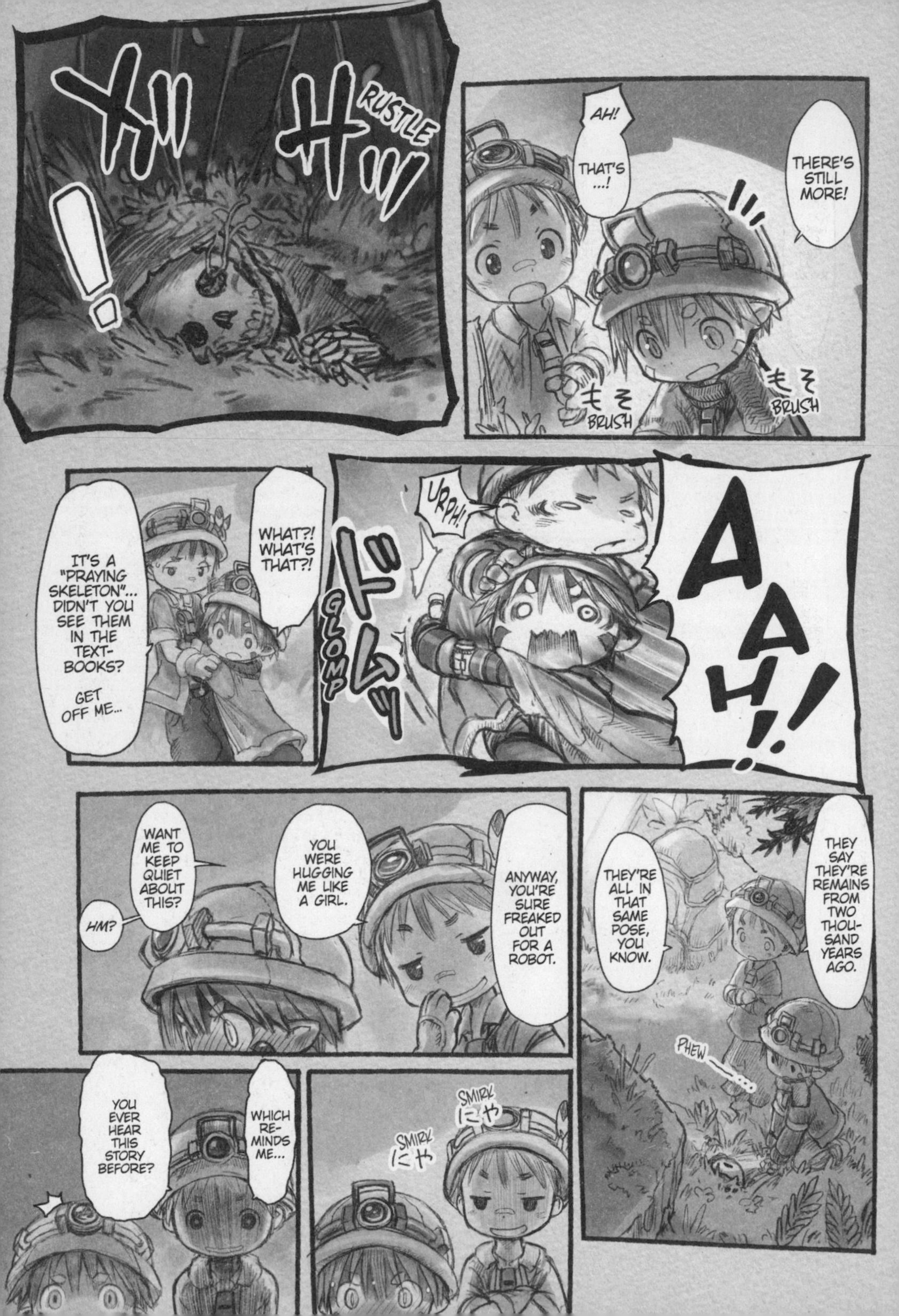
THERE'S STILL MORE!
AH! THAT'S ...!
もそ BRUSH
もそ BRUSH
RUSTLE
!
AAH!!
URPH!
GLOMP
WHAT?! WHAT'S THAT?!
IT'S A "PRAYING SKELETON"... DIDN'T YOU SEE THEM IN THE TEXT-BOOKS?
GET OFF ME...
THEY SAY THEY'RE REMAINS FROM TWO THOU-SAND YEARS AGO.
THEY'RE ALL IN THAT SAME POSE, YOU KNOW.
PHEW
ANYWAY, YOU'RE SURE FREAKED OUT FOR A ROBOT.
YOU WERE HUGGING ME LIKE A GIRL.
WANT ME TO KEEP QUIET ABOUT THIS?
HM?
SMIRK にや
SMIRK にや
WHICH RE-MINDS ME...
YOU EVER HEAR THIS STORY BEFORE?

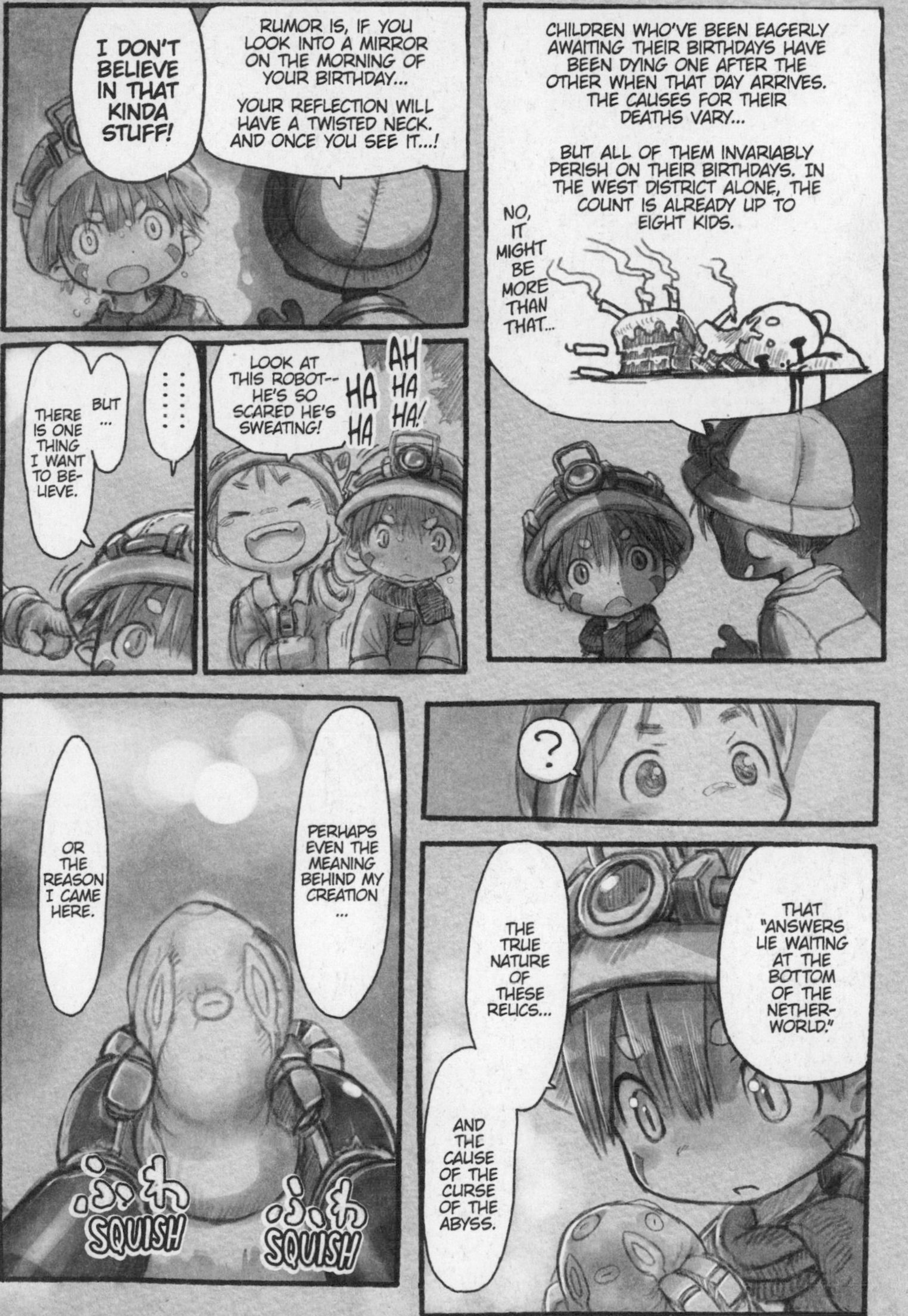
CHILDREN WHO'VE BEEN EAGERLY AWAITING THEIR BIRTHDAYS HAVE BEEN DYING ONE AFTER THE OTHER WHEN THAT DAY ARRIVES. THE CAUSES FOR THEIR DEATHS VARY...
BUT ALL OF THEM INVARIABLY PERISH ON THEIR BIRTHDAYS. IN THE WEST DISTRICT ALONE, THE COUNT IS ALREADY UP TO EIGHT KIDS.
NO, IT MIGHT BE MORE THAN THAT...
RUMOR IS, IF YOU LOOK INTO A MIRROR ON THE MORNING OF YOUR BIRTHDAY...
YOUR REFLECTION WILL HAVE A TWISTED NECK. AND ONCE YOU SEE IT...!
I DON'T BELIEVE IN THAT KINDA STUFF!
AH HA HA HA!
HA HA
LOOK AT THIS ROBOT-- HE'S SO SCARED HE'S SWEATING!
......
BUT ...
THERE IS ONE THING I WANT TO BE-LIEVE.
?
THAT "ANSWERS LIE WAITING AT THE BOTTOM OF THE NETHER-WORLD."
THE TRUE NATURE OF THESE RELICS...
AND THE CAUSE OF THE CURSE OF THE ABYSS.
PERHAPS EVEN THE MEANING BEHIND MY CREATION ...
OR THE REASON I CAME HERE.
ふわ SQUISH
ふわ SQUISH

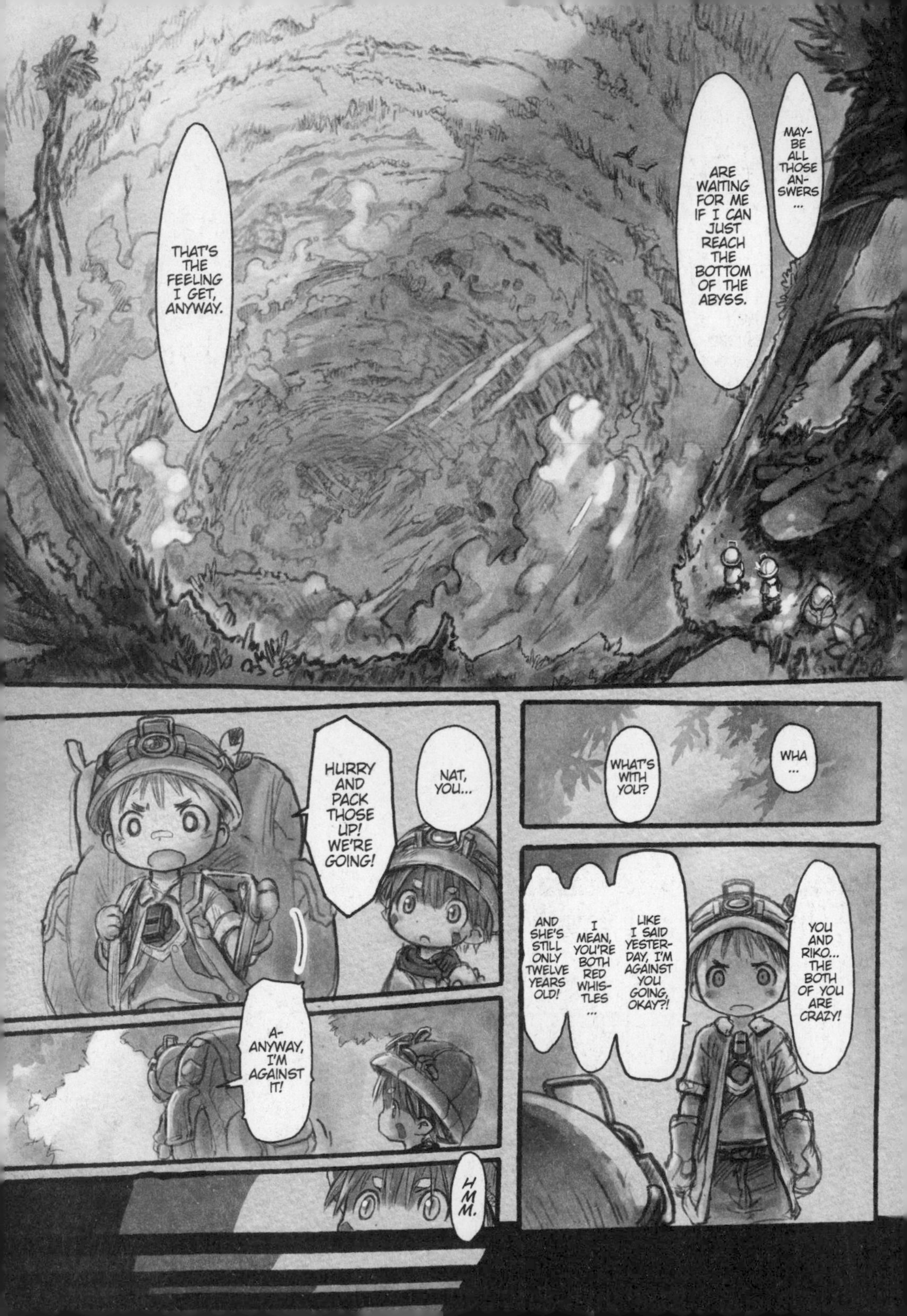
MAY-BE ALL THOSE AN-SWERS...
ARE WAITING FOR ME IF I CAN JUST REACH THE BOTTOM OF THE ABYSS.
THAT'S THE FEELING I GET, ANYWAY.
WHA...
WHAT'S WITH YOU?
YOU AND RIKO... THE BOTH OF YOU ARE CRAZY!
LIKE I SAID YESTER-DAY, I'M AGAINST YOU GOING, OKAY?!
I MEAN, YOU'RE BOTH RED WHIS-TLES...
AND SHE'S STILL ONLY TWELVE YEARS OLD!
NAT, YOU...
HURRY AND PACK THOSE UP! WE'RE GOING!
A-ANYWAY, I'M AGAINST IT!
HMM.

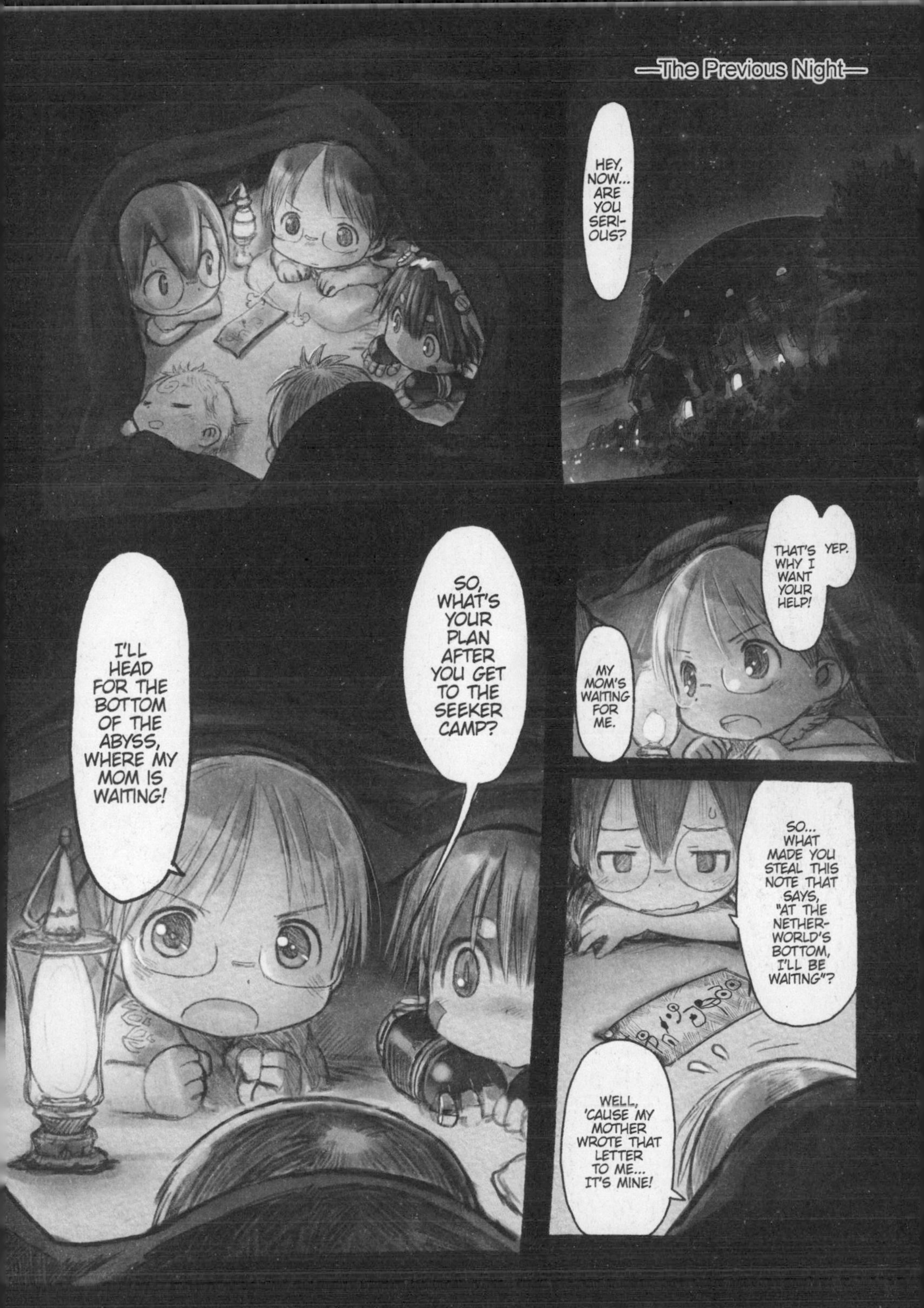
—The Previous Night—
HEY, NOW... ARE YOU SERIOUS?
YEP.
THAT'S WHY I WANT YOUR HELP!
MY MOM'S WAITING FOR ME.
SO... WHAT MADE YOU STEAL THIS NOTE THAT SAYS, "AT THE NETHER-WORLD'S BOTTOM, I'LL BE WAITING"?
WELL, 'CAUSE MY MOTHER WROTE THAT LETTER TO ME... IT'S MINE!
SO, WHAT'S YOUR PLAN AFTER YOU GET TO THE SEEKER CAMP?
I'LL HEAD FOR THE BOTTOM OF THE ABYSS, WHERE MY MOM IS WAITING!

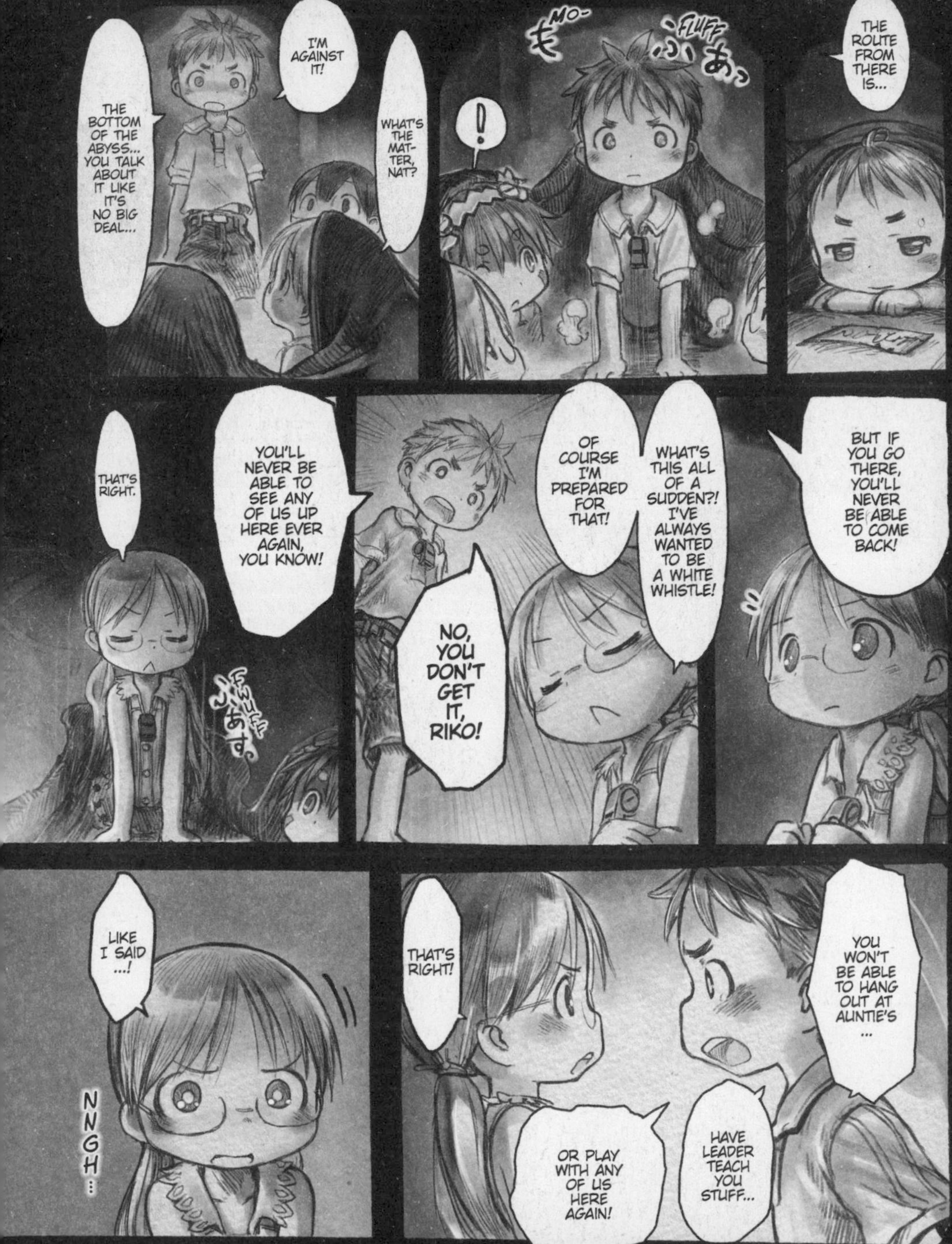
THE ROUTE FROM THERE IS...
MO-
FLUFF
!
WHAT'S THE MAT-TER, NAT?
I'M AGAINST IT!
THE BOTTOM OF THE ABYSS... YOU TALK ABOUT IT LIKE IT'S NO BIG DEAL...
BUT IF YOU GO THERE, YOU'LL NEVER BE ABLE TO COME BACK!
WHAT'S THIS ALL OF A SUDDEN?! I'VE ALWAYS WANTED TO BE A WHITE WHISTLE!
OF COURSE I'M PREPARED FOR THAT!
NO, YOU DON'T GET IT, RIKO!
YOU'LL NEVER BE ABLE TO SEE ANY OF US UP HERE EVER AGAIN, YOU KNOW!
THAT'S RIGHT.
FWUFF
YOU WON'T BE ABLE TO HANG OUT AT AUNTIE'S ...
THAT'S RIGHT!
HAVE LEADER TEACH YOU STUFF...
OR PLAY WITH ANY OF US HERE AGAIN!
LIKE I SAID ...!
NNGH...

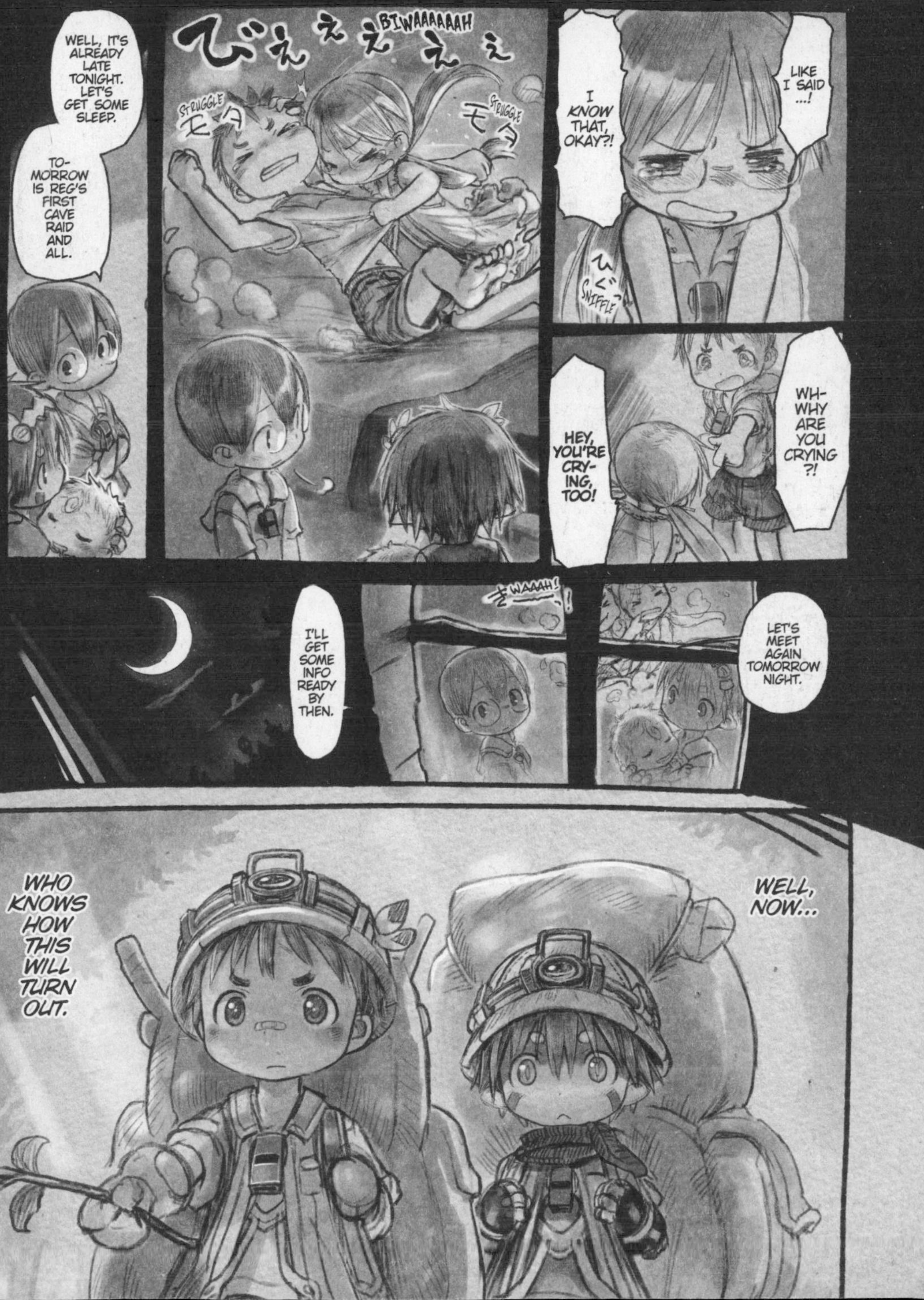
LIKE I SAID ...!
I KNOW THAT, OKAY?!
ひぐ SNIFFLE
WH-WHY ARE YOU CRYING?!
HEY, YOU'RE CRY-ING, TOO!
びえええええ BIWAAAAAAH
STRUGGLE モタ
STRUGGLE モタ
WELL, IT'S ALREADY LATE TONIGHT. LET'S GET SOME SLEEP.
TO-MORROW IS REG'S FIRST CAVE RAID AND ALL.
WAAAH!
LET'S MEET AGAIN TOMORROW NIGHT.
I'LL GET SOME INFO READY BY THEN.
WELL, NOW...
WHO KNOWS HOW THIS WILL TURN OUT.

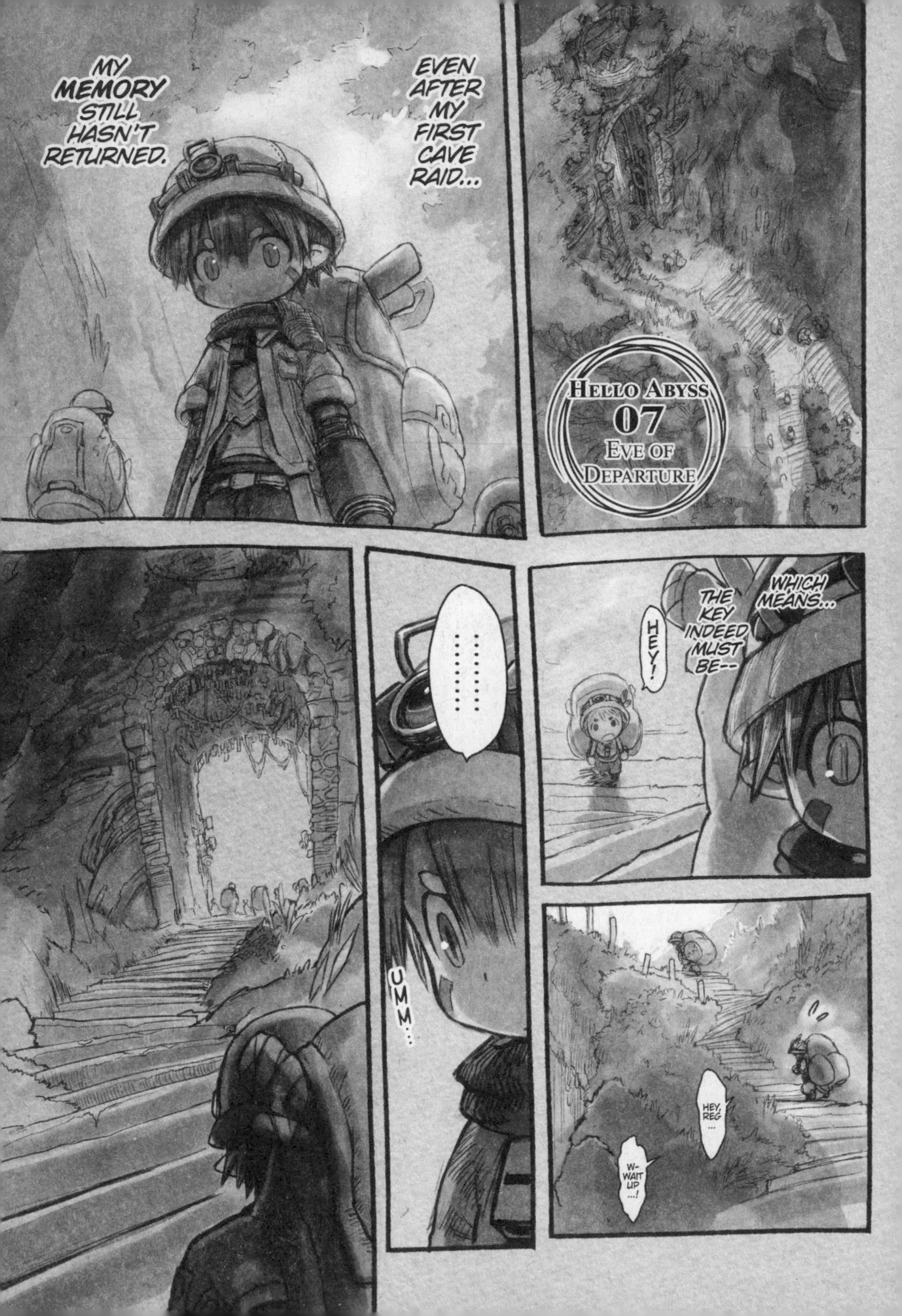
HELLO ABYSS
07
EVE OF DEPARTURE
EVEN AFTER MY FIRST CAVE RAID...
MY MEMORY STILL HASN'T RETURNED.
WHICH MEANS...
THE KEY INDEED MUST BE--
HEY!
HEY, REG...
W-WAIT UP...!
......
UMM..

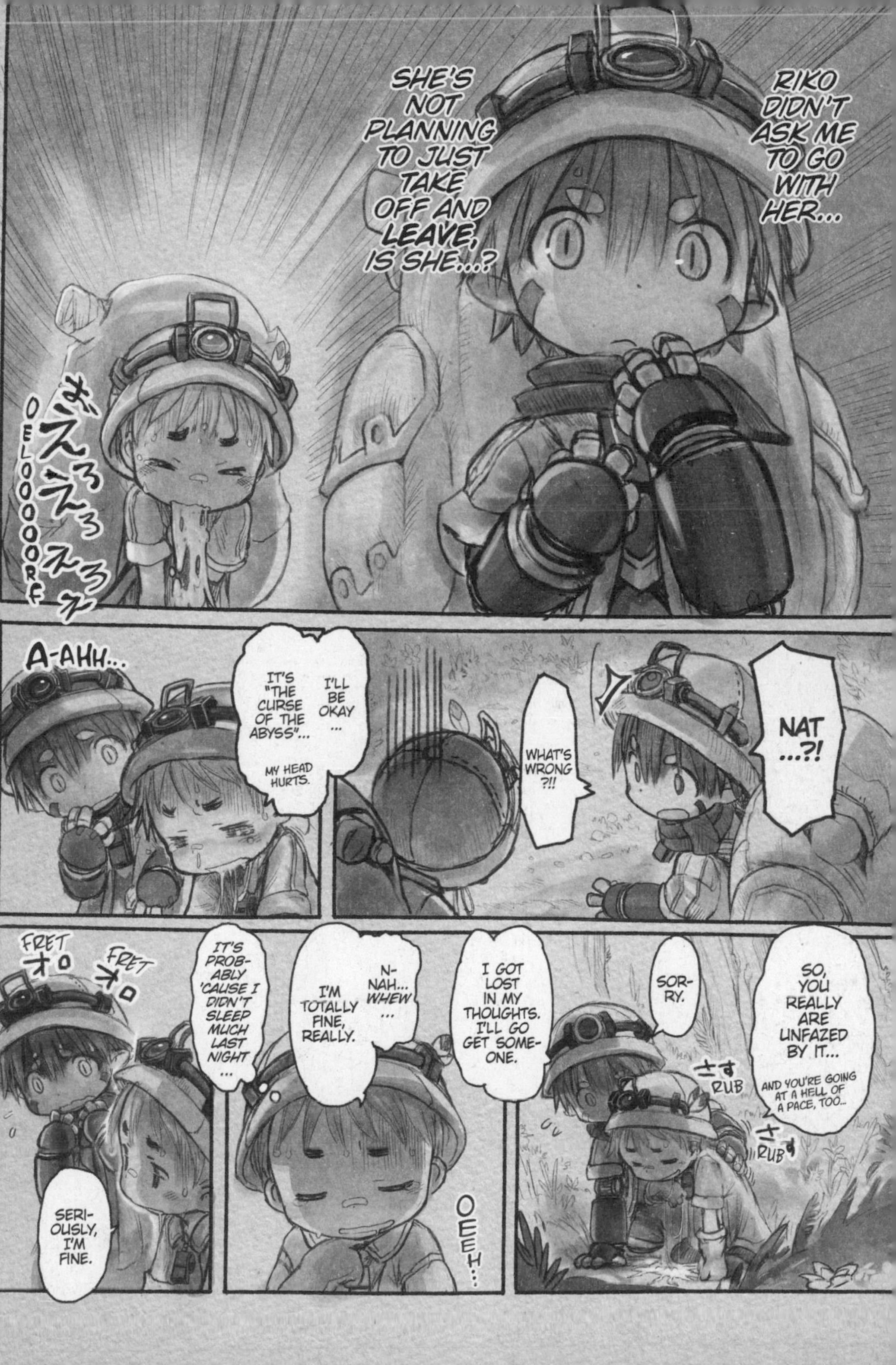
RIKO DIDN'T ASK ME TO GO WITH HER...
SHE'S NOT PLANNING TO JUST TAKE OFF AND LEAVE, IS SHE...?
おええろえろえ
OELOOOOOORF
NAT ...?!
WHAT'S WRONG ?!!
A-AHH...
I'LL BE OKAY ...
IT'S "THE CURSE OF THE ABYSS"...
MY HEAD HURTS.
SO, YOU REALLY ARE UNFAZED BY IT...
AND YOU'RE GOING AT A HELL OF A PACE, TOO...
SOR-RY.
さす RUB
さす RUB
I GOT LOST IN MY THOUGHTS. I'LL GO GET SOME-ONE.
N-NAH... WHEW ...
I'M TOTALLY FINE, REALLY.
OEEH...
FRET オロ
FRET オロ
IT'S PROB-ABLY 'CAUSE I DIDN'T SLEEP MUCH LAST NIGHT ...
SERI-OUSLY, I'M FINE.

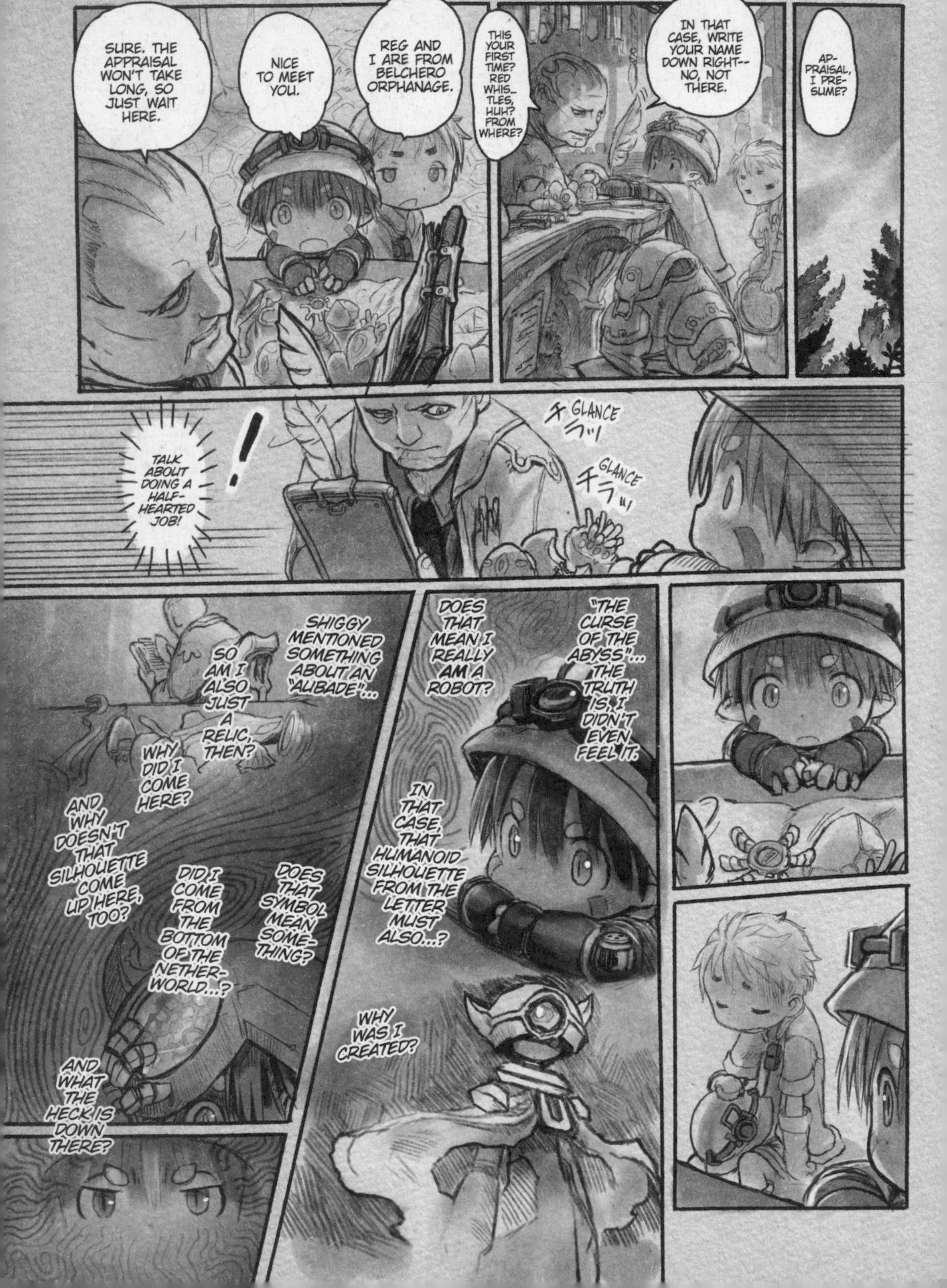
AP-PRAISAL, I PRE-SUME?
IN THAT CASE, WRITE YOUR NAME DOWN RIGHT--NO, NOT THERE.
THIS YOUR FIRST TIME? RED WHIS-TLES, HUH? FROM WHERE?
REG AND I ARE FROM BELCHERO ORPHANAGE.
NICE TO MEET YOU.
SURE. THE APPRAISAL WON'T TAKE LONG, SO JUST WAIT HERE.
GLANCE
GLANCE
!
TALK ABOUT DOING A HALF-HEARTED JOB!
"THE CURSE OF THE ABYSS"... THE TRUTH IS, I DIDN'T EVEN FEEL IT.
DOES THAT MEAN I REALLY AM A ROBOT?
IN THAT CASE, THAT HUMANOID SILHOUETTE FROM THE LETTER MUST ALSO...?
WHY WAS I CREATED?
SHIGGY MENTIONED SOMETHING ABOUT AN "AUBADE"...
SO AM I ALSO JUST A RELIC, THEN?
WHY DID I COME HERE?
AND WHY DOESN'T THAT SILHOUETTE COME UP HERE, TOO?
DOES THAT SYMBOL MEAN SOME-THING?
DID I COME FROM THE BOTTOM OF THE NETHER-WORLD...?
AND WHAT THE HECK IS DOWN THERE?

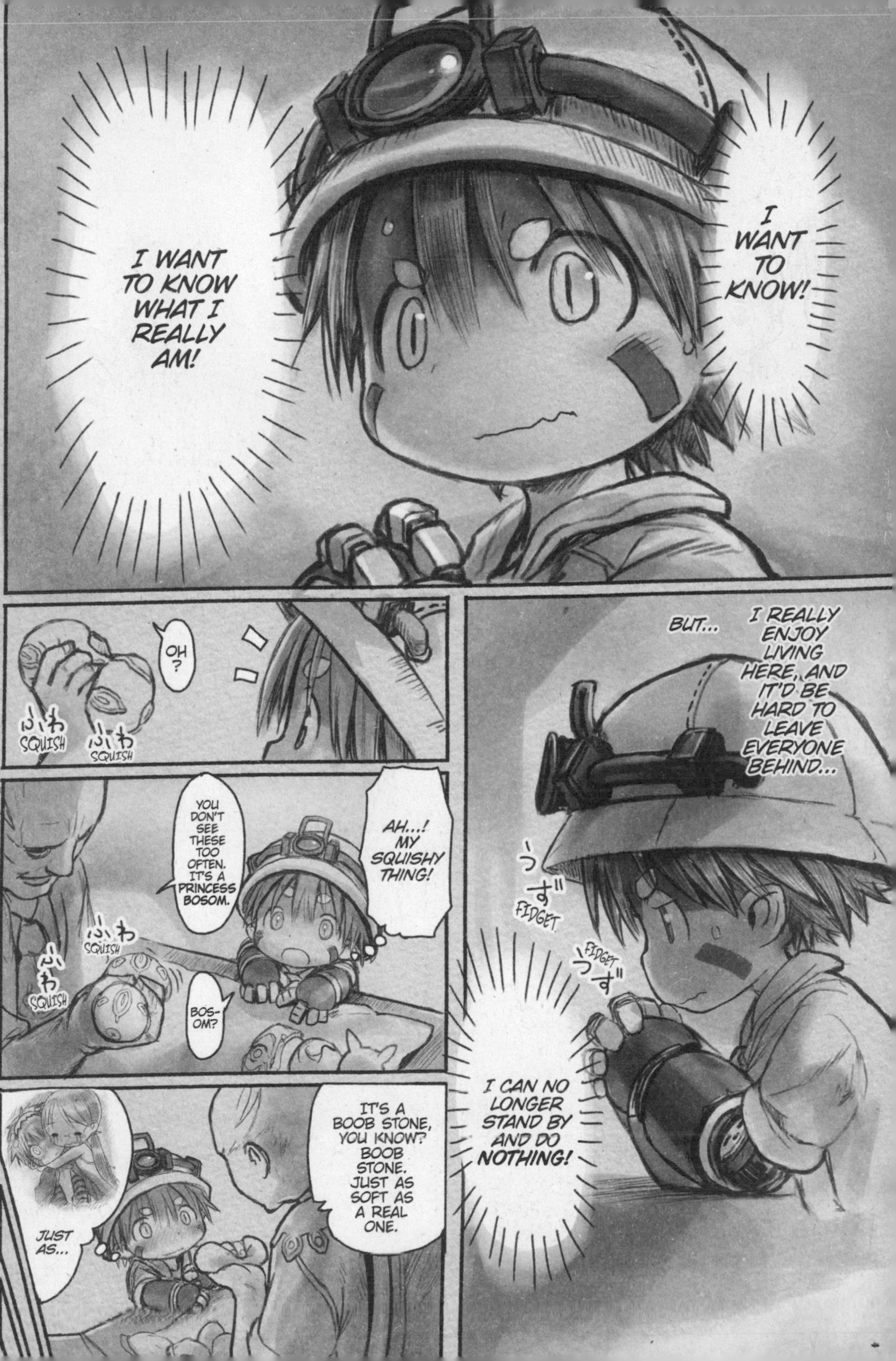
I WANT TO KNOW!
I WANT TO KNOW WHAT I REALLY AM!
BUT...
I REALLY ENJOY LIVING HERE, AND IT'D BE HARD TO LEAVE EVERYONE BEHIND...
うず FIDGET
うず FIDGET
I CAN NO LONGER STAND BY AND DO NOTHING!
OH?
ふわ SQUISH
ふわ SQUISH
AH...! MY SQUISHY THING!
YOU DON'T SEE THESE TOO OFTEN. IT'S A PRINCESS BOSOM.
ふわ SQUISH
ふわ SQUISH
BOS-OM?
IT'S A BOOB STONE, YOU KNOW? BOOB STONE. JUST AS SOFT AS A REAL ONE.
JUST AS...

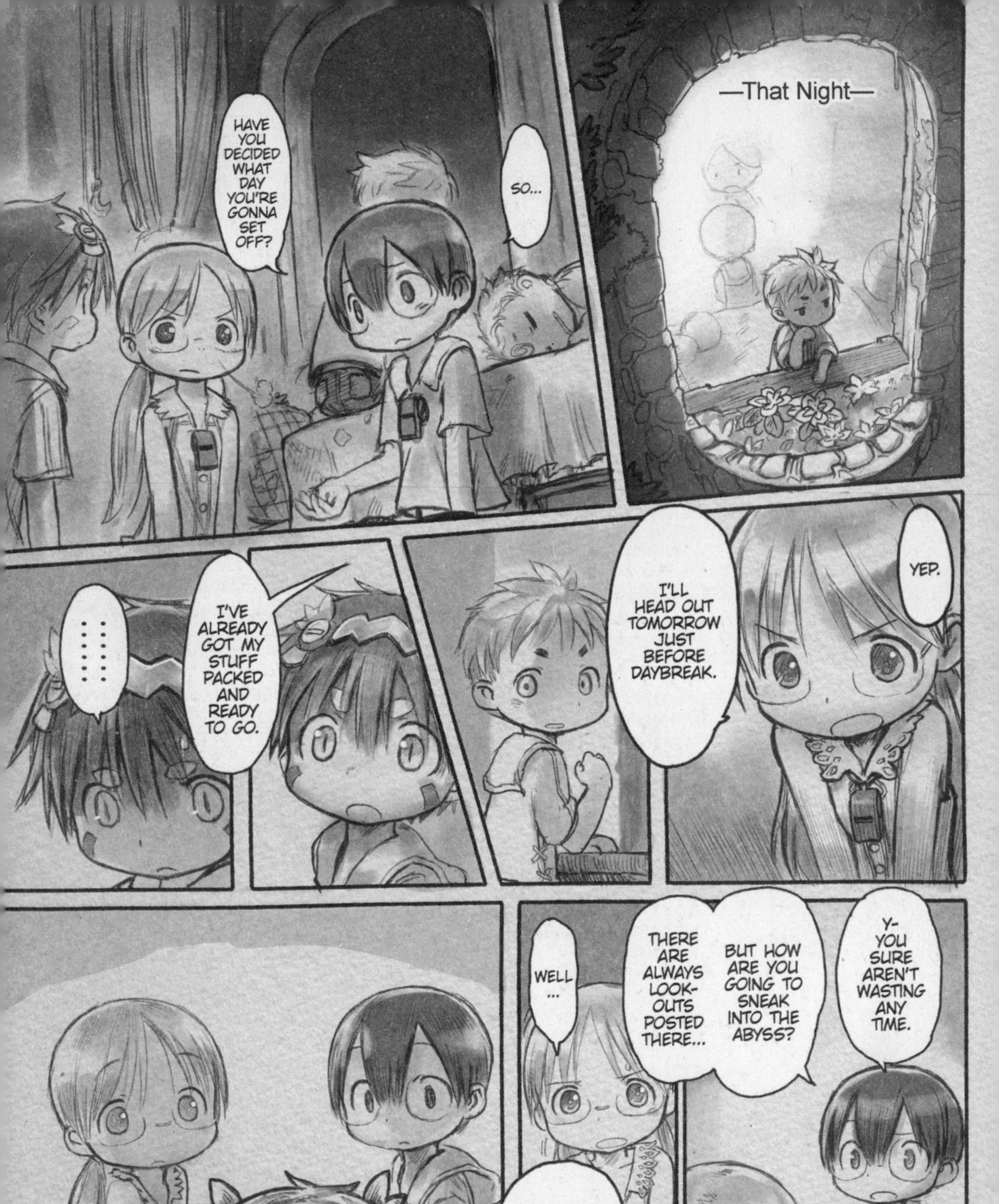
—That Night—
SO...
HAVE YOU DECIDED WHAT DAY YOU'RE GONNA SET OFF?
YEP.
I'LL HEAD OUT TOMORROW JUST BEFORE DAYBREAK.
I'VE ALREADY GOT MY STUFF PACKED AND READY TO GO.
......
Y-YOU SURE AREN'T WASTING ANY TIME.
BUT HOW ARE YOU GOING TO SNEAK INTO THE ABYSS?
THERE ARE ALWAYS LOOK-OUTS POSTED THERE...
WELL...
I'LL USE MY EXTENDABLE ARMS TO LOWER YOU DOWN.

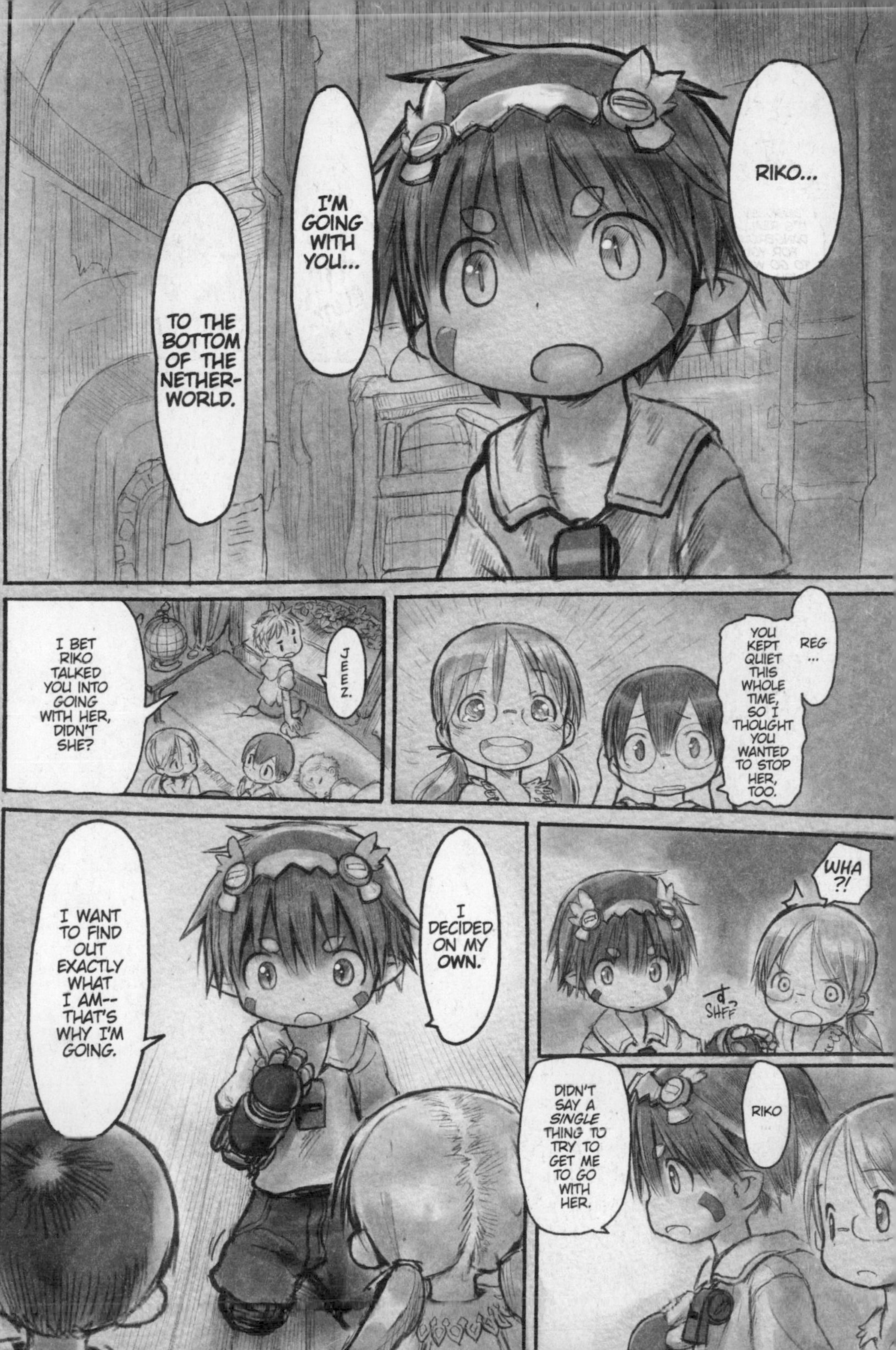
RIKO...
I'M GOING WITH YOU...
TO THE BOTTOM OF THE NETHER-WORLD.
REG ...
YOU KEPT QUIET THIS WHOLE TIME, SO I THOUGHT YOU WANTED TO STOP HER, TOO.
JEEZ.
I BET RIKO TALKED YOU INTO GOING WITH HER, DIDN'T SHE?
WHA ?!
SHFF
RIKO ...
DIDN'T SAY A SINGLE THING TO TRY TO GET ME TO GO WITH HER.
I DECIDED ON MY OWN.
I WANT TO FIND OUT EXACTLY WHAT I AM--THAT'S WHY I'M GOING.

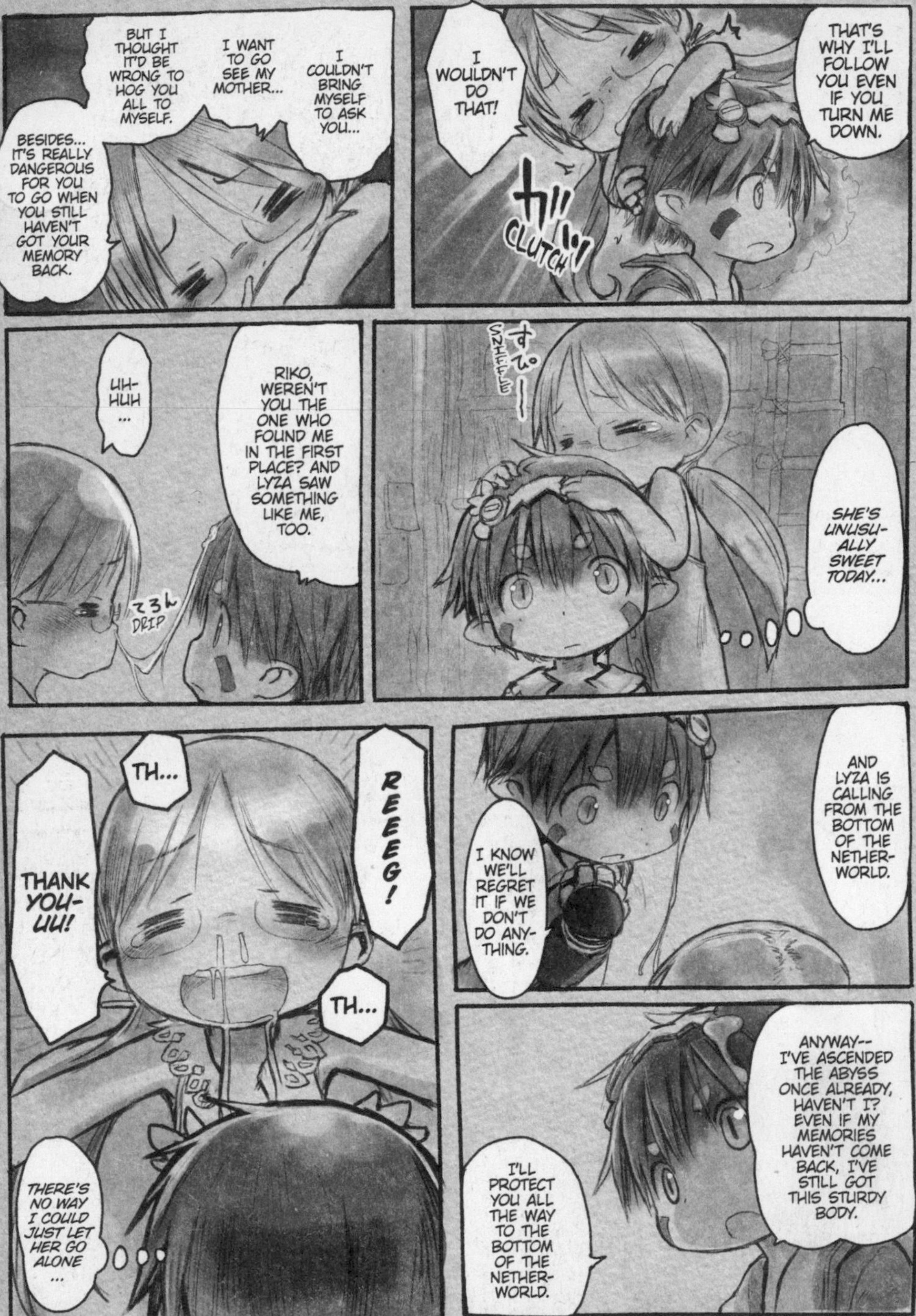
THAT'S WHY I'LL FOLLOW YOU EVEN IF YOU TURN ME DOWN.
I WOULDN'T DO THAT!
ガッ
CLUTCH
I COULDN'T BRING MYSELF TO ASK YOU...
I WANT TO GO SEE MY MOTHER...
BUT I THOUGHT IT'D BE WRONG TO HOG YOU ALL TO MYSELF.
BESIDES... IT'S REALLY DANGEROUS FOR YOU TO GO WHEN YOU STILL HAVEN'T GOT YOUR MEMORY BACK.
すぴー
SNIFFLE
SHE'S UNUSUALLY SWEET TODAY...
RIKO, WEREN'T YOU THE ONE WHO FOUND ME IN THE FIRST PLACE? AND LYZA SAW SOMETHING LIKE ME, TOO.
UH-HUH...
てろん
DRIP
AND LYZA IS CALLING FROM THE BOTTOM OF THE NETHERWORLD.
I KNOW WE'LL REGRET IT IF WE DON'T DO ANYTHING.
ANYWAY-- I'VE ASCENDED THE ABYSS ONCE ALREADY, HAVEN'T I? EVEN IF MY MEMORIES HAVEN'T COME BACK, I'VE STILL GOT THIS STURDY BODY.
I'LL PROTECT YOU ALL THE WAY TO THE BOTTOM OF THE NETHERWORLD.
REEEEG!
TH...
THANK YOU-UU!
TH...
THERE'S NO WAY I COULD JUST LET HER GO ALONE...

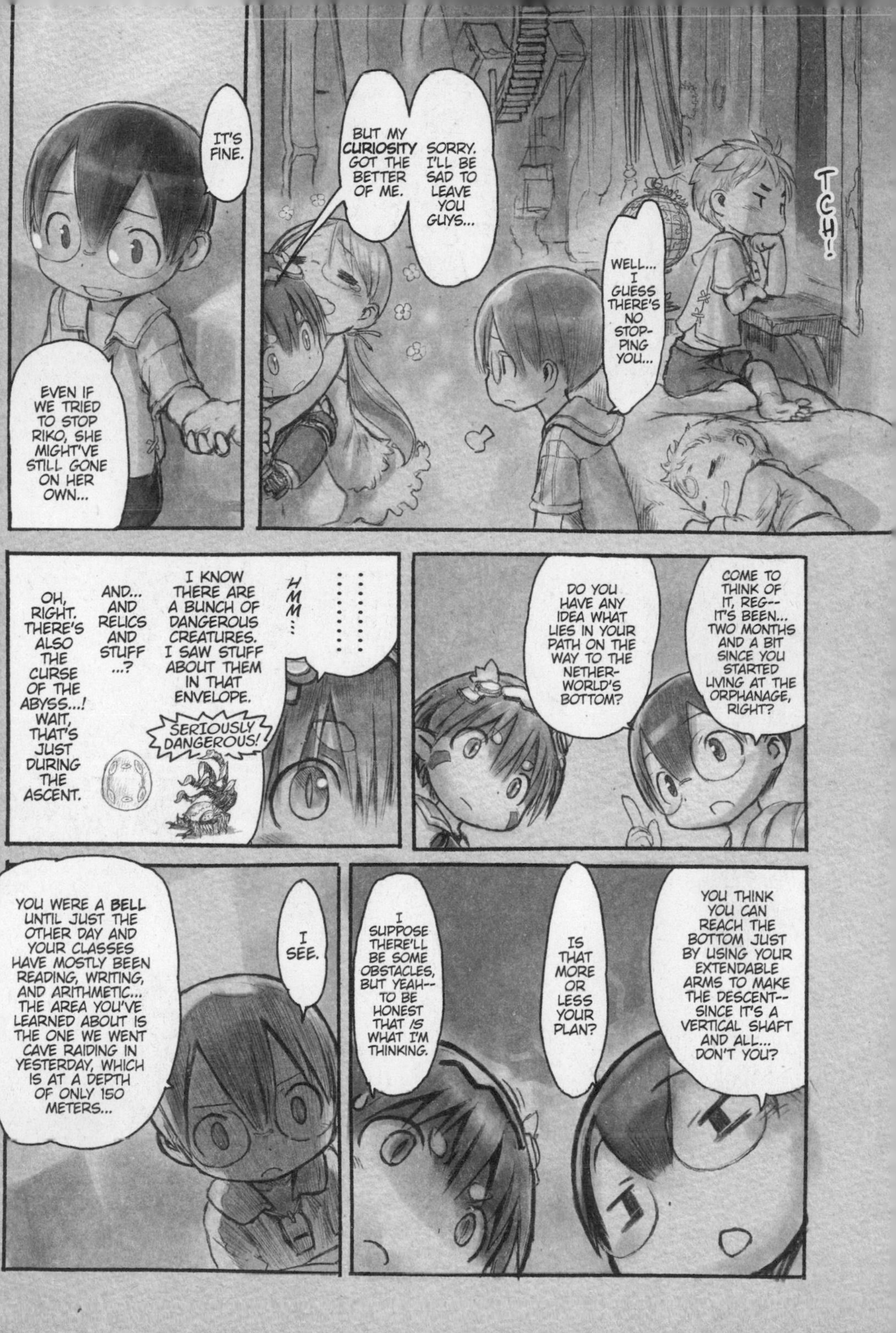
SORRY. I'LL BE SAD TO LEAVE YOU GUYS...
BUT MY **CURIOSITY** GOT THE BETTER OF ME.
WELL... I GUESS THERE'S NO STOPPING YOU...
TCH!
IT'S FINE.
EVEN IF WE TRIED TO STOP RIKO, SHE MIGHT'VE STILL GONE ON HER OWN...
COME TO THINK OF IT, REG--IT'S BEEN... TWO MONTHS AND A BIT SINCE YOU STARTED LIVING AT THE ORPHANAGE, RIGHT?
DO YOU HAVE ANY IDEA WHAT LIES IN YOUR PATH ON THE WAY TO THE NETHERWORLD'S BOTTOM?
......
HMM...
I KNOW THERE ARE A BUNCH OF DANGEROUS CREATURES. I SAW STUFF ABOUT THEM IN THAT ENVELOPE.
SERIOUSLY DANGEROUS!
AND... AND RELICS AND STUFF ...?
OH, RIGHT. THERE'S ALSO THE CURSE OF THE ABYSS...! WAIT, THAT'S JUST DURING THE ASCENT.
YOU THINK YOU CAN REACH THE BOTTOM JUST BY USING YOUR EXTENDABLE ARMS TO MAKE THE DESCENT--SINCE IT'S A VERTICAL SHAFT AND ALL... DON'T YOU?
IS THAT MORE OR LESS YOUR PLAN?
I SUPPOSE THERE'LL BE SOME OBSTACLES, BUT YEAH--TO BE HONEST THAT *IS* WHAT I'M THINKING.
I SEE.
YOU WERE A **BELL** UNTIL JUST THE OTHER DAY AND YOUR CLASSES HAVE MOSTLY BEEN READING, WRITING, AND ARITHMETIC... THE AREA YOU'VE LEARNED ABOUT IS THE ONE WE WENT CAVE RAIDING IN YESTERDAY, WHICH IS AT A DEPTH OF ONLY 150 METERS...

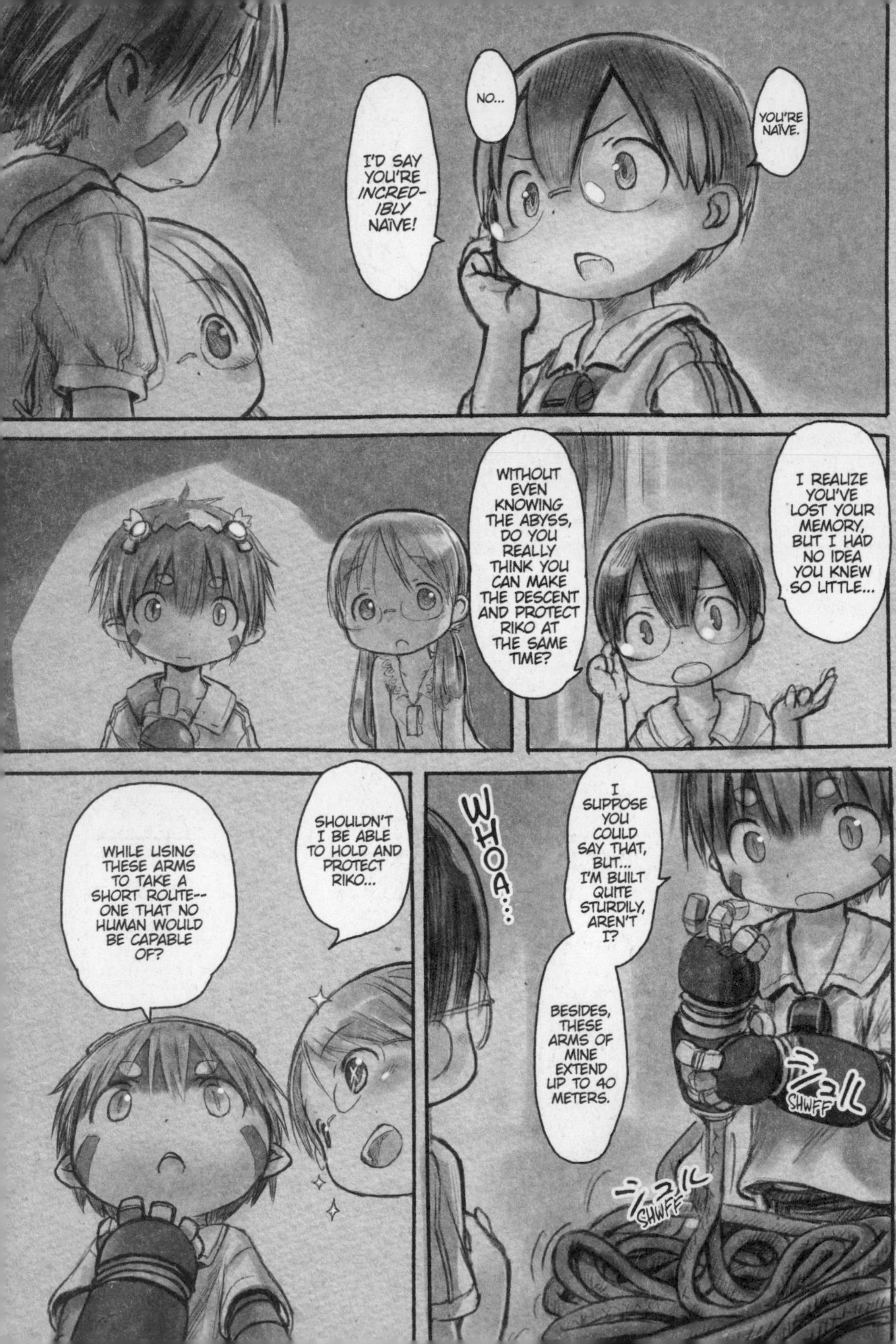
YOU'RE NAÏVE.
NO...
I'D SAY YOU'RE INCRED-IBLY NAÏVE!
I REALIZE YOU'VE LOST YOUR MEMORY, BUT I HAD NO IDEA YOU KNEW SO LITTLE...
WITHOUT EVEN KNOWING THE ABYSS, DO YOU REALLY THINK YOU CAN MAKE THE DESCENT AND PROTECT RIKO AT THE SAME TIME?
I SUPPOSE YOU COULD SAY THAT, BUT... I'M BUILT QUITE STURDILY, AREN'T I?
WHOA...
BESIDES, THESE ARMS OF MINE EXTEND UP TO 40 METERS.
シュル
SHWFF
シュル
SHWFF
SHOULDN'T I BE ABLE TO HOLD AND PROTECT RIKO...
WHILE USING THESE ARMS TO TAKE A SHORT ROUTE-- ONE THAT NO HUMAN WOULD BE CAPABLE OF?

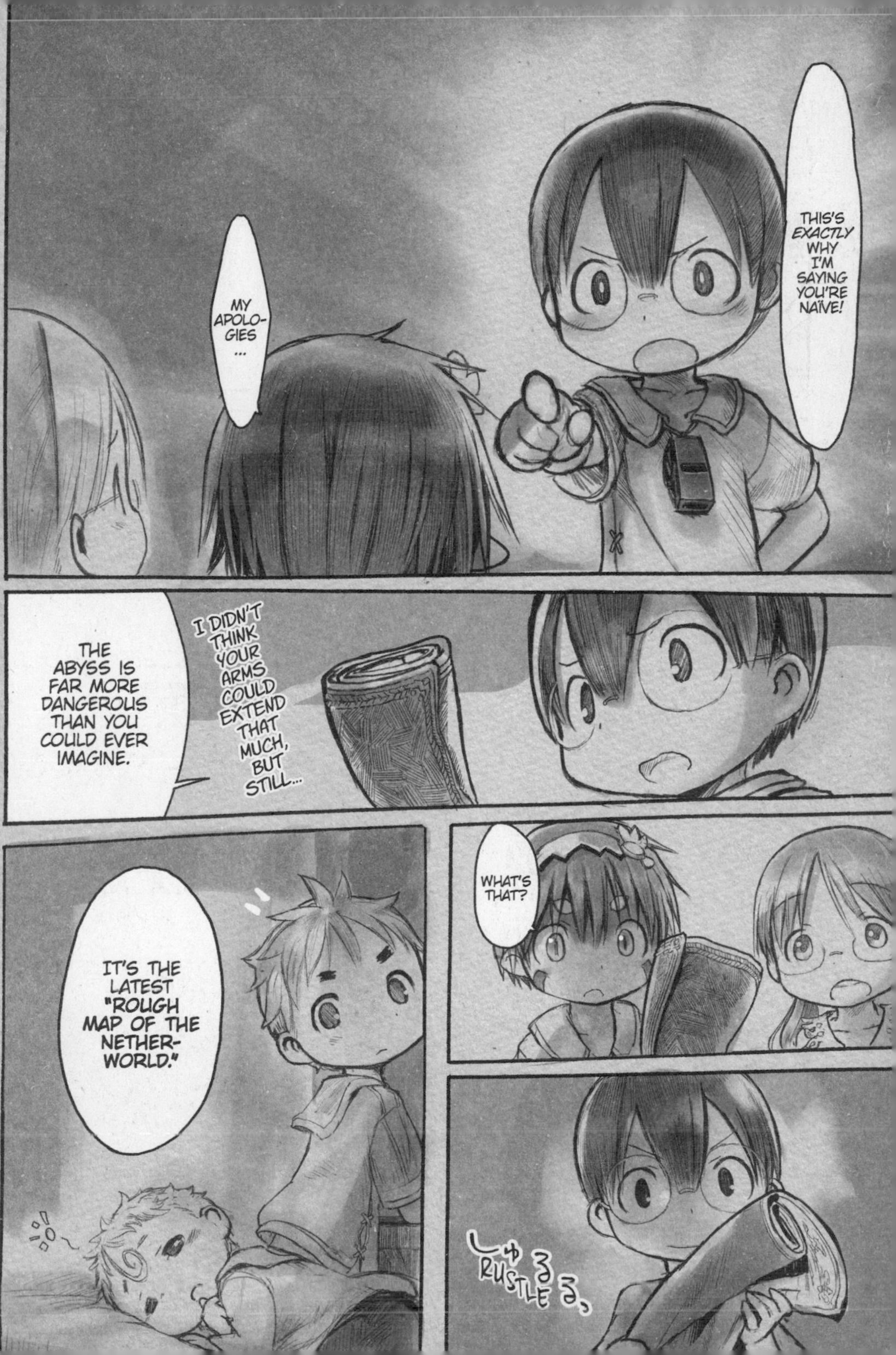
THIS'S EXACTLY WHY I'M SAYING YOU'RE NAÏVE!
MY APOLOGIES...
I DIDN'T THINK YOUR ARMS COULD EXTEND THAT MUCH, BUT STILL...
THE ABYSS IS FAR MORE DANGEROUS THAN YOU COULD EVER IMAGINE.
WHAT'S THAT?
RUSTLE
IT'S THE LATEST "ROUGH MAP OF THE NETHER-WORLD."

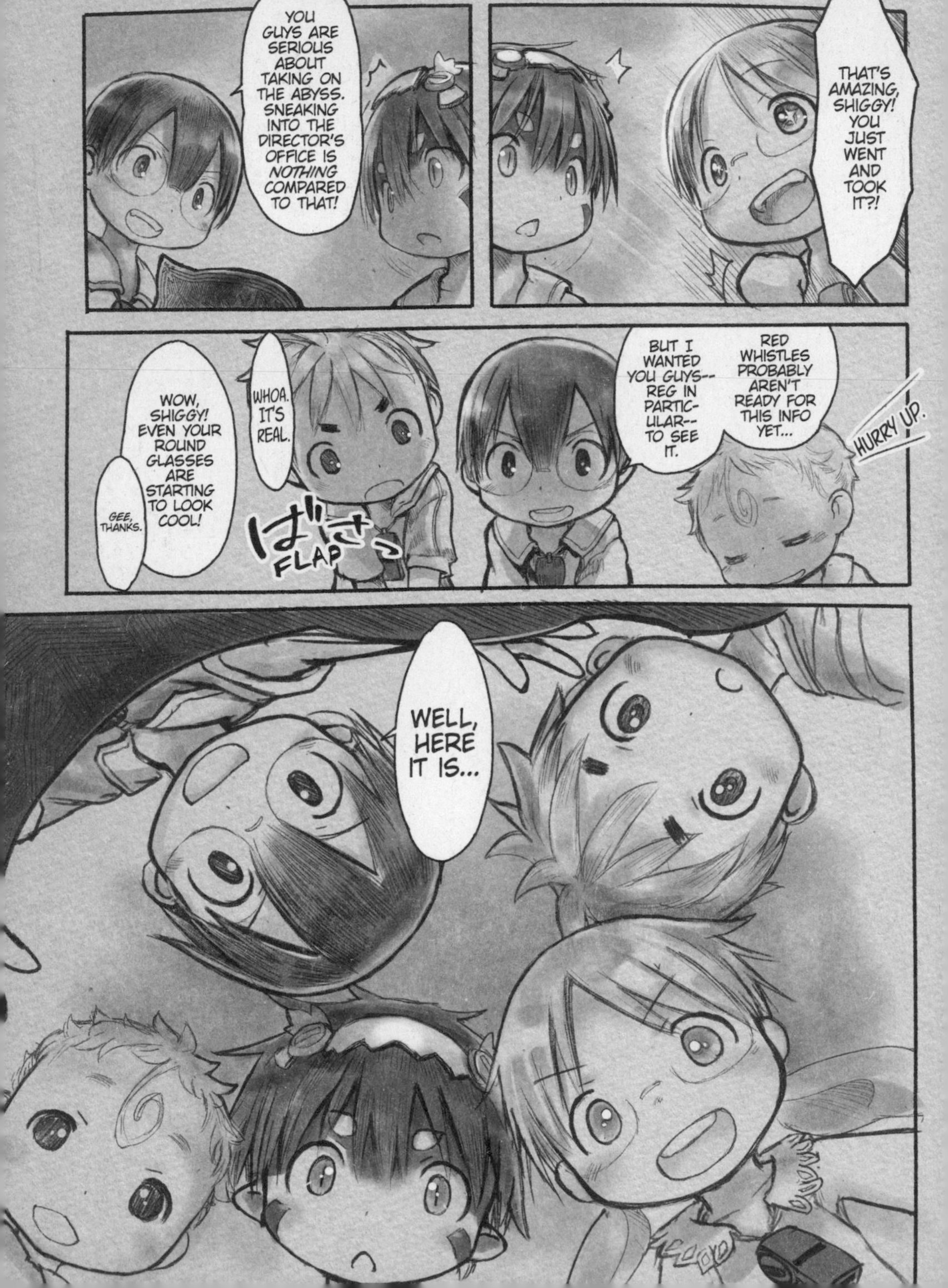
THAT'S AMAZING, SHIGGY! YOU JUST WENT AND TOOK IT?!
YOU GUYS ARE SERIOUS ABOUT TAKING ON THE ABYSS. SNEAKING INTO THE DIRECTOR'S OFFICE IS *NOTHING* COMPARED TO THAT!
HURRY UP.
RED WHISTLES PROBABLY AREN'T READY FOR THIS INFO YET...
BUT I WANTED YOU GUYS--REG IN PARTICULAR--TO SEE IT.
WHOA. IT'S REAL.
WOW, SHIGGY! EVEN YOUR ROUND GLASSES ARE STARTING TO LOOK COOL!
ばさっ
FLAP
GEE, THANKS.
WELL, HERE IT IS...

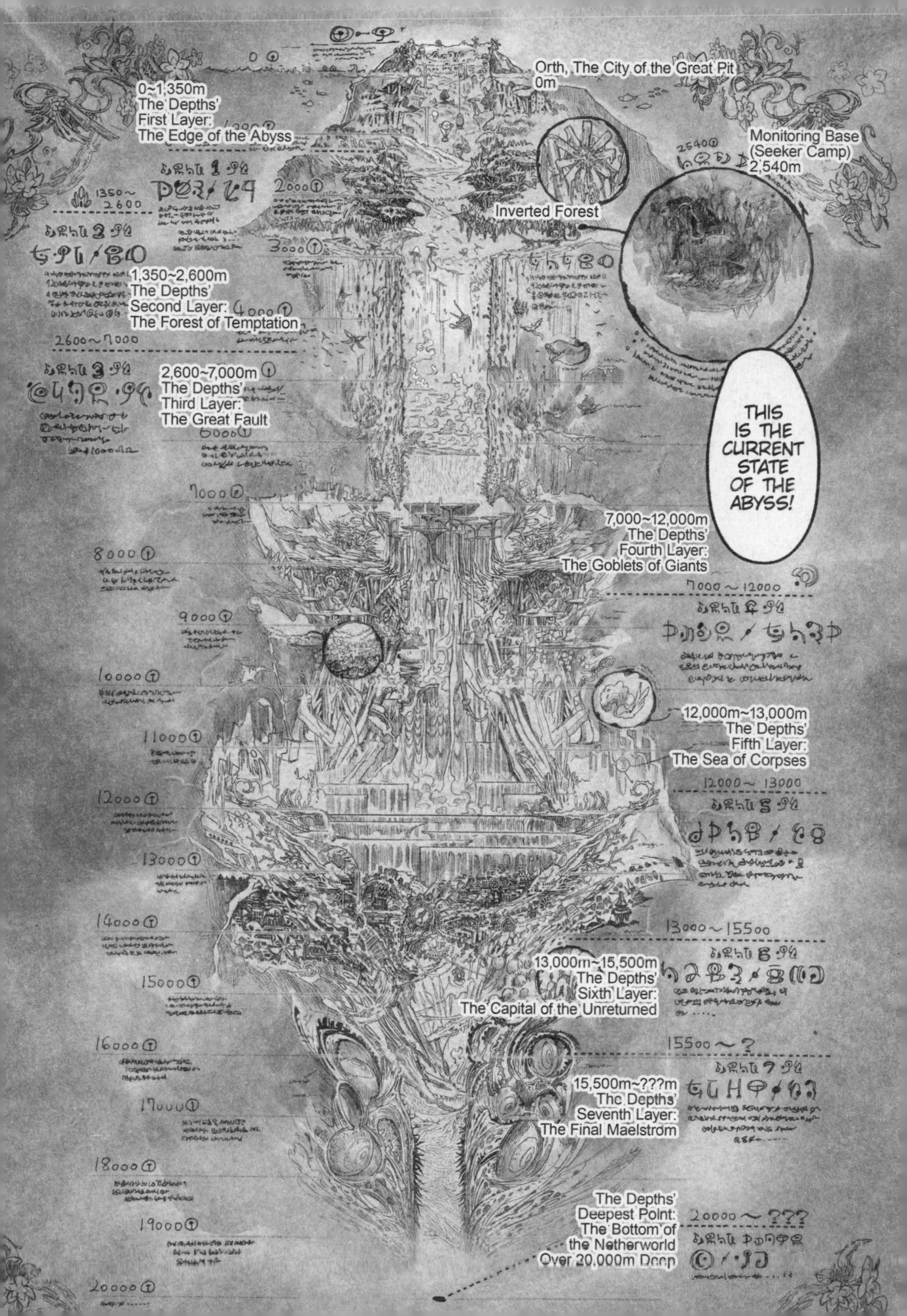
Orth, The City of the Great Pit
0m
Monitoring Base
(Seeker Camp)
2,540m
0~1,350m
The Depths'
First Layer:
The Edge of the Abyss
Inverted Forest
1,350~2,600m
The Depths'
Second Layer:
The Forest of Temptation
2,600~7,000m
The Depths'
Third Layer:
The Great Fault
THIS IS THE CURRENT STATE OF THE ABYSS!
7,000~12,000m
The Depths'
Fourth Layer:
The Goblets of Giants
12,000m~13,000m
The Depths'
Fifth Layer:
The Sea of Corpses
13,000m~15,500m
The Depths'
Sixth Layer:
The Capital of the Unreturned
15,500m~???m
Thc Depths'
Seventh Layer:
The Final Maelstrom
The Depths'
Deepest Point:
The Bottom of
the Netherworld
Over 20,000m Deep
1350~2600
2600~7000
7000~12000
12000~13000
13000~15500
15500~?
20000~???
2000
3000
4000
6000
7000
8000
9000
10000
11000
12000
13000
14000
15000
16000
17000
18000
19000
20000

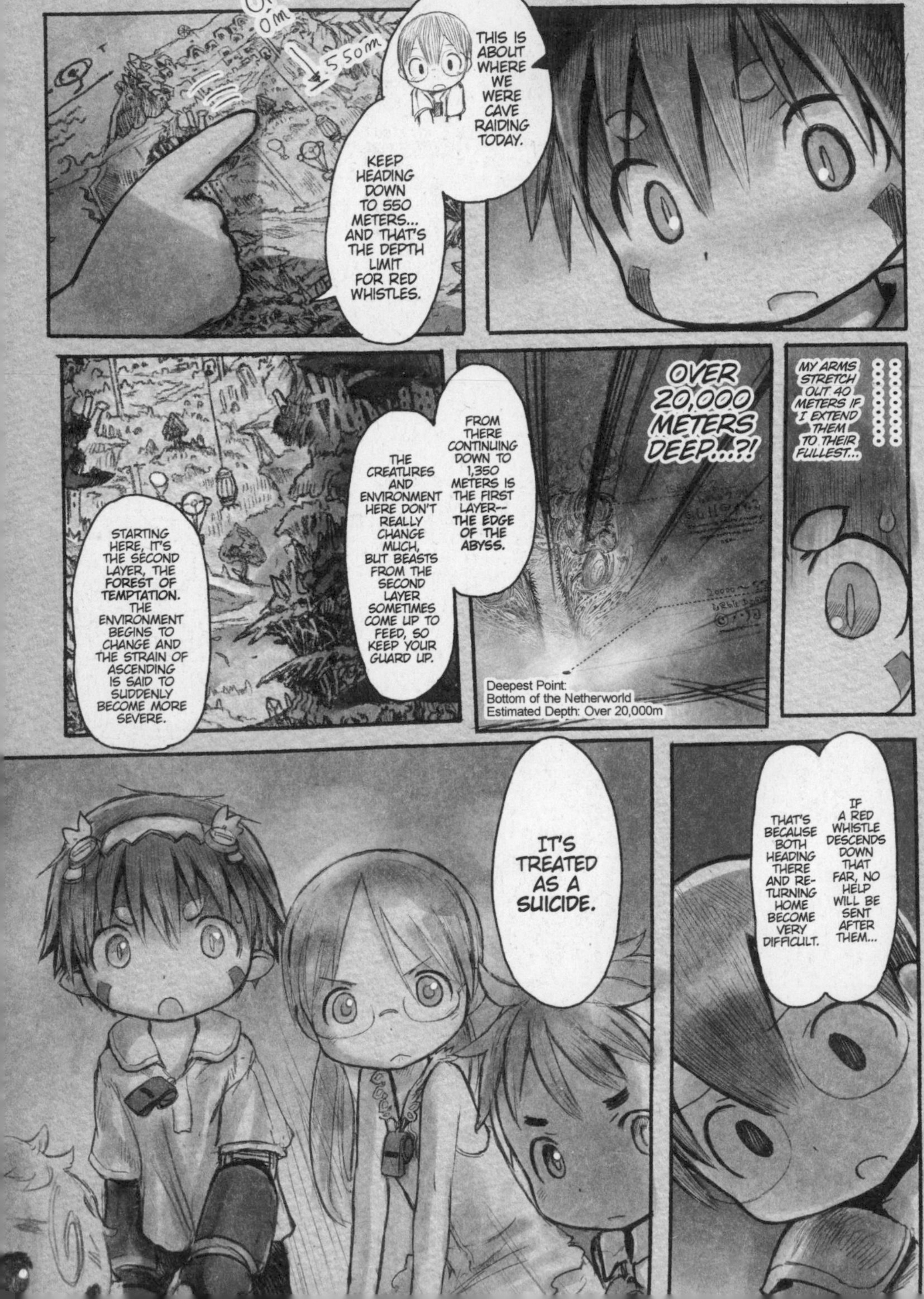
THIS IS ABOUT WHERE WE WERE CAVE RAIDING TODAY.
KEEP HEADING DOWN TO 550 METERS... AND THAT'S THE DEPTH LIMIT FOR RED WHISTLES.
Orth
0m
550m
MY ARMS STRETCH OUT 40 METERS IF I EXTEND THEM TO THEIR FULLEST...
OVER 20,000 METERS DEEP...?!
Deepest Point: Bottom of the Netherworld
Estimated Depth: Over 20,000m
FROM THERE CONTINUING DOWN TO 1,350 METERS IS THE FIRST LAYER-- THE EDGE OF THE ABYSS.
THE CREATURES AND ENVIRONMENT HERE DON'T REALLY CHANGE MUCH, BUT BEASTS FROM THE SECOND LAYER SOMETIMES COME UP TO FEED, SO KEEP YOUR GUARD UP.
STARTING HERE, IT'S THE SECOND LAYER, THE FOREST OF TEMPTATION. THE ENVIRONMENT BEGINS TO CHANGE AND THE STRAIN OF ASCENDING IS SAID TO SUDDENLY BECOME MORE SEVERE.
IF A RED WHISTLE DESCENDS DOWN THAT FAR, NO HELP WILL BE SENT AFTER THEM...
THAT'S BECAUSE BOTH HEADING THERE AND RE-TURNING HOME BECOME VERY DIFFICULT.
IT'S TREATED AS A SUICIDE.

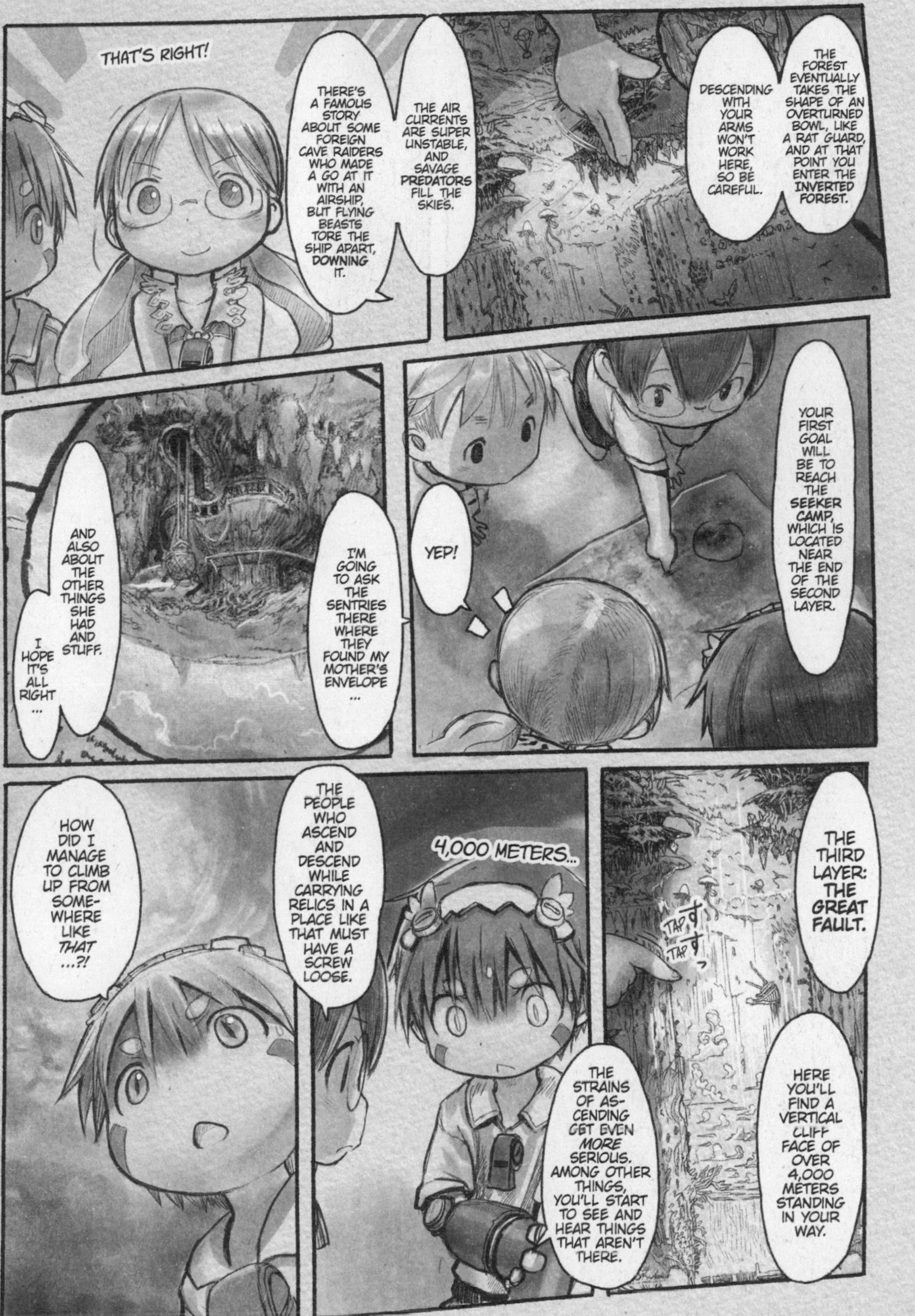

THE FOREST EVENTUALLY TAKES THE SHAPE OF AN OVERTURNED BOWL, LIKE A RAT GUARD, AND AT THAT POINT YOU ENTER THE **INVERTED FOREST.**
DESCENDING WITH YOUR ARMS WON'T WORK HERE, SO BE CAREFUL.
THE AIR CURRENTS ARE SUPER UNSTABLE, AND SAVAGE **PREDATORS** FILL THE SKIES.
THERE'S A FAMOUS STORY ABOUT SOME FOREIGN CAVE RAIDERS WHO MADE A GO AT IT WITH AN AIRSHIP, BUT FLYING BEASTS TORE THE SHIP APART, **DOWNING** IT.
THAT'S RIGHT!
YOUR FIRST GOAL WILL BE TO REACH THE **SEEKER CAMP,** WHICH IS LOCATED NEAR THE END OF THE SECOND LAYER.
YEP!
I'M GOING TO ASK THE SENTRIES THERE WHERE THEY FOUND MY MOTHER'S ENVELOPE ...
AND ALSO ABOUT THE OTHER THINGS SHE HAD AND STUFF.
I HOPE IT'S ALL RIGHT ...
THE THIRD LAYER: **THE GREAT FAULT.**
TAP TAP
HERE YOU'LL FIND A VERTICAL CLIFF FACE OF OVER 4,000 METERS STANDING IN YOUR WAY.
4,000 METERS...
THE PEOPLE WHO ASCEND AND DESCEND WHILE CARRYING RELICS IN A PLACE LIKE THAT MUST HAVE A SCREW LOOSE.
THE STRAINS OF AS-CENDING GET EVEN *MORE* SERIOUS. AMONG OTHER THINGS, YOU'LL START TO SEE AND HEAR THINGS THAT AREN'T THERE.
HOW DID I MANAGE TO CLIMB UP FROM SOME-WHERE LIKE *THAT* ...?!

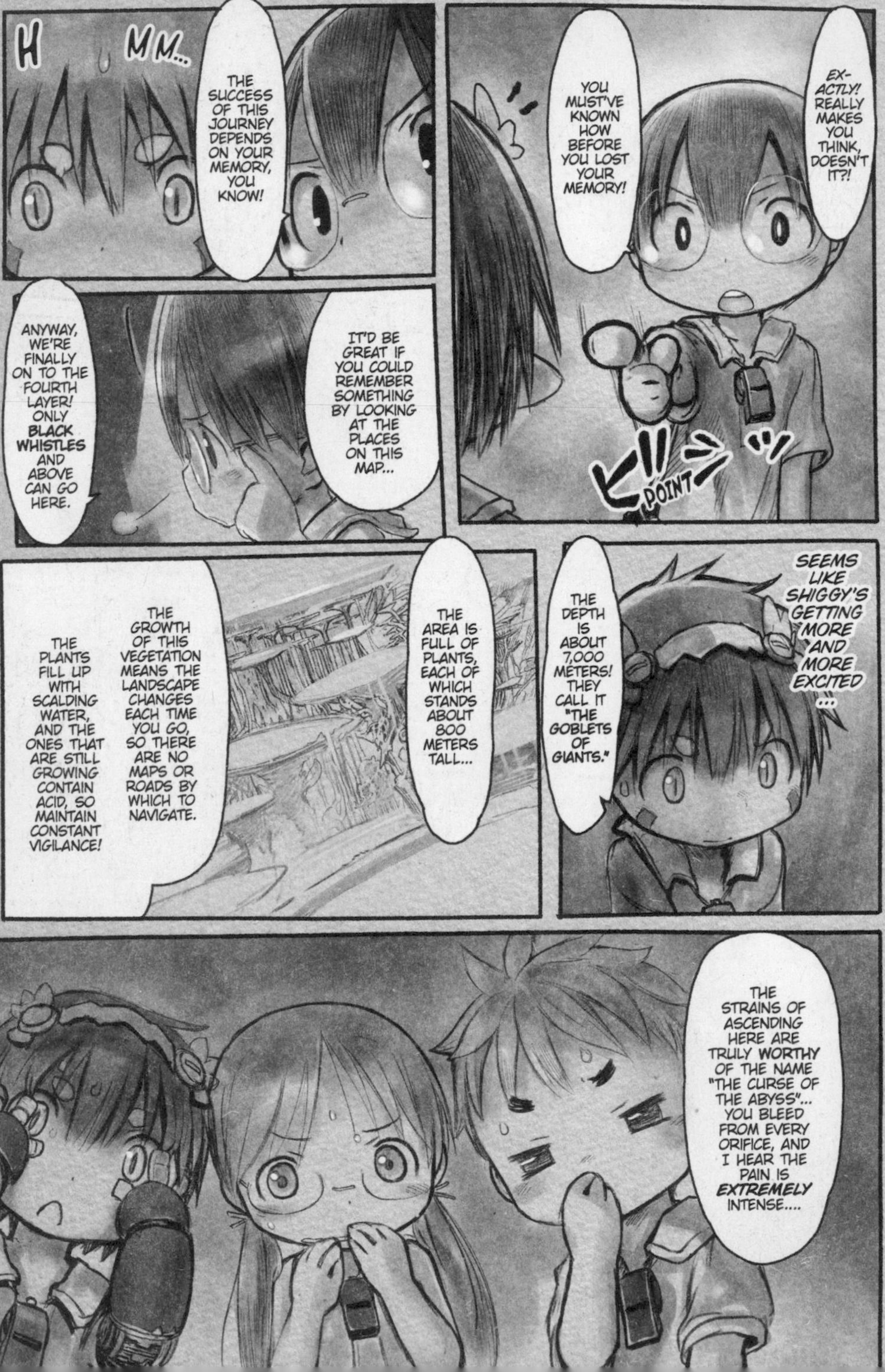
EX-ACTLY! REALLY MAKES YOU THINK, DOESN'T IT?!
YOU MUST'VE KNOWN HOW BEFORE YOU LOST YOUR MEMORY!
POINT
THE SUCCESS OF THIS JOURNEY DEPENDS ON YOUR MEMORY, YOU KNOW!
HMM...
IT'D BE GREAT IF YOU COULD REMEMBER SOMETHING BY LOOKING AT THE PLACES ON THIS MAP...
ANYWAY, WE'RE FINALLY ON TO THE FOURTH LAYER! ONLY **BLACK WHISTLES** AND ABOVE CAN GO HERE.
SEEMS LIKE SHIGGY'S GETTING MORE AND MORE EXCITED...
THE DEPTH IS ABOUT 7,000 METERS! THEY CALL IT "THE GOBLETS OF GIANTS."
THE AREA IS FULL OF PLANTS, EACH OF WHICH STANDS ABOUT 800 METERS TALL...
THE GROWTH OF THIS VEGETATION MEANS THE LANDSCAPE CHANGES EACH TIME YOU GO, SO THERE ARE NO MAPS OR ROADS BY WHICH TO NAVIGATE.
THE PLANTS FILL UP WITH SCALDING WATER, AND THE ONES THAT ARE STILL GROWING CONTAIN ACID, SO MAINTAIN CONSTANT VIGILANCE!
THE STRAINS OF ASCENDING HERE ARE TRULY **WORTHY** OF THE NAME "THE CURSE OF THE ABYSS"... YOU BLEED FROM EVERY ORIFICE, AND I HEAR THE PAIN IS ***EXTREMELY*** INTENSE....

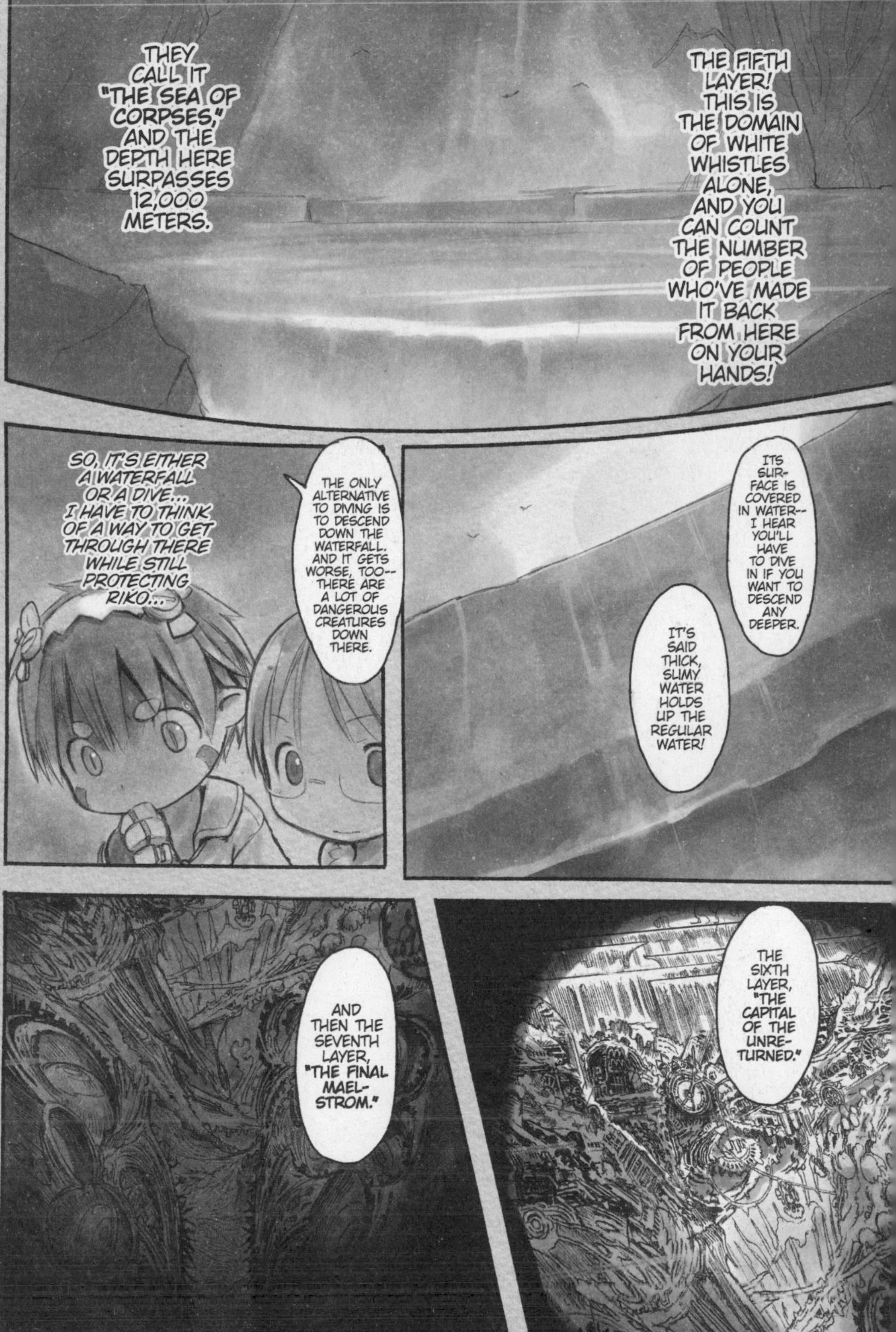
THE FIFTH LAYER! THIS IS THE DOMAIN OF WHITE WHISTLES ALONE, AND YOU CAN COUNT THE NUMBER OF PEOPLE WHO'VE MADE IT BACK FROM HERE ON YOUR HANDS!
THEY CALL IT "THE SEA OF CORPSES," AND THE DEPTH HERE SURPASSES 12,000 METERS.
ITS SURFACE IS COVERED IN WATER-- I HEAR YOU'LL HAVE TO DIVE IN IF YOU WANT TO DESCEND ANY DEEPER.
IT'S SAID THICK, SLIMY WATER HOLDS UP THE REGULAR WATER!
THE ONLY ALTERNATIVE TO DIVING IS TO DESCEND DOWN THE WATERFALL. AND IT GETS WORSE, TOO-- THERE ARE A LOT OF DANGEROUS CREATURES DOWN THERE.
SO, IT'S EITHER A WATERFALL OR A DIVE... I HAVE TO THINK OF A WAY TO GET THROUGH THERE WHILE STILL PROTECTING RIKO...
THE SIXTH LAYER, "THE CAPITAL OF THE UNRETURNED."
AND THEN THE SEVENTH LAYER, "THE FINAL MAELSTROM."

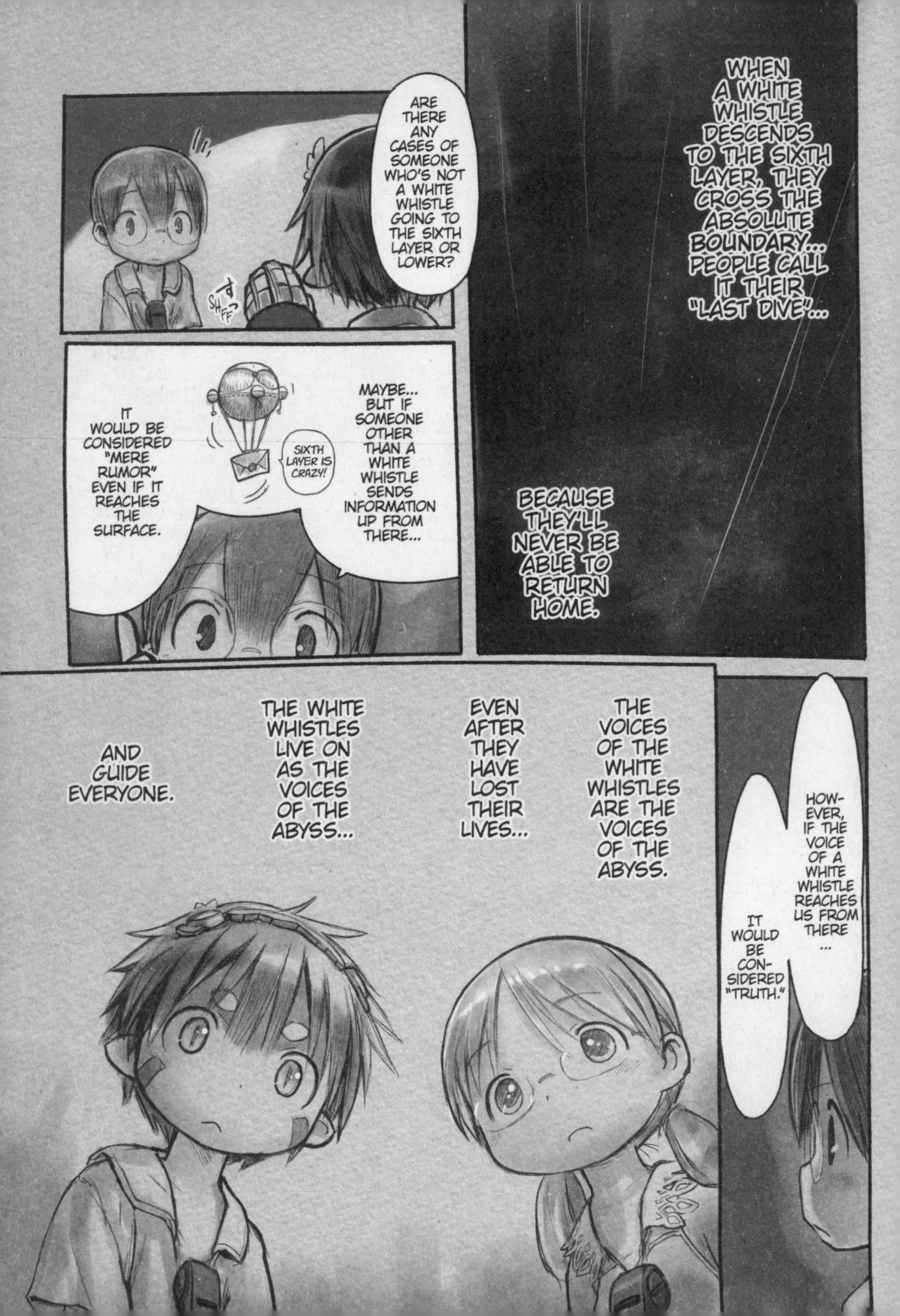
WHEN A WHITE WHISTLE DESCENDS TO THE SIXTH LAYER, THEY CROSS THE ABSOLUTE BOUNDARY... PEOPLE CALL IT THEIR "LAST DIVE"...
BECAUSE THEY'LL NEVER BE ABLE TO RETURN HOME.
ARE THERE ANY CASES OF SOMEONE WHO'S NOT A WHITE WHISTLE GOING TO THE SIXTH LAYER OR LOWER?
す
SHFF
MAYBE... BUT IF SOMEONE OTHER THAN A WHITE WHISTLE SENDS INFORMATION UP FROM THERE...
SIXTH LAYER IS CRAZY!
IT WOULD BE CONSIDERED "MERE RUMOR" EVEN IF IT REACHES THE SURFACE.
HOW-EVER, IF THE VOICE OF A WHITE WHISTLE REACHES US FROM THERE ...
IT WOULD BE CON-SIDERED "TRUTH."
THE VOICES OF THE WHITE WHISTLES ARE THE VOICES OF THE ABYSS.
EVEN AFTER THEY HAVE LOST THEIR LIVES...
THE WHITE WHISTLES LIVE ON AS THE VOICES OF THE ABYSS...
AND GUIDE EVERYONE.

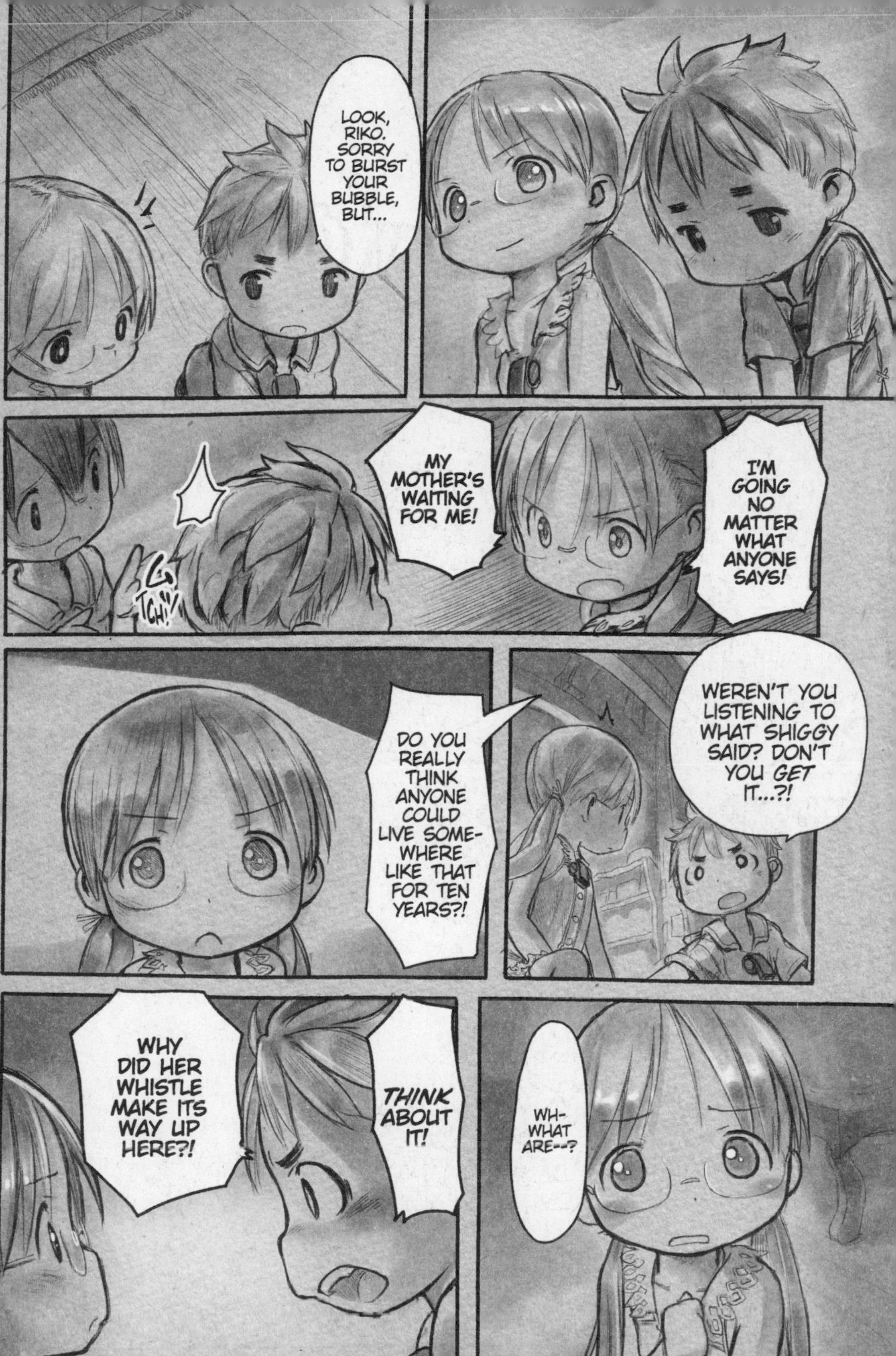
LOOK, RIKO. SORRY TO BURST YOUR BUBBLE, BUT...
I'M GOING NO MATTER WHAT ANYONE SAYS!
MY MOTHER'S WAITING FOR ME!
TCHI!
WEREN'T YOU LISTENING TO WHAT SHIGGY SAID? DON'T YOU GET IT...?!
DO YOU REALLY THINK ANYONE COULD LIVE SOME-WHERE LIKE THAT FOR TEN YEARS?!
WH-WHAT ARE--?
THINK ABOUT IT!
WHY DID HER WHISTLE MAKE ITS WAY UP HERE?!

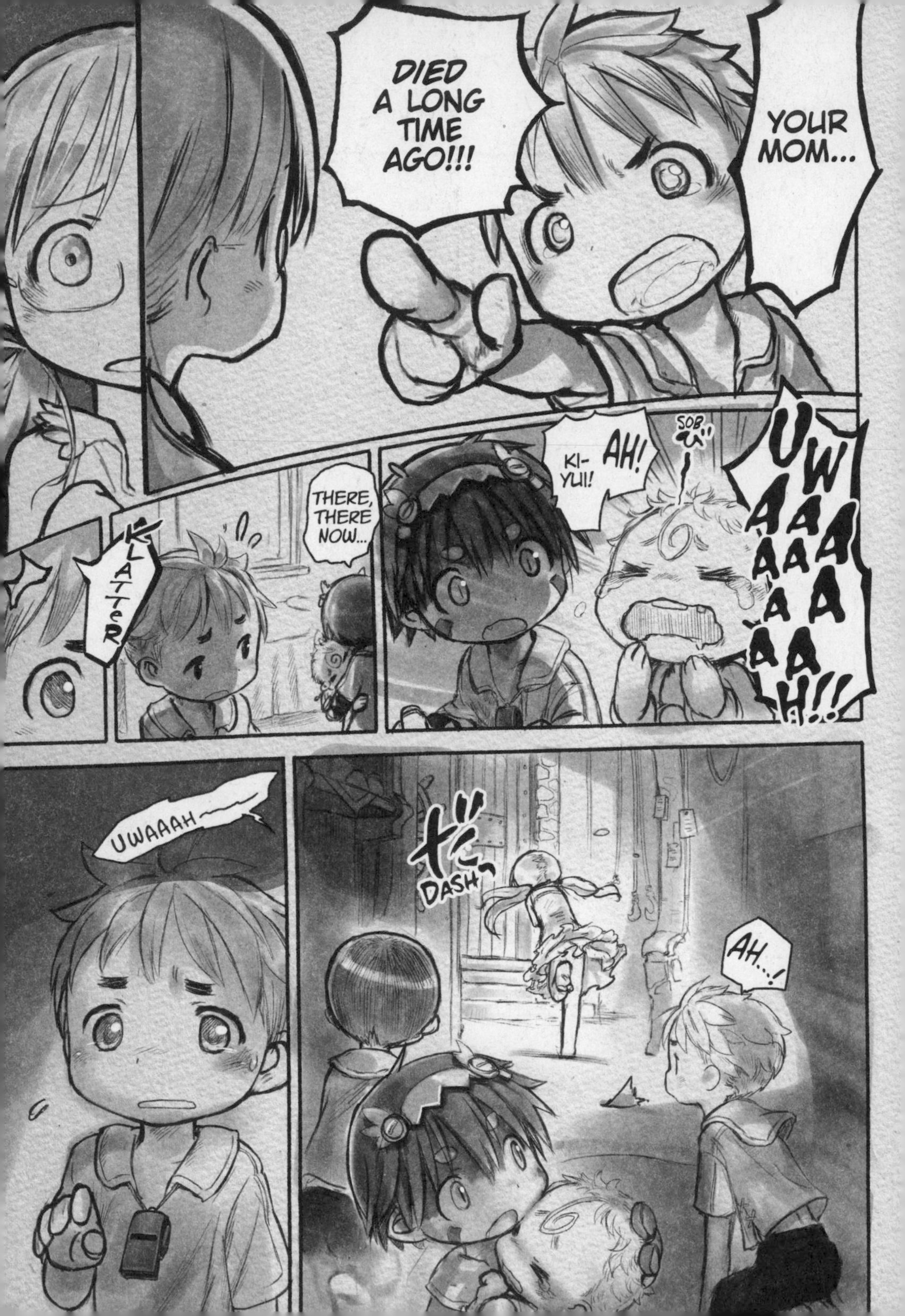
YOUR MOM...
DIED A LONG TIME AGO!!!
UWAAAAAAAAAAH!!!
SOB
AH!
KI-YUI!
THERE, THERE NOW...
KLATTER
DASH
AH...!
UWAAAH

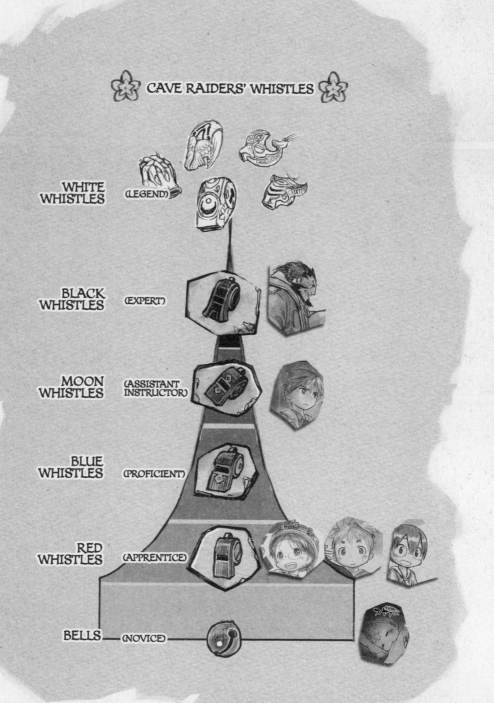

CAVE RAIDERS' WHISTLES

WHITE
WHISTLES — (LEGEND)

BLACK
WHISTLES — (EXPERT)

MOON
WHISTLES — (ASSISTANT INSTRUCTOR)

BLUE
WHISTLES — (PROFICIENT)

RED
WHISTLES — (APPRENTICE)

BELLS — (NOVICE)

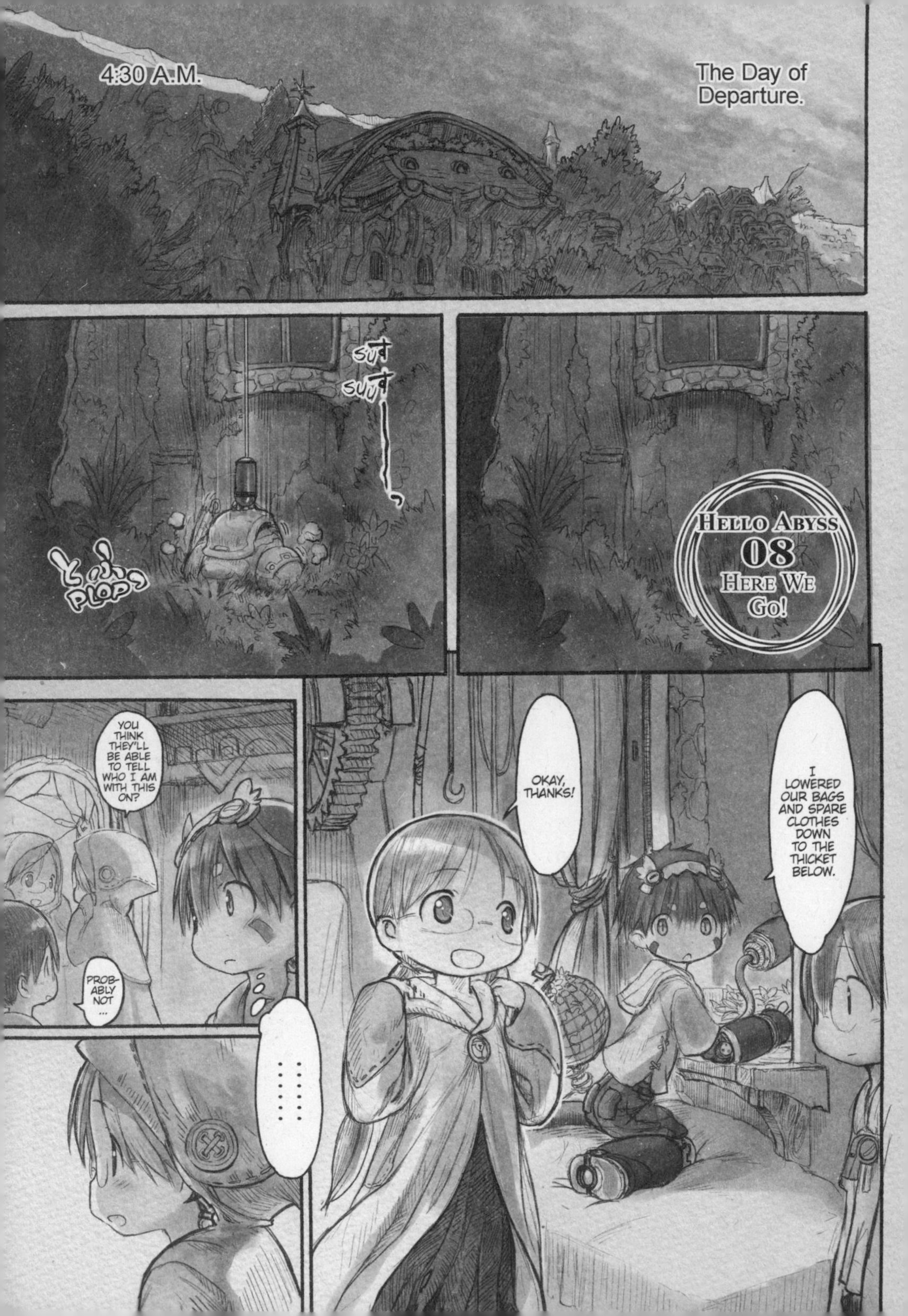
The Day of Departure.
4:30 A.M.
HELLO ABYSS 08 HERE WE GO!
SUU SUU
PLOP
I LOWERED OUR BAGS AND SPARE CLOTHES DOWN TO THE THICKET BELOW.
OKAY, THANKS!
YOU THINK THEY'LL BE ABLE TO TELL WHO I AM WITH THIS ON?
PROBABLY NOT ...
......

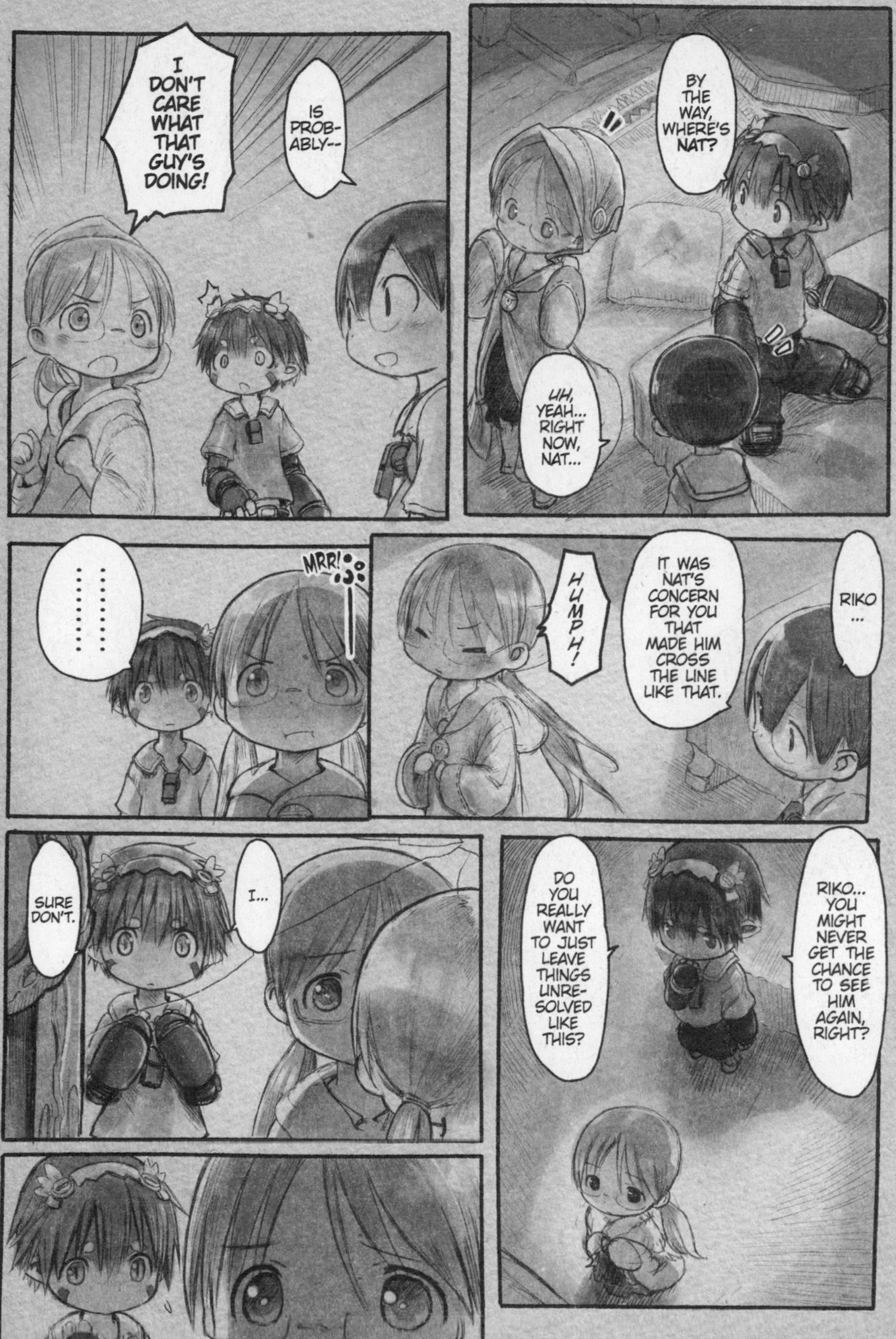
BY THE WAY, WHERE'S NAT?
UH, YEAH... RIGHT NOW, NAT...
IS PROBABLY--
I DON'T CARE WHAT THAT GUY'S DOING!
RIKO...
IT WAS NAT'S CONCERN FOR YOU THAT MADE HIM CROSS THE LINE LIKE THAT.
HUMPH!
MRR!
......
RIKO... YOU MIGHT NEVER GET THE CHANCE TO SEE HIM AGAIN, RIGHT?
DO YOU REALLY WANT TO JUST LEAVE THINGS UNRESOLVED LIKE THIS?
I...
SURE DON'T.

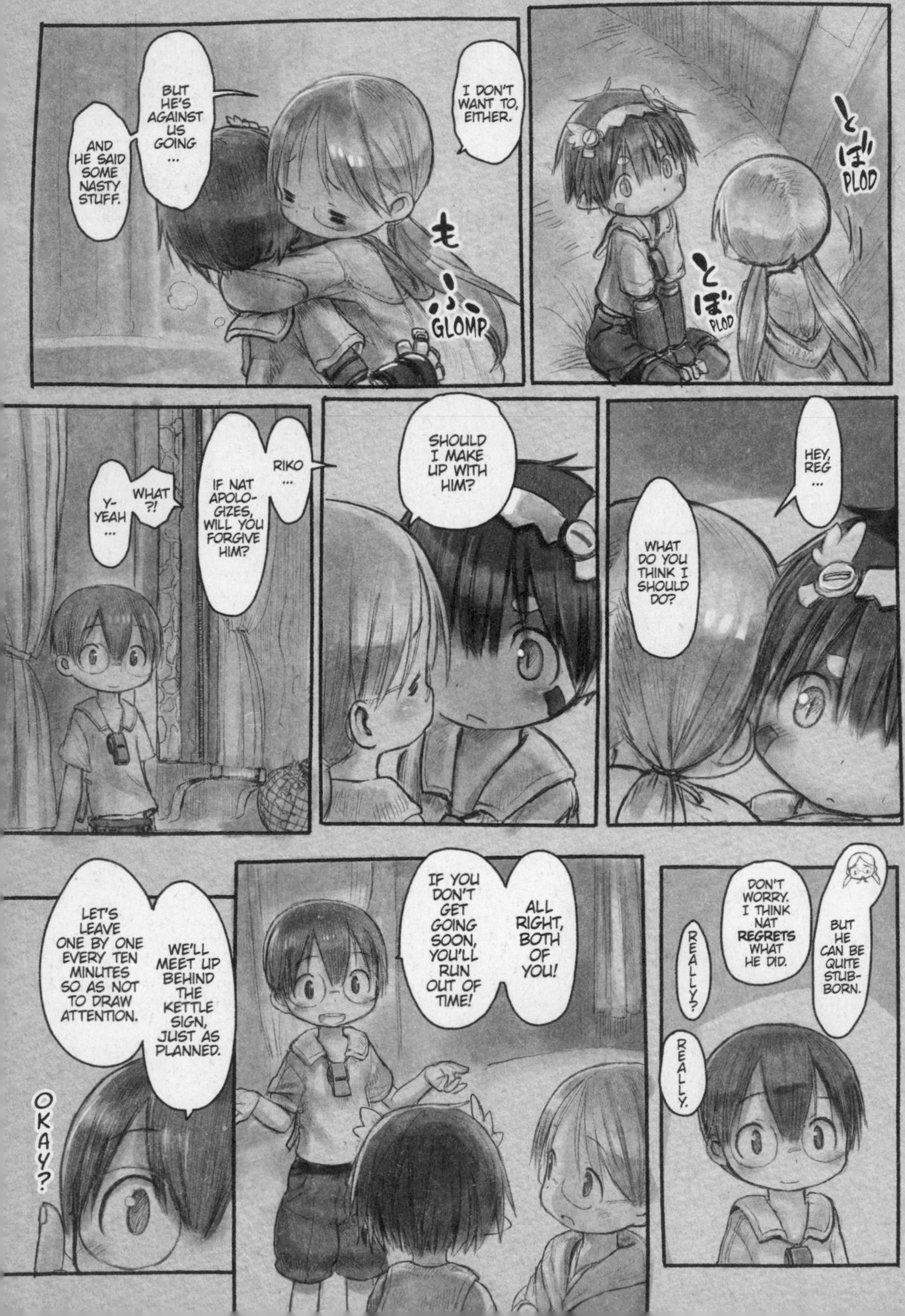
とぼ
PLOD
とぼ
PLOD
I DON'T WANT TO, EITHER.
BUT HE'S AGAINST US GOING...
AND HE SAID SOME NASTY STUFF.
もふ
GLOMP
HEY, REG...
WHAT DO YOU THINK I SHOULD DO?
SHOULD I MAKE UP WITH HIM?
RIKO...
IF NAT APOLOGIZES, WILL YOU FORGIVE HIM?
WHAT?!
Y-YEAH...
DON'T WORRY. I THINK NAT REGRETS WHAT HE DID.
BUT HE CAN BE QUITE STUBBORN.
REALLY?
REALLY.
ALL RIGHT, BOTH OF YOU!
IF YOU DON'T GET GOING SOON, YOU'LL RUN OUT OF TIME!
LET'S LEAVE ONE BY ONE EVERY TEN MINUTES SO AS NOT TO DRAW ATTENTION.
WE'LL MEET UP BEHIND THE KETTLE SIGN, JUST AS PLANNED.
OKAY?

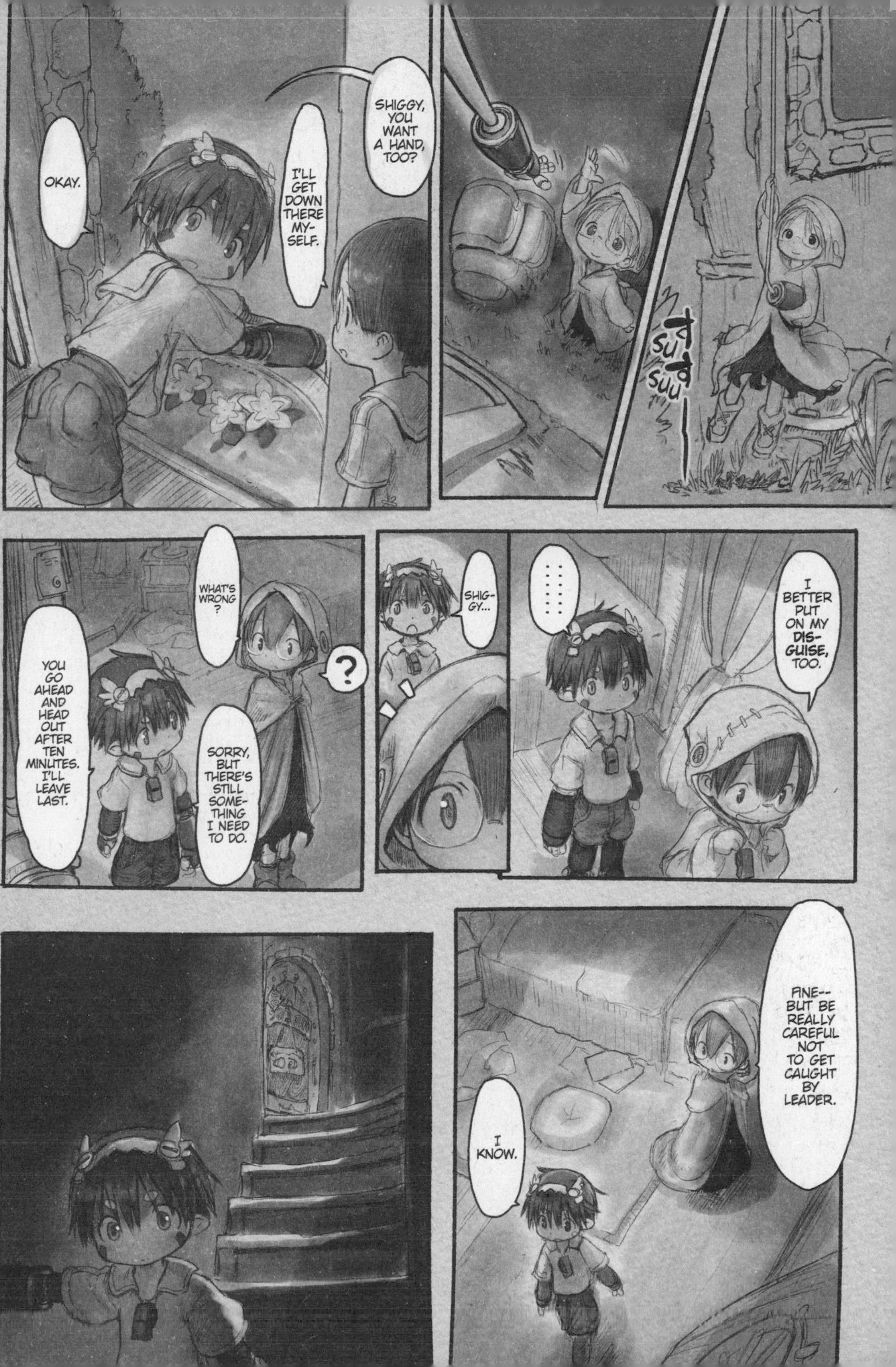
す SU す SUU
SHIGGY, YOU WANT A HAND, TOO?
I'LL GET DOWN THERE MYSELF.
OKAY.
I BETTER PUT ON MY DISGUISE, TOO.
......
SHIGGY...
WHAT'S WRONG?
?
SORRY, BUT THERE'S STILL SOMETHING I NEED TO DO.
YOU GO AHEAD AND HEAD OUT AFTER TEN MINUTES. I'LL LEAVE LAST.
FINE-- BUT BE REALLY CAREFUL NOT TO GET CAUGHT BY LEADER.
I KNOW.

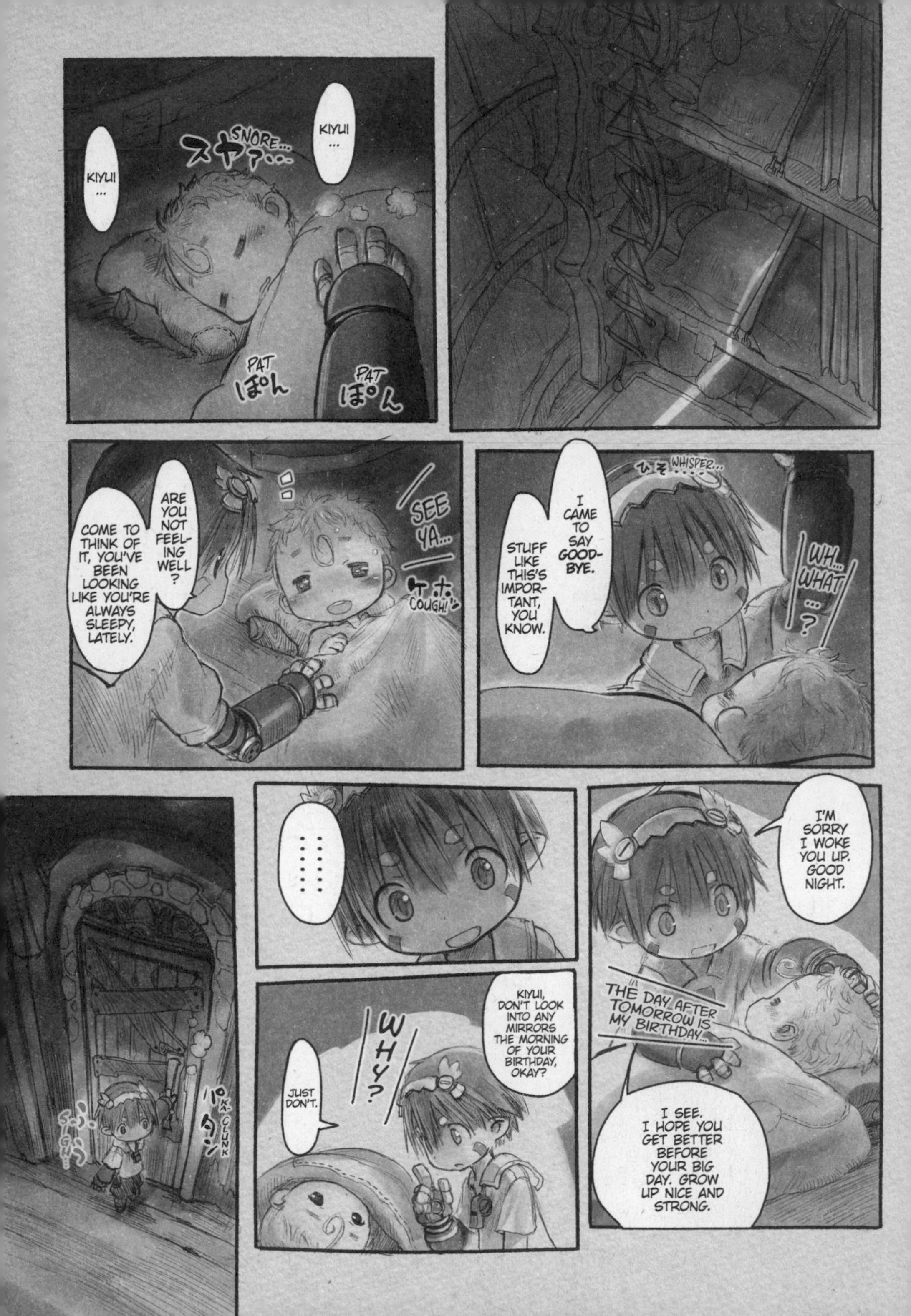
KIYUI...
SNORE... スヤァ...
KIYUI...
PAT ぽん
PAT ぽん
ひそ WHISPER...
WH... WHAT...?
I CAME TO SAY GOODBYE.
STUFF LIKE THIS'S IMPORTANT, YOU KNOW.
SEE YA...
ケホ COUGH!
ARE YOU NOT FEELING WELL?
COME TO THINK OF IT, YOU'VE BEEN LOOKING LIKE YOU'RE ALWAYS SLEEPY, LATELY.
I'M SORRY I WOKE YOU UP. GOOD NIGHT.
THE DAY AFTER TOMORROW IS MY BIRTHDAY...
I SEE. I HOPE YOU GET BETTER BEFORE YOUR BIG DAY. GROW UP NICE AND STRONG.
......
KIYUI, DON'T LOOK INTO ANY MIRRORS THE MORNING OF YOUR BIRTHDAY, OKAY?
WHY?
JUST DON'T.
パタン KA-CLUNK

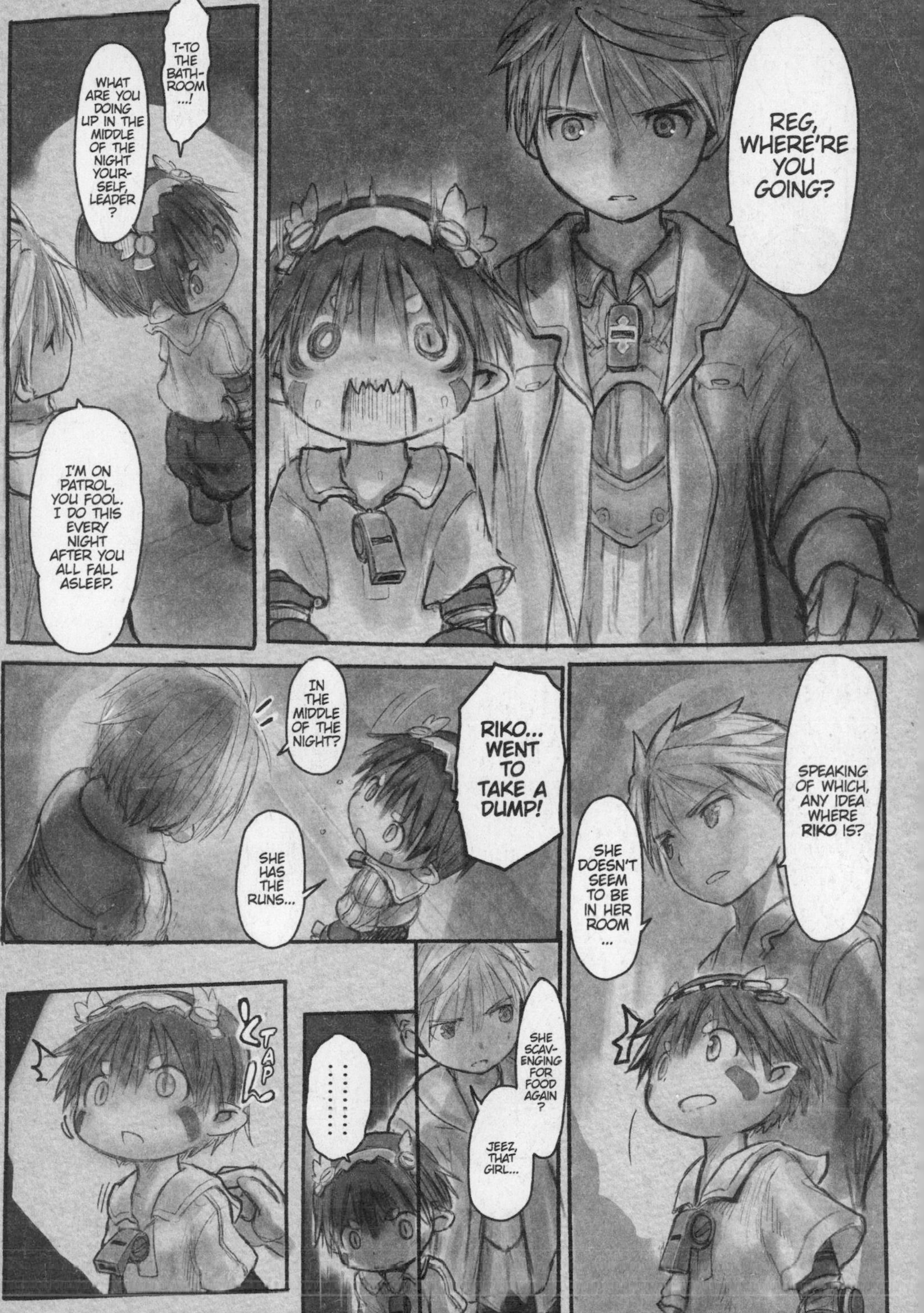
REG, WHERE'RE YOU GOING?
T-TO THE BATH-ROOM...!
WHAT ARE YOU DOING UP IN THE MIDDLE OF THE NIGHT YOUR-SELF, LEADER?
I'M ON PATROL, YOU FOOL. I DO THIS EVERY NIGHT AFTER YOU ALL FALL ASLEEP.
SPEAKING OF WHICH, ANY IDEA WHERE RIKO IS?
SHE DOESN'T SEEM TO BE IN HER ROOM...
RIKO... WENT TO TAKE A DUMP!
IN THE MIDDLE OF THE NIGHT?
SHE HAS THE RUNS...
SHE SCAV-ENGING FOR FOOD AGAIN?
JEEZ, THAT GIRL...
......
TAP

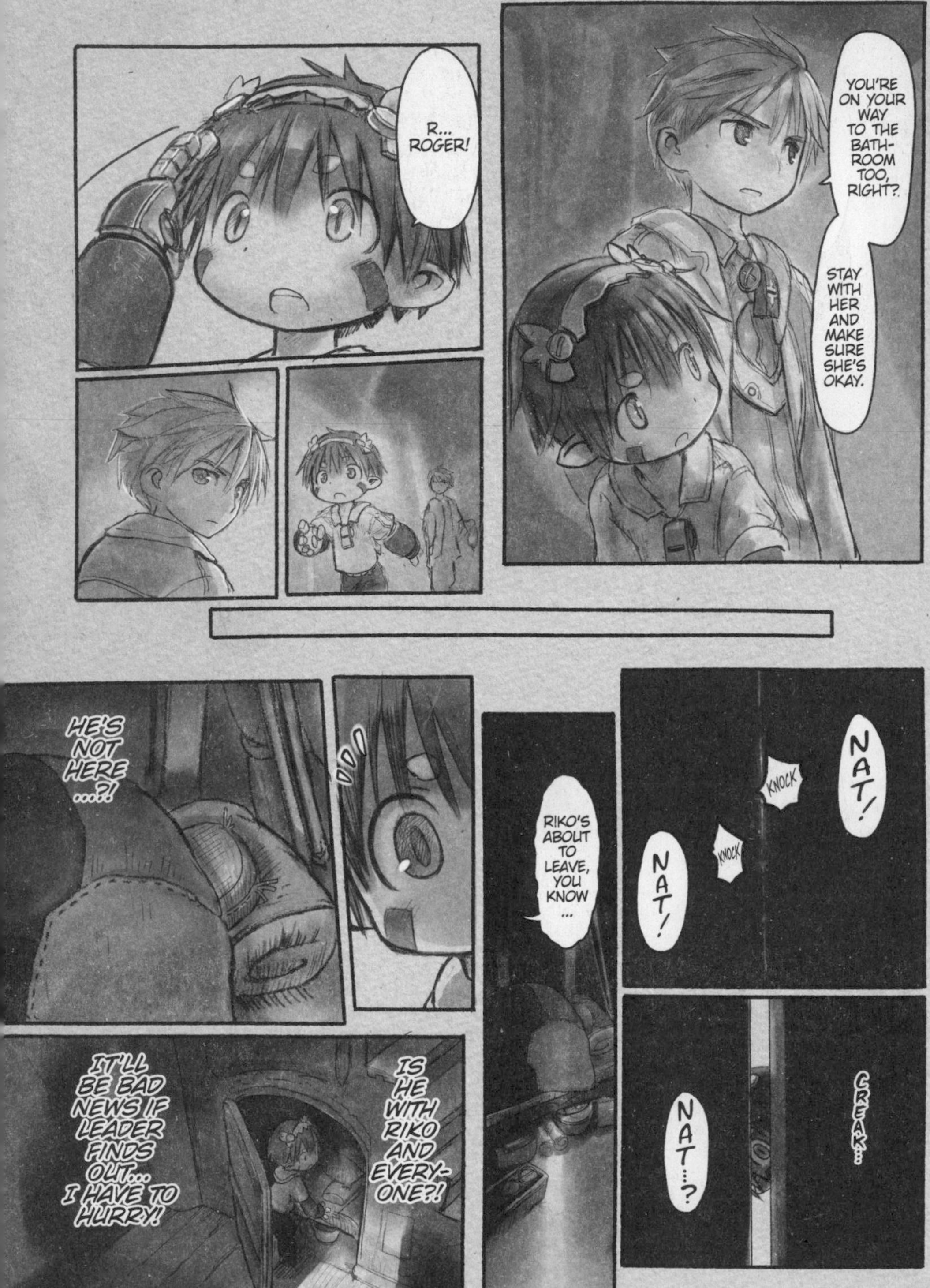
YOU'RE ON YOUR WAY TO THE BATH-ROOM TOO, RIGHT?
STAY WITH HER AND MAKE SURE SHE'S OKAY.
R... ROGER!
NAT!
KNOCK
KNOCK
NAT!
CREAK...
NAT...?
RIKO'S ABOUT TO LEAVE, YOU KNOW ...
HE'S NOT HERE ...?!
IS HE WITH RIKO AND EVERY-ONE?!
IT'LL BE BAD NEWS IF LEADER FINDS OUT... I HAVE TO HURRY!

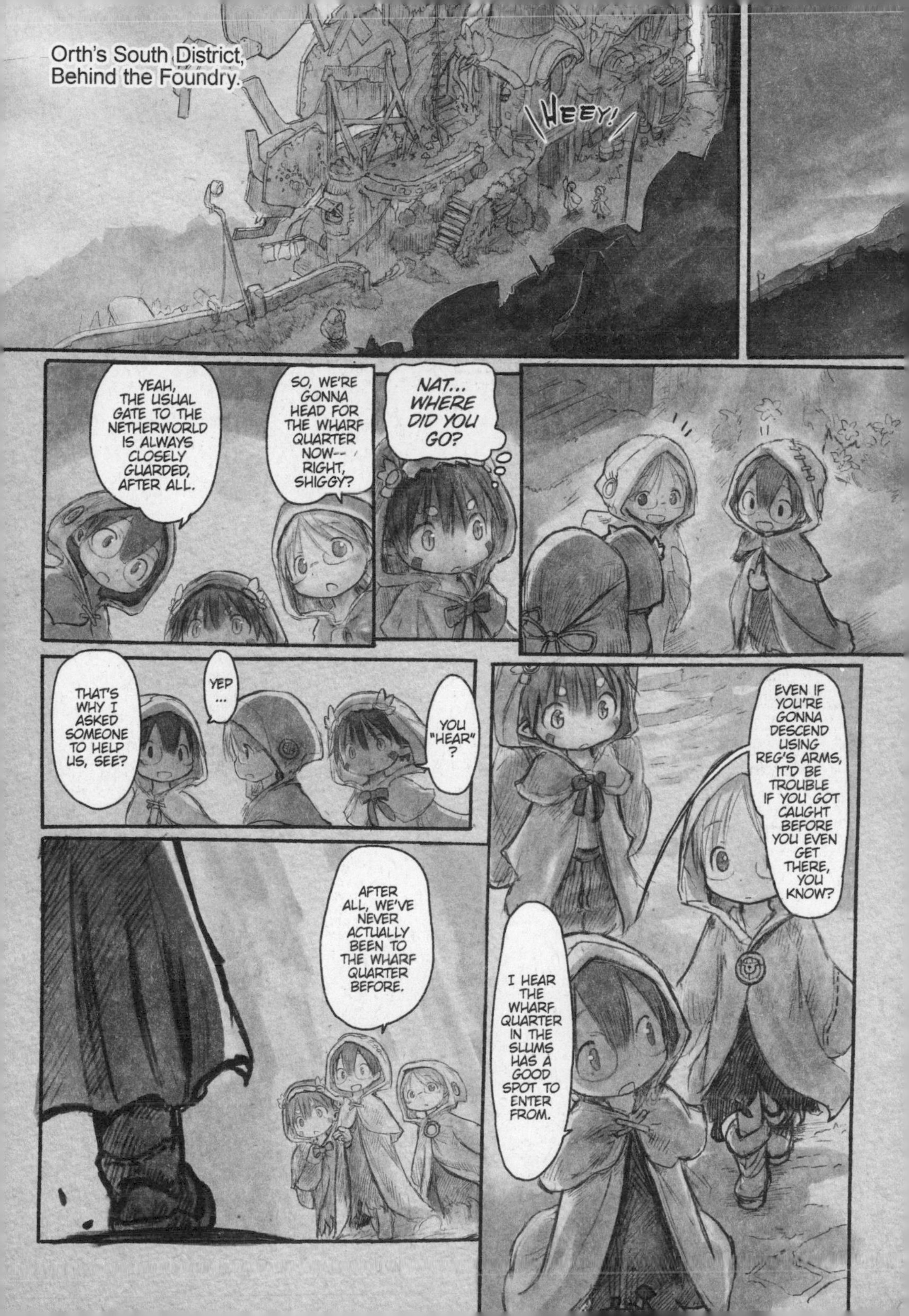
Orth's South District, Behind the Foundry.
HEEY!
NAT... WHERE DID YOU GO?
SO, WE'RE GONNA HEAD FOR THE WHARF QUARTER NOW-- RIGHT, SHIGGY?
YEAH, THE USUAL GATE TO THE NETHERWORLD IS ALWAYS CLOSELY GUARDED, AFTER ALL.
EVEN IF YOU'RE GONNA DESCEND USING REG'S ARMS, IT'D BE TROUBLE IF YOU GOT CAUGHT BEFORE YOU EVEN GET THERE, YOU KNOW?
I HEAR THE WHARF QUARTER IN THE SLUMS HAS A GOOD SPOT TO ENTER FROM.
YOU "HEAR"?
YEP...
THAT'S WHY I ASKED SOMEONE TO HELP US, SEE?
AFTER ALL, WE'VE NEVER ACTUALLY BEEN TO THE WHARF QUARTER BEFORE.

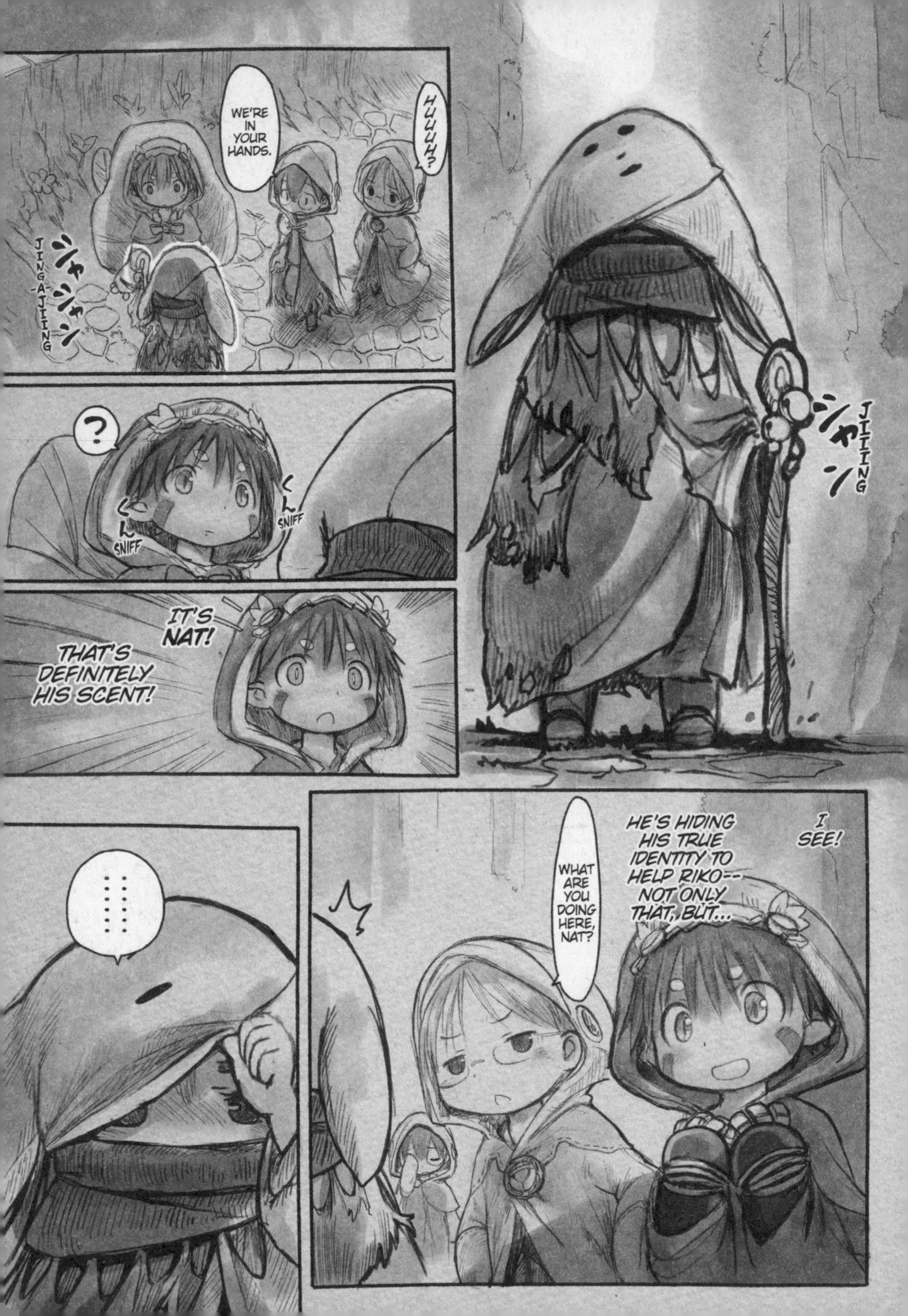

シャン
JIIING
HUUUH?
WE'RE IN YOUR HANDS.
シャシャン
JINGAJIING
?
くん
SNIFF
くん
SNIFF
IT'S NAT!
THAT'S DEFINITELY HIS SCENT!
I SEE!
HE'S HIDING HIS TRUE IDENTITY TO HELP RIKO-- NOT ONLY THAT, BUT...
WHAT ARE YOU DOING HERE, NAT?
......

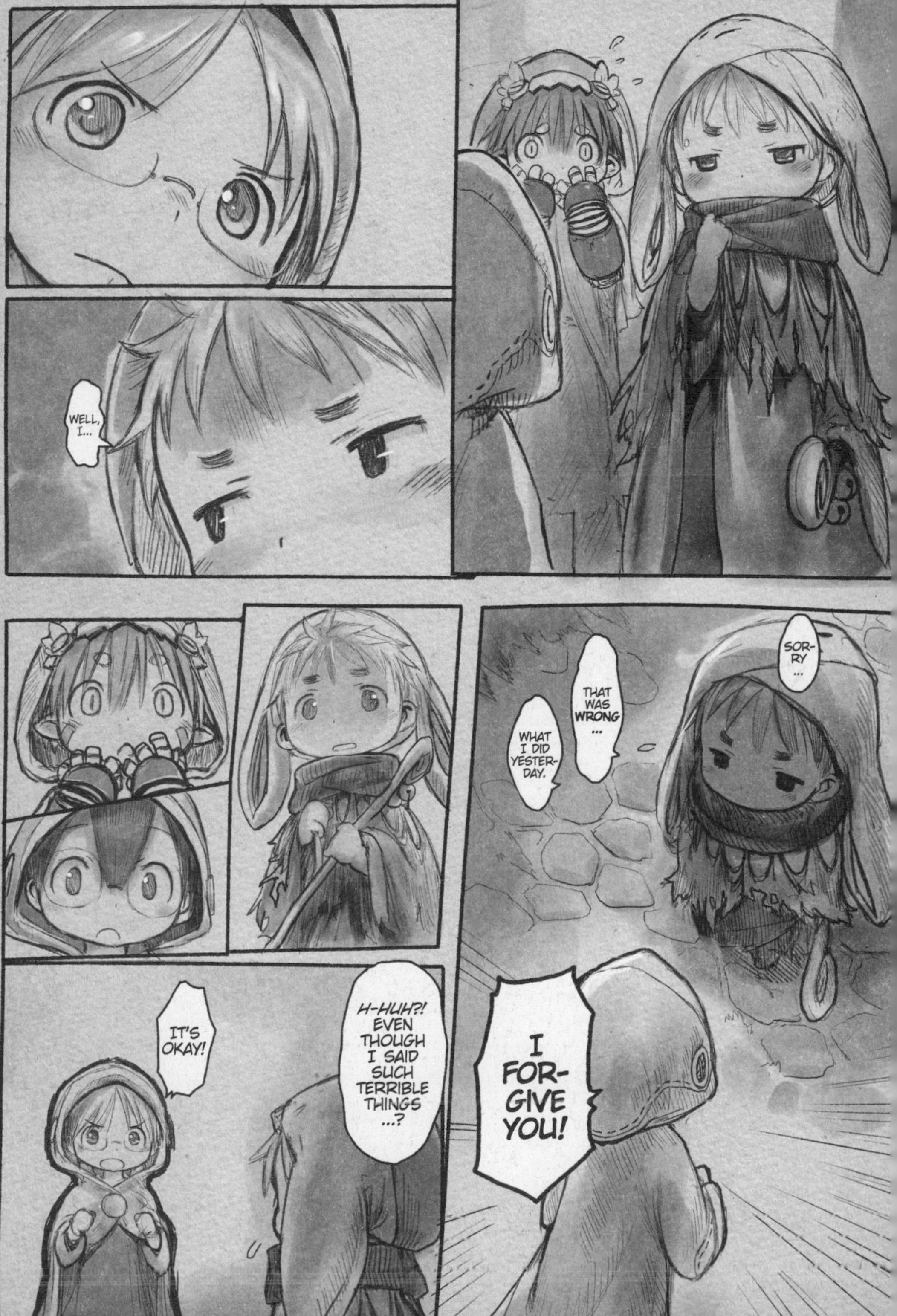
WELL, I...
SOR-RY...
THAT WAS WRONG...
WHAT I DID YESTER-DAY.
I FOR-GIVE YOU!
H-HUH?! EVEN THOUGH I SAID SUCH TERRIBLE THINGS...?
IT'S OKAY!

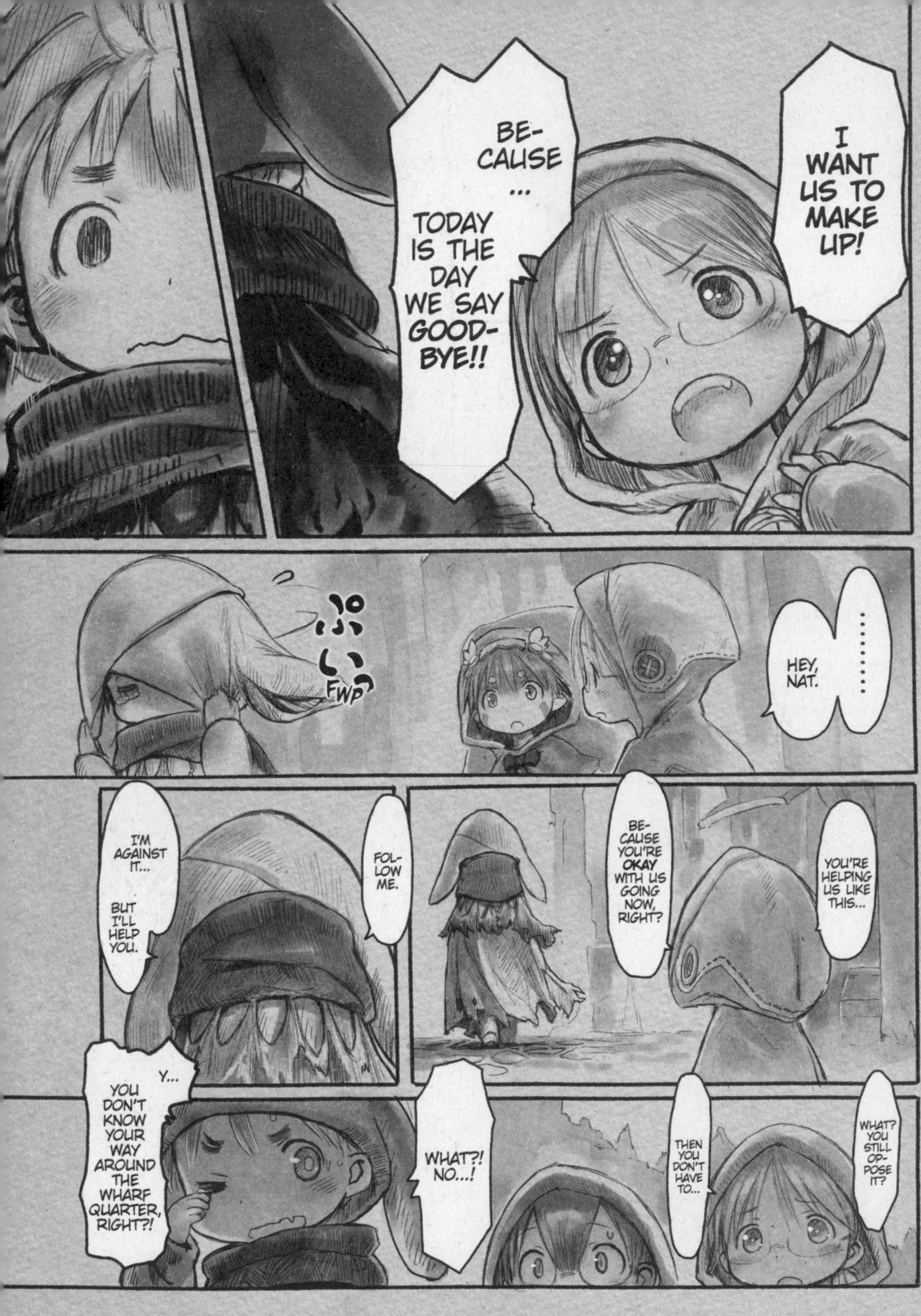
I WANT US TO MAKE UP!
BE-CAUSE ... TODAY IS THE DAY WE SAY GOOD-BYE!!
......
HEY, NAT.
ぷい
FWP
YOU'RE HELPING US LIKE THIS...
BE-CAUSE YOU'RE OKAY WITH US GOING NOW, RIGHT?
FOL-LOW ME.
I'M AGAINST IT...
BUT I'LL HELP YOU.
WHAT? YOU STILL OP-POSE IT?
THEN YOU DON'T HAVE TO...
WHAT?! NO...!
Y...
YOU DON'T KNOW YOUR WAY AROUND THE WHARF QUARTER, RIGHT?!

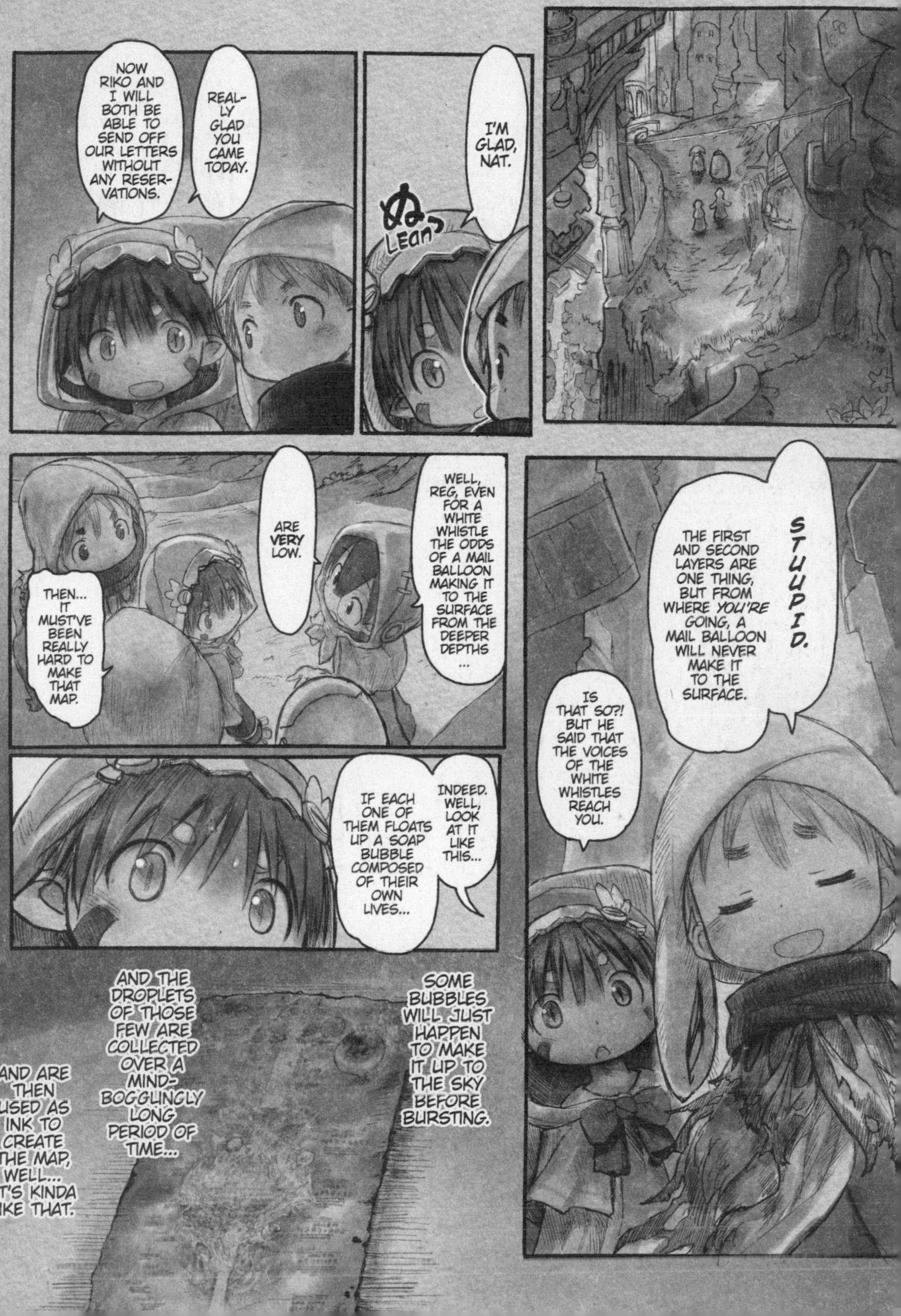
I'M GLAD, NAT.
ぬっ LEAN
REALLY GLAD YOU CAME TODAY.
NOW RIKO AND I WILL BOTH BE ABLE TO SEND OFF OUR LETTERS WITHOUT ANY RESERVATIONS.
STUPID.
THE FIRST AND SECOND LAYERS ARE ONE THING, BUT FROM WHERE YOU'RE GOING, A MAIL BALLOON WILL NEVER MAKE IT TO THE SURFACE.
IS THAT SO?! BUT HE SAID THAT THE VOICES OF THE WHITE WHISTLES REACH YOU.
WELL, REG, EVEN FOR A WHITE WHISTLE THE ODDS OF A MAIL BALLOON MAKING IT TO THE SURFACE FROM THE DEEPER DEPTHS ...
ARE VERY LOW.
THEN... IT MUST'VE BEEN REALLY HARD TO MAKE THAT MAP.
INDEED. WELL, LOOK AT IT LIKE THIS...
IF EACH ONE OF THEM FLOATS UP A SOAP BUBBLE COMPOSED OF THEIR OWN LIVES...
SOME BUBBLES WILL JUST HAPPEN TO MAKE IT UP TO THE SKY BEFORE BURSTING.
AND THE DROPLETS OF THOSE FEW ARE COLLECTED OVER A MIND-BOGGLINGLY LONG PERIOD OF TIME...
AND ARE THEN USED AS INK TO CREATE THE MAP, WELL... IT'S KINDA LIKE THAT.

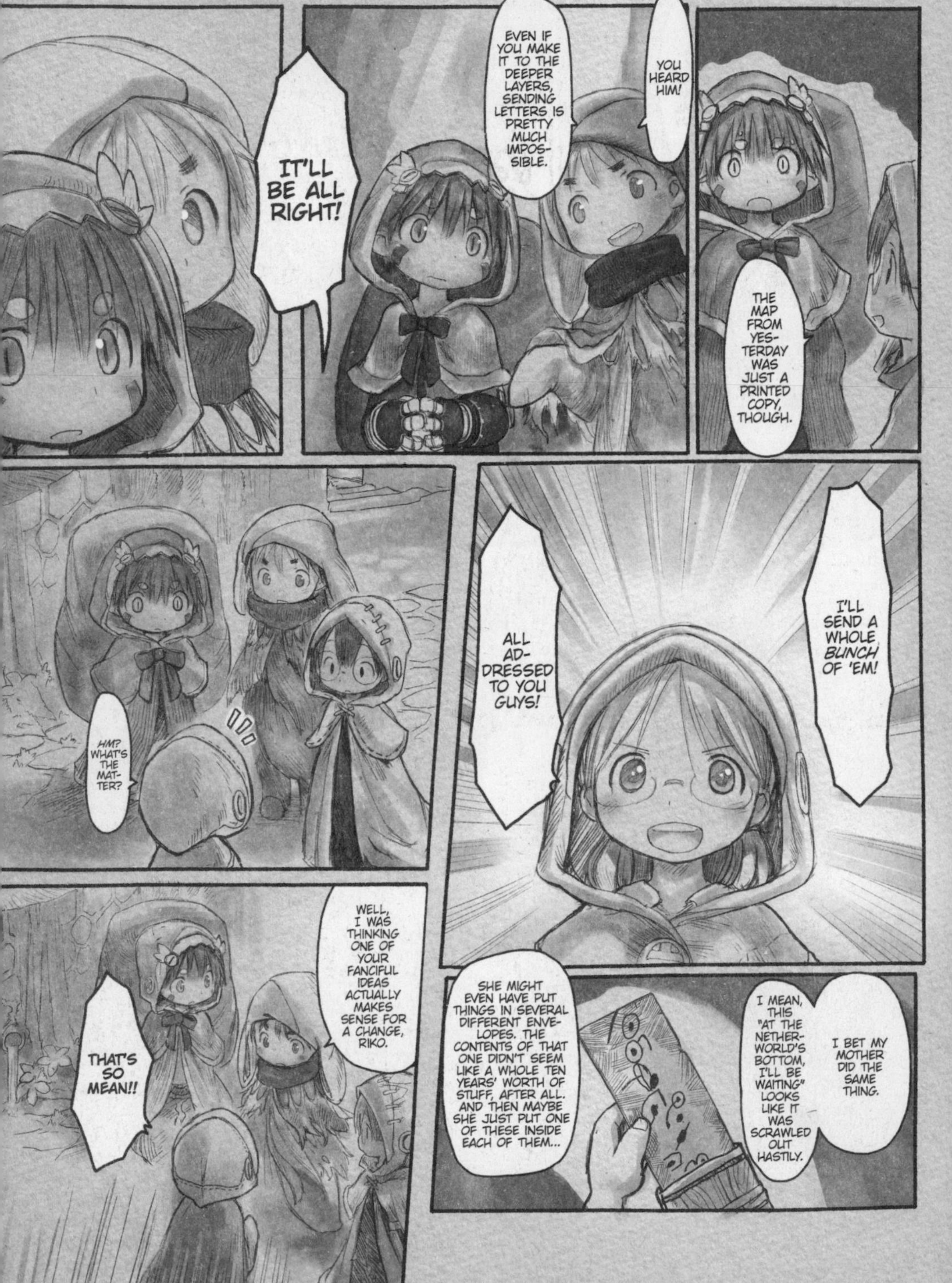
THE MAP FROM YESTERDAY WAS JUST A PRINTED COPY, THOUGH.
YOU HEARD HIM!
EVEN IF YOU MAKE IT TO THE DEEPER LAYERS, SENDING LETTERS IS PRETTY MUCH IMPOSSIBLE.
IT'LL BE ALL RIGHT!
I'LL SEND A WHOLE *BUNCH* OF 'EM!
ALL ADDRESSED TO YOU GUYS!
!!
HM? WHAT'S THE MATTER?
I BET MY MOTHER DID THE SAME THING.
I MEAN, THIS "AT THE NETHERWORLD'S BOTTOM, I'LL BE WAITING" LOOKS LIKE IT WAS SCRAWLED OUT HASTILY.
SHE MIGHT EVEN HAVE PUT THINGS IN SEVERAL DIFFERENT ENVELOPES. THE CONTENTS OF THAT ONE DIDN'T SEEM LIKE A WHOLE TEN YEARS' WORTH OF STUFF, AFTER ALL. AND THEN MAYBE SHE JUST PUT ONE OF THESE INSIDE EACH OF THEM...
WELL, I WAS THINKING ONE OF YOUR FANCIFUL IDEAS ACTUALLY MAKES SENSE FOR A CHANGE, RIKO.
THAT'S SO MEAN!!

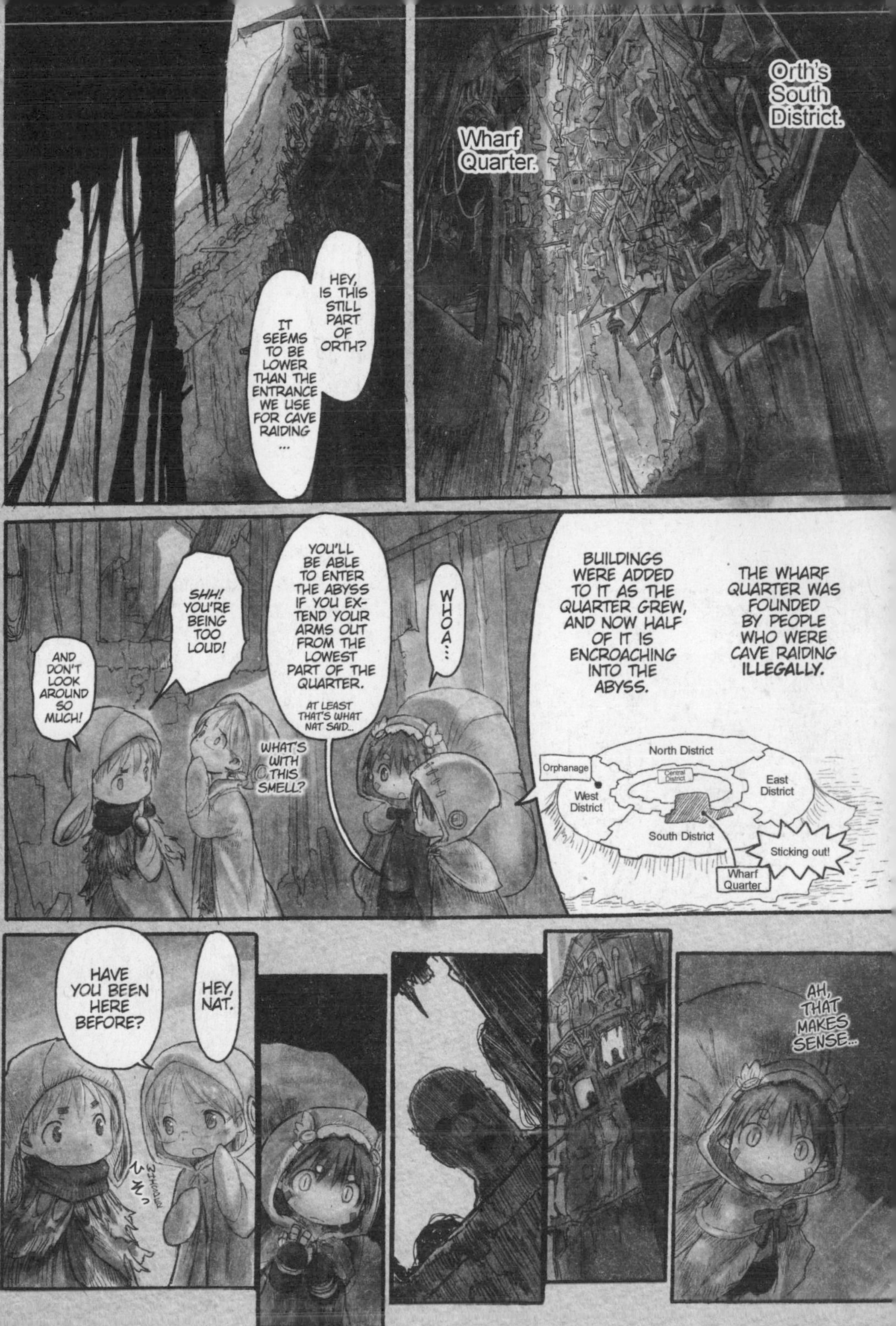
Orth's South District.
Wharf Quarter.
HEY, IS THIS STILL PART OF ORTH?
IT SEEMS TO BE LOWER THAN THE ENTRANCE WE USE FOR CAVE RAIDING ...
THE WHARF QUARTER WAS FOUNDED BY PEOPLE WHO WERE CAVE RAIDING ILLEGALLY.
BUILDINGS WERE ADDED TO IT AS THE QUARTER GREW, AND NOW HALF OF IT IS ENCROACHING INTO THE ABYSS.
North District
Orphanage
Central District
East District
West District
South District
Sticking out!
Wharf Quarter
WHOA...
YOU'LL BE ABLE TO ENTER THE ABYSS IF YOU EXTEND YOUR ARMS OUT FROM THE LOWEST PART OF THE QUARTER.
AT LEAST THAT'S WHAT NAT SAID...
WHAT'S WITH THIS SMELL?
SHH! YOU'RE BEING TOO LOUD!
AND DON'T LOOK AROUND SO MUCH!
AH, THAT MAKES SENSE...
HEY, NAT.
HAVE YOU BEEN HERE BEFORE?

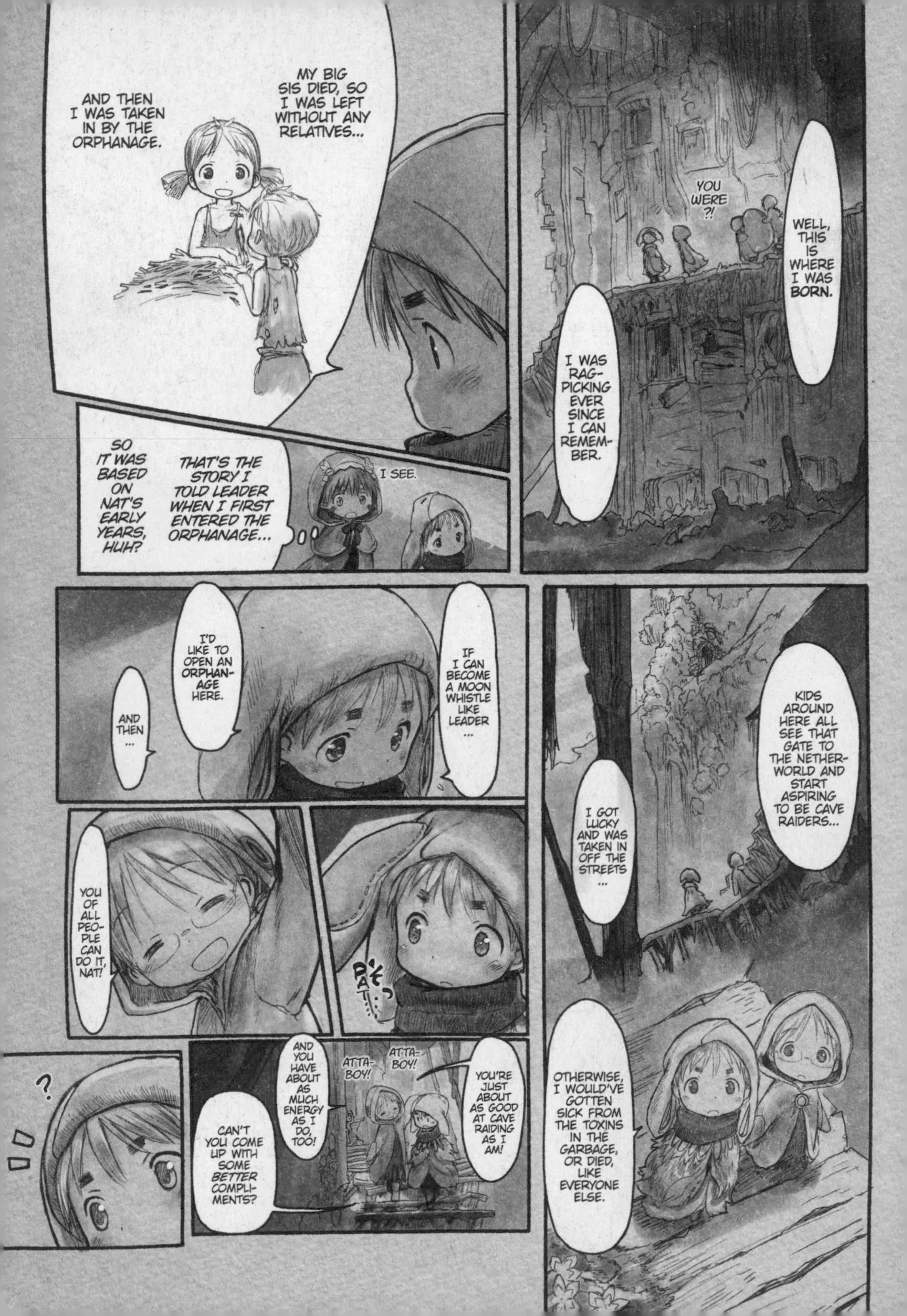

WELL, THIS IS WHERE I WAS BORN.
YOU WERE ?!
I WAS RAG-PICKING EVER SINCE I CAN REMEMBER.
MY BIG SIS DIED, SO I WAS LEFT WITHOUT ANY RELATIVES...
AND THEN I WAS TAKEN IN BY THE ORPHANAGE.
I SEE.
THAT'S THE STORY I TOLD LEADER WHEN I FIRST ENTERED THE ORPHANAGE...
SO IT WAS BASED ON NAT'S EARLY YEARS, HUH?
KIDS AROUND HERE ALL SEE THAT GATE TO THE NETHER-WORLD AND START ASPIRING TO BE CAVE RAIDERS...
I GOT LUCKY AND WAS TAKEN IN OFF THE STREETS...
OTHERWISE, I WOULD'VE GOTTEN SICK FROM THE TOXINS IN THE GARBAGE, OR DIED, LIKE EVERYONE ELSE.
IF I CAN BECOME A MOON WHISTLE LIKE LEADER...
I'D LIKE TO OPEN AN ORPHANAGE HERE.
AND THEN...
PAT PAT
YOU OF ALL PEOPLE CAN DO IT, NAT!
YOU'RE JUST ABOUT AS GOOD AT CAVE RAIDING AS I AM!
ATTA-BOY!
ATTA-BOY!
AND YOU HAVE ABOUT AS MUCH ENERGY AS I DO, TOO!
CAN'T YOU COME UP WITH SOME BETTER COMPLI-MENTS?
?

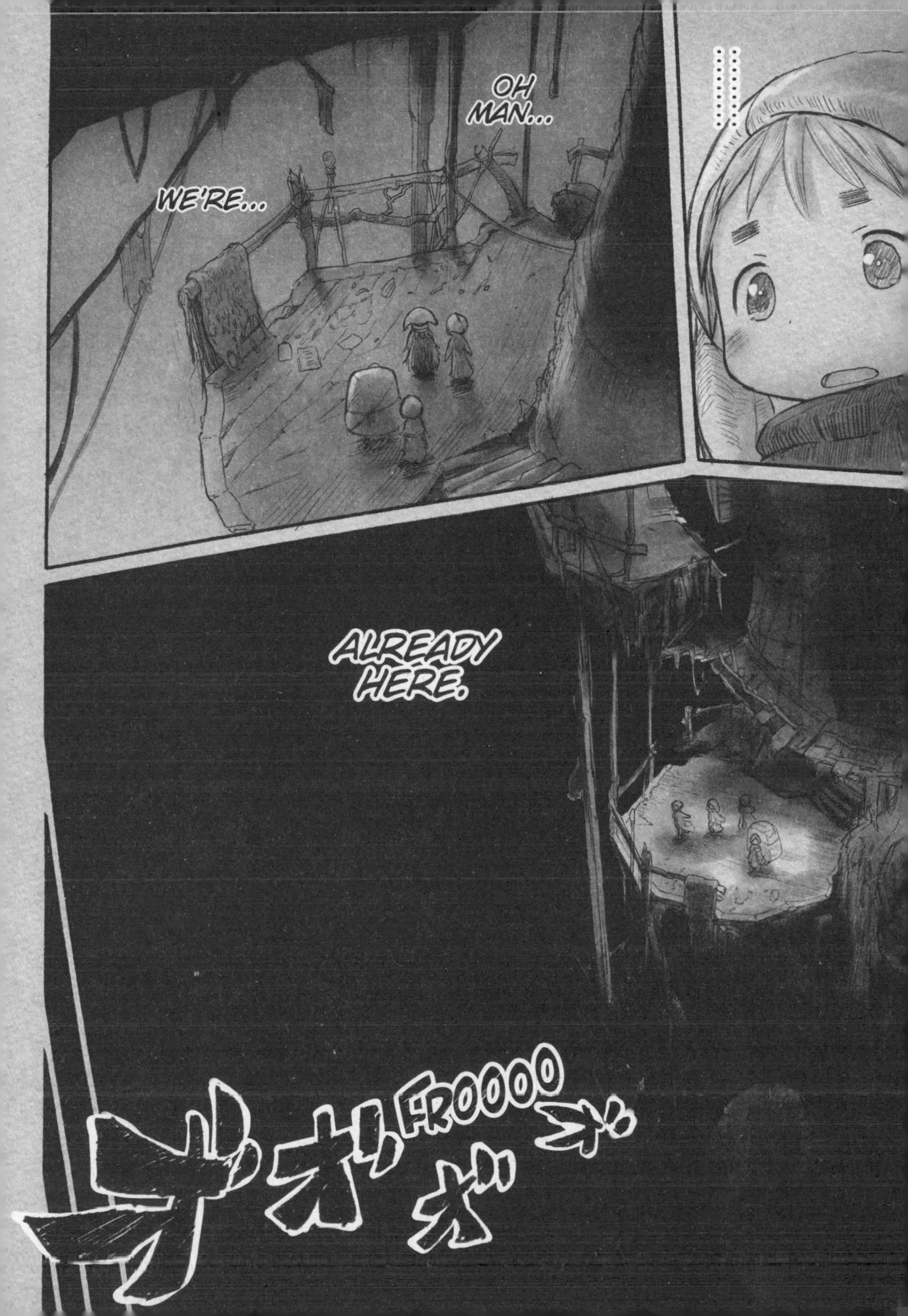
......
OH MAN...
WE'RE...
ALREADY HERE.
FROOOO

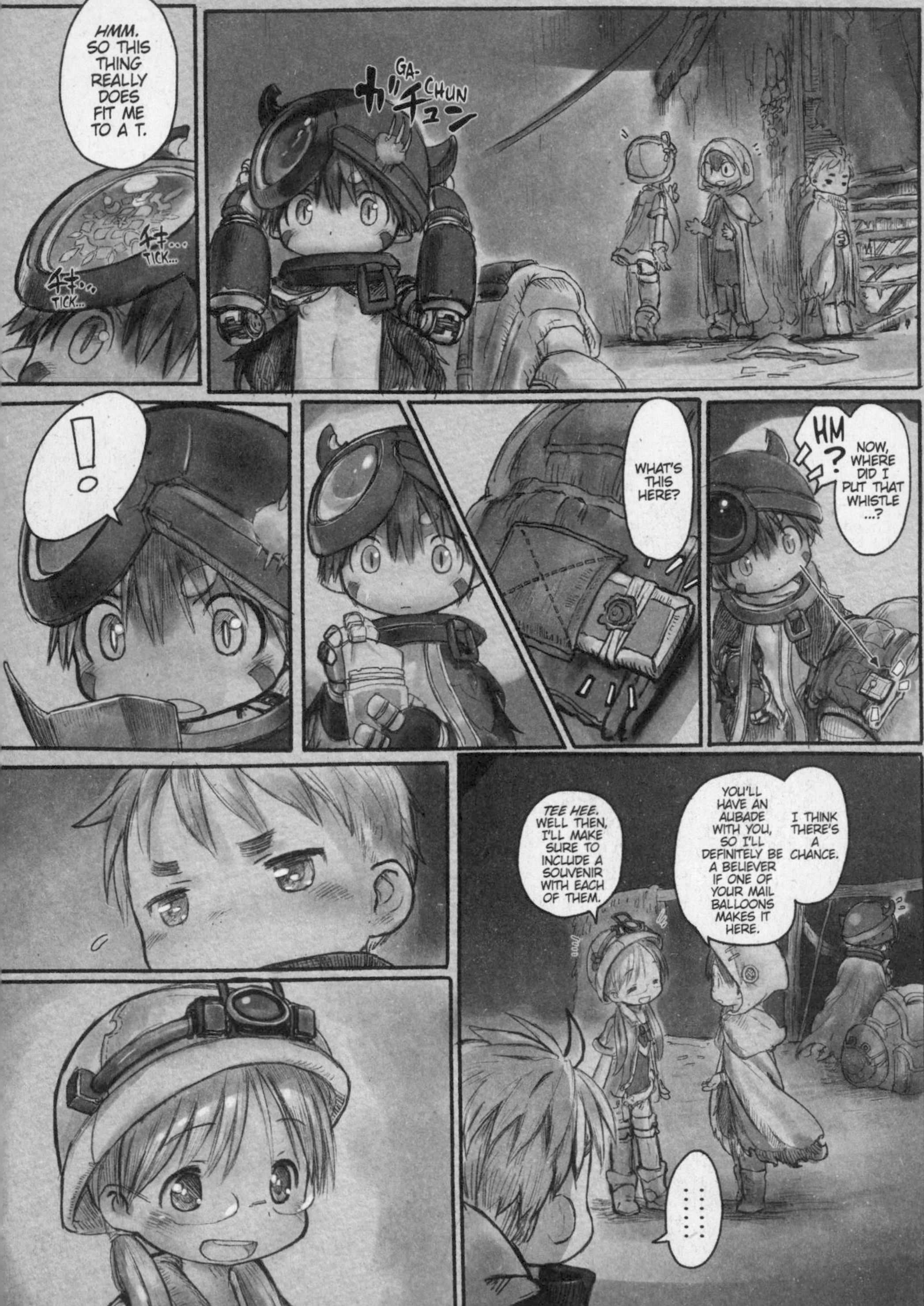
GA-CHUN
HMM. SO THIS THING REALLY DOES FIT ME TO A T.
TICK...
TICK...
HM?
NOW, WHERE DID I PUT THAT WHISTLE ...?
WHAT'S THIS HERE?
!
I THINK THERE'S A CHANCE.
YOU'LL HAVE AN AUBADE WITH YOU, SO I'LL DEFINITELY BE A BELIEVER IF ONE OF YOUR MAIL BALLOONS MAKES IT HERE.
TEE HEE. WELL THEN, I'LL MAKE SURE TO INCLUDE A SOUVENIR WITH EACH OF THEM.
......

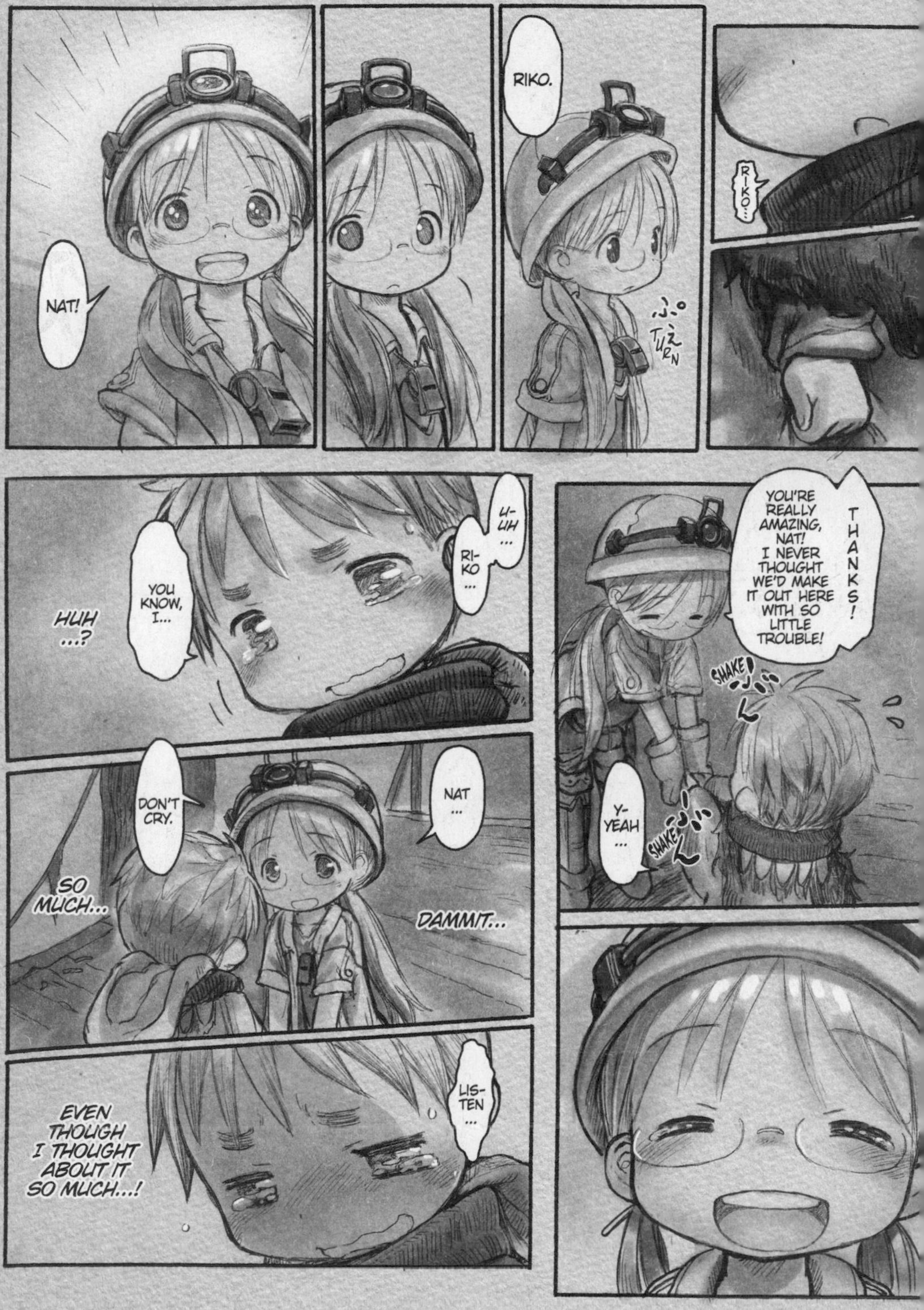

RIKO...
RIKO.
TURN
NAT!
YOU'RE REALLY AMAZING, NAT! I NEVER THOUGHT WE'D MAKE IT OUT HERE WITH SO LITTLE TROUBLE!
THANKS!
SHAKE
SHAKE
Y-YEAH...
U-UH...
RIKO...
YOU KNOW, I...
HUH...?
NAT...
DON'T CRY.
DAMMIT...
SO MUCH...
LISTEN...
EVEN THOUGH I THOUGHT ABOUT IT SO MUCH...!

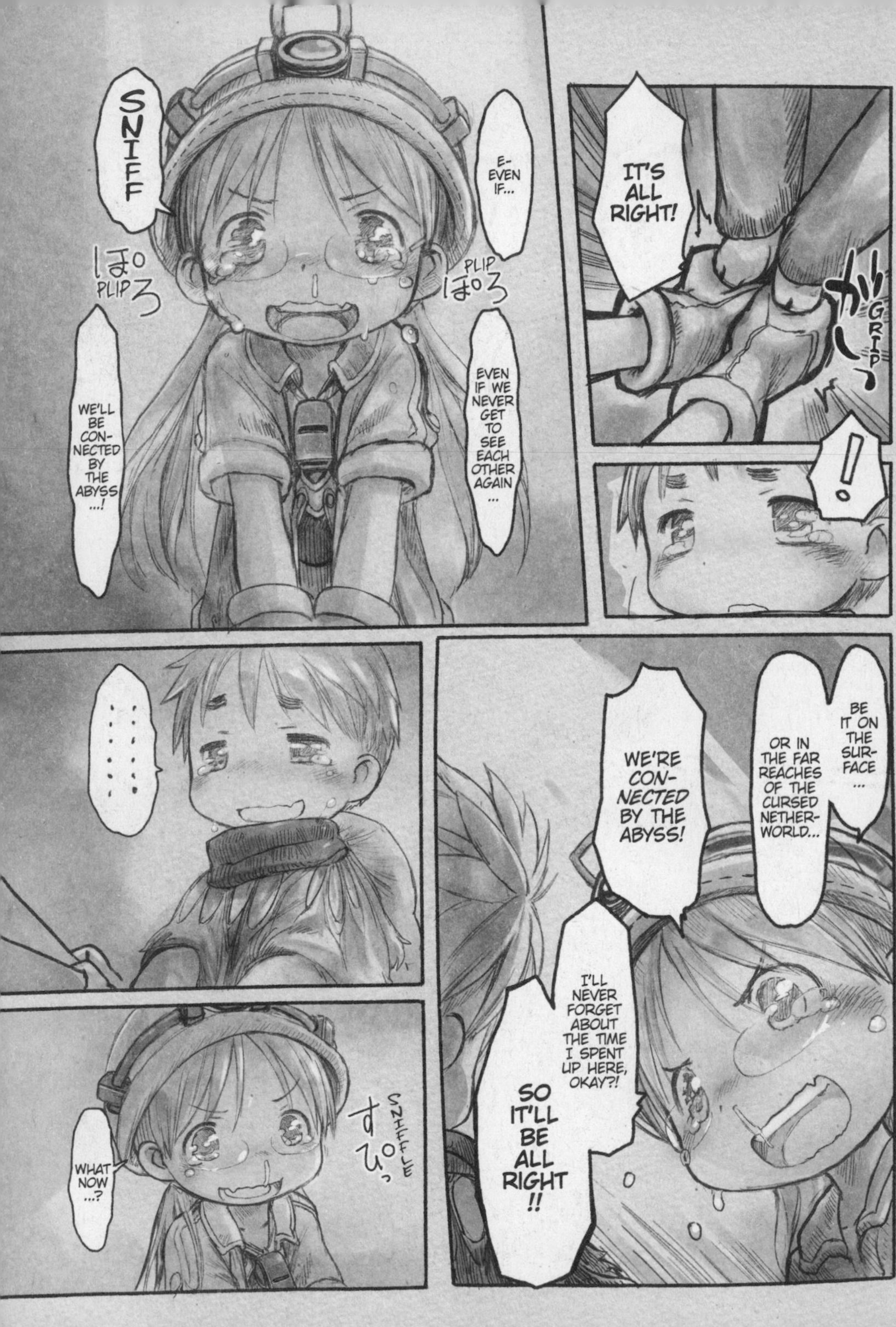
IT'S ALL RIGHT!
がしっ GRIP
!
E-EVEN IF...
SNIFF
ぽろ PLIP
ぽろ PLIP
EVEN IF WE NEVER GET TO SEE EACH OTHER AGAIN...
WE'LL BE CONNECTED BY THE ABYSS...!
BE IT ON THE SURFACE...
OR IN THE FAR REACHES OF THE CURSED NETHERWORLD...
WE'RE CONNECTED BY THE ABYSS!
I'LL NEVER FORGET ABOUT THE TIME I SPENT UP HERE, OKAY?!
SO IT'LL BE ALL RIGHT!!
......
すぴっ SNIFFLE
WHAT NOW...?

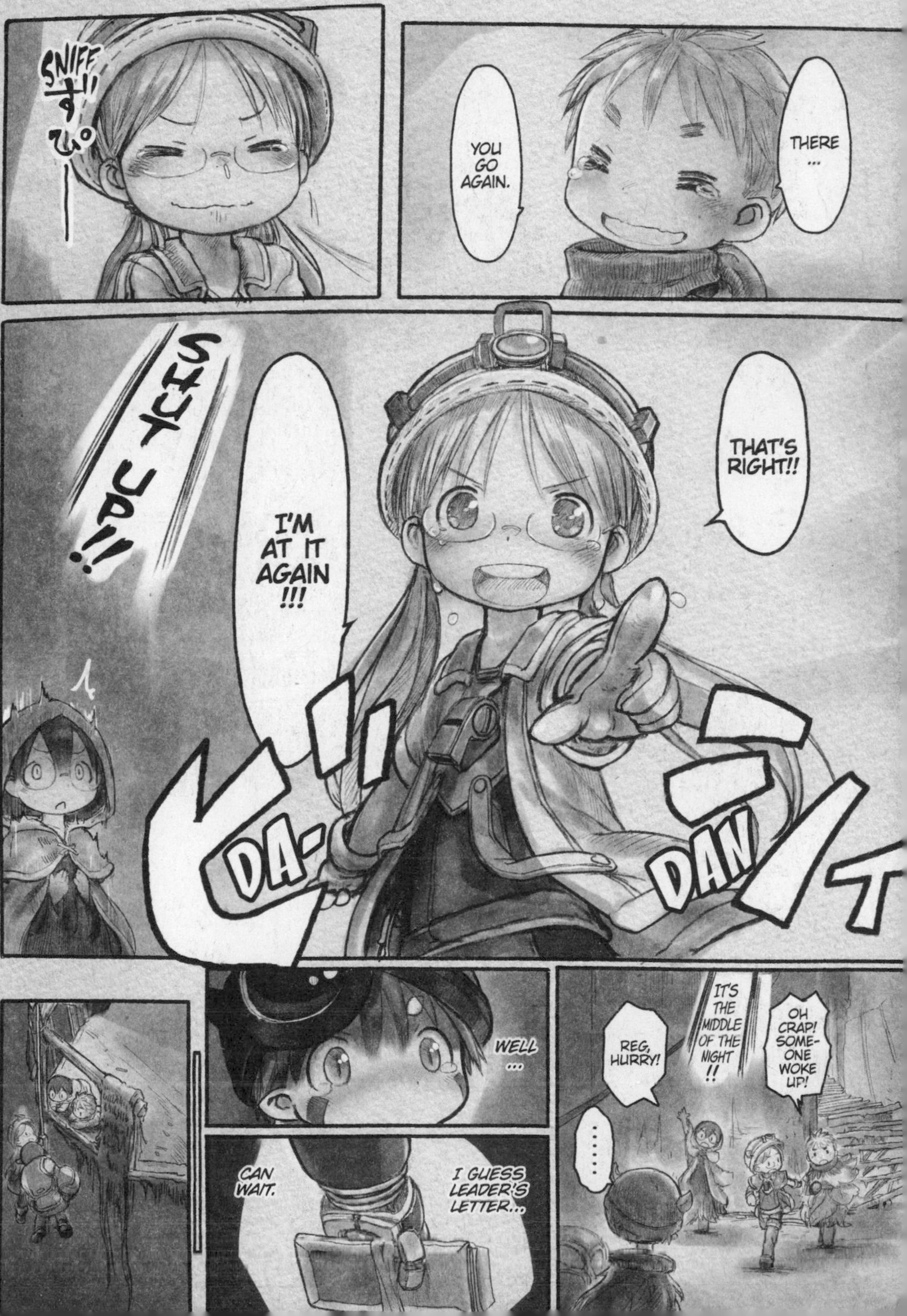
THERE ...
YOU GO AGAIN.
SNIFF すぴー
THAT'S RIGHT!!
I'M AT IT AGAIN !!!
SHUT UP!!
DA- DAN
OH CRAP! SOME-ONE WOKE UP!
IT'S THE MIDDLE OF THE NIGHT !!
REG, HURRY!
......
WELL ...
I GUESS LEADER'S LETTER...
CAN WAIT.

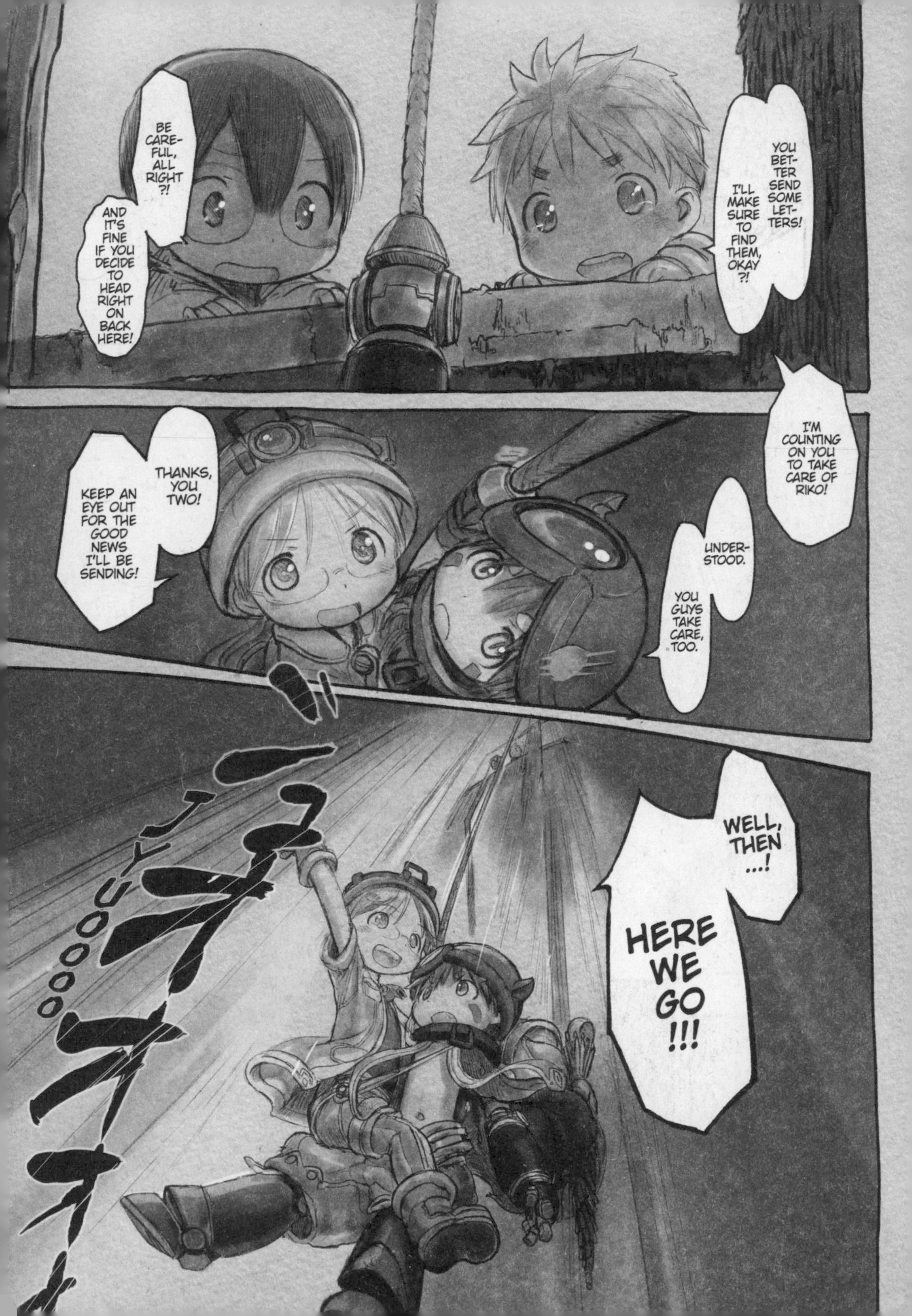
YOU BETTER SEND SOME LETTERS!
I'LL MAKE SURE TO FIND THEM, OKAY?!
BE CAREFUL, ALL RIGHT?!
AND IT'S FINE IF YOU DECIDE TO HEAD RIGHT ON BACK HERE!
I'M COUNTING ON YOU TO TAKE CARE OF RIKO!
UNDERSTOOD.
YOU GUYS TAKE CARE, TOO.
THANKS, YOU TWO!
KEEP AN EYE OUT FOR THE GOOD NEWS I'LL BE SENDING!
WELL, THEN...!
HERE WE GO!!!
JYUOOOOO

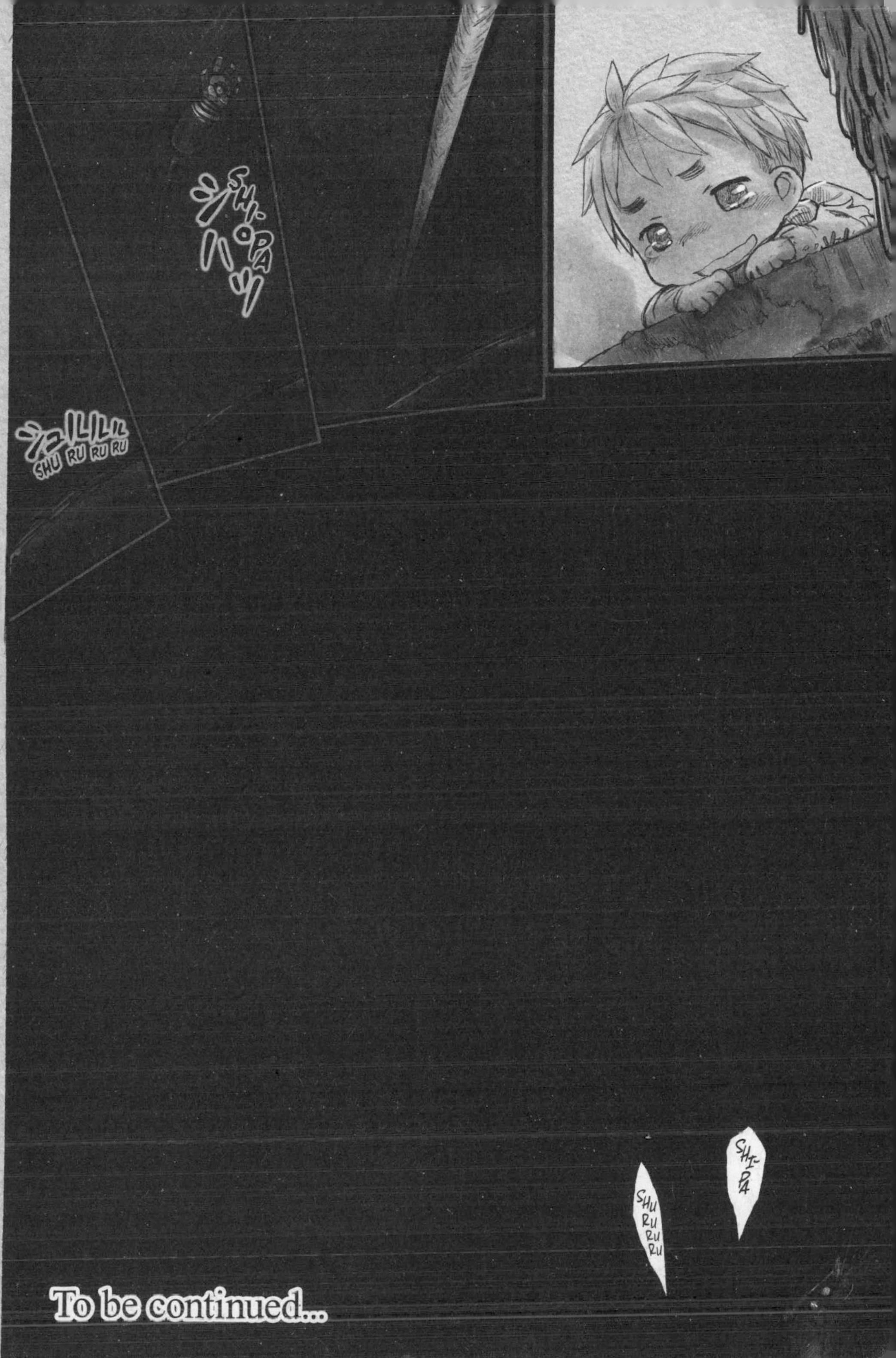
SHI-PA
SHU RU RU RU
SHI-PA
SHU RU RU RU
To be continued...